The Cavalry at Appomattox

A Tactical Study of Mounted Operations
During the Civil War's Climactic Campaign,
March 27–April 9, 1865

EDWARD G. LONGACRE

STACKPOLE
BOOKS

Copyright ©2003 by Stackpole Books

Published by
STACKPOLE BOOKS
5067 Ritter Road
Mechanicsburg, PA 17055
www.stackpolebooks.com

Printed in the United States of America

10 9 8 7 6 5 4 3 2 1

FIRST EDITION

Library of Congress Cataloging-in-Publication Data

Longacre, Edward G., 1946–
    The cavalry at Appomattox : a tactical study of mounted operations during the Civil War's climactic campaign, March 27–April 9 1865 / by Edward G. Longacre.— 1st ed.
        p. cm.
    Includes bibliographical references (p.) and index.
    ISBN 0-8117-0051-8
    1. Appomattox Campaign, 1865. 2. Virginia—History—Civil War, 1861–1865—Cavalry operations. 3. United States—History—Civil War, 1861–1865—Cavalry operations. 4. United States. Army. Cavalry—History—Civil War, 1861–1865. 5. Confederate States of America. Army. Cavalry—History. 6. United States. Army. Cavalry—Drill and tactics—History—19th century. 7. Confederate States of America. Army. Cavalry—Drill and tactics. I. Title.

E477.67.L66 2003
973.7'38—dc21

                                                                2002155313

For
Larry and Dorothy

CONTENTS

PREFACE

At war's outset, the cavalry of the Army of Northern Virginia over-awed the mounted wing of the Army of the Potomac. Conversant with horsemanship and firearms since early youth, the Confederate troopers were poised, experienced, and confident of their ability to outride and outfight their opponents, many of whom had never sat a horse or discharged a firearm prior to the outbreak of hostilities. Not surprisingly, for the two years that followed, the Virginians and Carolinians of James Ewell Brown Stuart's command consistently defeated, and sometimes humiliated, the New York mechanics and New England store clerks who appeared to predominate in the Union cavalry.

By the early spring of 1865, with the conflict nearing its climax and the Confederacy nearing oblivion, the opponents had experienced a dramatic reversal of fortune. The Confederate horsemen had lost much of their swagger, the result of depleted resources—human, equine, and inanimate. Nearly four years of unremitting attrition had reduced divisions to the size of brigades, brigades to the size of regiments, and regiments to battalion or even company strength. The Confederate cavalry's leadership base had been worn away. Gone was the brilliant, flamboyant Stuart, mortally wounded in battle outside Richmond. Gone, too, was his successor, the quietly competent Wade Hampton, who had been sent to his native South Carolina in January 1865 in a futile effort to curtail the advance of 60,000 Federals under William T. Sherman. In their place was twenty-eight-year-old Fitzhugh Lee, nephew of the army's commander, Robert E. Lee, an able officer but an inexperienced corps commander who lacked Stuart's strategic vision and Hampton's tactical expertise. Moreover, the weary, grim-faced troopers who would follow Fitz Lee into the final battles of the war lacked the mounts, equipment, firearms, and ammunition that would have made the coming struggle an even contest.

In contrast, the Confederates' once-downtrodden adversaries enjoyed in abundance every resource their adversaries lacked. They rode well-fed and well-groomed horses, and they could draw on a seemingly inexhaustible supply of remounts. Their equipment was notable for both quality and quantity, and their firearms included two especially effective breechloaders, the seven-shot Spencer carbine and the sixteen-shot Henry rifle. The men themselves were experienced in all aspects of combat, the fruit of rigorous training and long months of trial and error. Under commanders such as the fiery Philip H. Sheridan, the colorful George Armstrong Custer, and the hard-bitten Wesley Merritt, they had learned to fight with equal skill on foot and in the saddle as conditions dictated, in contrast to their enemy's seemingly stubborn reliance on mounted tactics. In fact, the blue-clad troopers had evolved—albeit slowly and painfully—into some of the finest horse soldiers in American history.

Given the disparity of manpower and supplies, one might assume that the last campaign in Virginia was short and one-sided, the result never in question. In fact, it was more protracted than it might otherwise have been, and its denouement remained in doubt to the end. One reason was that the opponents were more evenly matched than one might suppose. Factors such as determination, desperation, and pride brought an element of unpredictability to the contest. As a result, the campaign witnessed some of the most spirited cavalry combat of the war, featuring the imaginative application of both mounted and dismounted tactics. In fact, the quality of the contest was such that the Appomattox campaign marked the zenith of large-scale cavalry campaigning in America.

The Cavalry at Appomattox not only provides detailed coverage of the mounted operations between March 27 and April 9, 1865, but attempts to place those operations in proper context. Therefore, the movements of the main armies receive attention when warranted, especially those forces that played major roles in determining the outcome of the campaign. In the main, the book seeks to tell, in abundant detail, the story of a critical period of the Civil War, one that reflects credit on all involved—not only those who rode sleek horses, wielded state-of-the-art weaponry, and pursued final victory with single-minded determination, but also those few poorly mounted and ill-equipped soldiers who remained defiant and unbowed to the last, resolved to sell their lives, and the life of their nation, as dearly as possible.

ACKNOWLEDGMENTS

I AM INDEBTED TO MANY PERSONS WHO PROVIDED RESEARCH ASSISTANCE. Foremost is Patrick Schroeder, historian at Appomattox Court House National Historical Park, who not only gave access to the park's collection of research materials and answered numerous queries, but also critiqued this study in manuscript form.

Others to whom I owe a debt of gratitude include Rufus Barringer, Rocky Mount, N.C.; Ruth M. Blair and Eunice Gillman DiBella, Connecticut Historical Society, Hartford; DeAnn Blanton and Mike Musick of the Military Reference Branch, National Archives, Washington, D.C.; Mary Boccaccio and Martha G. Elmore, J. Y. Joyner Library, East Carolina University, Greenville, N.C.; Elva J. Bogert, Massachusetts Historical Society, Boston; Andy Boisseau and E. Lee Shepard, Virginia Historical Society, Richmond; John C. Broderick, Library of Congress, Washington, D.C.; Phyllis Burnham, University Archives and Regional History Collections, Western Michigan University, Kalamazoo; Marie Byrne, Bancroft Library, University of California, Berkeley; Marie T. Capps, United States Military Academy Library, West Point, N.Y.; Harris S. Colt, New York, N.Y.; Susan Cornett, Herbert Bateman Memorial Library, Langley Air Force Base, Va.; John and Ruth Coski, Eleanor S. Brockenbrough Library, Museum of the Confederacy, Richmond; John C. Dann and Mary Jo Pugh, University of Michigan Libraries, Ann Arbor; Rebecca Ebert, Handley Regional Library, Winchester, Va.; Leslie Fields, Gilder Lehrman Collection, New York, N.Y.; Connell Gallagher, Guy W. Bailey Library, University of Vermont, Burlington; Bill Godfrey, Hampton, Va.; Margaret Hrabe, Alderman Library, University of

Virginia, Charlottesville; Michele Leiser, C. H. Green Library, Stanford University, Palo Alto, Calif.; Paul McCarthy, Elmer E. Rasmuson Library, University of Alaska, Fairbanks; William Miles, Clarke Historical Library, Central Michigan University, Mount Pleasant; Mary Molineux, Earl Gregg Swem Library, College of William and Mary, Williamsburg, Va.; Reginald Pettus, Keysville, Va.; John Rhodehamel, Henry E. Huntington Library, San Marino, Calif.; Judith A. Schiff, Sterling Memorial Library, Yale University, New Haven, Conn.; Donald C. Skemer, New Jersey Historical Society, Newark; Thomas A. Smith, Rutherford B. Hayes Presidential Center, Fremont, Ohio; Richard J Sommers, U.S. Army Military History Institute, Carlisle Barracks, Pa.; Paul Spence, Illinois State Historical Library, Springfield; Kathy Stewart and Patricia Watkinson, Library of Virginia, Richmond; Valerie Wingfield, New York Public Library, New York, N.Y.; and Steve Zerbe, War Library, National Commandery, Military Order of the Loyal Legion of the United States, Philadelphia.

As so often in the past, I also thank my editor, Leigh Ann Berry; my cartographer, Paul Dangel; and my wife, Melody Ann Longacre.

THE ANTAGONISTS

AT HEADQUARTERS, ARMY OF NORTHERN VIRGINIA
34th Virginia Battalion (Capt. Samuel Brown)

CAVALRY CORPS, ARMY OF NORTHERN VIRGINIA
(Maj. Gen. Fitzhugh Lee)

FITZ LEE'S DIVISION (Brig. Gen. Thomas T. Munford)
Munford's Brigade (Col. William B. Wooldridge)
    1st Maryland Battalion (Lt. Col. Gustavus W. Dorsey)
    1st Virginia (Col. William A. Morgan, Maj. Charles R. Irving)
    2nd Virginia (Lt. Col. Cary Breckinridge)
    3rd Virginia (Lt. Col. William M. Feild, Capt. Jesse S. Jones)
    4th Virginia (Maj. Charles Old, Capt. Alexander D. Payne)
Payne's Brigade (Brig. Gen. William H. F. Payne, Col. Reuben B. Boston, Col. William A. Morgan)
    5th Virginia* (Col. Reuben B. Boston, Lt. Col. James H. Allen)
    6th Virginia (Maj. Daniel A. Grimsley)
    8th Virginia (Capt. Achilles J. Tynes)
Gary's Brigade (Brig. Gen. Martin W. Gary)
    Hampton Legion Cavalry (Lt. Col. Robert B. Arnold)
    7th Georgia (Capt. William H. Burroughs)
    7th South Carolina (Col. Alexander C. Haskell)
    24th Virginia (Col. William T. Robins)

*Officially known as the "5th Virginia Cavalry (Consolidated)," this regiment included four companies composed of former members of the 15th Virginia.

ROONEY LEE'S DIVISION (Maj. Gen. William H. F. Lee)
Barringer's Brigade (Brig. Gen. Rufus Barringer, Col. William H. Cheek)
    1st North Carolina (Col. William H. Cheek)
    2nd North Carolina (Col. James L. Gaines, Maj. John P. Lockhart)
    3rd North Carolina (Lt. Col. Roger Moore)
    5th North Carolina (Col. James H. McNeill, Capt. John R. Erwin)
Beale's Brigade (Brig. Gen. Richard L. T. Beale)
    9th Virginia (Col. Thomas C. Waller)
    10th Virginia (Col. Robert A. Caskie, Lt. Col. W. Bailey Clement)
    13th Virginia (Col. Alexander Savage)
    14th Virginia [six companies] (Capt. Edwin E. Bouldin)
Roberts's Brigade (Brig. Gen. William P. Roberts)
    4th North Carolina (Capt. Demosthenes Bell, Capt. Joseph B. Cherry, Capt. Thomas W. Moore)
    16th North Carolina Battalion** (Lt. Col. John B. Edelin, Maj. F. G. Pitts, Lt. E. J. Holt)

ROSSER'S DIVISION (Maj. Gen. Thomas L. Rosser)
Laurel Brigade (Brig. Gen. James Dearing, Lt. Col. Elijah V. White)
    7th Virginia (Maj. Daniel C. Hatcher)
    11th Virginia (Lt. Col. Mottrom D. Ball)
    12th Virginia (Maj. John L. Knott, Capt. George Grandstaff)
    35th Virginia Battalion (Lt. Col. Elijah V. White, Capt. Franklin M. Myers)
McCausland's Brigade (Brig. Gen. John McCausland)
    16th Virginia (Col. Milton J. Ferguson)
    17th Virginia (Capt. John T. Bland)
    21st Virginia (Col. William E. Peters)
    22nd Virginia (Capt. William W. Brown)

HORSE ARTILLERY (Maj. R. Preston Chew)
2nd Stuart Horse Artillery (Capt. George W. Brown)
Petersburg Artillery (Capt. Edward Graham)

**This unit, composed of nine companies, was a regiment in all but name. It was to have been redesignated the 7th North Carolina Cavalry, but the order was either not issued or not observed.

AT HEADQUARTERS, ARMIES OF THE UNITED STATES
5th United States [three companies] (Capt. Julius W. Mason)

ARMY OF THE SHENANDOAH
(Maj. Gen. Philip H. Sheridan)

CAVALRY, ARMY OF THE SHENANDOAH
(Bvt. Maj. Gen. Wesley Merritt)

FIRST DIVISION (Brig. Gen. Thomas C. Devin)
First Brigade (Col. Peter Stagg)
    1st Michigan (Lt. Col. George R. Maxwell, Capt. Edward L. Negus)
    5th Michigan (Lt. Col. Smith H. Hastings)
    6th Michigan (Lt. Col. Harvey H. Vinton)
    7th Michigan (Lt. Col. George G. Briggs)
Second Brigade (Col. Charles L. Fitzhugh)
    1st New York Dragoons (Maj. Howard M. Smith)
    6th New York (Maj. Harrison White)
    9th New York (Maj. James R. Dinnin)
    17th Pennsylvania (Lt. Col. Coe Durland)
    20th Pennsylvania (Lt. Col. Gabriel Middleton)
Reserve Brigade (Brig. Gen. Alfred Gibbs)
    2nd Massachusetts (Col. Casper Crowninshield)
    6th Pennsylvania [six companies] (Col. Charles L. Leiper)
    1st United States (Capt. Richard S. C. Lord)
    5th United States (Capt. Thomas Drummond, Lt. Gustavus Urban)
    6th United States (Maj. R. Murray Morris)
Horse Artillery
    Batteries C/E, 4th United States (Capt. Marcus P. Miller)

THIRD DIVISION (Bvt. Maj. Gen. George A. Custer)
First Brigade (Col. Alexander C. M. Pennington)
    1st Connecticut (Col. Brayton Ives)
    3rd New Jersey (Lt. Col. William P. Robeson, Jr.)
    2nd New York (Col. Alanson M. Randol)
    2nd Ohio (Capt. Albert Barnitz)
Second Brigade (Brevet Brig. Gen. William Wells)
    8th New York (Maj. James Bliss)
    15th New York (Col. John J. Coppinger)
    1st Vermont (Lt. Col. Josiah Hall)

Third Brigade (Col. Henry Capehart)
  1st New York (Lt. Col. J. C. Battersby)
  1st West Virginia (Maj. S. B. Howe, Lt. Col. Charles E. Capehart)
  2nd West Virginia [seven companies] (Lt. Col. James Allen)
  3rd West Virginia (Maj. John S. Witcher)

SECOND CAVALRY DIVISION, ARMY OF THE POTOMAC
(Maj. Gen. George Crook)

First Brigade (Brevet Maj. Gen. Henry E. Davies)
  1st New Jersey (Col. Hugh H. Janeway, Maj. Walter R. Robbins)
  10th New York (Col. M. Henry Avery)
  24th New York (Col. Walter C. Newberry, Lt. Col. Melzer Richards,
    Maj. William A. Snyder)
  1st Pennsylvania [five companies] (Maj. Hampton S. Thomas, Lt. War-
    ren L. Holbrook)
  Battery A, 2nd United States Artillery (Lt. James H. Lord)
Second Brigade (Bvt. Brig. Gen. J. Irvin Gregg, Col. Samuel B. M. Young)
  4th Pennsylvania [eleven companies] (Col. Samuel B. M. Young, Lt. Col.
    Alexander P. Duncan)
  8th Pennsylvania [eight companies] (Lt. Col. William A. Corrie)
  16th Pennsylvania (Lt. Col. John K. Robison, Maj. William H. Fry)
  21st Pennsylvania [eleven companies] (Col. Oliver B. Knowles)
Third Brigade (Bvt. Brig. Gen. Charles H. Smith)
  1st Maine (Lt. Col. Jonathan P. Cilley)
  2nd New York Mounted Rifles (Maj. Paul Chadbourne, Col. John Fisk)
  6th Ohio (Capt. Matthew H. Cryer)
  13th Ohio (Lt. Col. Stephen R. Clark)

AT ARMY/CORPS/DIVISION HEADQUARTERS,
ARMY OF THE POTOMAC

  1st Indiana [one company] (Lt. William O. Hedrick)
  3rd Indiana [two companies] (Lt. Benjamin F. Gilbert)
  1st Massachusetts [ten companies] (Maj. John Tewksbury)
  2nd Pennsylvania (Col. William W. Sanders)
  3rd Pennsylvania (Lt. Col. James W. Walsh)
  4th Pennsylvania [one company] (Capt. Napoleon J. Horrell)
  21st Pennsylvania [one company] (Capt. William H. Boyd, Jr.)
  Independent Company, Oneida Cavalry (Capt. James E. Jenkins)

CAVALRY DIVISION, ARMY OF THE JAMES*
(Brig. Gen. Ranald S. Mackenzie)
First Brigade (Col. Robert M. West)
    20th New York [one company] (Capt. Thomas H. Butler)
    5th Pennsylvania (Lt. Col. Christopher Kleinz)
Second Brigade (Col. Samuel P. Spear, Col. Andrew W. Evans)
    1st District of Columbia [four companies] (Maj. J. Stannard Baker)
    1st Maryland (Col. Andrew W. Evans, Lt. Col. Jacob H. Counselman)
    11th Pennsylvania (Lt. Col. Franklin A. Stratton)
Horse Artillery
    4th Wisconsin Battery (Capt. Dorman L. Noggle)

AT HEADQUARTERS, ARMY OF THE JAMES
4th Massachusetts [five companies] (Col. Francis Washburn]

IN FORCES, ARMY OF THE JAMES, BESIEGING RICHMOND
4th Massachusetts [two companies] (Col. Atherton H. Stevens, Jr.)
5th Massachusetts (Col. Charles F. Adams, Jr.)
20th New York [eleven companies] (Lt. Col. David M. Evans)
2nd United States Colored (Col. George W. Cole)

*On April 8, 1865, Mackenzie's regiments were consolidated into a single brigade.

ONE

"There Are So Many Things Calculated to Depress"

FOR THE ARMY OF NORTHERN VIRGINIA, IT WAS THE WORST OF TIMES. Spring was on the land, bringing pleasant weather, turning the foliage from a dismal brown to a vibrant green, and drying roads recently crusted over with frozen mud. Rather than the promise of new life, however, the season draped a pallor over the poorly armed, ill-clothed, inadequately fed troops of Robert E. Lee. Combat attrition and disease had played hob with the army's health throughout the winter now ending. Barely 56,000 troops, not all of them "effectives," remained to man the nearly forty miles of picket posts, trenches, rifle pits, redans, and redoubts that defended the Confederate capital at Richmond; its support center to the south, Petersburg; and the hotly contested ground in between.

Opposing this meager remnant were the 90,000 members of Maj. Gen. George Gordon Meade's Army of the Potomac, and the 30,000 troops of the Army of the James, commanded by Maj. Gen. Edward O. C. Ord. The combined armies were under the leadership of Lt. Gen. Ulysses S. Grant. Despite having forged a reputation as the Union's most consistently successful commander, Grant had been battling Lee's savvy, tenacious veterans for nearly a year without having won a decisive victory. At last, however, he had run his enemy to earth. Since laying siege to Petersburg and Richmond the previous June, Grant had continually strengthened and lengthened his lines, as if to surround his objectives. In the end, he knew, this slow strangling of Lee's army would exact a toll greater than any battle could inflict.[1]

Given the Confederates' dwindling resources, and the ever-growing strength of the troops facing them, even the least introspective defender should have sensed the approach of the end—the end of the Confederacy's greatest army, the end of the dream of Southern nationhood. Many had given up hope of continued resistance. Writing to his family in February, an infantryman in the division of Maj. Gen. George E. Pickett put it succinctly: "The Confederacy is gone. . . ." Some who appreciated the magnitude of their predicament took steps to avoid being caught up in the final result. Throughout the winter, officers and men had quit the army in droves. Most had made their way inside enemy lines to surrender and then to enjoy their first full meal in weeks or months. A few comrades struck out for home by routes roundabout and often perilous.[2]

Lee's mounted arm shared with the rest of the army the doldrums, discomforts, and dangers of the siege. Perhaps because of its perceived status as an elite branch—cavalrymen rode to war, after all, while the infantry slogged through mud and artillerymen jounced over rutted roads atop limbers and caissons—the gray troopers managed to keep their morale tolerably high throughout the winter. To be sure, depression and despair infected a certain number. One North Carolinian, whose regiment picketed the Petersburg & Weldon Railroad below Petersburg, wrote his wife in late February of the "gloomy mood" that had been oppressing him for weeks: "It is a hard matter for me to keep lively & in good spirits these times. There are so many things calculated to depress," including rumors of the impending evacuation of the besieged cities. Of more immediate concern for this man was the general lack of warm clothing and adequate food, as well as the impossibility—especially with the approaching resumption of active campaigning—of securing a furlough.[3]

Thoughts of home were always on the soldiers' minds, and the fear that loved ones were suffering even more than they was another source of gloom. Writing after the war, an officer in the 3rd Virginia Cavalry recalled that by the early months of 1865, "the physical & financial resources" of the Confederacy "had been taxed to their utmost—and beyond that they could not be carried. While our soldiers were fighting & freezing in the damp cold rifle pits their wives & children were <u>naked</u> & <u>starving</u> at home. It was impossible to do more. All that statesman could do—all that bravery could accomplish—all that patriotic, self-sacrificing manhood could endure—all that ever faithful, patient, constant woman could sacrifice & suffer—had been done."[4]

Yet not everyone gave way to fatalism; some refused to believe defeat was inevitable. Lt. Col. William W. Blackford of the 1st Confederate Engineers, who had served for almost two years on the staff of Lee's late, lamented cavalry commander, Maj. Gen. James Ewell Brown Stuart, asserted that despite the odds facing them, those in the ranks "looked forward to beating the enemy when the campaign opened, as a matter of course." Throughout the winter,

Blackford and his comrades had received grim news from other theaters of combat, including the near-destruction of the Army of Tennessee outside Nashville; Maj. Gen. William T. Sherman's occupation of Savannah, Georgia; and the capture of the Confederacy's last operating seaport, Wilmington, North Carolina. Yet Blackford maintained that the rank and file "never troubled [themselves] much about events so far away."[5]

The trooper-turned-engineer was not the only optimist in Lee's army; at times, the cavalry seemed rife with them. Toward the end of February, a member of the 9th Virginia declared, "I do firmly believe we will gain our independence & that the day is not far distant." Like many of his comrades, he conceded that, whatever its outcome, the war had irrevocably changed the social and economic structure of his region. Although he called slavery "a dead letter in Va.," a more important goal—independence—was still attainable. More cautious in his outlook, but just as resolute in his will to fight, was a member of the 24th Virginia, whose regiment occupied the Richmond suburbs. He believed the Army of Northern Virginia capable of months of continued resistance: "I see . . . another year of war before us, and perhaps war to the end of the Lincoln Administration. I think our people and soldiers will be aroused to renewed effort. We held a meeting in our Regiment this morning expressing our willingness and determination to prosecute the war." A few weeks after this man's declaration, an officer in the 1st North Carolina opined, "Our Army is strengthening, and the men are in fine spirits and determined." He added: "We are going to whip [the enemy in] every fight hereafter. Grant is 'trembling in his shoes,' already."[6]

Even those who fully appreciated the disadvantages under which Lee's army labored saw reason for hope. A South Carolina trooper recalled after the war that as spring 1865 approached, the A.N.V., "wasted and reduced to skeleton battalions, was still an army of veteran material, powerful yet for attack or defence, all the more dangerous from its desperate condition." This view was shared by some of the commanders, including Col. Thomas Taylor Munford, leader of a brigade of Virginia horsemen. Wherever Munford looked along the siege lines, he saw

> the trusted veterans of a hundred battles. Their countenances were cheerful and bright, though their rations were pinched and scanty, their blankets thin and worn, their clothing tattered and of various colors. Many were shod with moccasins, fresh from slaughtered cattle. Some were housed in patched tents, and others in daubed huts, through which the cold winds might whistle . . . notwithstanding all, they hopefully awaited the dawn of a brighter morrow. The old Con-

federates knew that it <u>was their own fight,</u> and they felt sure that those of their old comrades who acted as spies and scouts . . . would keep their General accurately informed as to every movement of the enemy.

Thus forewarned, the army would counter every effort to pry it out of its trenches.[7]

Munford, for one, believed that, in time, stasis and enemy attrition would achieve dramatic results. Sherman's well-timed seizure of Atlanta and a series of Union victories in the Shenandoah Valley had prompted a war-weary North in November 1864 to elect President Abraham Lincoln to a second term. Yet if Petersburg and Richmond continued to remain in Confederate hands, the inconclusiveness of Grant's campaign might pressure the politicians into suing for peace.

But even the most optimistic Confederate expressed some concern over his army's condition. One of the most vexing problems was the state of the cavalry's mounts. The recent winter had been especially hard on the horse herds, hundreds of animals having died from overwork, lack of regular forage, and exposure to the elements. A general scarcity of hay and grain had hit the cavalry particularly hard, the result of pastures ravaged and crops burned or confiscated by the enemy. As one North Carolinian complained on March 27: "Our Horses look bad. We don't get any thing to feed on but Corn. The horses is going up fast."[8]

For the third winter in a row, cavalry leaders had been forced to detach companies, regiments, and even brigades to regions dozens of miles behind the siege lines, where provender could still be obtained. At one point during the winter, Robert E. Lee had complained to Confederate Secretary of War John C. Breckinridge that the army's troopers were "scattered for want of provisions & our supply and ammunition trains, which ought to be with the army in case of a sudden movement, are about collecting provisions and forage," some as far off as western Virginia and North Carolina. On February 5, when the Yankees tried to capture the Boydton Plank Road southwest of Petersburg, Lee was forced to move the cavalry division commanded by his son, Maj. Gen. William Henry Fitzhugh ("Rooney") Lee, forty miles until it was in position to block the advance. But the situation persisted; as spring approached, many troopers, as well as artillery comrades foraging for their battery horses, remained far from the point at which they would be needed when full-scale campaigning resumed.[9]

At times, even dispersal proved inadequate to the needs of the cavalry. On several occasions, Stuart and his successors had resorted to disbanding whole regiments and sending their men home for the winter. There they could subsist themselves as well as their horses without burdening the army's deteriorating supply system, before returning to the ranks in the spring. This practice, although undesirable for a number of reasons—one being the tendency of some men to remain at home indefinitely—had a certain logic. Every Confederate trooper furnished his own horse, whose health he was personally responsible for maintaining. If the animal was lost to the army, whether through wound or disease, the trooper had to procure a remount as quickly as possible.[10]

This situation contrasted dramatically with that of the enemy. Since the war's start, Federal troopers had been the beneficiaries of a large-scale remount system, operated more or less efficiently by the U.S. War Department. Union troopers could be prolifigate with their steeds, knowing they would be replaced, without cost to the rider, not only if killed or injured in combat, but also if disabled through want of care. A Confederate who found himself dismounted, even if through no fault of his own, faced the prospect of being transferred to a less mobile, and therefore less desirable, branch of the service.

The temporary disbanding of Confederate units had one beneficial effect. It enabled officers who had been sent home to recruit among the local population. The results were sometimes dramatic. After a winter at home, the number of able-bodied men in the 5th Virginia Cavalry increased from about 150 to nearly 600. Furthermore, when spring came, the regiment's horses were in better condition than they had been for months, while deficiencies in weaponry and tack had been made good.[11]

Still, the benefits of wintertime recruitment were unevenly felt. As March 1865 neared its close, Lee's cavalry continued to number well below maximum effective strength. Rooney Lee's division, which consisted of eight regiments, each of which had begun the war approximately 1,000 strong, now comprised fewer than 2,000 officers and men. One of the brigades in the division of Maj. Gen. Fitzhugh Lee, Rooney's cousin, had a paper strength of 2,730 but fewer than 1,000 troopers "effective for the field." The third division in the cavalry corps, Maj. Gen. Thomas L. Rosser's, which had spent the winter campaigning in western Virginia and the Shenandoah Valley, appeared even worse off. A member of Rosser's 6th Virginia complained in a letter home that a season of raiding and fighting had "ruined our Brigade," and especially the 6th Virginia: "We have not over a hundred men in my Regt."[12]

The odds against the Army of Northern Virginia only seemed to get longer. Rumors had the Yankees expanding their strength through conscription and effective recruiting, even as Confederate resources drained away. Under these circumstances, the men of R. E. Lee's cavalry needed a powerful brand of stoicism to see them through the coming spring. Yet many seemed to possess this trait in abundance. One who did, Edwin H. Claybrook of the 9th Virginia, wrote his little sister that it did neither of them any good to dwell on the adversity the army would face in the weeks ahead: "We must not think of it darling, lest it might serve in some slight manner even to slacken our energies in the prosecution of this war, & keep us from doing our whole duty." Even many of the fatalists vowed to fight unstintingly to the end. As one of Claybrook's comrades in the 9th, Andrew Kay, put it: "I do firmly believe that the intention of the enemy is not only to subjugate but to exterminate our whole race. . . . Better [by] far an honorable death than to live an ignominious life and perish at last in degradation."[13]

Such sentiments indicated that the fighting that lay ahead would be desperate and sanguinary, even if brief.

A worrisome future was something Robert E. Lee's troopers were not used to confronting. Their history was one of almost unbroken success, the result not only of native ability and an enviable work ethic, but also of the patent inferiority of their opponents. From the outset of the war, the country boys in gray—many of whom had ridden and wielded firearms since early youth— had dominated the city dwellers who appeared to predominate in the ranks of the Yankee cavalry. This dominance begun to be felt in the spring of 1861, even before the first large-scale land battles of the war, with a series of small-scale victories by Confederate horsemen—most of them veterans of mounted militia service—on the Virginia Peninsula below Richmond. Not only did the Union cavalry, including Regulars, flee before the charging Rebels, so too did well-armed infantrymen and even artillerymen protected by formidable defenses.[14]

Unsurprisingly, the situation did not change after 36,000 pea-green Federals under Brig. Gen. Irvin McDowell marched out of Washington in mid-July, intent on capturing the Confederate capital. In their path were two dozen companies of Virginia horsemen, part of a 20,000-man force under Brig. Gen. Pierre G. T. Beauregard that had assembled near Manassas Junction and along Bull Run, eighty miles northwest of Richmond. The preponderance of raw recruits ensured that for both armies, the coming battle would be a series of missed opportunities. That the Confederates had any opportunity at all was largely due to Lt. Col. "Jeb" Stuart, whose 1st Virginia had screened the departure from the Shenandoah Valley of Gen. Joseph E. Johnston's army. Johnston's command was relatively small, some 12,000 troops of all arms. But after slipping away from Federal forces assigned to keep him in the Valley, Johnston linked with Beauregard hours before McDowell could strike. His arrival dramatically lowered the odds against the troops on Bull Run.

When McDowell attacked on the sultry morning of the twenty-first, most of Johnston's and Beauregard's troopers saw little action. The exception was Stuart, whose regiment, at the height of the contest, charged and scattered a phalanx of Yankee infantry before it could strike the flank of Brig. Gen. Thomas Jonathan Jackson's newly christened "Stonewall Brigade." When late in the day McDowell's exhausted recruits began to leave the field in retreat, the rest of the Southern horsemen were unleashed to hasten them on their way. Spurred on by energetic officers, they pursued with such speed and tenacity, taking so many prisoners, including several of high rank, that an orderly retreat became a rout. While most of the fugitives made it back to the Washington defenses, the gray riders not only gobbled up stragglers, but also collected an immense haul of materiel, including dozens of artillery pieces.

From July 21 can be dated the general perception, in the North as well as in the infant Confederacy, of the marked superiority of the Confederate cavalryman. In actuality, the battle did not prove the point, for McDowell's mounted arm had consisted of barely six companies of Regulars. They had seen little or no action until all was lost; then they did a tolerable job of protecting some of the retreat columns. Presumably, once adequate numbers of cavalrymen became available to the Federal government, Rebel supremacy would end.

Yet it quickly became clear that the Union faced a daunting challenge. Its first response was to create and fill a sixth regiment of Regular cavalry. When this measure proved inadequate to the army's needs, the War Department—which had long been wary of forming regiments of volunteer horsemen—reluctantly bowed to the demands of the situation, only to find that volunteer cavalry was not a short-term solution, either.

It seemed as if every youngster south of the Mason-Dixon line intended to ride to war, the gentleman's preferred mode of soldiering. Almost to a man, the later recruits could ride and shoot as well as those who had preceded them into the field. Moreover, like the earlier enlistees, they were commanded by natural leaders. Men who had risen to positions of civil authority now gravitated to high military command. When the officials in Washington finally conceded that they must recruit a large force of volunteers, they offered commissions to the politically powerful. Unlike their Southern counterparts, however, a preponderance of the Union recipients—especially, it seemed, those who found their way into the cavalry—displayed little or no military talent. In consequence, through the first half of the conflict, the North's mounted units were poorly organized, poorly led, and poorly disciplined.

In stark contrast, command of the cavalry in what become known as the Army of Northern Virginia was assumed by Stuart, a strict disciplinarian, an efficient administrator, a gifted tactician, and a resourceful intelligence gatherer. Early on, the "Beau Sabreur of the Confederacy" won the confidence and respect of most of his men, and the esteem and affection of many. His most valuable trait was the ability to make his officers and troopers believe themselves invincible—which, under his guiding hand, they appeared to be.

Stuart's talents were exhibited for all to see in the spring of 1862, when Maj. Gen. George B. McClellan, McDowell's successor, led the 120,000-man Army of the Potomac toward Richmond via the Virginia Peninsula. Barring the way was Joseph E. Johnston, commanding two-thirds as many able-bodied Confederates, including Stuart's several regiments and battalions. First at Yorktown, later outside Williamsburg, and later still along the siege lines at Richmond, Stuart's people successfully opposed many times their number of Yankees, including Regular and volunteer cavalry under their leader's father-in-law, Philip St. George Cooke.

When Johnston fell wounded while leading a sortie from Richmond on the last day of May, Robert E. Lee—heretofore military advisor to Confederate president Jefferson Davis—succeeded him. Like his predecessor, Lee quickly developed an appreciation of Stuart's gifts. Desperate to locate a weak point in McClellan's siege lines, in mid-June Lee dispatched Stuart, with 1,000 riders, to probe the Union right flank astride the Chickahominy River. Stuart not only gained critical intelligence that enabled Lee to attack the flank, precipitating a Union withdrawal, but he also rode along the length of the enemy army, sacked supply depots and rail lines, and outdistanced a phalanx of pursuers. Passing around McClellan's left, he returned his men to home base with minimal loss and to the cheers of Richmond's populace. The "Chickahominy Raid" made Stuart's name familiar in all quarters of the war-torn nation.

Bedeviled by Stuart and frightened by Lee's surprise offensive, McClellan withdrew from Richmond to Harrison's Landing, a distance of almost thirty miles. Although pleased by the outcome and his role in it, Stuart refused to rest on his new-won laurels. Supported closely by subordinates, including Fitz and Rooney Lee, as well as by the Stuart Horse Artillery under a handsome young daredevil named John Pelham, Stuart followed and harassed the Yankees, while keeping Robert E. Lee apprised of their movements. Thereafter he monitored McClellan's extended stay on the James River. Displaying a touch of audacity, on July 3 he showered the enemy's camps with shells from Pelham's batteries, heaping both insult and injury on a once-formidable foe.

In the first half of August, a thoroughly beaten McClellan withdrew to northern Virginia, while adding portions of his army to the recently organized Army of Virginia, which was operating more than fifty miles to the north and west under Maj. Gen. John Pope. Even before the last Yankees left the Peninsula, however, Stuart prepared to accompany the main army to the new field of action. While a few thousand horsemen under his newest subordinate, Brig. Gen. Wade Hampton of South Carolina, remained behind to watch McClellan, Stuart ranged deep inside enemy lines with the remainder of his newly organized division to strike Pope's supply base at Catlett's Station on the Orange & Alexandria Railroad. By sacking that lightly guarded depot, he forced Pope to abandon his apparently impregnable position along the Rappahannock River and withdraw to Manassas Junction.

Robert E. Lee, whom Stuart had provided with captured documents that shed light on enemy numbers and dispositions, followed up Pope's withdrawal and brought him to bay late in August on the fringes of the Bull Run battlefield. In the ensuing fight, Stuart thrust aside cavalry guarding the Union left, ensuring that no stand would be made in that sector when Pope fell back under the heavier blows of Lee's infantry. For the second time in a little over a year, a Yankee army sought refuge in the Washington defenses.

Lee and Stuart refused to copy their enemy's inactivity. On September 4, the Army of Northern Virginia began to cross the Potomac into lower Maryland, then ranged northwestward. That border state, whose Unionist governor had refused to permit its secession, had nevertheless furnished thousands of recruits to Lee's army. By moving north, the Confederate commander intended not only to recruit further, but also to subsist his troops outside war-ravaged Virginia.

Following Pope's relief from command, McClellan returned to power. When "Little Mac" finally departed Washington to pursue Lee, Stuart's horsemen slowed his march through South Mountain and the neighboring Catoctins. Eventually the Army of the Potomac muscled its way through those ranges and confronted Lee along Antietam Creek, near Sharpsburg. Lee's defensive tactics combined with the local terrain to limit the service of Stuart's troopers throughout the fighting on September 17, the bloodiest single day of the war.

Fought to a tactical draw at Sharpsburg, Lee ended his invasion and quickly recrossed the Potomac. It took McClellan a month to muster the nerve to follow; when he did, Stuart ably screened the movements of James Longstreet's infantry as it withdrew from the Shenandoah Valley to its old haunts along the Rappahannock. By then Stuart had successfully executed a second raid inside McClellan's lines. From October 9 to 12, he and 1,800 of his men had encircled their enemy, ranging as far north as Chambersburg, Pennsylvania. The raiders brought Robert E. Lee intelligence on enemy positions, secured hundreds of remounts, emptied Union warehouses, and by a combination of skill and daring, eluded forces of all arms sent to run them down.

McClellan's delay in pursuing Lee, combined with Stuart's embarrassing foray in his rear, cost Little Mac his job in early November. His innovative but stubborn successor, Maj. Gen. Ambrose Burnside, moved quickly in the direction of Richmond. Stuart kept tabs on the suddenly speedy Yankees, but only the lack of intact bridges on the Rappahannock prevented Burnside from crossing at Falmouth and sweeping down on the Confederate capital, via Fredericksburg, before Lee could stop him. By the time Burnside finally crossed the river on pontoon bridges, the Army of Northern Virginia held commanding terrain outside Fredericksburg. Incredibly, Burnside attacked, losing 13,000 men killed or wounded to no strategic purpose. As at Sharpsburg, Stuart's troopers were restricted to the sidelines, mostly in Stonewall Jackson's sector. Even so, John Pelham immortalized himself and the Stuart Horse Artillery. Supported by two guns, the young captain shelled the flank of one of Burnside's attack columns from a close-in position, causing consternation and carnage and preventing many soldiers from attacking at all.

As if he had not done enough to hurt and frustrate the Army of the Potomac, two weeks after the bloodletting of December 13 Stuart led yet another raid into the enemy's rear. Again he wrecked supply depots and captured quartermasters' and sutlers' wagons. This time his 2,000 riders drove to the outskirts of Washington, D.C., spreading panic wherever they turned, before returning home at a leisurely pace. The spoils secured on the "Dumfries Raid" complemented those Wade Hampton had taken during a series of earlier, smaller-scale expeditions in the same region.

The winter of 1862–63 was the first to take a heavy toll of Stuart's command. Hundreds of horses died of equine diseases, exposure to freezing temperatures, and a lack of adequate forage. The season also revealed that the enemy's cavalry, once the playthings of the gray cavaliers, had acquired enough training and experience to vie with them on something uncomfortably close to even terms. On March 17, 1863, reacting to an embarrassing series of attacks on its picket lines northwest of Falmouth, Brig. Gen. William W. Averell's division surprised and nearly routed a slightly smaller contingent of Confederates under Fitz Lee. Although Stuart arrived to take charge in midfight, he was unable to prevent each of Lee's regiments from being shot, shelled, and sabered into retreat near Kelly's Ford. At the height of the contest, the irreplaceable Pelham took a mortal wound. Although the day closed with the enemy's withdrawal, many of Stuart's men had the nagging feeling they had been outfought for the first time.

During the subsequent Chancellorsville Campaign, Stuart and his troopers recouped any prestige they had lost on St. Patrick's Day. Late in April and early in May, they deftly parried the first large-scale Union raid of the war in the eastern theater, while also helping foil an offensive by Burnside's successor, Maj. Gen. Joseph Hooker. On May 2, 1863, the second day of combat in the Virginia Wilderness west of Fredericksburg, Fitz Lee's scouts discovered that the right flank of the Army of the Potomac was unanchored and vulnerable. Stuart then guided Stonewall Jackson's troops into position for a daring assault that shattered not only Hooker's flank, but also his confidence. On May 3, the versatile Stuart, who had commanded combined arms on several occasions, helped ensure Hooker's withdrawal to the north side of the Rappahannock by skillfully leading the corps of the mortally wounded Jackson against several points of the Union line.

Buoyed by this latest success, Lee again took the war into the North, this time as far as south-central Pennsylvania. But on June 9, just before Stuart's men could join the invasion column, the seemingly rejuvenated Union cavalry attacked their camps near the Orange & Alexandria Railroad depot at Brandy Station. Five hours of charges and countercharges ended, as had the fighting of March 17, with a Union withdrawal. But again the Yankees had given as good as they got, thanks to an effective mix of mounted and dismounted tactics, fighting fiercely with saber, pistol, and carbine. In contrast, their opponents had displayed their preference for fighting in the saddle, mainly with sidearms, although tactical versatility would have served them better.

Within a week, Stuart and his men had essentially recovered from the effects of Brandy Station. It took longer, however, to salve injured pride and rise above the criticism that the Southern public and press heaped upon them in the wake of their near disaster. Soon after joining the march north, Stuart, with a sizable portion of his division, was again tilting with the upstart Yankees, this time in Virginia's Loudoun Valley. A week of spirited clashes ended on terms favorable to the Confederates, who did an excellent job of screening the movements of Lee's infantry and artillery farther west. Even so, the encounters at Aldie, Middleburg, and Upperville revealed the growing confidence and ability of the Yankees under Maj. Gen. Alfred Pleasonton and such seasoned subordinates as John Buford, David McMurtrie Gregg, and H. Judson Kilpatrick.

On June 22, Stuart secured Lee's permission to cut loose from the main army and raid through Maryland to link with the advance wing in Pennsylvania. The Beau Sabreur left behind enough troopers to escort Lee through enemy territory, although due to miscommunication and distracted attention, they were used ineffectively. With 3,500 others, Stuart rode through the elongated lines of the Union army, command of which was soon to pass from Joe Hooker to George Gordon Meade. En route to their destination along the Susquehanna River, the riders were delayed at several points as well as slowed by the integration of 125 captured supply wagons. For several days unable to locate Lee's whereabouts, Stuart reached Gettysburg on the afternoon of July 2, more than twenty-four hours after a battle had broken out there between major elements of both armies. Although no proof exists that Lee rebuked the cavalry chief for tardiness or disobedience of orders, contemporary and latter-day critics would accuse Stuart of allowing his superior to stumble blindly into a fight that ultimately helped doom the Confederate cause.

After rejoining the main army, Stuart and his men fought long and hard at Gettysburg as well as at nearby Hunterstown. In the climactic struggle of July 3, they inflicted heavy casualties on their adversaries—principally Gregg's division—but suffered just as heavily, including the wounding and disabling of Wade Hampton. When Lee withdrew from Pennsylvania, Stuart guarded the army's flanks and rear as it moved to the rain-swollen Potomac. In a score of skirmishes between July 5 and 14, until the river receded to the point that fording was possible, the Confederates kept their pesky opponents at arm's length. Although beset by adversity, Stuart's officers and men appeared to have lost none of their spirit and determination.

After the war returned to Virginia, Stuart and his opponents squared off in a series of clashes amid the Rappahannock-Rapidan basin. The running war continued into the autumn of 1863, both sides losing heavily in officers, enlisted men, and horseflesh. Active operations did not cease until the close of Meade's ill-fated Mine Run Campaign of November-December, which Lee, armed with timely intelligence from Stuart, effectively countered. By then Stuart nominally commanded a corps, although its components remained so far understrength that he was denied the lieutenant general's rank due him by regulations. Even so, he continued to enjoy Robert E. Lee's confidence and respect, both as an intelligence analyst and as a field leader.

In May 1864, following an eventful winter in which he helped stymie more than one raid on the Confederate capital, Stuart prepared to oppose the Overland Campaign of Grant, the newly appointed commander of all Union land forces, who had chosen to make his headquarters with Meade's army. Stuart's close support of Robert E. Lee's troops helped cause Grant's offensive to bog down in the Wilderness. Then Jeb rode hard at the head of four brigades to deflect yet another strike at Richmond, this by 10,000 Yankees under Meade's new cavalry commander, Maj. Gen. Philip H. Sheridan. On the eleventh, Stuart barred Sheridan's path a dozen miles above the capital. In a desperate battle near Yellow Tavern, the Beau Sabreur received a mortal wound from a pistol ball, from which he died the following day. Sheridan routed the leaderless enemy but elected not to attack Richmond, bypassing it on his way south.

Although grateful that his capital had been spared, Robert E. Lee keenly felt Stuart's loss. For several months, he refused to appoint an official successor, although Hampton, who had recovered from his Gettysburg wounds, exercised overall command whenever his division served alongside Fitz or Rooney Lee's.

Not till early August did Lee gain enough confidence in Hampton to bestow on him titular authority. By then the South Carolinian had demonstrated high aptitude in several clashes between the Chickahominy and James Rivers, especially in the sanguinary action at Haw's Shop, May 28. Then, too, early in June he had curtailed Sheridan's raid on Trevilian Station, a Virginia Central depot sixty miles west of Richmond. In two days of desperate combat, he had decisively defeated his opponent despite being heavily outnumbered and lacking the close cooperation of a seemingly apathetic Fitz Lee, who considered himself the rightful heir to Stuart's mantle. Hampton's preference for dismounted fighting, and his reliance on firepower over horsemanship, contrasted sharply with his predecessor's tactics. In time, however, he gained the trust and respect even of those who revered Jeb Stuart's memory.

Hampton, this time with the full support of Fitz Lee, harassed Sheridan's return march to the James, taking a heavy toll of the Union rear guard at Samaria Church. After following the Yankees over the river toward Grant's latest objective, Petersburg, the gray troopers fell upon a Yankee column that had been raiding the railroads west and south of the "Cockade City," cuffing it about at Sappony Church and Reams's Station.

Both armies then settled down to siege operations outside Petersburg. In mid-August, Robert E. Lee tried to end the stalemate by sending 3,000 cavalry under his nephew to the Shenandoah Valley, where a small army under Maj. Gen. Jubal A. Early was opposing a larger force of all arms recently placed under Sheridan. In September and October, while Hampton continued to oppose Meade's investment, Fitz Lee's horsemen supported Early in battle outside Winchester, atop Fisher's Hill, and along Cedar Creek. Thanks to the greater strength of the enemy as well as to some lost opportunities, each fight closed with Early's withdrawal up (south through) the Valley.

In the midst of the melee outside Winchester, Fitz Lee was wounded in the thigh and incapacitated. During his recuperation, subordinates including

Rosser, Munford, Lunsford Lomax, and Williams Wickham tried to keep pressure on Sheridan's Army of the Shenandoah. When cold weather ended active operations, many troopers ranged into West Virginia to attack Union outposts and secure provisions for what remained of Early's army as it went into winter quarters. Upon returning to the Valley, the troopers found they could do little to discomfit the better-fed, better-armed, better-equipped troops under Sheridan.

When spring returned and roads began to dry, the Yankees were in fighting trim and eager for the fray, their opponents less so on both counts. Rosser, Munford, and their colleagues could only observe as Sheridan, on February 27, 1865, led 7,500 cavalrymen on the first leg of their march to rejoin Grant and Meade. At Waynesboro on March 2, Little Phil halted long enough to assault, uproot, and scatter the fragments of Early's decimated command, before continuing east by south with an air of invincibility. Horsemen under Rosser dogged his heels as Sheridan moved on to Charlottesville, but they remained powerless to slow the little Irishman.

By the third week in March, Sheridan's destroyers were nearing Petersburg, which, along with Richmond, had seen bitter fighting in the months since Fitz Lee followed Early to the Valley. Hampton, with such resources as he could gather, had done his utmost to counter a series of Union offensives, many of them spearheaded by the cavalry Sheridan had left behind: Gregg's division of the Army of the Potomac and the small cavalry division of the Army of the James, under Brig. Gen. August V. Kautz. Hampton had stubbornly resisted Grant's advance toward and beyond the Petersburg & Weldon Railroad. On August 25, he had helped break the lodgment made by Meade's II Corps at Reams's Station. On September 16, Hampton launched a raid of his own, directed not at enemy works, but at the cattle herd that fed the combined Union armies, corralled at Coggins's Point on the James. The strike into the Federal rear was a dramatic success. Hampton and his second in command, Rosser, captured and drove off 2,500 head of cattle, a gift that their hungry comrades at Petersburg gratefully accepted.

Two weeks after the "Beefsteak Raid," when Grant launched a coordinated offensive on both sides of the James, Hampton's horsemen teamed with an infantry division to halt an advance by Meade's troops near Peebles's Farm, south of Petersburg. But in later weeks, despite Hampton's best efforts, the Army of the Potomac extended its lines west of the Weldon line. A growing number of defenders began to suspect that the railroads in Petersburg's rear would soon be in Yankee hands.

Although outgunned, with their backs to the wall, the Rebel troopers refused to quit. In late October, Meade sent infantry and cavalry toward the

Boydton Plank Road in Lee's rear. Two gray infantry divisions, supported closely by Hampton's riders, interposed between the attacking columns, forcing the Federals to pull back. A little more than three months later, however, as Sheridan poised to leave the Valley for the siege lines at Petersburg, a new offensive ended with the Boydton Plank Road in Meade's hands. Union success at Hatcher's Run had so stretched the enemy's flank that Lee's men now held a line almost forty miles long, from north of Richmond to southwest of Petersburg. Observers on both sides realized that some links in this human chain were so weak that an assault in moderate strength might break them. In that event, the life span of Lee's army would be measurable in days.

Given their mobility, Early's horsemen had cleared the scene of the disaster at Waynesboro more quickly than their luckless comrades in the infantry; thus the arm remained relatively intact as it followed Sheridan east toward Charlottesville. A few hundred horsemen under Col. William A. Morgan of the 1st Virginia kept watch over the Federals throughout their two-day layover in the college town, and when Sheridan pressed on to the James River on March 6, Morgan staged a cautious pursuit. Another, larger contingent under Thomas Rosser—who had succeeded to the command of Early's cavalry following Fitz Lee's wounding—attempted to overawe the column that Sheridan had sent back to Winchester along with the hundreds of Confederates who had been captured on the second. But the escort, 1,200 strong, proved too hefty and too vigilant. Despite his best efforts, Rosser proved unable to liberate more than a few dozen captives.[15]

Confederate bridge burners prevented Sheridan from crossing the James at amd near Columbia, and his pontoon train was of limited capacity. Thus he started east along the upper bank of the river. For the next two weeks, he marched toward Richmond and Petersburg at a pace slow enough to permit his men to wreck sections of the Virginia Central and the James River Canal. As before, the Confederate cavalry—not only Rosser's and Morgan's contingents, but also miscellaneous detachments that had survived the fiasco at Waynesboro—followed at a respectful distance. Chagrined by their inability to bring the enemy to heel, by midmonth many Rebels had turned toward the siege lines via more direct routes. The decision to abandon the pursuit seemed to be validated when a large force of infantry under Longstreet, bolstered by cavalry under the fully recuperated Fitz Lee (now commanding all Confederate horsemen north of the James), failed to intercept the Yankees as they neared the end of their march.[16]

Rosser's arrival from the Valley, combined with some recent personnel shifts, changed the face of the Confederate cavalry on the Richmond-Petersburg front. In August, on the eve of Fitz Lee's departure to join Early, the Cavalry Corps, A.N.V., now officially under the command of Hampton, had consisted of the divisions of Fitz Lee, Rooney Lee, and Brig. Gen. M. Calbraith Butler, Hampton's most trusted subordinate. When Fitz went west, he took his two brigades of Virginians, Lomax's and Wickham's. At Petersburg, Hampton retained Butler's two brigades of South Carolinians and Georgians, Rosser's "Laurel Brigade" of Virginia troopers, and Rooney Lee's two brigades, one composed of Virginians under Brig. Gen. John R. Chambliss, Jr., the other made up of North Carolinians under Brig. Gen. Rufus Barringer.[17]

When he reached the Valley, Fitz Lee had assumed command not only of his own division, but also of four small brigades that had been supporting Early since the previous June. He grouped the imperfectly organized and poorly disciplined "Valley Cavalry" into a division under Lomax. Thus Fitz became in effect a corps commander. His old division was assigned to Tom Munford, who gave way to Rosser when the Laurel Brigade was called to the Valley following its stint as cattle rustlers. It was from this post that Rosser ascended to overall command upon Fitz's wounding.[18]

By January 1865, R. E. Lee's nephew was back on active duty, managing the cavalry defending Richmond. In size and ability, his command did not compare with the one Early had assigned him. It consisted mainly of a heterogeneous group of Virginia, South Carolina, and Georgia horsemen under the direct command of Brig. Gen. Martin W. Gary. Rooney Lee's and Butler's divisions, under Hampton's overall command, continued to support the Confederate forces on the Southside.[19]

Then came the changes at the top. Late in January, with Sherman's legions poised to move from Georgia into South Carolina en route to Petersburg, Joe Johnston, recently reinstated to command of what remained of the Army of Tennessee, called on Lee for reinforcements. Lee, who now had authority over all Confederate forces, believed he could spare some cavalry, but only temporarily. He consented to send Butler's division south, with Wade Hampton, who was anxious to defend his native state, at its head. Lee even persuaded Jefferson Davis to appoint Hampton a lieutenant general, at which rank he would command all of Johnston's horsemen, heretofore led by the fiery but erratic Maj. Gen. Joseph Wheeler.

Hampton and Butler went to Johnston with the stipulation that they would return to the A.N.V. when active campaigning returned to the Richmond-Petersburg front. As Lee ought to have foreseen, however, no troopers returned from the Carolinas. He came to consider his act of generosity a major mistake, writing Hampton after the war, "You cannot regret as much as I did that you were not with us at our final struggle."[20]

Upon Hampton's departure, Lee reacted as he had in the aftermath of Stuart's death by electing not to appoint a titular commander of cavalry. By seniority, however, Fitz Lee assumed effective control of the horsemen at Richmond and Petersburg, not only Gary's brigade on the James and Rooney Lee's division along the Petersburg & Weldon Railroad, but also the troopers returning from the Valley. When Rosser's people arrived near Richmond, Fitz oversaw a small-scale reorganization, the first element of which involved demoting Rosser to command of the brigade formerly led by Brig. Gen. John McCausland—the only element of Lomax's Valley Cavalry to make the trip to Richmond.

Rosser filled the lesser position only briefly. Perhaps at the urging of Robert E. Lee, who was sensitive to matters of seniority, his nephew returned Rosser to division command by assigning him not only McCausland's troopers, but also the Laurel Brigade. Command of the latter unit—once Rosser's own, more recently led by Brig. Gen. Henry B. Davidson, who appears to have lacked the clout to retain the position—had recently devolved upon a close friend of Rosser's, Brig. Gen. James Dearing, like Rosser a former artillery commander. At the same time, Fitz instigated some actions that irked the prideful Rosser. Soon after Rosser bivouacked his men at Spencer's Mill on the Nottoway River southeast of Petersburg, Fitz detached the 8th Virginia from McCausland's brigade and assigned it to Rooney Lee's division near Stony Creek Station. This was the second such loss McCausland's brigade had suffered in less than a month. Sometime prior to mid-March, the 14th Virginia had also been transferred to Rooney Lee's command.[21]

The loss of even two regiments rankled, but Rosser was even more dismayed when Fitz Lee restored Munford to the command of the brigade once led by Fitz himself and later by Williams Wickham—the oldest and most prestigious brigade in the Cavalry, A.N.V., consisting of the 1st, 2nd, 3rd, and 4th Virginia regiments. Rosser and Munford had been at odds throughout their service together under Early. On one occasion, the prickly tempered Rosser had preferred court-martial charges against the colonel for some trivial offense. A military court promptly dismissed the case, but the spiteful Rosser had long denied Munford the brigade his seniority entitled him to, restricting him to command of his own 2nd Virginia.[22]

The new assignments having been made, Lee and his subordinates could focus attention and energy on countering any moves that Grant, Meade, and Sheridan made on either side of the James. Some such move was surely imminent—it was a matter of time before the enemy struck hard at those weak points on the Richmond-Petersburg line. It was the job of the cavalry of the Army of Northern Virginia not only to alert the main army to the coming blows, but to commit every resource—every man and beast—to parry them and, if possible, counterattack.

Fulfilling the demands of this mission would tax everyone to the limit, and beyond. But there was no viable alternative to resistance and retaliation.

TWO

"We Are . . . Going to Take Richmond and Finish the Rebels Up"

IF THE CONFEDERATE CAVALRY AWAITED EVENTS WITH A MIXTURE OF RESOLVE and trepidation, their opponents looked to the future with quiet confidence. Not that they believed the coming campaign would be brief and bloodless. A trooper in the 2nd Pennsylvania, a member of the provost guard at Meade's headquarters, wrote his family in the waning days of March: "We are I firmly believe going to take Richmond and finish the rebels up . . . but there will be a good many lives lost yet."[1]

Years of hard-won experience, of trial and error, of mistakes surmounted and limitations expanded, had brought the horsemen of the Armies of the Potomac and the James to a high degree of effectiveness, and the sometimes painful lessons they had learned were about to pay off. A lieutenant in the 6th New York believed that the tactics and training he and his comrades had absorbed "were more practical and efficient than those of any regular cavalry in Europe." The high command held as firmly to this belief as the rank and file. Bvt. Maj. Gen. Wesley Merritt, the thirty-year-old commander of the two divisions that had accompanied Sheridan from Waynesboro to Petersburg, described the troopers at Meade's and Ord's disposal as "about twelve thousand as good cavalry as the world ever saw."[2]

The road to proficiency had been long, rocky, and replete with detours and dead ends. The Union cavalry in the eastern theater had entered the war, as had their enemy, imbued with a cavalier tradition that stressed horsemanship over firepower, the mounted charge over fighting afoot. Such concepts had been drummed into the Federals by European drillmasters, veterans of the light and heavy cavalry of the French and Prussian Armies. Tutors, nostalgic for the warfare of Napoleon, failed to take into account the emergence of the rifle-musket. This relatively new firearm, which doubled the effective range of the smoothbore weapons long wielded by armies, had revolutionized cavalry tactics as well as infantry formations. The rifle, in the hands of soldiers who knew how to use it, had rendered the mounted charge obsolete except under highly controlled conditions.

A major factor in the Federal cavalry's slow but steady ascendancy was that its people outstripped their adversaries in grasping the importance of rifled arms and integrating them into their tactics. Another factor was the greater availability in the North of carbines, the principal shoulder arm of the cavalry, which enabled companies and regiments to dismount and fight on foot behind good cover, from which they could decimate charging Confederates. The preponderance in the Union ranks of breech-loading carbines, including repeaters able to discharge several rounds without reloading, increased the firepower troopers could unleash, enabling them to halt and scatter attackers.[3]

Perceiving an advantage to dismounted fighting, the Federals worked hard to perfect this mode of warfare. They fought so often on foot that they developed an identity as something other than conventional horse soldiers. "Our cavalry," observed an artillery commander on the eve of the war's final campaign, "are more mounted infantry than anything else." In a sense the officer was correct, but in another sense he was short-sighted. By March 1865, the troopers of the armies under Grant fought in the saddle with saber and pistol just as effectively as they did afoot. In acquiring this versatility, they had rediscovered their roots as dragoons—hybrid soldiers of the prewar army, armed, equipped, and trained to fight mounted and dismounted as conditions dictated. This split personality had been fostered by influential commanders including Merritt, Gregg, and Buford, each of whom had won his spurs in the dragoon regiments of the Old Army.[4]

The dragoon tradition was something that the average Confederate neither understood nor adopted. The Federal trooper of 1865 professed to view his mount as a vehicle—an instrument of mobility that did not constitute his only, or even his primary, resource. By contrast, the typical Confederate, in the words of one Virginian, "considered himself only half a man when separated from his horse." The cavalry of the Army of Northern Virginia had suffered for its single-minded devotion to this mode of thinking. It would continue to suffer as long as the conflict lasted.[5]

In the early going, the Federals had a difficult time inculcating *any* tactics — staying in the saddle long enough to acquire even a semblance of professionalism constituted their foremost challenge. The relatively brief training most volunteer cavalry units received in their home regions was insufficient to make horsemen of recruits who had rarely, if ever, ridden in civilian life. Nor did they become horse soldiers during the more extended training periods they experienced in camp outside Washington, D.C., and across the Potomac in northern Virginia. For many months, drillmasters shook their heads at the quality of the material at their disposal. Many came to doubt the validity of the old adage that two years' service would produce a fully developed trooper. A typical reaction to the mistakes the would-be cavaliers made on the drill field was the exclamation of one disgusted European: "Oh, stupid! stupid! even an ox may be taught to know right from left, but ye will never learn!"[6]

One reason for such exasperation was the dread with which would-be troopers regarded their mounts. Looking back, one veteran recalled that most of his comrades "showed much more fear of their horses than they ever did afterward of the enemy. The wild fumbling after mane or saddle-straps, the terror depicted on some faces . . . are a lasting source of amusement." So it might have seemed in the warm glow of memory, but at the time, the situation was anything but humorous.

Predictably, when the first volunteer units were placed in the field, error, defeat, and occasionally disaster resulted. One reason was that the high command of the Army of the Potomac, including George B. McClellan's well-intentioned but shortsighted cavalry commander, Brig. Gen. George Stoneman, tended to reduce regiments to two-company squadrons and four-company battalions for active service. When these detachments encountered larger units of polished Confederates, the Yankees usually broke and ran, often in abject terror. The outcome was often the same even when they outnumbered their enemy.

The situation had improved only marginally by the time McClellan invaded southeastern Virginia in the spring of 1862. Little Mac, like his predecessor, McDowell, aimed his army at Richmond, seat of the Confederate government. Unlike McDowell, he advanced on the city from the southeast, shipping his more than 100,000 men down the coast to Fort Monroe, then leading them on foot up the Virginia Peninsula. At first McClellan's strategy looked promising, but it fell apart outside Yorktown, whose tiny garrison bluffed him into believing it too formidable to take by storm. The upshot was a month-long siege that furnished his troops, including his understrength mounted arm, with limited experience in active operations.

On the evening of May 3, only hours before McClellan could open on Yorktown with carefully emplaced cannons and mortars, the reinforced garrison—now under Joe Johnston, the hero of Manassas—suddenly evacuated and headed to Williamsburg, en route to Richmond. Stoneman's cavalry pursued with the enthusiasm of rookies, but on the fifth, Stuart's people struck them outside the colonial capital. Showing flashes of poise, the Federals held on until McClellan's infantry spelled them. But when Johnston resumed his retreat following a day of indecisive battle, the Federals saw only fitful skirmishing on the road to Richmond.

The cavalry were similarly idle through the early days of McClellan's investment of the enemy capital. They played a negligible role in the first engagement of the siege, Seven Pines (Fair Oaks), May 31-June 1, which ended with Robert E. Lee succeeding the wounded Johnston. They played a larger, but humiliatingly unsuccessful, part in countering Stuart's Chickahominy Raid, perhaps because the slow-moving Philip St. George Cooke, who led the pursuit, was unwilling to overtake his quarry for fear of being captured by his son-in-law.

Cooke's failure brought him a certain amount of criticism, but it paled in comparison to the censure he attracted less than two weeks later at Gaines's Mill, third of the so-called Seven Days' Battles. When Lee, fresh from strategic victories at Oak Grove and Mechanicsville, attacked the retreating Federals along Boatswain's Swamp on the afternoon of June 27, the fighting swirled in the direction of Cooke, whose Regulars had been posted, without orders, in the Union left rear. Brigade after brigade of Confederate infantry struck the left flank, only to recoil against the resistance of thousands of steadfast Yankees. Eventually, however, a portion of the flank gave way, threatening a bank of strategically positioned artillery. Without the requisite authority, Cooke ordered one of his Regular regiments to move forward and counterattack. Reluctantly, the unit's leader led 250 of his men, at a rapid gait, toward the enemy force. The surprised attackers halted only long enough to train their rifles on the approaching horsemen. With a single massed volley, they blew almost half of the Regulars out of their saddles. Survivors galloped back in confusion, leaving behind almost sixty dead, dying, wounded, or captured comrades. For exceeding the norms of cavalry employment, Cooke (a noted theorist and tactician who ought to have foreseen the folly of such a charge) was placed on inactive service for the rest of the war.

McClellan's cavalry was relegated to picket and scouting duty through the balance of the campaign, which ended with their demoralized army far from the city it had come within five miles of entering. While the command sat immobile, junior officers such as John F. Farnsworth, William W. Averell, and Alfred Pleasonton rose in rank and authority to replace those, such as Cooke, who had been found wanting. But once Lee left McClellan's front to oppose John Pope, these officers had no opportunity to validate their promotions.

On those few occasions when allowed to display his ability, no newcomer covered himself with distinction. During the pursuit of Stuart's

Chambersburg raiders, for example, neither Averell nor Pleasonton showed a burning desire to overtake the Rebels, and they made mistakes that enabled Stuart to escape the punishment his audacity surely merited. The same lack of aggressiveness characterized the pursuit of the graybacks who sacked Occoquan and Dumfries, although this time most of the blame attached itself to the cavalry of the Defense Forces of Washington. When, following the carnage at Fredericksburg, Averell attempted to launch an expedition of his own into the enemy's rear, he was thwarted by logistical foul-ups and the obstructionism of jealous colleagues. Little wonder that by the end of 1862, the army's opinion of its horsemen found expression in the sneering observation of its chief provost marshal: "With the exception of a few regulars and two or three other regiments . . . our cavalry is an awful botch."

Ambrose Burnside's mishandling of the army at Fredericksburg—one blunder being his failure to assign his cavalry a productive role in the battle— had beneficial long-term effects. When the army leader lost his job following a late January 1863 offensive hampered by roads so boggy it came to be known as the "Mud March," his successor, "Fighting Joe" Hooker, vowed to improve the efficiency of every unit he had inherited. Hooker's coming paid especial dividends for the cavalry, which he supplied with more and better arms, equipment, and remounts. He also pledged to provide it with a more reliable leadership base, but he failed to follow through, keeping in power plodders such as Stoneman and Averell.

Perhaps Fighting Joe's most welcome reform was his massing of the well-scattered arm into a full-fledged corps, one removed from the jurisdiction of infantry commanders. The result was a force 12,000 strong under Stoneman, with Pleasonton, Averell, and Gregg as his senior subordinates. The foursome was backed by lower-ranking cavalry officers of ability, including Buford, Benjamin F. ("Grimes") Davis, and Thomas C. Devin, and by such talented horse artillerymen as John C. Tidball and James Madison Robertson.

Having invested time, energy, and resources on his new mounted wing, Hooker was understandably chagrined when, within weeks of the corps' formation, troopers picketing the upper Rappahannock were uprooted and scattered by Stuart's lieutenants. Following a particularly embarrassing strike by Fitzhugh Lee on Averell's lines near Hartwood Church, a livid Hooker demanded retaliation. The result was the March 17 attack on Lee's bivouacs near Culpeper Court House, in which Averell's troopers for the first time propelled not one regiment of Virginians, but five of them into hasty and indecorous retreat. A jittery Averell betrayed his shortcomings not only by delaying his initial offensive until too late in the day to finish the job, but also by withdrawing prematurely. Even so, the high spirits of his men communicated themselves to the rest of the corps. In time, even those who had yet to cross paths with the Rebels looked forward to leaving the imprint of their boots on Jeb Stuart's hide.

While corporate morale was at its peak, George Stoneman started on his raid to Richmond, the first large-scale operation of the rejuvenated cavalry. Originally, the expedition was to have been the centerpiece of Hooker's grand scheme to flank the Confederates out of their impregnable positions near Fredericksburg and attack them on open ground. Like Burnside's Mud March, however, Stoneman's Raid ran afoul of an extended spell of bad weather, which delayed its start for two weeks and forced Hooker to revamp his strategy.

When the rains and high winds finally ceased and the Rappahannock receded to fording depth, Stoneman crossed into the Rebel rear and headed south in multiple columns. Over the next week, his raiders levered up railroad track, torched supply depots, and took prisoners. One wing, led by the feisty Judson Kilpatrick, penetrated to the gates of Richmond before withdrawing inside Union lines at Yorktown to avoid pursuit. Other columns, including Averell's, found their paths blocked by the few Rebels who trailed them. Sensing correctly that the expedition was a glorified diversion, Stuart kept his main body well in hand and within supporting distance of its army, thus contributing greatly to Robert E. Lee's success against Hooker at Chancellorsville. By the time Stoneman rejoined him, Hooker had retreated to his old base at Falmouth. The raid, which had laid waste to large sections of middle Virginia, had no lasting, strategic effect. Hooker, seeking scapegoats for his defeat, pounced on Stoneman and Averell. Both officers lost their commands within days of their return to the army.

Again, new blood rose to the top. Alfred Pleasonton, a master self-promoter, succeeded Stoneman, while Buford and Kilpatrick eventually joined Gregg in division command. At Hooker's urging, the newcomers seized the offensive, on June 9 launching a surprise attack on Stuart's bivouacs between the Rappahannock and Culpeper Court House. The inhabitants, who had expected to join the vanguard of R. E. Lee's invasion force before dawn, were awakened even earlier when two columns of Yankees came splashing across the river at Kelly's and Beverly Fords. The wings attempted to unite at Brandy Station on the Orange & Alexandria, but belated Rebel resistance, combined with blunders by Pleasonton and the early loss of Grimes Davis, prevented the link-up until the battle became a stalemate and the Federals withdrew. Yet Pleasonton's troopers, most of whom had fought afoot against charging Rebels, had given their enemy all they could handle. At several points in the battle, which had involved no fewer than 17,000 combatants, the upstarts in blue seemed on the verge of routing Stuart's vaunted horsemen. The Cavalry Division, A.N.V., had survived a violent test, but by the narrowest of margins.

Despite another retreat from a hard-fought field, the Federals could take pride and satisfaction in their achievements. Their morale remained high when, a few days later, they trailed Lee's army northward, seeking to determine its heading. The battering he had absorbed prevented Stuart from renewing combat until midmonth. While screening the right flank of Lee's main army, his men again crossed swords with the feisty enemy. At times during the fighting in the Loudoun Valley, Pleasonton's troopers and horse artillerymen pressed Stuart back upon the Blue Ridge gaps he had been ordered to block. They failed, however, to penetrate the Confederates' counterreconnaissance barrier until the close of the fighting near Upperville on June 21, when scouts from Buford's division climbed foothills that provided a view of Lee's infantry camps in the Shenandoah. But by then it was too late to prevent the Army of Northern Virginia from crossing the Potomac into Maryland and Pennsylvania.

When Stuart cut loose from his army, intending to ride through Hooker's elongated ranks and rejoin his infantry friends on the Susquehanna River, unanticipated events helped foil his plans. He had not foreseen that a part of Pleasonton's command—Kilpatrick's division, including the brigade of twenty-three-year-old George Armstrong Custer—would bar his path outside Hanover, Pennsylvania, twelve miles east of Gettysburg, on June 30. Due as much to Custer's combativeness as to any other factor, the Confederates were pinned down for several hours before they could break free and resume their march in search of comrades whose location remained a mystery to them.

Kilpatrick, whose forte was combat, not reconnaissance, lost touch with the raiders once they cleared Hanover. Meanwhile, Buford, who was proficient in both capacities, led his troopers out of Emmitsburg, Maryland, and into Gettysburg just shy of noon on the thirtieth. As commander of the advance element of the army that had recently passed into Meade's hands, Buford scrutinized the presence of Confederate infantry west and north of town. He correctly surmised that Lee was concentrating his far-flung troops in and near the road hub the cavalry had occupied.

An expert evaluator of terrain, Buford viewed Gettysburg's ridges and valleys as good defensive ground. Regardless of the consequences, he determined to hold that ground until relieved by Meade's infantry. As the old dragoon feared, before supports could reach Gettysburg on the morning of July 1, thousands of Rebels swept down on the town from two, and later three, directions. Outnumbered nearly twenty to one, fighting afoot from behind any cover they could find, Buford and his men slowed the Rebel advance so drastically that when the I and XI Army Corps finally reached the field, the contest was still in doubt. Buford's eye for topography also enabled his infantry comrades to occupy and, when outpositioned, to withdraw from successive

positions, staving off annihilation until nightfall—and additional reinforcements—came to Gettysburg. Buford's against-all-comers defense permitted
the fighting to continue into a second, and a decisive third, day.

On July 3, Buford's colleague David Gregg, closely supported by Custer's
brigade, also delayed an enemy force, this one composed of horsemen, and
prevented it from accomplishing a mission assigned it by Robert E. Lee. After
Stuart rejoined him, Lee ordered his cavalry leader, with four of his brigades,
to circumvent Meade's right, gain his rear, and from that direction attack the
midpoint of the Union line on Cemetery Ridge. Apparently Lee believed that
Stuart, even if unable to break through, might distract enemy attention from
an infantry strike on the front of the same sector. Stuart started out in good
order, but Gregg and Custer met him as he swung south toward the Federal
rear. An hours-long succession of thrust and parry rendered 250 Federals and
200 Rebels *hors de combat* and closed with Stuart miles from his objective. By
then the offensive later known as Pickett's Charge had run its bloody course,
and Lee was left with no alternative to ending his Pennsylvania excursion.

Over the next two weeks, the cavalries slugged it out on an almost daily
basis as the once-confident invaders struggled to reach and cross the Potomac
into Virginia. Meade's overcaution prevented a decisive confrontation, while
tactical blunders by Kilpatrick killed a promising effort to cut off Lee's rear
guard at the river. The horsemen of the Army of the Potomac had yet to learn
how to finish off an opponent they had put on the ropes.

For five months after Gettysburg, the armies jockeyed for position in Virginia, most often in the corridor formed by the Rappahannock and Rapidan.
Pleasonton's troopers—more confident than ever of their ability to prevail in
an open fight—frequently got the better of their antagonists, outmaneuvering
and outfighting them at Culpeper Court House (August 1), again at Brandy
Station (September 13), and at Liberty Mills (September 22), as well as in several engagements of lesser magnitude. In October, however, the Federals for-
feited some of their hard-won success. In response to orders from
Washington, Meade withdrew from the Rappahannock to the heights of Cen-
treville. Lee pursued, but the new position proved impregnable, prompting
him to return south. Meade pursued in turn, but at a more moderate pace.
When the impetuous Kilpatrick, leading the Union column, outdistanced his
supports, Stuart faced his men about at Buckland Mills and thudded into the
head of the blue column while Fitz Lee struck it in the flank and rear.
Stunned by the unexpected blow, Kilpatrick lost scores of men killed,
wounded, or captured, while hundreds fled in every direction.

At Washington's urging, Meade in late November launched an offensive
before cold weather paralyzed his army. Despite the good work of Gregg, who
led the way across the Rapidan, and Custer, who staged a loud diversion on

the north bank, the attempt to flank Lee out of his entrenchments bogged down along a Rapidan tributary known as Mine Run.

During the winter that followed, Meade and Grant (the latter being appointed general-in-chief early in March 1864) consolidated corps and shifted personnel. Although the cavalry's organization was lightly affected, its leadership changed radically. Phil Sheridan, one of only two field commanders who had come east with Grant, replaced the uninspired and uninspiring Pleasonton, while an ex-infantryman, Brig. Gen. Alfred T. A. Torbert, succeeded John Buford, who had died of typhoid fever in mid-December. Gregg remained the commander of the 2nd Cavalry Division, while a Grant protégé, Brig. Gen. James Harrison Wilson, took the place of Judson Kilpatrick. The less-than-brilliant "Kill-Cavalry" had seen his already spotty reputation fatally soiled when he botched a 3,500-man raid on lightly guarded Richmond in February and March.

In May 1864, when the officers and men under Torbert, Gregg, and Wilson retook the field, they were in peak condition, the result of not only Grant's and Meade's solicitude, but also that of the War Department, which the previous July had established an agency to meet the special needs of the mounted arm. The most visible element of the Cavalry Bureau was a huge remount depot on the Anacostia River, where thousands of horses were stabled, maintained, and distributed to needy regiments.

Campaigning recommenced with the cavalry leading the way across the Rapidan into the defeat-haunted Wilderness. This new attempt to flank Lee out of his works failed as signally as the last one: Again Stuart alerted Lee to the Union advance, and again the A.N.V. rushed up to strike its enemy in the vision-obscuring, movement-stifling woods. Two days of desperate fighting ended on May 6 with Grant stymied and frustrated. Cavalry had seen only intermittent action among the trees and foliage. There Wilson's division, which led the advance, had been cut off from its supports and savagely pummeled until David Gregg broke through to rescue it.

Bloodied but unbowed, on the seventh Grant resumed his movement toward Lee's right. He ordered Meade's army in the general direction of Richmond, which, even if found to be impervious to attack, might fall to the kind of siege McClellan had hoped to clamp on it. Any such investment would require cooperation between Meade's troops and those of the Army of the James, under Benjamin F. Butler. That newly formed command, only one-third the size of the Army of Potomac, was moving against the city from the south via its namesake river.

As it turned out, the armies were unable to join hands for six weeks after the fighting in the Wilderness died out. In the interim, Sheridan launched the raid toward Richmond that ended with Stuart's mortal wounding. Two weeks later, "Little Phil" battled Wade Hampton to an exhausting draw at Haw's Shop. Three weeks after that, to his regret, he encountered Hampton at Trevilian Station. By the time Sheridan's weary, dusty troopers rejoined their army, they found Grant and Meade, as well as Butler, immersed in siege warfare south of Richmond and east of Petersburg. Grant had decided that to take the lower city was to force the evacuation of the capital. By all indications, however, gaining that result would take much time and cost hundreds of casualties.

Sheridan did his best to quicken the pace of operations. In late July, he took his troopers above the James to threaten the approaches to Richmond and divert the attention of Petersburg's defenders from the activation of an unusual weapon: A regiment of former coal miners had dug a gunpowder-filled shaft beneath an enemy salient east of the city. The mine was detonated as planned on July 30, but the breakthrough it promised died when a follow-up attack was botched.

Sheridan returned his disappointed troopers to their camps, where they rested and refit until called west early in August to battle Jubal Early. In the Valley of Virginia, Sheridan became an army commander, taking charge of the VI, VIII, and XIX Corps of infantry plus three divisions of cavalry grouped under his senior subordinate, Torbert. The mounted arm consisted of Merritt's and Wilson's troopers, now styled, respectively, the 1st and 3rd Divisions, Army of the Shenandoah. The 2nd Division comprised units that had been campaigning in the Valley and western Virginia under William Averell, whose mostly successful record in those theaters had restored some of the luster his reputation had lost under Joe Hooker.

In his first weeks in the Valley, Sheridan chafed under demands by his superiors that he proceed cautiously lest he err in a way that would hurt Abraham Lincoln's chances for reelection. Little Phil's cautious maneuvering in the face of Early's smaller force made the Confederate commander believe his opponent lacked energy and fortitude. By appearing to avoid a confrontation, Sheridan lulled Early into a sense of complacency that was shattered as soon as Grant, in mid-September, gave his subordinate the go-ahead to attack. Three days later, Sheridan struck Early's carelessly deployed troops outside Winchester. After a fifteen-hour fight that featured heavy cavalry participation, he sent the Confederates into full retreat.

While Sheridan pursued the fugitives with his infantry (supported so poorly by the 2nd Cavalry Division that the luckless Averell again lost his command), he sent Torbert, with the horsemen under Merritt and Wilson, to get ahead of Early and cut him off. The foot soldiers did their job well, savaging the Confederates as soon as they halted atop Fisher's Hill. When the survivors resumed their flight, Sheridan believed he had them trapped. He was wrong: Torbert's people were kept at arm's length by the battle-thinned brigades of Williams Wickham. When Torbert's superior learned of the failure, he ascribed it to the same faintheartedness that Early believed he had seen in Sheridan.

Torbert tried mightily to make amends. When Early took up an inaccessible position near the top of the Valley, Sheridan broke contact and headed north to Cedar Creek, fourteen miles below Winchester. En route, he resumed the destruction of farms and crops that he had begun soon after reaching the Valley, a campaign of destruction and terror urged on him by the authorities in Washington and known ever afterward as "The Burning." Hungry for revenge, the horsemen of Lomax and Rosser struck the Union rear a series of blows so painful that Sheridan ordered Torbert to face about, engage the foe, and "whip or be whipped." On October 9, Torbert complied, attacking the Rebels near Tom's Brook with the 1st and 3rd Divisions (the latter now under Custer, Wilson having gone west to command William T. Sherman's horsemen). The result was the Buckland Races with roles reversed: a furious, running battle that ended with Lomax and Rosser almost thirty miles south of the point of first contact. They had suffered several dozen casualties, as well as the loss of seventy horses and mules and forty-some supply wagons.

When the victors moved to join Sheridan along Cedar Creek, the Rebels pursued, albeit at a more respectful distance than before. Moved to desperation, Early gambled on a surprise assault while Sheridan was away from the Valley, conferring with superiors in Washington. The attack, which began in the small hours of October 19, was initially successful, especially on the VIII and XIX Corps' front. The troopers under Merritt and Custer, however, held their ground against mounting pressure. By early afternoon, the Confederates were in possession of most of the field, but their attack was spent. When the now-returning Sheridan galloped up from Winchester on his black charger, demoralized Yankees took heart and followed him into the fray. Although Early's assault had already been contained, Sheridan, by his morale-raising heroics, provided the stimulus for a counterblow that stunned the Rebels, rolled back their lines, and transformed a near rout into a decisive victory.

Once again, Torbert's horsemen pursued the defeated enemy. They chased their quarry as far south as New Market, then returned to Sheridan to report an obvious fact: The Confederates would never again operate freely anywhere in the Valley, much less threaten the jittery politicians in Washington. Another result of Early's latest defeat came to light a few weeks after

Cedar Creek. Coupled with the dramatic news from Atlanta, Sheridan's defeat of his once-formidable adversary helped extend Abraham Lincoln's lease on the White House.

Throughout the winter that followed, Sheridan's troopers completed the job of pacifying the lower Valley, leaving their camps outside Winchester to run down enemy guerrillas and strike the Virginia Central near Gordonsville. What remained of Early's infantry spent the cold-weather season shivering and starving, although many of their mounted comrades remained active, raiding Union outposts in search of foodstuffs and remounts.

Except during the weather-plagued strike on Gordonsville, most of Sheridan's people kept warm and comfortable through the winter, as did their well-sheltered horses. When, in February, Little Phil prepared to finish off Early and then head east, men and mounts were in top physical condition. Only a single cog in Sheridan's war machine was missing: Alfred Torbert had gone on leave, against his superior's wishes, shortly before the return march began. Still stewing over Torbert's inability to overtake Early after Fisher's Hill, as well as his failure to render the Virginia Central unusable to the enemy, Little Phil did not recall him. He replaced Torbert with Wesley Merritt, who had proven his mettle numerous times between Williamsburg and Cedar Creek. When he finally returned to the army, Torbert found himself in command of the 3,000 troopers Sheridan had left behind, including hundreds who lacked horses. Sheridan's action may have smacked of vindictiveness, but this was war.

The 6,000 officers and men who made the journey from Winchester to Petersburg via Waynesboro, Charlottesville, and points east included some of the most able and experienced Federals to wear blue jackets trimmed in yellow. The 1st Division, commanded by Brig. Gen. Thomas C. Devin, was a particularly solid component of this impressive aggregation. Although, at forty-two, a good fifteen years older than many of his colleagues, the even-tempered, unflappable Devin had been a mainstay of the Cavalry Corps since 1862 and '63, when he gained a reputation as John Buford's strong right arm. A fondness for alcohol did not appear to dilute his leadership abilities. A staff officer who observed him closely over several months cited Devin's "blunt soldiership, sound judgment, his prompt and skillful disposition for battle, his long period of active service, his bulldog tenacity, and his habitual reliability."[7]

Devin's three brigades overflowed with savvy veterans. The four Michigan regiments of his "Wolverine Brigade," once George Custer's and now Col.

Peter Stagg's, were the most celebrated Western horsemen to serve in an eastern army. The hard-fighting quartet had been known for its spirit and skill since Custer led them in a succession of saber charges on the third day at Gettysburg. The 2nd Brigade, formerly Devin's own, was composed of five stalwart outfits from New York and Pennsylvania. Now, as had been the case over the past few months, it was led by a former artilleryman of proven versatility, Col. Charles L. Fitzhugh. Finally, Devin's ranking subordinate, Brig. Gen. Alfred Gibbs, led the so-called "Reserve Brigade," made up of two volunteer outfits—the 2nd Massachusetts and the erstwhile lancers of the 6th Pennsylvania—as well as three Regular outfits, the 1st, 5th, and 6th U.S. Cavalry, whose thinned ranks testified to the hard service each had seen and to the lax efforts of government recruiters. Despite their relative paucity of manpower, the Reserves represented a reliable source of reinforcement, as they had since John Buford led them in the operations of 1863. Although his facial features resembled those of an oriental sage, Gibbs was a hard-bitten old dragoon in temperament and demeanor. Like his superior, he had a fondness for liquor—one he appears to have controlled except on rare occasions.[8]

The 3rd Division had recently become the showpiece of the cavalry, Army of the Shenandoah, following years of faithful service in relative obscurity. Originally Judson Kilpatrick's, then James H. Wilson's, the command had prospered under neither man, failing to live up to the potential that Sheridan saw in it. Little Phil finally gave it the leader it deserved when Wilson went west early in October 1864. The stern disciplinarian was succeeded by the free spirit George Custer, who had transferred out of the division months before because of his intense dislike of Wilson.[9]

Under Custer, the 3rd Division was transformed. At Cedar Creek, it dealt the men of Tom Rosser blows harder and more frequent than it had ever landed under Wilson. Ten days earlier, it had propelled the same Rebels into their longest, most chaotic retreat of the war. The men of the 3rd had come to think of themselves as an elite force. As one of them later boasted, Custer took a command that under his predecessors "had only held its reputation with respectability, and transformed it into the most brilliant one of the whole Army (east or west) and so much impressed it with his individuality that every officer in the command was soon copying his eccentricities of dress and ready to adore his every motion and word."[10]

Custer's three brigades were led by subordinates fiercely loyal to him, and he to them. The 1st had been entrusted to another former cannoneer, one with a name as impressive as his record: Col. Alexander Cummings McWhorter Pennington. As the longtime commander of Battery M, 2nd U.S. Artillery, Pennington had closely supported Custer's Wolverines on many fields. On the day Custer replaced Wilson, he had appointed Pennington colonel of a mounted regiment from his native state, the 3rd New Jersey, more popularly known as "the Butterflies" for the gilt-encrusted uniform of its troopers. Having proven himself not only adept at handling horsemen, but also worthy of higher responsibility, Pennington now commanded, in addition to his spangled Jerseymen, three regiments from Connecticut, New York, and Ohio.[11]

Another Custer protégé, Bvt. Brig. Gen. William Wells, headed the boy general's 2nd Brigade. The twenty-seven-year-old Vermonter had already made an enviable record in command of his state's single regiment of volunteer cavalry, the only non-Michigan outfit to serve in the Wolverine Brigade. Wells had advanced to the brigade level just before the fight at Winchester, and he had done well enough to be considered a candidate for a star. His command consisted of his old regiment, plus the 8th and 15th New York—the first a veteran outfit, the second a recent transferee from garrison service.[12]

Col. Henry Capehart, a trained physician who had entered the war as chief surgeon of the 1st Virginia (Union) Cavalry, had risen through native ability and hard work to command his regiment (after May 1863 known as the 1st West Virginia). A man of courage and vision, Capehart now also commanded two other regiments from his home state, as well as the 1st New York, the first mounted unit to be recruited in the North; organized at the behest of Abraham Lincoln, it had long been known as the "Lincoln Cavalry."

The mountaineers who populated Capehart's 1st, 2nd, and 3rd West Virginia were worth a second look, but not for appearance's sake. Few were fashion plates; fewer could be considered models of soldierly deportment, at least not on a consistent basis. Even so, they numbered among the fiercest fighters in the Army of the Shenandoah, as well as some of its most gifted horsemen. The hill-country Unionists had forged such a bond with their mounts that even under artillery fire, the animals would maintain cohesion and marching formation. "There was not another Brig. in the Cav. Corps that had such trained horses," wrote an admiring Ohioan. Under the most trying conditions, "they kept in line almost as well as on parade."[13]

On March 27, Sheridan's officers and men, having trod the pontoons over the James, went into bivouac near Hancock's Station, a depot on the military railroad that coursed in rear of Meade's lines. There, late in the day, Sheridan was reunited with the troopers he had left behind when starting for the Valley, the 2nd Cavalry Division, Army of the Potomac. That command, 3,300 strong, had made its reputation under David Gregg, but the stalwart Pennsylvanian was not on hand to greet Sheridan upon his return.[14]

Gregg had served faithfully and well through the greater part of the Petersburg siege. His services had been merited the praise of his superiors and the brevet of major general of volunteers. As if this recognition were inadequate or unconscionably tardy, Gregg had submitted his resignation late in January 1865; he had said his good-byes on February 10. Although he never provided a clear explanation, observers ascribed his action to various motives, including an unwillingness to serve under the bluff, hard-to-please Sheridan. Whatever the reason, he was gone; Sheridan and his subordinates would miss him.[15]

In Gregg's place was a full major general of volunteers, a former infantryman from Ohio, George Crook. Recently a corps commander in West Virginia and the Shenandoah Valley (he had led the ill-starred VIII Corps at Cedar Creek), in late March the thirty-six-year-old Crook had been captured at his headquarters in Cumberland, Maryland, by Rebel partisans. He had served a brief confinement in Richmond's Libby Prison before being exchanged and assigned to the Army of the Potomac, apparently at the behest of Sheridan, his West Point classmate. Crook's command would retain its designation as a component of Meade's army, while Devin's and Custer's divisions would continue to be known as members of the Army of the Shenandoah.[16]

If not to Sheridan, Crook was an unknown quantity to the men of the 2nd Division. As one of his recently acquired troopers put it, Gregg's successor might be "the best cavalry commander in the world," but "he had not been tried by our fire." For his part, Crook expressed no great pleasure upon assuming his new position. In a letter to a former colleague, Brig. Gen. (and future U.S. President) Rutherford B. Hayes, he strongly implied that, given the rank and authority he had formerly wielded, the assignment was beneath him. Crook believed that his superiors felt the same way. He quoted Grant to the effect that "my present position was merely temporary & intimated that he was having the 8th Corps filled up for me—meaning the remnants of our old Command & the 19th Corps." Until then, Crook would apply himself faithfully to cavalry service, although the coming campaign was a source of unease: "I feel fearful for the results, although I am satisfied we have at least two men to the enemies [sic] one." The army's enlisted force might be "confident & eager for the fray," but I fear some of our officers are whipped before they start. My hope is that Grant will take command in person."[17]

While Grant would exercise close supervision of the campaigning to come, he would give Sheridan a free hand to lead not only the cavalry, but as many elements of Meade's army as would come within his area of operations.

Sheridan was grateful for the addition of Gregg's old command, which gave him a force of 9,000 effectives, but the augmentation posed a problem. Sheridan wished to keep Wesley Merritt in command of the cavalry of the Army of the Shenandoah. Yet Merritt, despite his *de facto* position as corps commander, was junior to Crook. The solution was to have Crook report directly to Sheridan's headquarters, as Merritt did. The system would prove somewhat awkward for all involved, but there appeared to be no clear alternative.

Since the 2nd Division had served under him for three months prior to the outset of the Valley Campaign, Sheridan was familiar with its organizational structure and personnel. As currently constituted, the command embraced three brigades. The 1st, which consisted of four regiments from Pennsylvania, New York, and New Jersey, was led by Bvt. Maj. Gen. Henry E. Davies, a dapper, diminutive lawyer, one of very few nonprofessional soldiers to win star rank in the Union cavalry in the East. This distinction appeared to testify to his high competence, and Davies's men were known to be, as one knowledgeable staff officer observed, "as fine a body of cavalry for their size as could be found in the service."[18]

Bvt. Brig. Gen. John Irvin Gregg, David Gregg's cousin, commanded the 2nd Brigade, 2nd Division. Brash and impatient, "Long John" Gregg was also a hard fighter who took calculated risks but never gambled with the lives of his men. Gregg commanded four Pennsylvania regiments, including the 16th, which he had led to war in 1861 and with which he had made a notable record dating from Kelly's Ford. Less flamboyant, perhaps less volatile, was the leader of Crook's 3rd Brigade, Bvt. Brig. Gen. Charles H. Smith, a soft-spoken volunteer from Maine who in numerous fights had proven his high competence in deeds rather than in words. In addition to the venerable 1st Maine, Smith commanded the 2nd New York Mounted Rifles and two regiments from Ohio, the 6th and 13th.[19]

On the whole, the force assigned to Sheridan for the coming campaign—a campaign he was determined to make the last ever waged in Virginia—was seasoned, tactically proficient, and imbued with the success ethic. Little Phil did not share George Crook's doubts about its morale or self-confidence. With these men, and with the support of God, Grant, and the Cavalry Bureau, Sheridan expected not only to defeat any Rebels who got in his way—regardless of their branch of the service—but to grind them beneath his boots. He had his sights set on the annihilation of his enemy, and he would accept nothing less, even if to achieve it he had to make the sacred soil of Virginia run red with blood.

THREE

"Sleeping with One Eye Open and One Foot Out of Bed"

HAD THEY BEEN STEALTH INCARNATE, SHERIDAN'S TROOPERS, MARCHING from Charlottesville to Petersburg, could not have escaped the enemy's attention. In mid-March, when it appeared that they might be intercepted en route to Richmond, James Longstreet, commanding Confederate forces north of the James, had started after the cavalry at the head of Pickett's division. He had failed to overtake his quarry, but thereafter scouts from the Northside had kept tabs on the returning Federals.

For a time late in March, however, as Sheridan's men left White House Landing on the Pamunkey River and passed inside the Union lines farther south, the lookouts lost contact with them. During this period, the troopers crossed the James at the pontoon bridge Ben Butler's army had constructed at Deep Bottom, on the northern flank of the contested peninsula known as Bermuda Hundred. On the morning of the twenty-seventh, when outriders from Martin Gary's brigade finally sighted Sheridan's people trotting along the south bank of the James, Longstreet rushed the news to Robert E. Lee at Petersburg.[1]

Upon learning of Sheridan's proximity, the Confederate commander tried to discern his ultimate destination. That the cavalry leader had departed quickly from the supply depot at White House suggested that he was making haste to join some movement at Petersburg. Perhaps Grant intended to add Sheridan's men to a new advance against the railroads in Lee's rear. Thanks to the recent Union gains at Hatcher's Run, the left flank of the Army of the

Potomac extended to the crossing of the Vaughan Road, seven miles south-west of Petersburg. The Confederacy's last open supply line, the Petersburg & Lynchburg (more familiarly known as the South Side Railroad), which lay just beyond the Federals' reach, was a prize that Grant would surely make another attempt to seize. On the other hand, rumors emanating from the enemy's lines suggested that at least some cavalrymen were bound for North Carolina, either to join forces with Sherman or to waylay the communication lines that linked Lee's army with Joe Johnston's.[2]

Hoping to cover all eventualities, Lee opted to augment his lower flank by detaching heavily from Longstreet's command, including Fitz Lee's troop-ers. When Longstreet learned of his superior's intention, he counseled against it as a case of putting too many eggs in one basket. He recommended, in-stead, that Lee counter any move Sheridan made with Pickett's infantry, the only maneuverable reserve on the siege lines. Pickett's division, although a shadow of the command that had gone into the fighting at Gettysburg, em-braced more than 6,000 effectives, and it could be spared from its most recent position, opposite the Army of the James at Bermuda Hundred.

Over the past several weeks, Pickett's men had been shuttled to and fro, not only to track Sheridan, but also to support Lee's attack on Fort Stedman, along the northeastern corner of the Union lines opposite Petersburg. That bold but poorly conducted offensive of March 25—the last Lee would ever launch—had failed even before most of Pickett's troops reached the scene of fighting via the Richmond & Petersburg Railroad. Although Pickett had begun to return to the Northside as soon as the assault spent itself, his com-mand had been halted along Swift Creek, just north of Petersburg, where it continued to await further orders.

Now Longstreet suggested that Lee use the division, strengthened by a cavalry force and a couple of reliable batteries, to pursue and waylay Sheridan. If the Irishman headed for the railroad in Lee's rear, Pickett would have enough men, and enough long-range rifles, to halt him indefinitely. If, in-stead, Sheridan turned south, Pickett could reinforce Johnston within hours of Sheridan's joining Sherman. As Longstreet explained, "Such a force in proper hands, will be able to frustrate [the] object of [the] enemy, as nearly all of his horses must be somewhat exhausted."[3]

Longstreet's choice of Pickett as expeditionary commander was open to criticism, since the division leader had never been considered a model soldier or even a bright one (he had, after all, graduated at the foot of his West Point class). Since Gettysburg, Pickett's performance in the field had been less than inspired, and his morale had been noticeably low. He was, however, a great favorite of Longstreet's, who in 1862 had helped secure two promotions for Pickett, honors that more than a few colleagues doubted he deserved. Even with Longstreet's patronage, Pickett had not risen above the rank he had gained two and a half years before.[4]

If Robert E. Lee had qualms about assigning Pickett to the post Longstreet had proposed, he failed to show it. Bowing to his subordinate's logic, he directed Longstreet to order most of Fitz Lee's cavalry to Petersburg, preparatory to joining Pickett athwart Sheridan's path. Even after giving up Pickett and Lee, Longstreet would retain enough infantry to ease his peace of mind: two divisions of Regular troops, plus local defense forces and the troops of the Department of Richmond, under the immediate command of Lt. Gen. Richard S. Ewell. He would also enjoy the continued support of Gary's horsemen, as well as that of dozens of troopers who, having lost their mounts to disease or bullets, could not accompany Fitz Lee to Petersburg.[5]

In forming Pickett's expeditionary force, Lee found it necessary to shift about some forces in order to avoid disarranging the defensive perimeter southwest of Petersburg. When he moved toward Sheridan's position, Pickett would leave behind a brigade that had remained on the Northside when the rest of the command entrained for Fort Stedman. In addition to his remaining troops—the battle-scarred brigades of Brigadier Generals George H. Steuart, Montgomery D. Corse, and William R. Terry—Pickett would advance at the head of two brigades from the division of Maj. Gen. Bushrod Rust Johnson, whose men occupied the trenches along the White Oak Road southwest of the embattled city. These brigades, commanded by Brigadier Generals Matt Ransom and William H. Wallace, could vacate their positions without compromising the integrity of the right flank. To the infantry under Pickett, Lee planned to add six cannons under one of the army's younger and more gifted artillerists, Col. William J. Pegram.[6]

Lee considered Pickett's infantry and artillery sufficient to the task assigned them, but he doubted that two-thirds of Fitz Lee's division would provide enough mounted support. Thus he made plans to add the division of his son, Rooney, as well as that under Tom Rosser, to the expedition, a move that would increase Pickett's strength to around 12,000. The augmentation would strip the siege lines of almost all its cavalry, but with the Confederate right under such a heavy threat, now was no time to withhold critical resources.

Other commanders did not see it that way. Desperate to secure additional horsemen for both Pickett and Petersburg, Lee briefly inquired into the possibility of transferring from Jubal Early's command one brigade of Valley Cavalry. The initiative came to naught when Early, despite lacking any realistic hope of renewing operations against the troops Sheridan had left behind, announced that he could not spare a single trooper.[7]

⸺⸺⸺⸺⸺

While Robert E. Lee's primary concern was how to parry a coming thrust, his opponent worried that when the thrust was made, it would hit open air. Since midwinter, Ulysses S. Grant had suspected that Lee's next move would be to abandon Richmond and Petersburg and, by stealing a march on the Federals, force them to follow him far from their base of supply. As Lt. Col. Horace Porter of the Commanding General's staff put it: "General Grant . . . had been sleeping with one eye open and one foot out of bed for many weeks, in the fear that Lee would thus give him the slip."[8]

Grant was not a habitual worrier; still, his mind did not begin to ease until the last week in March. By then the local roads had sufficiently dried to permit a rapid pursuit should Lee pull up stakes—which, however, he showed no sign of doing. By then, too, Grant had the opportunity to share his concerns, as well as his plans for the coming campaign, with his commander-in-chief. He usually felt better after conversing with Abraham Lincoln, who always gave the impression of having the best interests of his troops—and those of his most successful field leader—at heart.

On Saturday, the twenty-fifth, the day that Lee launched his desperate assault on the Union right, Lincoln came down from Washington aboard the presidential yacht *River Queen* to Grant's headquarters at City Point, eight miles northeast of Petersburg. President and general had a private conversation, then rode south to inspect the field of combat at Fort Stedman. Lincoln spent that night at City Point; the next day, he went to Bermuda Hundred to confer with General Ord and review a large segment of the Army of the James that included a division of African-American infantry. These troops were members of the XXV Corps, which was made up entirely of United States Colored Troops. On hand for the occasion were dignitaries who had accompanied the president, including cabinet members and congressmen. Yet another spectator was Rear Adm. David Dixon Porter, just arrived from North Carolina after helping another portion of Ord's army capture Fort Fisher.[9]

Porter's presence at the review indicated that Lincoln had called his ranking military and naval commanders to a strategy session. This was to be a lengthy affair, held on the twenty-seventh and twenty-eighth aboard the *River Queen,* berthed at City Point. The council would include a special guest, William T. Sherman, who had come up from recently occupied Goldsboro,

North Carolina. There the 60,000 soldiers who had accompanied Sherman from Atlanta and Savannah had linked with almost 40,000 other Federals under Maj. Gen. John McAllister Schofield to help complete the subjugation of the Tarheel State.[10]

In advance of the shipboard meeting, Grant wished to flesh out one part of the strategy he intended to apply to the coming campaign—the role the cavalry would play. Recent events had changed his thinking on that matter, and before the army moved, he wished to reevaluate his course and make certain it was the correct one.

Grant's original plan had been to move against Richmond and Petersburg with Meade's and Ord's infantry, supported only by Crook's division and the small mounted contingent of the Army of the James, command of which had recently passed from August Kautz to Brig. Gen. Ranald Slidell Mackenzie. Grant had not expected Sheridan and Merritt to return from the Valley with 7,500 additional troopers. He had intended that the cavalry of the Army of the Shenandoah, after leaving Waynesboro, should cross the James at Columbia, damaging the enemy-controlled railroads below it, then enter North Carolina to augment Sherman.

Grant had a number of reasons for wanting Sheridan out of Virginia when the armies moved against Petersburg. The effort to turn Lee's troops out of their works might prove a more difficult task, and take more time to accomplish, than anyone anticipated. In that event, Sheridan could help Sherman finish off Johnston's army and still take part in the operations in Virginia. Furthermore, Sherman's cavalry was commanded by the erratic Judson Kilpatrick; Grant preferred that Sheridan take his place.

Another problem associated with Sheridan's early return to Grant—one that would merely be postponed by his joining Sherman—concerned a clash of high-level personalities. During any offensive at Petersburg, Little Phil would have to serve with, if not under, Meade. The two men, both of whom were known for their temper (Meade's nickname was the "Old Snapping-Turtle"), had never gotten along. On more than one occasion, they had engaged in a shouting match over the roles and missions of the cavalry and its relationship to the main army. Meade viewed the cavalry's job as close tactical support of infantry; Sheridan habitually argued for a strategic role for his horsemen, whom he regarded as an independent strike force. Sheridan considered his superior an old fogy, set in his ways and ignorant of the needs, wants, and capabilities of his mounted arm. In turn, Meade regarded Sheridan as a selfish and sometimes insubordinate glory hound. A few weeks hence, the army leader would complain in a letter to his wife that throughout the campaign just ended, Sheridan's "conduct towards me, has been beneath contempt." The men's squabbling had already exerted a divisive influence on the army, one that distracted it from more important issues that required complete attention. Grant did not relish a resumption of this friction-laden relationship.[11]

But he may not have a choice: Sheridan's apparent inability to ford or bridge the rain-swollen James at Columbia had knocked Grant's plans askew. Even so, the commanding general still appeared to favor a union between Sheridan and Sherman, if it could be arranged to the satisfaction of both men. He wished, at least, to discuss the issue with each of them. Thus, while Lincoln reviewed the troops at Bermuda Hundred, Grant summoned Sheridan to City Point for a private talk.

Sheridan was aware of Grant's preferences; for this reason, he made the boat trip from Harrison's Landing to army headquarters with some misgivings. The commander of the Army of the Shenandoah was firmly and unalterably opposed to any union with Sherman in North Carolina. With the end of the war in the East fast approaching, he was anxious to get in on the kill— he could not bear the thought of serving hundreds of miles away when Robert E. Lee was cornered and forced to surrender. This desire was so strong that Sheridan's failure to cross at Columbia may have been due to unwillingness rather than physical inability.

When he arrived at the log cabin that housed Grant's headquarters at City Point, Sheridan's worst suspicions appeared to be confirmed. After welcoming his subordinate and inquiring about his recent operations, Grant outlined his thinking on how to use the men who had accompanied Little Phil from the Valley. He desired Sheridan to mass all available horsemen, including Crook's, then "cut loose" from the siege lines, pass south around the Army of the Potomac's left flank via the Richmond & Danville Railroad, and, by crossing the Roanoke River, join Sherman near Goldsboro.

Grant emphasized his intentions by showing Sheridan a copy of a letter of instructions intended for distribution throughout Meade's army. A quick perusal told his guest all he needed to know, and he reacted to it strongly. As Sheridan later recalled, by both words and gestures, "I showed plainly that I was dissatisfied" with the orders. He argued vehemently against Grant's strategy, calling it "bad policy" to send him against what remained of Johnston's army before dealing with the enemy's primary force, that defending Petersburg. Moreover, regardless of their official designation, the troopers of Merritt, Devin, and Custer continued to think of themselves as members of the Army of the Potomac. It would hurt their morale and tarnish their hard-won record to send them against an opponent other than the one they had been battling for the past four years.

To Sheridan's surprise, as well as to his immense relief, Grant agreed with his criticisms of the North Carolina plan: the lieutenant general "quietly told me that the portion of my instructions from which I so strongly dissented was intended as a 'blind' to cover any check the army in its general movement to the left might meet with, and prevent that element in the North which held that the war could be ended only through negotiation, from charging defeat." Sheridan was likewise gratified by Grant's assurance that in any cooperative movement between the Armies of the Potomac and the Shenandoah, Sheridan would exercise independent command as he had in the Valley, unless and until Grant decreed otherwise. If Grant could prevent it, there would be no resumption of the Sheridan-Meade relationship.[12]

His peace of mind restored, Sheridan accompanied Grant and Lincoln up the James to the point at which Sheridan's troopers, under Merritt's supervision, continued to cross the river. En route, Little Phil discussed the upcoming military operations with the president and tried to answer the many questions Lincoln directed at him. Despite the president's interest in the coming campaign, Sheridan got the impression that he had only a general understanding of Grant's strategy. After inspecting Merritt's crossing site, the party returned to City Point, where Sheridan spent the night.

Next morning, the commander of the Army of the Shenandoah rejoined his troopers at Hancock's Station, only to return to army headquarters upon receiving an invitation to accompany Grant, Lincoln, Sherman, and Admiral Porter aboard the *River Queen*. Delayed by an accident to the locomotive that pulled the military train on which he was riding, Sheridan failed to reach Grant's cabin until near midnight. There he found Grant and Sherman deep in conversation, long after the other conferees had gone to bed. Sherman greeted the latecomer cordially, but to Sheridan's dismay, he immediately brought up the instructions Grant had drafted for the cavalry. Sherman tried to persuade both Grant and Sheridan to stick to the original strategy, which he himself favored.[13]

Sheridan found that he had to explain his opposition to the plan once again. He recalled, "My uneasiness made me somewhat too earnest, I fear, but General Grant soon mollified me, and smoothed matters over by practically repeating what he had told me in regard to this point at the close of our interview the day before." With that, Sherman appeared to drop the matter—only to pick it up the next morning when visiting Sheridan at his overnight quarters at City Point. Again Little Phil argued his case, with even more vehemence than the previous day. Apparently convinced that his colleague's mind was made up, Sherman finally changed the subject. Sheridan considered the discussion over.

Little Phil turned his attention to carrying out an assignment much more to his liking: to break camp along the military railroad at an early hour on the twenty-ninth and head for the Confederate right below Petersburg in cooperation with Meade's II Corps, under Maj. Gen. Andrew A. Humphreys, and the V Corps of Maj. Gen. Gouverneur K. Warren. But Sheridan had barely begun to tackle the logistics involved when the North Carolina project resurfaced. Only hours after having apparently won Sherman to his point of view, Sheridan received additional instructions from Grant's headquarters, "the general tenor of which again disturbed" him. Scrutinizing the document, he had the uncomfortable suspicion that Grant had changed his mind yet again, perhaps under pressure from his old subordinate in the West.

The supplemental orders called for the cavalry of the Armies of the Shenandoah and the Potomac to move on the morning of the twenty-ninth toward Lee's rear. En route, Sheridan was to pass around the left flank of Warren's corps and make for Dinwiddie Court House, a road hub five miles southwest of the Confederate right flank. "It is not the intention," Grant had written, "to attack the enemy in his intrenched position, but to force him out if possible. Should he come out and attack us, or get himself where he can be attacked, move in with your entire force in your own way, and with the full reliance that the army will engage or follow the enemy, as circumstances will dictate." If Sheridan was unable to lure the defenders out of their works, he was to "cut loose and push for the Danville [Rail]road" near Burkeville Junction, where that line crossed the South Side. Sheridan was to damage both rail lines to the maximum extent, thereby preventing Lee from using the South Side to retreat westward and the R & D to move into North Carolina.

Then came the clause that suggested Grant was backsliding: "After having accomplished the destruction of the two railroads . . . you may return to this army, selecting your road further south, or you may go on into North Carolina and join General Sherman. Should you select the latter course, get the information to me as early as possible, so that I may send orders to meet you at Goldsboro.'"[14]

After mulling over the document, Sheridan soothed himself by thinking: "Those instructions did not alter my line of march for the morrow, and I trusted matters would so come about as not to require compliance with those portions relative to the railroads and to joining Sherman." When he finally got to bed, he spent a restless night, so eager was he for morning to come. He could hardly wait to join in the operation that would mark the beginning of the end for the Army of Northern Virginia.[15]

The men of Merritt, Devin, and Custer were not the only Federals marching long and hard to get in on the coming movement. On March 26, following Lincoln's review of the Army of the James at Bermuda Hundred, Grant briefed Edward Ord on the part his command would play in the days and weeks ahead. The forty-six-year-old Marylander listened intently, asked a few questions, and vowed to strive mightily to ensure the success of Grant's strategy. It was clear that like Phil Sheridan, Ord was grateful to have been included in that strategy, even though little more than half of his troops would accompany him into action.[16]

He need not have worried that he would be left out of Grant's planning. The general-in-chief thought too highly of the man's abilities and his past services to leave him behind while Meade and Sheridan went forth to reap final victory. Ord had been a prized subordinate of Grant's since mid-1862, first as a division commander in the Army of the Tennessee, then as leader of the XIII Corps, formerly Grant's own command. Despite the caliber of his field service, however, Ord, a conservative Democrat with Southern roots, had run afoul of army politics. As a result, he lost his command after his patron left Tennessee for Washington early in 1864.

Ord had remained unemployed until July, when Grant tendered him command of one of the two corps that made up Butler's army. He did well in his new position—and this time he kept his political beliefs to himself. In December, after Ben Butler made a botch of the first Fort Fisher expedition (the garrison finally fell to a second offensive, mounted by Maj. Gen. Alfred H. Terry), Grant installed Ord as the politician-general's successor. Grant's protégé tightened up administrative practices that had been allowed to lapse under Butler, while increasing the strength and raising the morale of his new command, almost half of which consisted of African-American units.[17]

When Grant briefed him on the twenty-sixth, Ord was instructed to prepare to transfer almost 16,000 of his 30,000 soldiers from above the James to the Petersburg front. Late the following day, he was to remove two divisions of white infantrymen—those commanded by Brigadier Generals Robert S. Foster and John Wesley Turner—plus the all-black division of Brig. Gen. William Birney and most of the cavalry under Ranald Mackenzie from their entrenched positions south and east of Richmond. With as much speed as possible, the infantry, under Maj. Gen. John Gibbon, the newly appointed commander of the all-white XXIV Army Corps, would cross the James and the Appomattox and take up positions southwest of Petersburg. There they would relieve the II and V Corps for service farther west in company with Sheridan. Only Mackenzie's troops would not transfer to Meade's bailiwick. After escorting Ord's supply wagons over the rivers, the little force—three regiments, two squadrons of a fourth, and a single company from a fifth—would report to Sheridan and take orders from him.[18]

The troops that Ord would leave outside Richmond when he headed south would have to keep a sharp eye on the capital's defenders. The 14,000 who would remain north of the James would be under the command of Maj. Gen. Godfrey Weitzel, a holdover from the Butler regime who lacked vision and initiative but who would follow instructions. Weitzel's depleted garrison would consist of one white and one African-American division (the latter led by Mackenzie's predecessor, Kautz), both stationed outside Richmond, plus, at Bermuda Hundred, a division of infantrymen and heavy artillerists under Maj. Gen. George L. Hartsuff. The troops on the Northside would include a small mounted contingent: the 2nd U.S. Colored Cavalry and the 5th Massachusetts, also composed of black enlisted men; plus eleven-twelfths of the 20th New York (the twelfth company would accompany Mackenzie) and a single squadron of the 4th Massachusetts. The remainder of the 4th, along with the regiment's commander, Col. Francis Washburn, would march with Ord's column to provide it with a mobile reconnaissance capability essential to navigating the country west and south of Petersburg.[19]

Yet another mounted regiment was available to Weitzel, but only nominally. Within hours of beginning his movement south, Ord would dispatch the 1st New York Mounted Rifles, commanded by Col. Edwin V. Sumner, son and namesake of the late commander of the II Corps, Army of the Potomac, on a raid into upper North Carolina. In that region, Sumner was to cut two railroads via which Lee might shuttle reinforcements to Petersburg.[20]

Ord's task, to transfer thousands of troops of all arms, plus a long supply column, to a new front almost forty miles away, could have been a logistical nightmare; to complicate matters, the movement had to be completed within seventy-two hours of the receipt of Grant's instructions. Fortunately, the army commander had anticipated a movement of this type and magnitude. A few days before his meeting with the Commanding General, he had begun to withdraw troops from the front line and place them in camps so remote from the enemy that their concentration would go unnoticed. "The remainder of my command," Ord noted, "I kept in motion, changing camps frequently. Pickets for several nights previous to the move were detailed only from the regiments to remain behind." Indeed, the March 26 review had been made possible by the partial withdrawal from the siege lines of Foster's, Turner's, and Birney's divisions.[21]

Ord had replaced these troops with members of Kautz's division, whose new line extended northeastward from Dutch Gap on the James to a point above Fort Burnham, at the southwest corner of the exterior defense line of Richmond. The other infantry to remain on the Northside, Brig. Gen. Charles Devens's division of the XXIV Corps, extended its flanks to cover a line running from Fort Burnham north to the Charles City Road, and then southeastward toward the James. The area between Devens's right and the river had recently been patrolled by Mackenzie's horsemen; when their commander pulled out of position preparatory to accompanying the infantry to Petersburg, the gap was filled by the few outfits that remained.[22]

On the morning of the twenty-seventh, Ord issued marching orders to his maneuver units. Shortly after darkness fell, everyone took to the roads leading to and across the James. As they moved out, prearranged acts of deception were set in motion. Fires in the camps of the departing troops continued to burn, tents remained standing, buglers stationed in the deserted camps blew the usual calls, and here and there army bands played for a phantom audience.[23]

The lead elements of the command, including a small artillery contingent, crossed the James on the floating bridge at Dutch Gap, which had been covered with moistened straw and compost to muffle the shuffling of feet. They were followed over the river by Turner's Independent Division, XXIV Corps. Most of Birney's African-Americans fell in behind Turner's men; the rest had crossed the previous evening, shortly after the review. Meanwhile, Foster's soldiers, who held a more exposed position and therefore had to disengage more slowly and carefully, crossed farther downstream at Deep Bottom.

Once on the south bank, both columns trekked across the rear of Hartsuff's lines at Bermuda Hundred. When they reached the end of the peninsula, they crossed the Appomattox River on two pontoon bridges, Foster's men at Broadway Landing and Turner's and Birney's a few miles farther west at Point of Rocks. Below the Appomattox, the trail led southwestward across the City Point Railroad and the railroad that connected Petersburg with Norfolk, Virginia.[24]

Throughout the twenty-eighth, the men slogged over roads turned into lagoons by a steady rain. They marched through the night as well, taking only occasional rest stops. Their perseverance was awarded when, early on the twenty-ninth, they reached Globe Tavern on the Weldon Railroad, in the sector of the Army of the Potomac. Already they had passed the breastworks and entrenchments occupied by the IX Corps of Maj. Gen. John G. Parke, on the eastern and southeastern sectors of Meade's siege lines. By 8:00 A.M., the rain having ceased, the men of the "flying column" route-stepped past the position of Maj. Gen. Horatio G. Wright's VI Corps. A short distance farther west, General Gibbon, at the head of the column, was joined by staff officers from Meade's headquarters, who guided his soldiers to the camps of the II and V Corps along the east bank of Hatcher's Run. Shortly after noon, Gibbon's men moved up to relieve elements of both corps, freeing them for the advance they were to commence the next morning.[25]

Despite the unfavorable weather, which not only soaked the roads and those moving on them, but also raised the James and Appomattox to alarming heights, the march had been remarkably trouble-free and therefore relatively swift. The rivers had risen so high that Ord had decided to leave his supply train—seventy-some ambulances and ordnance wagons—north of the James until the infantry and artillery had crossed. He entrusted the vehicles to General Mackenzie, whose troopers would escort them to Petersburg beginning on the morning of the twenty-ninth.

Having made such good time, Ord was in a lofty mood as his men settled into position near the point at which the Vaughan Road crossed Hatcher's Run. His spirits rose even further when he went forward under escort to observe the works facing him across the stream. Ord's initial impression, that the defenses were imperfectly constructed and lightly manned, convinced him that when Grant gave the order to attack, they would crumble at first contact. His belief grew with passing time; on April 1, it prompted him to boast to Colonel Porter that his men would slice through the barriers "as a hot knife goes into butter."[26]

Despite its imaginative use of deception and its wide circuit of Petersburg, Ord's column failed to escape detection. The initial report of its movements, however, reached R. E. Lee not from his army's scouts, but from an eighteen-year-old girl whose home lay within the Union lines. Seeing her duty clearly, the teenager made her way through the no-man's-land between the armies to bring word of the movement to Confederate outposts. By morning of the twenty-eighth, a report that the Army of the James had crossed its namesake river as well as the Appomattox had made its way to Petersburg. Lee relayed the report to the Northside, where members of Longstreet's command checked it out. Some hours later, they confirmed the girl's story, although they could not determine the size or the destination of the Yankee column. Nor could Longstreet provide additional information on Sheridan's movements south of the James.[27]

In telegraphing Lee, Longstreet took the opportunity to expound on his suggestion to dispatch Pickett and every trooper except Gary's to points southwest of Petersburg. He reiterated his belief that Sheridan was going to either attack the railroads in Lee's rear or join Sherman near Goldsboro:

> I do not think that we can well spare the division [Pickett's], but I think that we would choose a lesser risk by sparing it in case Sheridan's cavalry makes either of these moves contemplated than we would by holding him here to await the result of these operations. The enemy seems now to count upon taking Richmond by raiding upon our lines of communication and not by attacking our lines of work. I think, therefore, that we should endeavor to put a force in the field that can contend against that of the enemy.

Longstreet's assessment of Grant's strategy, while well taken, was not wholly accurate: The Yankee commander intended to strike not only his enemy's communications, but also his works—first those below Petersburg and then, if necessary, the city's interior defenses.[28]

Longstreet's argument was also moot; by this time, preparations were under way to carry out his proposal. That afternoon Fitz Lee, at his headquarters near Hanover Court House, fourteen miles north of Richmond, received a cable from his uncle. Fitz was directed to lead Munford's and Payne's brigades to Sutherland's Station on the South Side Railroad, almost ten miles west of Petersburg. On the way, he was to report at army headquarters in the city. To ensure that Longstreet retained enough mobile support, he was to leave behind not only Gary's brigade, but every dismounted member of his command.[29]

Upon receipt of these instructions, Fitz took steps to concentrate his far-flung command, calling in pickets and outpost forces and replacing them with Gary's men. At the same time, he massed his horseless troopers and placed them under Maj. William F. Graves of the 2nd Virginia. When formed, Graves's contingent turned out to consist of five officers and 385 enlisted men—only the officers had horses. The size of the force may have surprised Maj. Graves, if not Fitz Lee himself. Comprising as it did enough men to fill two or three regiments in the battle-decimated division, it was a graphic indication of how immobile the mobile arm of the A.N.V. had become in this fifth spring of the war.

Lee's division had been so widely dispersed that the most outlying elements could not be called in before the rest started for Petersburg. One of these, the 1st Maryland Battalion of Munford's brigade, had been picketing near Gordonsville, more than forty miles northwest of Hanover Court House.

Aware of the distance to be covered, Fitz Lee instructed its commander, Lt. Col. Gustavus W. Dorsey, to meet him at or near Sutherland's. Dorsey, long a member of the cavalry's inner circle (at Yellow Tavern, he had lifted his friend, the mortally wounded Stuart, from the saddle), obeyed promptly, but not until April 3 did he reach his assigned post with what remained of his depleted unit, fewer than 100 officers and men.[30]

Similarly scattered, and in no condition to make the march to Sutherland's Station, were the two batteries of horse artillery that days earlier had been assigned to Fitz Lee's command. One of these, the Baltimore Light Artillery, commanded by Lt. John R. McNulty, lacked enough men and horses to take the field. The other unit, Capt. John J. Shoemaker's Lynchburg Battery, which had been decimated during the Valley campaigning, was refitting in its home city, a week's march from Petersburg. In fact, of the ten horse artillery batteries nominally a part of the Army of Northern Virginia under the overall command of Lt. Col. R. Preston Chew, only two—Capt. William M. McGregor's 2nd Stuart Horse Artillery, attached to Rooney Lee's division south of Petersburg, and Capt. Edward Graham's Petersburg Artillery, which had been assigned to Butler's cavalry division but had remained behind when that command went to North Carolina—were combat-ready and able to play an active part in the operations ahead. The sorry state of the horse artillery, which from 1862 to 1864 had been such a potent adjunct to the mounted units under Stuart and Hampton, led some observers to express thanks that John Pelham had not lived to witness the decline of his war child.[31]

Even without having to wait for some detachments to reach him, Fitz Lee was unable to start for Sutherland's Station until the unseasonably chilly morning of the twenty-ninth. En route south, he left the marching column and, accompanied by a small escort, made his way through the Petersburg lines to his uncle's headquarters. Fitz recalled their meeting fifteen years later: "He told me that General Sheridan's cavalry were concentrating in the vicinity of Five Forks," a crossroads formed by the White Oak Road and other thoroughfares about eighteen miles southwest of the besieged city. Sheridan was "bent upon a raid upon our communications, with the intention of breaking up the South Side Railroad, and that it was important for us to maintain that [rail line] intact. He desired me to move my cavalry up to the vicinity of Five Forks; and told me that he had ordered the other two cavalry divisions under General W. H. F. Lee and General Rosser to report to me." The army commander made clear what the foregoing instructions implied: As soon as the units assembled, Fitz would lead it as *de facto* commander of the cavalry, Army of Northern Virginia.[32]

Fitz was highly gratified by the assignment. The authority it conferred upon him he had quietly sought ever since May 11, 1864. Although too much the gentleman to regard it as his due, he knew he was the only legitimate claimant to the position. He, and he alone, had been the embodiment of the Stuart ethos, the glorious tradition upon which the Confederate cavalry in the East had been founded. More than anyone else—certainly more than Wade Hampton or any other non-Virginian—he had kept the votary lights glowing throughout the long night that followed the Beau Sabreur's passing. He had remained true to his first commander's ideas, even after (as it seemed) Hampton turned his back on Virginia to defend South Carolina.

Long overdue or not, Fitz accepted the honor with quiet composure. And yet it appears to have gone to his head, if ever so slightly. As he recalled, his uncle had not told him that *he* was to support Pickett's foot soldiers at Five Forks, but that the army "would send infantry to *my* support, and that we must attack, and, if possible, disperse the cavalry corps of General Sheridan, then concentrating in the vicinity of Dinwiddie Court House [five miles south of Five Forks], as the best means of breaking up any object that General Sheridan might have in view in that concentration."[33]

The conference at an end, Fitz Lee saluted his superior with an extra flourish, departed army headquarters, remounted, and rode hard to overtake his column short of the South Side. He spent that night in its midst, and in a downpour, at Sutherland's Station. The next morning, the thirtieth, he led his division south and west across pastureland and gentle ridges toward Five Forks. Despite the continuing rain, Fitz sat comfortably in the saddle, chatting with his staff officers when not issuing orders or interviewing his outriders. He was happily aware that his first outing in command of the most celebrated mounted force in American history lay just up the road. Having anticipated this opportunity for what seemed like a lifetime, he looked forward to validating the trust and confidence his nation's army had placed in him, however belatedly.

Before Fitz Lee reached the South Side Railroad, the other elements of the expeditionary force that would occupy Five Forks got moving. At about the time Fitz conferred with Robert E. Lee, George Pickett, at his headquarters along Swift Creek, three miles above Petersburg, received orders to move to Sutherland's with those elements of his division close at hand. As soon as he could prepare the men for the march, he moved south at the head of Corse's and Terry's brigades. Crossing the Appomattox via the Turnpike Bridge, the column made for Petersburg Station on the South Side Railroad.

Then began a vexing ordeal. After waiting for a train with enough boxcars and flatcars to transport not only Corse's and Terry's men, but also George Steuart's, who had joined the others en route to the railroad, Pickett finally loaded everyone aboard. The embarkation alone probably took an hour or more. When the train began to lumber westward, its hissing engine puffed along at a couple miles per hour, all the speed its overage boilers could muster. Not until 9:00 that evening did it complete the twenty-mile run to Sutherland's, where the troops, cursing their cramped accommodations and the extended travel time, piled out of the cars. Their spirits did not improve when they were ordered to leave the station platform and form ranks in the drizzling rain.

While his men stood in formation beside the tracks, Pickett received an order from Lt. Gen. Richard H. Anderson, commanding the fortifications along the Confederate right, to join him in the trenches on the White Oak Road east of Five Forks. Temporarily, Pickett was to occupy a sector of rifle pits alongside Bushrod Johnson's men. With a sigh of resignation, Pickett gave the necessary instructions to his subordinates. After some further delay, the head of the expeditionary force took to the mud-coated roads leading south and east.[34]

Upon his sprightly mare, Lucy, Pickett avoided the mud but endured the same chilly rain that made the marching men increasingly miserable. Although he tried not to show it, the raw weather bothered him more than most of those trudging through the muck. Pickett was in poor physical condition—forty years old, he looked closer to sixty. At war's start, he had been robust and bright-eyed, lithe in his movements, and fit of physique. Now his frame sagged with excess flesh; his curly, once-lustrous hair hung limply to his shoulders; and his face, bloated from years of food and drink, wore a haggard look. A variety of ills bothered him on a regular basis, including gastrointestinal distress and a sometimes crippling case of piles. Although neither Pickett nor those who remarked on his changed appearance knew it, a more serious problem had begun to plague him: the onset of the coronary disease that would take his life ten years hence.[35]

Pickett's decline had a psychological aspect. Many observers dated its inception from the day in southern Pennsylvania when he beheld his division mowed down like wheat before the thresher as it tried to break the center of the Union line on Cemetery Ridge. During the year and a half since, Pickett's career had dipped as steeply as his health. Unable to recruit his command back to its original size, and concerned about Pickett's post-Gettysburg frame of mind, Robert E. Lee had tendered him ever less important assignments.

Eventually his division had been reduced to the status of an all-purpose re-serve, holding the least active sector of the defense lines between Richmond and Petersburg. Only through the patronage of Longstreet, who had watched out for Pickett since the 1840s, when they served as captain and lieutenant, respectively, in the 6th U.S. Infantry, had the Virginian been tendered his pre-sent assignment.[36]

Considering the magnitude of the responsibilities conferred on him, Pickett might have viewed the defense of Five Forks as an opportunity for re-demption, a chance to prove that he had not lost the skill, the spark of leader-ship, the thirst for combat that in 1862–63 had made him one of the more promising young commanders in the A.N.V. And yet by all indications, Pick-ett felt no urgency to comport himself energetically on this outing. Since leav-ing Swift Creek, he had exhibited a general disinterestedness, keeping aloof from all but essential members of his staff, allowing his subordinates to over-see the division's embarkation, disembarkation, and march. It was as though he regarded the present assignment as nothing out of the ordinary, some per-functory detail to carry out and be done with. His attitude would jeopardize not only his career, but also the continued existence of his army and the na-tion it defended.

The roads that drew Fitz Lee and George Pickett into the open country of Dinwiddie County attracted their opponents as well. Late on the morning of the twenty-ninth, Phil Sheridan led his newly supplied and recently re-mounted command southeastward from Hancock's Station along the Jerusalem Plank Road. The recent rains had left that usually reliable route of advance in what Little Phil called "a frightful state." Alternate routes were no better: "To make a detour was to go from bad to worse. In the face of these discouragements we floundered on, however, crossing on the way a series of small streams swollen to their banks."[37]

Leaving the plank road failed to speed up the march. Near Reams's Sta-tion on the Weldon Railroad, the mud-spattered column veered sharply west-ward and proceeded to Malone's Bridge, where Sheridan hoped to cross rain-swollen Rowanty Creek. To his disgust, he found the span in charred ruins, the work of Rebels who had gathered on the west bank. From there they pelted the head of the column, Irvin Gregg's brigade of Crook's division, with rifle fire.

Once Gregg's men dismounted and drove off the enemy with a heavier, more concentrated fire, Sheridan set his pioneers to constructing a makeshift bridge sturdy enough to support the weight of horses, cannons, and wagons.

While the work went on, patrols ranged south, where they encountered more graybacks. These were driven toward Stony Creek, and a few were taken prisoner. They informed Sheridan that Rooney Lee, with the main body of his division—the size of which the captives undoubtedly exaggerated—was stationed only ten miles farther down the railroad, at Stony Creek Station. Whatever its size, the force did not trouble Sheridan, who assumed it would remain where it was as long as he did not stir it up. Hedging his bets, the general had his men destroy the plank road bridge over Stony Creek, a move that would stymie any pursuers.

As soon as the replacement bridge was in position over Rowanty Creek, Devin's and Crook's divisions crossed. They left behind two batteries of horse artillery that had failed to keep pace with the cavalry due to the bottomless roads. Also left in the rear were the men of Custer's division, who were formed into fatigue parties. Sheridan had discovered that his subsistence and ammunition trains were "stuck in the mire at intervals all the way back to the Jerusalem plank-road." Custer's people would remain at Malone's Crossing until the wagons could be extricated and brought to the front. Theirs was not an enviable task; as Sheridan noted, the labor teams "often had to unload the wagons and lift them out of the boggy places."[38]

Onward trotted the rest of the command, now reduced to about 6,000 officers and men. Beyond the wretched roads that wound through dense groves of pine, and a few bands of would-be ambushers, the riders encountered no further obstacle on the road to Dinwiddie Court House, which they reached, under growing darkness, at about 5:00 P.M. Finding no Rebels in the immediate vicinity, Sheridan bivouacked the men in such a way as to cover the Dinwiddie (or Five Forks), Flat Foot, and Boydton Plank Roads, all of which met at the courthouse. Inspecting the area, Sheridan found it made up of "a half-dozen unsightly houses, a ramshackle tavern propped up on two sides with pine poles, and the weather-beaten building that gave official name to the cross-roads."[39]

The weather beat on the cavalry as well as the tavern. Within minutes of Sheridan's arrival, the skies, which had been threatening all day, let loose with a downpour. The general kept dry in the tottering tavern, which he appropriated for his headquarters and where he and his staff were served coffee by the proprietor's family. Less fortunate were the thousands of officers and men camped in the fields around the settlement. Having left their tents in the Shenandoah Valley, they had no protection against the cold, wind-whipped rain.

In addition to dry quarters and a hot beverage, Sheridan enjoyed the receipt of welcome news. Within a few hours of the cavalry's arrival, a courier reached the tavern with a dispatch from Grant. The general-in-chief, who that day had moved his headquarters to Gravelly Run, a few miles northeast of Dinwiddie, instructed Sheridan to abandon all thought of raiding the railroads and linking with Sherman. The cavalry was now free to cooperate with the II and V Corps in striking the Rebel right. Sheridan, his mind suddenly "easy with respect to the objectionable feature of [his] original instructions," spread blankets on the tavern floor and propped his head on his saddle. Impervious to the caffeine he had consumed, he "slept most soundly."[40]

When Pickett's foot soldiers departed Swift Creek for the South Side Railroad, the cavalrymen and horse artillerists under Rooney Lee were breaking camp at Stony Creek Station, and those of Tom Rosser were packing up to leave Spencer's Mill. Lee's men had occupied the area around the depot, which lay roughly halfway between Petersburg and the North Carolina line, since just after siege operations had begun the previous summer. Rosser's men had moved into the Nottoway River country east of Lee's position only two days before, after leaving a post of only slightly longer duration, Atlee's Station on the Virginia Central, eight miles north of Richmond.

The orders that both generals had recently received—to move to the Dinwiddie Court House-Five Forks vicinity, there to link with Fitz Lee—were imperative. Even so, Rooney Lee must have obeyed with some reluctance. Shortly before, his scouts had come in from points north to report the approach, along the east side of the Weldon Railroad, of a heavy column of Union horsemen—the vanguard of Sheridan's 9,000 sabers. To counter the Yankees in the event they continued south, Lee, when departing Stony Creek, left behind detachments of Col. Robert A. Caskie's 10th Virginia and Capt. Edwin E. Bouldin's 14th Virginia (the latter only six companies strong). These men were to keep tabs on the enemy and, if possible, divine their intentions. Except for those required to picket up and down the railroad, Caskie's and Bouldin's men would rejoin their division, at or near Five Forks, the following day.

The march west was hard on both man and beast, because of the soupy roads as well as the need to detour widely around the Yankee column, which was heading in the same general direction. The terrain was so difficult, the pace so aggravating, and the weather so foul that when the troopers and gunners reached their destination, they found themselves, as a member of the 14th Virginia phrased it, "nearly broke down."[41]

Some made the trip in a better frame of mind than others. Tom Rosser, for one, could look forward to a good meal at journey's end. During his brief stay on the Nottoway, his staff had hunted up a seine, with which they caught a mess of shad, a delicacy their commander was fond of. Because he was obliged to leave the area before he could devour the catch, Rosser had seen to it that the shad were packed in ice and stored carefully in the ambulance he used as his personal conveyance. Though he could not be sure when he would enjoy the tasty morsels, he was certain they would make a fine feast in the not-distant future.[42]

FOUR

"We Were Overpowered...
But Not Driven"

WHILE SHERIDAN'S TROOPERS SPENT THE TWENTY-NINTH SPARRING WITH THE enemy, their friends in the infantry had been seeing hard service, and gaining important objectives, farther to the north and east. In its first significant action since leaving winter quarters, Warren's V Corps had made steady progress toward Anderson's works on the White Oak Road. Under heavy rifle and shell fire, the corps had moved up the Quaker Road, then cross-country over swampy bottomland to take possession of a section of the Boydton Plank Road, Sheridan's avenue of advance to Dinwiddie Court House.

Bushrod Johnson's division had left its defenses to oppose the advance, but in stubborn fighting, the Federals had pushed it back across the Lewis Farm. By day's end, one of Warren's three divisions, under Bvt. Maj. Gen. Charles Griffin, held the junction of the Quaker and Boydton Roads, nearly within rifle range of Johnson's defenses. Throughout the fight, Humphreys's II Corps had supported Warren's right flank as closely as intervening forests permitted. In turn, Humphreys's right flank had been covered by Ord and Gibbon, whose men advanced to within four hundred yards of the Rebel works in their front.[1]

The infantry had done its part in the opening round; now it was the cavalry's turn. Morning of March 30 found Sheridan not only ready, but eager to tackle the task at hand. In his evening communiqué, Grant had ordered his subordinate, now relieved of his railroad mission, to "push round the enemy if you can and get onto his right rear. The movements of the enemy's cavalry may, of course, modify your action." Sheridan fully intended to do what Grant expected of him; he did not intend, however, to allow anyone to modify any action he took.[2]

Sometime before dawn, with the rain still pouring down, Sheridan's officers shook the men out of their bedrolls and ordered them to breakfast as quickly as possible. As the bivouacs stirred into life, Sheridan directed Wesley Merritt to send Devin's division on a reconnaissance toward the White Oak Road, supported closely by Davies's brigade of Crook's command. With Irvin Gregg's brigade, Crook would guard Devin's right near where the Boydton Plank Road crossed Stony Creek, while Smith's brigade of the same division would remain near Dinwiddie "for use in any direction required." Smith's would be the only cavalry retained at or near the courthouse. Custer's troopers were still in the rear, struggling with mud-encased wagons and recalcitrant mules.[3]

No sooner had Devin and Crook started out than Sheridan received an unexpected message from Grant's headquarters. Concerned by the effect of the continuing rain on the army's movements, the lieutenant general had decided to suspend operations until the skies cleared and the roads either dried or could be sufficiently "corduroyed"—firmed up with timber. In the meantime, Sheridan was to abandon his position and fall back to the military railroad, leaving behind only as many men as required to hold the crossroads at Dinwiddie.

The message not only shocked and dismayed Sheridan, it also spurred him into action. Without ordering a halt to the movements just begun, he mounted his gray pacer, Breckinridge, and galloped off through the downpour to Gravelly Run. Escorted by a dozen troopers and his adjutant, Col. Frederic C. Newhall, Sheridan splashed up the Boydton Plank Road, where he so startled a force of Union pickets that he had to duck a volley of friendly fire. Once the mistake had been rectified, the riders cut across the spongy fields till they gained the Vaughan Road, which led to Grant's camp. There Sheridan found the headquarters staff "standing around . . . on boards and rails placed here and there to keep them from sinking into the mire."[4]

Horace Porter, among other aides, greeted the visitors and inquired enthusiastically about operations in their sector. He recalled:

[Sheridan] took a decidedly cheerful view of matters, and entered upon a very animated discussion of the coming movements. He said he could drive in the whole cavalry force of the enemy with ease, and if an infantry force were added to his command he would strike out for [Robert E.] Lee's right and either crush it or force him so to weaken his intrenched lines that the troops in front of them could break through and march into Petersburg.

Porter observed that Sheridan's animation increased as he warmed up to his topic. When asked how he would procure enough forage to sustain an advance against Lee's infantry, the cavalryman snorted: "Forage? I'll get all the forage I want. I'll haul it out if I have to set every man in the command to corduroying roads, and corduroy every mile of them from the railroad to Dinwiddie. I tell you I'm ready to strike out to-morrow and go to smashing things."[5]

When Grant learned that Sheridan had come to see him, he invited the visitor into his personal tent. Sheridan found his host in earnest conversation with his chief of staff, the dour but able Brevet Maj. Gen. John A. Rawlins. The staff officer, who shared Sheridan's view of things, had been arguing rather heatedly that his boss should continue the offensive regardless of the weather.

When he learned that so far only the cavalry had been informed of Grant's intentions, Sheridan took up the argument. He stated the case for going on by drawing parallels with Burnside's notorious Mud March, which had destroyed the army's morale and undermined its confidence in its leader. He then alluded to a point Grant had made at City Point: "Although a suspension of operations would not be fatal," it would embolden those politicians who believed that the army could not prevail in the field and that the war could be ended only by negotiation.[6]

Midway through his appeal, it occurred to Sheridan that Grant was looking for an excuse to be dissuaded from his announced course. Therefore, he was not surprised when the commanding general gazed hard at him, chomped on his ever-present cigar, and announced in a voice rich with determination, "We will go on."[7]

The three men spent the rest of the impromptu war council discussing tactics. His mission accomplished, Sheridan left the tent, remounted, and, trailed by his escort, rode back to Dinwiddie Court House. En route, he encountered his second Doubting Thomas of the day.

Midway down the Boydton Plank Road, Sheridan reined in at the headquarters of G. K. Warren, whose left flank the cavalry had been tasked to support. Hoping to discuss matters of mutual concern, Sheridan was disappointed to find Warren inaccessible. He remained at the encampment to call upon an Old Army comrade, one of Warren's officers. Minutes before Sheridan left his friend to return to Dinwiddie, the corps commander made his appearance. "We had a short conversation," Sheridan recalled, although he never revealed its content. He noted only that Warren appeared to be in a gloomy mood, speaking "rather despondently of the outlook"—meaning, presumably, the army's chances of circumventing or breaking Lee's flank and forcing the evacuation of Petersburg.[8]

Host and visitor shared a regional identity, both having grown up in up-state New York, as well as a burning ambition and a desire to snuff out the rebellion by all permissible means. And yet they were, in many ways, a study in contrasts. Sheridan sprang from working-class immigrants who had had to scrap for the smallest piece of the American dream. He spoke loudly and brusquely, in ways intended to hide, but that merely emphasized, an imperfect education and a lack of social grace. The taller, more handsome, more cultured Warren, whose family connections included men of national as well as local distinction, was wont to assume the manners—or perhaps only the mannerisms—of the aristocrat.

Although Sheridan outranked him by date of commission, Warren may well have given his guest, as he gave others, the impression that he had been denied authority commensurate with his abilities. It was common knowledge that when he could get away with it, Warren would substitute his own ideas for those that underlay the orders of Meade and Grant. Sheridan, when he considered it absolutely essential, would remonstrate against given orders, as he did today. But he did not appreciate other people who did the same thing.

Although he did not fully understand the forces that drove Warren—in fact, he claimed not to know him well—Sheridan may have suspected that the man had his demons. Beneath Warren's placid exterior lurked a temper as volatile as his own, one often expressed in volleys of blood-curdling oaths. Just as often, it seemed, Warren gave vent to the gloomy musings of a born pessimist, as he did on this occasion. The corps leader's critics considered him a prissy egotist crippled by self-defeating behavior. Whether or not Sheridan shared this view, it seems clear that he neither admired nor trusted Warren.[9]

While the Union forces sat immobile, if only temporarily, George Pickett's expeditionary force kept moving despite rain, wind, high water, and other agents of human misery. By daybreak on the thirtieth, his foot soldiers had filed inside a section of trenches along the White Oak Road, where they remained pending receipt of further orders. About noon, with the rain coming down in sheets, General Anderson relayed him a message from army headquarters in Petersburg. Pickett was to continue on to Five Forks with Corse's, Terry's, and Steuart's brigades, supplemented by Ransom's and Wallace's men plus Pegram's cannons and an ordnance train. At the Forks he would meet Fitz Lee, who had arrived there in advance of Rooney Lee and Rosser.

At Pickett's direction, the soldiers of his suddenly enlarged command clambered up muddy trench walls and slogged through inundated fields toward the southwest. What followed was a true ordeal—not only because of the weather, but also due to the intervention of enemy horsemen, who charged, ghostlike, out of the mist to lash the marching men with carbine and pistol fire. Every minute or two, it seemed, the head of the column would recoil against these hit-and-run assaults. Occasionally dismounted Yankees would materialize along the flanks of the column, firing from behind trees and fences. Each time this occurred, infantrymen would go sprawling in the mud, while comrades searched frantically for the assailants.

Inevitably, the ammunition train became a target. Several attacks on the wagons were driven off only through the tenacity of Pickett's rear guard. As if fearful of the train's continuing vulnerability, its commander turned several wagons about and led them back to the White Oak Road. Apparently Pickett did not learn of their loss until much later; when he did, he surmised, rather curiously, that it was the work of Robert E. Lee himself. The vehicles' absence worried him, for without them he had to rely on the few ammunition wagons that had accompanied Ransom's brigade. Everything considered, the initial phase of Pickett's operations along the far right flank could hardly have been less auspicious.[10]

Fitz Lee reached Five Forks, at the head of Payne's and Munford's brigades, on the morning of the thirtieth. He did not intend to remain at that site, which was formed by the northward-leading Ford's (or Church) Road; the east-west-running White Oak Road; Scott's Road, which ran directly south; and the southeasterly Dinwiddie Court House (or Adams) Road. Fitz's destination was Dinwiddie, where, as his scouts told him, Sheridan's men had bivouacked. He did not know how many troopers had accompanied Little Phil, although he must have suspected they outnumbered his own force.[11]

The number of men at Fitz Lee's disposal is a matter of conjecture. Years later, he estimated that as of April 1, 1865, his single division comprised 1,300 officers and men, while Rooney Lee's and Rosser's commands fielded a combined total of 1,900. Yet Munford asserted that on the first, his brigade numbered about 2,000, including at least 1,800 effectives. Even taking into account the heavy losses Payne's brigade had suffered to this time, it seems likely that upon reaching Five Forks, Fitz's division amounted to nearly, if not quite, 3,000. Fitz also underestimated the size of the force under Pickett that joined him on the thirty-first, putting the combined total of all arms at 7,000. Counting the additions from Johnson's division, Pickett's infantry and artillery alone commanded that many men, if not more. If Fitz Lee, before Pickett's arrival, believed himself outnumbered by Sheridan's cavalry, he would have been correct, although not by the wide margin he cited in postwar years.[12]

The newly assigned commander of Robert E. Lee's cavalry reported that upon reaching the strategic crossroads, he found no enemy in the immediate vicinity. This seems strange, given that Sheridan's headquarters lay only four miles to the south; surely Little Phil would have placed pickets within observation distance of Five Forks. At once Fitz took steps to seek out the Yankees.[13]

He assigned the task to his senior subordinate, William Payne, whose brigade led Lee's advance. The job could not have rested in better hands, for the twenty-five-year-old native of Fauquier County, Virginia, was adept at reconnaissance, although his greatest skills were displayed in battle. His fighting spirit was illustrated by the rubber mask he had only recently discarded. The invention of a Yankee surgeon who had treated the captive Payne after the latter had been struck in the face by a Yankee bullet at Williamsburg in May 1862, the mask had held the bones of his shattered jaw together until they healed.

Exchanged and paroled, Payne had rejoined the army after the briefest of recuperations, his surgical contrivance partially hidden beneath muttonchop whiskers. Despite the suffering he had endured, he refused to spare himself. During the Gettysburg Campaign, he had again been unhorsed and captured, and this time spent a long stint in the prison camp near Sandusky, Ohio. With good reason, Fitz Lee considered Payne a "bold, capable officer" richly deserving of his new-won wreathed stars.

Huddling with him now, Lee directed him to head south, fix the location of the enemy's outposts, and feel Sheridan's main force. Payne saluted and was off at the head of his brigade. As he rode, many of Munford's men dismounted, some to cover Payne's advance, others to construct breastworks at the forks.[14]

According to Munford, the three regiments in Payne's command moved south not by the direct road to Dinwiddie but farther to the left, along a road leading south from a ford on Gravelly Run. The brigade was barely under way when it encountered the head of Merritt's command coming up from Dinwiddie; a firefight erupted a short distance below the White Oak Road. At once Munford led his brigade south to cover Payne's right flank. Before he could get into action, however, Payne was again wounded and forced to the rear. His injury was so severe that it was obvious he would not rejoin his brigade any time soon. According to Fitz Lee, the brigadier's loss was "severely felt in all subsequent movements."[15]

Command of both of Lee's brigades temporarily passed to Munford, who deftly handled the added responsibility. Almost immediately the combined force thrust the less numerous Yankees back from the White Oak Road. Resistance stiffened, but eventually the Federals were forced south on either side of the road to the courthouse, past its intersection with the Crump Road, beyond the J. Boisseau House, and then below the Brook (or Turkey Egg) Road.

Observing Munford's skillful movement, Fitz Lee made a mental note to secure for him promotion to brigadier general. Lee, as well as virtually everyone else in the cavalry, A.N.V., knew that such an honor was seriously overdue. The thirty-four-year-old Munford, a native of Lynchburg and a graduate of his state's military institute, had been one of first Virginians to organize a regiment of volunteer cavalry, whose lieutenant colonel he had quickly become. He had served capably at First Manassas, as well as in the Shenandoah Valley under Jackson and on the Peninsula under Stuart. If the man had a weakness, it was his bluff and sometimes abrasive demeanor. He had clashed with both Stuart and Jackson, who had criticized him, much as Tom Rosser had in 1864, for mistakes that appeared not to be Munford's fault.[16]

Munford served competently—and at times with distinction—during the Maryland operations that culminated at Sharpsburg. For much of this period, he commanded not only his 2nd Virginia, but also the brigade of which it was a part, although always as a colonel. Then, at the outset of the Gettysburg Campaign, he ran afoul of Jeb Stuart in a way that killed any hope of future promotion. When the Yankee cavalry surprised Stuart's men at Brandy Station, Munford, commanding Fitz Lee's brigade while Fitz was on medical leave, received Stuart's imperative order to leave his assigned post on the Hazel River, almost eight miles northwest of Brandy, and hasten to the scene of action. As Stuart saw it, Munford did not respond in timely fashion, a failing the Beau Sabreur held against him ever afterward. Munford claimed that Stuart's courier, after delivering the order, rode off without indicating where, and by what road, Munford should reach the battlefield. Being unfamiliar not only with the local geography, but also with his regimental commanders, Munford failed to secure their help in solving his problem. He later claimed to have started south as soon as ordered but through an unfortunate choice of routes reached Stuart too late to help turn the near disaster into a victory.[17]

Munford always believed he had been made a scapegoat for a badly managed fight that soiled Stuart's till-then-pristine reputation. His arguments, if he made them to Stuart's face, had no effect on his superior; over the next several months, Stuart passed him over when promoting junior officers such as Rosser and Wickham. When he succeeded the Beau Sabreur, Wade Hampton made no effort to rectify the situation. Through it all, Munford continued to serve faithfully and well, refusing to succumb to resentment or bitterness.

Now, at last, Fitz Lee hoped to reward the man's perseverance while also recti-
fying what appeared to be a grave injustice.[18]

About 6:00 that morning, March 30, despite the continuing rain, Wesley
Merritt fulfilled the orders he had received from Sheridan, orders that remained in effect even after Little Phil received Grant's message about suspending operations—to reconnoiter the Rebel works along the White Oak
Road east of Five Forks. At Merritt's direction, Tom Devin led his division,
Gibbs's Regulars and volunteers in advance, up the road connecting Dinwiddie Court House with Five Forks. About two miles above Dinwiddie, Devin
halted Gibbs near the home of J. Boisseau. At and near that point, intersect-
ing roads snaked east, northeastward, and west, the last cutting through pine
groves and farmland toward a marshy stream known as Chamberlain's Bed.

Uncertain of the enemy's location, Devin had Gibbs send scouting parties
along each of these roads. Within minutes, the division leader had a better
idea of Rebel dispositions: The party that ranged up the northeastward-run-
ning byway, under Col. Charles L. Leiper of the 6th Pennsylvania, quickly encountered the head of Payne's brigade, moving in its direction. A detachment
of Gibbs's command, under Maj. R. Murray Morris, which continued up the
road to Five Forks, also ran into enemy troopers, probably members of Munford's brigade. Observing from the rear, Merritt believed that each party had
run into Rebel infantry—in fact, they were facing Confederate cavalry in the
unaccustomed role of fighting afoot. The Federals, who were much more familiar with that mode of warfare, dismounted to show the enemy how it was
done.[19]

As fighting heated up north and east of J. Boisseau's, Devin fed in additional troops. And yet, apparently because of detaching units to serve as flank
guards, he failed to match the manpower arrayed against him. Merritt, as
though unconcerned about the result, did not order Davies's brigade into action when that portion of Crook's division came up in midafternoon to lend
support. Merritt noted approvingly that though outgunned, Devin's men put
up a strong fight, thereby giving an indication "of the good work that might
be expected of them in the future."[20]

Perhaps he should have been less complacent. At about 3:00 P.M., Morris's
party—approximately 150 men of the 5th and 6th Regulars—encountered
serious trouble. Having forced the enemy in his immediate front to remount
and withdraw to within a mile of Five Forks, Morris followed, only to see his
men bog down on swampy terrain. Worse, Morris found himself suddenly

surrounded by Rebels who had advanced stealthily on his flanks and rear. Forced to fight his way out of encirclement, the major lost three officers and twenty men killed, wounded, or captured. The enemy pursued, determined to increase the toll.

Apprised of his subordinate's predicament, Devin sent a rescue force consisting of the 1st United States, under Capt. Richard S. C. Lord, two of Colonel Fitzhugh's regiments, and elements of Stagg's command. Riding at the head of these reinforcements, Alfred Gibbs took charge of the fight, only to find himself in much the same predicament as Morris—hemmed in by hordes of advancing Confederates, many afoot, most mounted. Although forced to fight in several directions simultaneously, Gibbs held the line below Five Forks until sunset, whereupon he skillfully disengaged and withdrew to the road junction at Boisseau's. Most of Devin's division remained in that area throughout the night, picketing every road against the possibility of a surprise assault.[21]

Before evening, Sheridan had returned to Dinwiddie from his visit to Grant and Warren. He conferred with Merritt and Devin, approved their dispositions, and expressed general satisfaction with the day's events. He had not intended to force a full-scale battle, merely to develop the enemy's dispositions and strength, and this his subordinates had done, albeit at considerable loss. The following day, in conjunction with major movements off his right flank by Meade's infantry, Sheridan intended to return to Five Forks in greater strength, prepared to challenge Fitz Lee, no holds barred and devil take the hindmost.

———————

Just before sunset, as the cavalry's fight was winding down, the advance guard of Pickett's weather-plagued column drew within sight of Fitz Lee's position. Pickett rode on ahead for a preliminary consultation with the cavalry leader. Recalling the meeting a month later, the expeditionary commander claimed that his initial intention had been to move at once against Sheridan, despite the rain and the approach of night. He implied that Fitz dissuaded him, although he came to agree with his colleague that the move would have subjected the command to inordinate risk. In addition to being unfamiliar with the local terrain, Pickett's foot soldiers and artillerymen were "much in need of rest—having been marching nearly continuously for eighteen hours." In the end, Pickett contented himself with pushing portions of Corse's and Terry's brigades down the road to the courthouse, "so as to keep the enemy at a respectable distance during the night." He maintained that the detachments advanced south for nearly a mile, "driving the enemy's cavalry who, however, being dismounted and armed with the repeating rifles [carbines], made quite a stout little fight."[22]

Stout fight or not, Pickett did not fear the proximity of Sheridan's troopers. In fact, his subsequent actions suggest that he held his adversaries in contempt. Like many another infantry commander, even after four years of war, he refused to acknowledge that a skillfully managed force of dismounted cavalry could contend successfully against an equal numbers of foot soldiers. He intended to prove as much on the morrow.

A couple hours after Pickett's arrival at the Forks—its commander put the time at 8:00—Rosser rode up from the southeast at the head of Dearing's and McCausland's brigades. The newcomer, who lacked a knowledge of the enemy's positions, immediately conferred with his superiors, who filled him in. Pickett, Lee, and Rosser then began to plan their itinerary for March 31. They were still hashing things out when, shortly after midnight, Rooney Lee's men came in from the south. The division had recently completed a time-consuming circuit of Sheridan's position, just as the Union commander had foreseen. The protracted detour had irritated and frustrated everyone in Lee's column, as had the weather. The rain had soaked the troopers to the skin, while swelling the many watercourses they encountered, making for what one enlisted man called "dreadful fording."[23]

By the wee hours of the thirty-first, Pickett's strategy was still in the developmental stage. Its completion would have to wait until daylight, when he could observe, and respond to, Sheridan's latest dispositions. Whatever the tactical situation, however, Pickett intended to seize and maintain the offensive. By superior management and force of numbers, he would push Sheridan's troopers completely off the board, where they would pose no threat to the Rebel right.

When Pickett's offensive got under way, Fitz Lee would take part not as a division leader, but as head of his army's cavalry. Acting under the authority granted him two days before, he informed Rooney Lee and Rosser that they were now under his command. To lead the division he thus relinquished, he announced the appointment of Munford and let it be known that in his new position, the colonel enjoyed his full support. The vacancy created by Munford's rise was filled by his ranking subordinate and close friend, Col. William B. Wooldridge of the 4th Virginia, whose ability to walk, but not to fight, had been compromised by the wooden leg he had received as a result of battle wounds. At the same time, Col. Reuben B. Boston of the 5th Virginia, who had distinguished himself in many campaigns, especially Gettysburg, assumed command of Payne's brigade.[24]

Munford spent the better part of the morning expanding his staff to division size. He enjoyed the experience immensely. He had almost despaired of rising to so lofty a position as he now held. He intended to make the most of it—such an opportunity might never come again.[25]

During the night, Sheridan received another dispatch from Grant, this one urging him to hold his position as close to the White Oak Road as possible. The lieutenant general also inquired whether, after sunup, Sheridan could push some troopers as far north and east as Burgess's Mill, where the White Oak Road met the plank road. Sheridan was warned that in the morning the V Corps, which had been held idle for most of the day just ended, might be subjected to a heavy assault on its left flank. Originally Grant had hoped that if this occurred, Sheridan would come to Warren's assistance. Now, given Sheridan's preparations to deal with Pickett, Grant doubted that the cavalry would have the time or the manpower to support Warren. Significantly, perhaps, Sheridan did not dissuade his superior from this view.[26]

One reason Grant believed Sheridan would be unavailable to support the infantry was Little Phil's intimation that come morning, he would be tangling with a force larger than his own. From prisoners, he had learned that thousands of foot soldiers under Pickett had recently joined Fitz Lee. Ordinarily a mounted commander would be wary of taking on so large a force of infantry, but Sheridan suspected that the division facing him had been whittled down by casualties to the point of vulnerability. He fully expected to push Pickett back from Five Forks and then occupy that strategic landmark almost within reach of the enemy's rear.

As always, Grant approved of his subordinate's aggressiveness. Mindful of his intention to return Sheridan to command of combined arms, Grant informed him: "If your situation in the morning is such as to justify the belief that you can turn the enemy's right with the assistance of a corps of infantry, entirely detached from the balance of the army, I will so detach the Fifth Corps, and place the whole under your command for the operation."[27]

Early on the thirty-first, Sheridan replied that while he would like to try to turn or break through the Rebel flank, he preferred to do so with the VI Corps, which had served him so well in the Shenandoah (Wright's command had been the only element of the army to stand firm against the Rebel onslaught at Cedar Creek). Sheridan added pointedly: "I would not like the Fifth Corps to make such an attempt."[28]

By midmorning on the last day of March, Sheridan found himself sad-
dled with problems other than choosing his infantry support. Sometime after
9:00, Merritt sent most of Devin's division up roads leading to various sectors
of the Confederate line on the White Oak Road. Peter Stagg's Wolverines ascended the Crump Road, while a large detachment of Fitzhugh's brigade advanced on foot up the direct road from Dinwiddie. Gibbs massed his brigade
at Boisseau's for use wherever needed. The Reserve Brigade spent the balance
of the morning, as it had much of the night, building breastworks in the
clearing around the farmhouse. The sound of axes felling trees was clearly
heard in the Confederate bivouacs to the north. Davies's brigade of Crook's
division also congregated near Boisseau's to provide Devin, once again, with
flank coverage. Patrols from the support force ranged westward toward Chamberlain's Bed, alert to signs of an enemy presence along the Union left.

Soon after starting toward the White Oak Road, the troopers of Stagg
and Fitzhugh attracted rifle and carbine fire in heavy volume. Both brigades
promptly fell back, Stagg's to establish a blocking position on the Crump
Road, Fitzhugh's to build a line of defense along a branch of Chamberlain's
Bed about a mile southeast of Five Forks. When the enemy's fire slackened,
detachments of Fitzhugh's command probed the breastworks that Fitz Lee had
begun to build at Five Forks and that Pickett, soon after his arrival, had improved. Although they continued to draw fire, both brigades remained in
close contact with the foe, whose dispositions they scrutinized despite the
continuing rain and the ubiquitous clouds of powder smoke.[29]

Late in the morning, the standoff appeared to turn in favor of the Confederates, who, it became apparent, were not content to pop away at their opponents from behind barricades. One of Davies's more enterprising patrols
splashed over Chamberlain's Bed, captured a Rebel infantry post, and learned
from its captives that Pickett commanded not only his own division, but also
a large part of Johnson's, and that every cavalryman in the Army of Northern
Virginia was supporting him. Furthermore, Johnson's troops, accompanied by
Rooney Lee's horsemen, Barringer's brigade in the lead, were moving down
the west side of the stream, seeking to turn Devin's left, strike his rear, and cut
him off from his comrades at Dinwiddie.

Rushed to cavalry headquarters, the news resulted in a shoring up of the
Union left. Sheridan sent Davies's 1st New Jersey across Chamberlain's Bed to
locate the oncoming Rebels. The balance of the brigade, along with Charles
Smith's troopers, originally stationed at Dinwiddie, were ordered into position
to block the most likely routes of enemy advance. These were the roads that
approached Danse's Ford and, almost a mile to the south, Fitzgerald's Ford.
Davies guarded the upper ford from the east side, while Smith sent a regiment

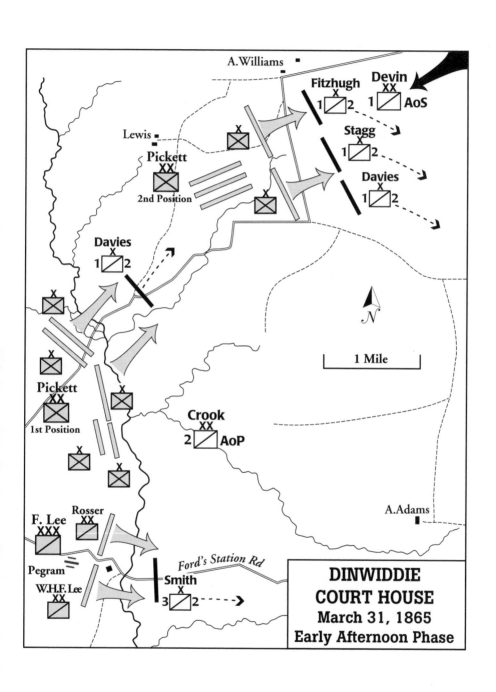

A.Williams

Devin
XX
1 ◨ AoS

Fitzhugh
X
1 ◨ 2

Stagg
X
1 ◨ 2

Lewis

Pickett
XX
2nd Position

Davies
X
1 ◨ 2

Davies
X
1 ◨ 2

N

1 Mile

Crook
XX
2 ◨ AoP

Pickett
XX
1st Position

A.Adams

F. Lee
XXX

Rosser
XX

Pegram

Ford's Station Rd

Smith
X
3 ◨ 2

W.H.F. Lee
XX

**DINWIDDIE
COURT HOUSE**
March 31, 1865
Early Afternoon Phase

across Fitzgerald's to establish an outpost and provide advance warning of Pickett's approach.

After approving these dispositions, Sheridan sat back to await events. He did not like the apparent fact that he was facing a body of infantry larger than a division. While still confident of halting Pickett's troops, he had the nagging suspicion that control of the developing fight was slipping away from him.[30]

When, sometime before 9:00 A.M., Pickett learned that Devin's men were in his immediate front in strong force, he improvised a plan to strike them from the blind side. The result was an ambitious but promising piece of strategy, one worthy of a better soldier than Pickett had become. While Munford's main body held, and strengthened, its position on the upper reaches of the road to Dinwiddie, and while detachments moved down the Crump and Gravelly Run Church Roads to threaten the Union right, Pickett's foot soldiers, their lower flank covered by the horsemen of Rooney Lee and Rosser, would descend the west bank of Chamberlain's Bed until able to cross into Sheridan's left rear. The attackers would ford the stream in two columns—the cavalry at Fitzgerald's Ford, the infantry at Danse's.[31]

Despite its strong points, Pickett's strategy went awry almost from the start—largely the fault of Fitz Lee. After reaching its assigned crossing point, the cavalry, instead of waiting for Pickett's men to get into position to the north, attacked on its own. Rosser's division, leading the column, rammed into the 2nd New York Mounted Rifles, the unit Smith had sent across the river at Fitzgerald's, and shoved it back to the east bank. There the New Yorkers were joined by the 6th Ohio, also of Smith's brigade, whose men, fighting dismounted, held back the attackers for an extended period through the sheer power of their repeating carbines.

To exploit his temporary advantage, Smith sent another force—a battalion of the 1st Maine, a regiment that had been a force in battle ever since the fight at Kelly's Ford—across the stream to take Rosser's men in flank. The tactic backfired: As the brigade commander admitted, the Mainers were the ones outflanked and "driven back in confusion, the men seeking refuge among the led horses and fording the stream up to their necks."

The North Carolinians of Barringer's brigade pursued with wild abandon, splashing through the water while screeching the Rebel yell. They suffered for their impetuosity. The water had risen so high from the recent rains that horses foundered and riders toppled into the stream; a few of both species drowned. When the first pursuers reached dry ground, Rooney Lee ordered a regiment of Brig. Gen. Richard L. T. Beale's brigade to charge Smith's Ohioans and New Yorkers. Through some error, only one squadron of the outfit did so; lacking close support, it was repulsed with "frightful loss."[32]

When enough Confederates had reached the east bank to place Smith's command in jeopardy, the brevet brigadier called up his remaining units, the 13th Ohio and the balance of the 1st Maine, and led them in a dismounted advance up the ford road. The Federals slowly but steadily pushed back the Confederates, who had yet to solidify their hold on the east side. Rooney Lee's division, especially Barringer's brigade, suffered severely as it recrossed the stream, losing an inordinate number of field and line officers. In a matter of minutes, the only soldiers in gray and butternut-colored uniforms on the east bank were prisoners. Looking on from the rear, Sheridan exulted that, as he later informed Grant, Smith's assailants had "got cleaned out."[33]

Smith's success endured for perhaps three hours. By then Pickett's infantry had forced its way across Danse's Ford to threaten the Federals' right and rear while, at the same time, a four-gun battery from Pegram's battalion was, from across the stream, subjecting the troopers to a destructive fire. Smith's flank and rear were quickly covered, however, by the men of Davies's brigade, who, desiring to help their comrades but restricted to a road so narrow they could not do so mounted, had come down on foot just before Pickett crossed at Danse's. Davies's movement, though well intentioned, was poorly timed, for by leaving his assigned position, the brigade commander ensured that the detachment of the 1st New Jersey he had left behind would be overwhelmed by the Rebel infantry.

Despite the size of the opposition, the New Jerseymen, under Maj. Walter Raleigh Robbins, made a good fight. From behind serviceable breastworks, they peppered Pickett's advance, Corse's brigade, as it moved to cross the stream. The first attack wave recoiled, but other elements of Pickett's column rolled forward, eventually lapping around Robbins's flanks and threatening his rear. The major gave the order to pull out only minutes before the screaming, shouting foot soldiers surrounded him. Minutes later, the bulk of Davies's brigade reached the ford, having countermarched from Fitzgerald's to try to stem the onslaught. Exhausted from their recent footwork, they failed to generate as much resistance as they would have had they arrived on horseback. Against dwindling opposition, the remainder of Pickett's command followed Corse's brigade across Chamberlain's Bed. Unable to hold back the gray tide, Davies's weary, sweat-stained troopers fled down the Dinwiddie Court House Road. Their withdrawal was covered by the remainder of Robbins's regiment, under Col. Hugh H. Janeway, a stalwart fighter whose reputation rested on the dozen wounds he had accumulated over the past three and a half years.[34]

At about 2:30 P.M., Tom Devin personally led one of Stagg's regiments to Davies's assistance. Forming beside the 1st New Jersey, the Michiganders did their best to blunt Pickett's drive, which had accumulated great momentum. Once Devin saw how difficult the task would be, he sent back for supports—Fitzhugh's brigade, minus one regiment (Maj. Harrison White's 6th New York, which was left behind to hold the Dinwiddie Court House Road). But the additions failed to stop Pickett—for one thing, the newcomers' formation was broken by the rush of Davies's fugitives to the rear. A charitable staff officer observed that "Davies with his regiments dismounted, had made a gallant stand against overwhelming numbers; but had been obliged to give way, and he was now retiring by the right flank." Scooping up the 1st New Jersey, Davies led his embattled troopers to the Boisseau place, where he sought desperately to regroup. On the way, dozens of his men fell to the infantry's rifles, including Maj. James Hart, long a mainstay of the 1st New Jersey.[35]

Pickett's men continued to cross Chamberlain's Bed in great volume. As soon as it secured a foothold on the east bank, Corse's brigade struck Fitzhugh's just-arrived troopers with intimidating force. While attempting to parry the blow in front, Fitzhugh found his left flank under threat by Terry's brigade, which had crossed the stream below its comrades. To save Fitzhugh from annihilation, Devin bolstered his flanks with Stagg's brigade, but when that tactic failed to relieve the pressure, Devin pulled Fitzhugh to the rear. Eventually the embattled brigade joined Davies's men at Boisseau's, although under pressure all the way. Devin reported that "twice the brigade was obliged to halt and charge the enemy while retiring."[36]

By now Fitzhugh's 6th New York was also in trouble. About 2:00 P.M., elements of Munford's division, which had largely been confined to diversionary movements and limited advances, suddenly pushed south and, as its leader wrote, "got a move on the enemy." It crushed its initial target, White's regiment. Although Devin rushed a portion of the Wolverine Brigade to its support, the 6th New York broke apart under Munford's pounding, pieces flying south and east in wild retreat.[37]

Fitzhugh's pullback meant that Stagg's belatedly positioned brigade received the full attention and motive force of Pickett's infantry. After a few minutes of spirited but futile resistance, the Wolverines fell back to avoid extinction. They followed their comrades eastward, linking near Boisseau's with Davies and Fitzhugh, whose troopers had re-formed and dug in to resist further pressure against front or flank.

With Sheridan still in the rear at Dinwiddie, Merritt galloped up to Boisseau's to assume personal control of the fighting. To ease the congestion in that crowded sector, he placed Fitzhugh and Stagg on the right of the Dinwiddie Road and Davies's brigade to the left. He sent patrols from each command to link with the troopers who remained near Sheridan's headquarters.

By now the troops at Dinwiddie included the horse artillery units that had sunk so deeply into the mud they had failed to keep pace with the cavalry on the twenty-ninth. Of greater importance, also on hand were two-thirds of Custer's division, the brigades of Pennington and Capehart. These had been called to Dinwiddie at about 3:30 to help contain Pickett. As described by Sgt. Roger Hannaford of Pennington's 2nd Ohio, the hastily assembled reinforcements had been brought up from the rear at the double-quick:

> Some Officer (Staff) came dashing down toward us, & in a moment we were in [column of] fours & . . . dashing up the road. Faster & faster we go, & when near a mile from the Court House, we [see] Custer & his Staff, who are waiting for us, dash to the head of the column, & we turn into a field on the right & form in line on a gallop. "Dismount! Prepare to fight on foot" is the word, before our horses have time to be still. Then, before we have time to tie our horses together, or those who have sabres on their belts time to unloosen them, the word is given "Forward march," & away we go on a dead run, making for a little knoll 450 or 500 yds. in a right oblique direction. Scattered all over the fields before us are our men, now rapidly falling [back], occasionally turning to fire at the swift[ly] advancing rebel skirmishers, they give us a hearty cheer as we draw toward them.[38]

The presence of Custer and the artillery, as well as the sudden cessation of the several-day rainfall, must have comforted Sheridan. For some hours, his men had been on the defensive, hard-pressed on all parts of the field. Through staunch fighting, however, they had staved off defeat; by all indications, their energy and enthusiasm remained high. By utilizing that spirit, Sheridan hoped to turn the tables on his opponents. Even with his back to the wall, he was plotting a counterattack.

Little Phil may have planned boldly, but Pickett continued to make bold moves. By the middle of the afternoon he had advanced a large portion of his force along the road from Danse's Ford to its intersection with the road to Dinwiddie Court House. Despite Merritt's near-desperate efforts to avoid it, this movement effectively cut off Devin and Davies from the troopers at Dinwiddie. From his new position, Pickett could attack toward Boisseau's or swing south against Sheridan's isolated position.

Merritt, who fully appreciated the gravity of the situation, acted swiftly to keep it from spiraling out of control. He sent Devin's and Davies's men on a detour as far east as the Boydton Plank Road. Both commands were able to disengage from Boisseau's thanks to Munford's sudden quiescence. The Virginians recovered in time, however, to harass the rear of the moving columns with both mounted and dismounted attacks. When Stagg's 6th Michigan whirled about and cut loose with its Spencer repeaters, the pressure abruptly lessened, and in the gathering darkness of late afternoon, the Federals made their roundabout way to the vicinity of the courthouse, passing behind a line of breastworks thrown up the night before and now held by the new arrivals under Custer. Only then were Davies's people, who had been serving on foot since morning, reunited with their horses, which had been held well behind the front.[39]

The run to safety down the plank road was a near thing. As Devin wrote a few weeks later:

> They surrounded me . . . and nearly got me and would have done so if their Cavalry had pluck enough to charge me or if my gallant lads had wavered for a moment. . . . Every body supposed I was captured as it was known that we were cut off and I thought I did a "big thing" in getting out with my whole command but all the praise I got from Sheridan was a grin and "O I knew you would get out somehow."[40]

Upon the arrival of Merritt's refugees, Sheridan called in Smith's men, who had been holding on at Fitzgerald's Ford, effectively preventing the horsemen of Rooney Lee and Rosser (the latter had taken a severe wound in the action, as had Smith) from joining their infantry friends on the east side of Chamberlain's. With Smith's men came Irvin Gregg's brigade, which had supported the holding action at Fitzgerald's almost to the point of being surrounded ("I thought everything was gone up," admitted a field officer in the 21st Pennsylvania). Then Gibbs's Reserves, backed by a two-gun section of horse artillery, trotted down to Dinwiddie from their former post at the intersection of the Court House and Brook Roads. Alluding to the circumstances surrounding their pullout, a lieutenant in Gibbs's 2nd Massachusetts insisted, "We were *overpowered*—badly whipped but not *driven* nor *routed* nor *demoralized*."[41]

With most of his men, and all of his horse artillery, in hand, Sheridan dug in for a final defense. Maj. Henry E. Tremain of Crook's staff observed that "every nerve was strained; all was life, activity, and industry. Sheridan seemed

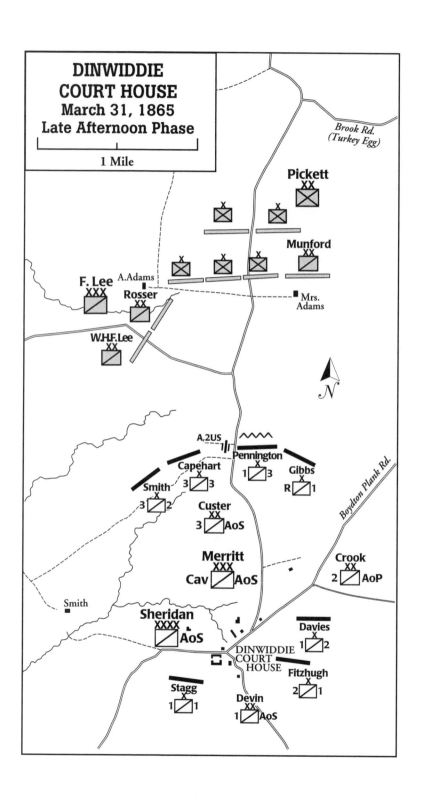

DINWIDDIE
COURT HOUSE
March 31, 1865
Late Afternoon Phase

1 Mile

Brook Rd.
(Turkey Egg)

Pickett
XX

Munford
XX

A. Adams

F. Lee
XXX

Rosser
XX

Mrs.
Adams

W.H.F. Lee
XX

N

A, 2US

Pennington
X
1   3

Capehart
X
3   3

Gibbs
X
R   1

Smith
X
3   2

Custer
XX
3   AoS

Merritt
XXX
Cav   AoS

Crook
XX
2   AoP

Smith

Sheridan
XXXX
AoS

Davies
X
1   2

DINWIDDIE
COURT
HOUSE

Boydton Plank Rd.

Fitzhugh
X
2   1

Stagg
X
1   1

Devin
XX
1   AoS

to have infused his own indomitable spirit among his subordinates. . . . If the enemy could not be conquered today at least he must be overawed."[42]

Sheridan's troopers had deployed both above and around Dinwiddie. Their front line, about three-quarters of a mile north of the courthouse, consisted of (from west to east) the brigades of Smith, Capehart, Pennington, Gregg, and Gibbs. Farther to the rear, in a more sheltered area, were the men of Stagg, Fitzhugh, and Davies—those who had borne the brunt of the fighting, and the losses, this day. Yet every component of Sheridan's force, those in front and those in rear, took up their posts on the firing line when, sometime after 5:00, the enemy advanced on them, spoiling for a fight. The attack column comprised Pickett's foot soldiers, their right guarded by Rooney Lee's division, their left and rear by the horsemen of Munford.

Pickett's men came on confidently, convinced of their superiority. Colonel Newhall later recalled that the Confederates "had an air of *abandon,* a sort of devil-may-care swing in their long stride . . . that was rather disheartening to men that did not want to get shot." Their attitude did not, however, concern Newhall's boss. Sheridan was content that "we were now in good shape behind the familiar barricades."[43]

In a gesture either courageous or foolhardy, just before the Rebels struck, Little Phil, fully exposed to enemy fire, rode the length of his line in company with subordinates including Merritt and Custer and trailed by civilian visitors at cavalry headquarters. As he trotted past, Little Phil shouted words of encouragement and advice to all within earshot. Whether or not his words had an effect, his conspicuous presence attracted a volley of rifle fire. Although the general escaped unhurt, some of those near him reeled in their saddles, including *New York Herald* reporter Theodore Wilson, who was slightly wounded. "In reply," Sheridan recalled, "our horse-artillery opened on the advancing Confederates, but the men behind the barricades lay still till Pickett's troops were within short range. Then they opened, Custer's repeating rifles pouring out such a shower of lead that nothing could stand up against it." Newhall marveled at the firepower generated by "the carbines of five brigades . . . blazing in the twilight, the repeating Spensers [*sic*] puffing out their cartridges like Roman candles."[44]

Although initially staggered by the fusillade, Pickett's men gave almost as good as they got. To Sheridan's dismay and concern, their fire dislodged a section of Pennington's brigade, which held a position slightly in advance of its comrades on either side and thereby vulnerable to an enfilade. Little Phil was relieved, however, when the displaced men withdrew in good order to more defensible terrain, where they planted themselves like concrete pillars. Twice Pickett's men attacked the new position, and twice they were thrown back.

Then Custer led Capehart's men in a dismounted charge that caused the enemy line to waver and, after a few minutes, to fall back. "The repulse was very quick," wrote Sheridan, "and as the gray lines retired to the woods from which but a few minutes before they had so confidently advanced, all danger of their taking Dinwiddie or marching to the left and rear of our infantry line was over, at least for the night."[45]

Custer's movement—the only counterattack Sheridan had managed that afternoon—appeared to drain Pickett's troops not only of momentum, but also of confidence. The infantry made no additional efforts to advance in force. Thus, for all intents and purposes, ended what would become known as the battle of Dinwiddie Court House.

It had been a frustrating experience for the Confederates, who by every rule of logic should have overwhelmed the smaller cavalry force before them. At such close quarters, however, their long-range rifles had counted for little. Then, too, the darkness of early evening had hampered their attack formations. Only an eleventh-hour assault by dismounted troopers on Pickett's right achieved some limited success, and then only because Smith's brigade, which held that part of the line, had been forced to the rear by empty ammunition boxes. Like Pennington's fugitives, they took up a stronger position farther south, which they held by bluffing the enemy into believing their carbines were fully loaded.[46]

The victor this day was hard to determine. Through most of the fight, the Confederates appeared to hold the advantage. Their greater strength and staying power had enabled them to shove their enemy from point to point, inflicting on Sheridan nearly 500 casualties, including one-third the effective force of Crook's division. For these and other reasons, many, perhaps most, Southerners considered the fight a great success. General Barringer later called it "the last marked victory of our armies." Some of their opponents agreed. Tom Devin, for one, claimed that he and his comrades had been "walloped like thunder."[47]

But Confederate resources and options were so limited that Pickett could not profit from a draw—which is how the engagement truly ended. Although cuffed about on many quarters of the field, Sheridan's men had also fought stubbornly and skillfully in a tactical situation that most cavalrymen could not have handled. At day's end, they had rallied to hold their final position with a degree of tenacity that must have warmed their leader's heart. Significantly, Pickett himself refused to claim a victory, commenting only that the engagement had been "quite a spirited one, the men and officers behaving most admirably."[48]

FIVE

"Don't Talk to Me, My Lines Are Broken!"

IN THE AFTERMATH OF THE FIGHTING NEAR DINWIDDIE COURT HOUSE, EACH side believed the other to be in dire straits. The more numerous Confederates had shoved their enemy inside a compact perimeter that appeared to be vulnerable at many points, the combativeness of the defenders notwithstanding. In so doing, they had driven a wedge between Sheridan's men and the rest of the forces under Grant, although at what Robert E. Lee called a "severe" loss in the Rebel ranks. In his official report of the fight, Pickett insisted that only the coming of night had saved his adversary from being dispersed, if not destroyed: "Half an hour more of daylight and we would have gotten to the Court-House." The implication was that soon after sunup on April 1, he would finish the job.[1]

Not everyone in gray shared Pickett's view of things, but his words later gave rise to a pointed question. Looking back, Tom Munford called the general's claim "a mere hypothesis." "Why was a halt necessary?" he asked. "We had Sheridan in full retreat, and had driven him between three and four miles almost at a run, and General Pickett's orders from General R. E. Lee . . . [were] to drive him out, <u>and to break him up.</u> The golden opportunity was lost,—egregiously lost. . . . We think daylight had nothing to do with it." Munford never forgave his superior for halting his offensive before it was fully effective.[2]

For their part, the officers and men under Sheridan appeared to believe that their enemy had no realistic hope of driving them from their final positions. Ensconced behind solid works, armed with repeating carbines, and as capable of fighting afoot as any infantrymen, they felt certain of holding the line against additional attacks until the Rebels' ammunition ran out. Had they known that many of Pickett's ordnance wagons had not made it to Five Forks, they would have considered their claim strengthened.

Their commander appears to have entertained conflicting opinions on the subject. While the battle raged, Horace Porter of Grant's staff joined Sheridan at Dinwiddie to get his impressions of the fight. The Irishman was in high spirits; Porter quoted him as saying that "he had had one of the liveliest days in his experience, fighting infantry and cavalry with cavalry only, but that he was concentrating his command on the high ground just north of Dinwiddie, and would hold that position at all hazards." In a later communiqué to headquarters, however, Sheridan revealed a different outlook. "The men have behaved splendidly," he assured Grant, but far from boasting that he could hold the position indefinitely, he opined: "[Pickett's force] is too strong for us. I will hold on to Dinwiddie Court-House until I am compelled to leave."[3]

On one point, however, Sheridan would not equivocate. He told Porter, as he told others then and later, regarding Pickett's command: "[It] is in more danger than I am—if I am cut off from the Army of the Potomac, it is cut off from Lee's army, and not a man in it should ever be allowed to get back to Lee. We at last have drawn the enemy's infantry out of its fortifications, and this is our chance to attack it."[4]

By "our chance," Sheridan did not mean that his horsemen alone should assault Pickett; he had in mind cavalry supported by a hefty force of foot soldiers. Grant's offer to lend him the V Corps was fresh in Sheridan's mind, but he continued to reject the idea of working closely with Gouverneur Warren. In addition to doubting Warren's ability to subordinate himself to a colleague known primarily as a cavalry commander, Sheridan was uncertain of the caliber of the man's command. He had heard reports that more than once during the siege the corps had failed to give maximum effort when cooperating with other elements of the army. When Porter reached cavalry headquarters, he surely informed Sheridan of the day's operations farther to the right, where the V Corps had attempted to extend its reach to and, if possible, across the White Oak Road near Burgess's Mill. Warren, however, had gone forward sluggishly; then one of his divisions had withdrawn in disorder under an attack by a smaller force. Another element of the corps had recovered the lost ground, but the day's action had not testified to V Corps steadfastness.[5]

As he had earlier that day, Sheridan begged Porter, as the latter related, "to go to General Grant at once and again urge him to send him the Sixth Corps, because it had been under him in the battles in the Valley of Virginia, and knew his way of fighting." Shaking his head, the aide reiterated Grant's earlier reply, that Wright's corps was too far to the right to be available to Sheridan: "The only one which could reach him by daylight was the Fifth." This was news Sheridan did not wish to hear, but he digested it, taking note of Warren's ability to reach him by sunup. Either overtly or tacitly, he finally consented to the substitution.[6]

Porter rode off to bring word of the cavalry's operations to the commanding general and to expedite transfer of the V Corps to Dinwiddie Court House. Some hours later, another emissary from Grant's headquarters, which had been moved to Dabney's Mills, between the Boydton Plank Road and the Vaughan Road, reached Sheridan with a message dated 10:45 P.M. It informed the recipient that Grant had ordered Warren to the cavalry's support. Two of his three divisions would reach Sheridan by marching westward to J. Boisseau's; the third would come down the plank road. Grant added that he had ordered Mackenzie's cavalry, which had crossed the James to the outskirts of Petersburg, to report to Sheridan as well.

Despite his doubts about Warren and the quality of his command, Sheridan determined to make the most of his new resources. Given the magnitude of the pending reinforcement and the fact that "discretionary authority was given to me to use all my forces against Pickett," Sheridan stated in his memoirs, "I resolved to destroy him, if it was within the bounds of possibility, before he could rejoin Lee."[7]

In so deciding, Sheridan was heavily influenced by an assurance Grant had given him in his orders of 10:45. The commanding general revised the timetable Horace Porter had laid out, telling Sheridan the troops to be sent to Dinwiddie Court House, "except the cavalry, should reach you by 12 tonight." Sheridan would hold Warren accountable for meeting that deadline.[8]

After dark, when the fighting ceased on Pickett's front, most of his troops remained within rifle range of Sheridan's defenses. Some of Pegram's guns had already started back to Five Forks, but for hours the infantry traded shots with Custer's men. The latter had moved up to take possession of all parts of Sheridan's line, giving comrades who had seen heavier fighting the chance to rest and refit. Fitz Lee's cavalry was similarly active in the night, keeping up a carbine fire on the Union works, as well as scouting the roads in Pickett's rear and on his flanks.

The gray troopers were especially busy reconnoitering toward the east, where, only a few miles off, Federal infantry was known to be lurking. While dismounted members of Munford's division filled the gap between Pickett's left (Corse's position) and the Boydton Plank Road, mounted patrols searched for stragglers from both armies. As Munford recalled, sometime after 9:00 P.M., a party from Capt. Jesse S. Jones's 3rd Virginia (the regiment's longtime commander, Lt. Col. William M. Feild, had been knocked out of action during the day) brought him two Union prisoners. The Yankees were not cavalrymen, but foot soldiers. Upon questioning them, Munford discovered they were members of the V Corps brigade of Brig. Gen. Joseph J. Bartlett. Although he did not leave a full account of his interrogation, it appears that Munford learned that the captives had been moving, with the rest of their brigade, down the plank road to Dinwiddie Court House. In the darkness, they had wandered from the route of march and had run into Munford's videttes.[9]

Whether or not he appreciated the full significance of this information, the cavalry leader hastened the Yankees to Fitz Lee, who was resting in rear of the lines in company with General Pickett. Within minutes of hearing the prisoners' story, Lee, and presumably Pickett as well, realized that, as Fitz wrote, "the infantry confronting the right of our line of battle at Burgess' Mills . . . had about-faced and was marching to the support of Sheridan and his discomfited cavalry, which would have brought them directly upon our left flank." Pickett's command may have been large enough to "discomfit" 9,000 cavalrymen, but it could not be expected to oppose successfully the same force augmented by 15,000 foot soldiers. Moreover, Pickett's primary objective was not to capture Dinwiddie Court House, but to defend Lee's far right and especially to block enemy access to the South Side Railroad. Under the circumstances, it was imperative that he withdraw to Five Forks and strengthen the works there against an assault by combined arms.[10]

In hasty consultation, Pickett and Lee determined to send back at once their ambulances, ordnance wagons, and what remained of the artillery. According to Lee, the first of these resources reached Five Forks by 11:00 P.M., and the last wagon was put in motion before midnight. For another four hours or more, Pickett's infantry and cavalry held their positions in close proximity to Sheridan, even after receiving indications that a full division of the V Corps was coming down the Plank Road to challenge them. Between 4:00 and 5:00 A.M., Pickett's main body began to move north over the same road it had taken from Five Forks the previous morning. Corse's brigade, which held the flank most threatened by the newcomers, was the last infantry unit to disengage. Its withdrawal was screened by Munford's men, most of them deployed on foot. After the infantry had moved on, the troopers remounted and followed them, covering their rear.[11]

When he discovered the enemy was pulling out, Sheridan's natural reaction was to pursue. This he did, moving out with Custer's division, mostly dismounted, on the left, its far flank resting on Chamberlain's Bed, and Devin's mounted men on the right, angling in the direction of their old position at J. Boisseau's. A few horse artillery pieces advanced in rear of the cavalry, although the fields were still too muddy to admit of their employment in all sectors. Sheridan permitted the majority of Crook's battle-scarred division to remain in bivouac below Dinwiddie Court House, although Irvin Gregg's brigade later moved north to guard Custer's left flank.

The men of the 1st and 3rd Divisions sparred with the Confederates at medium and long range, but Sheridan did not compel them to pursue closely enough to overtake the escapees. He no longer intended to smite the enemy with his horsemen alone, not when so many foot troops were hastening to his side. Or were they? Sheridan had expected that at least the advance guard of Warren's corps would reach him by midnight, as Grant had promised. However, by 3:00 A.M. on April 1, with Pickett's pullout well under way, the V Corps was nowhere in sight. From some source, however, Sheridan had gotten the mistaken impression that the vanguard of the corps was, or should have been, in Pickett's left rear near Boisseau's. Instead of having Warren continue down the plank road and from there to Dinwiddie, Sheridan now sent a message urging him to move directly west, cutting Pickett off from Five Forks. While the V Corps struck from that direction, Sheridan would pile into the Rebels from the south.

But the trap Sheridan envisioned never closed. Warren was in no position to hit the Confederates from above; in fact, he remained hours away from a linkup with the cavalry. As Sheridan speculated in his memoirs, when Pickett's retreating column was passing the point at which the Union leader hoped it would be intercepted, "Warren's men were just breaking from the bivouac in which their chief had placed them the night before, and the head of Griffin's division did not get to Boisseau's till after my cavalry."[12]

Sheridan would never forgive his subordinate for what he considered Warren's unconscionable dawdling. Although Little Phil professed to believe that "there were good reasons for its [the V Corps'] non-appearance" by midnight, he blamed Warren for his inability to strike Pickett at or shortly after 3:00 A.M., which Sheridan viewed as the loss of an enormous opportunity. In his memoirs, he reduced to mere disappointment his reaction to Warren's failure to cut off Pickett's retreat. In reality, Warren's performance—so lacking in the energy and precision that invariably characterized Sheridan's operations—prompted the Irishman to lodge against Warren's name a mark so black it could not be cleansed by the most assiduous polishing.

Despite Sheridan's pursuit, the retreat to Five Forks proceeded with relative smoothness, at an unhurried pace, and in two columns. Most of the foot soldiers, Munford's horsemen close behind, proceeded up the direct road from Dinwiddie Court House. Fitz Lee recalled that his cousin Rooney's troopers, as well as those of Tom Rosser, marched up a road farther west, one that crossed Chamberlain's Bed.[13]

In after years, Munford took pains to note the leisurely nature of the withdrawal. Commenting on the postbattle reports of Sheridan and Merritt, both of which spoke of "pressing" the Confederates nearly to the crossroads, Munford called his opponents "entirely mistaken," adding, "The roads were very narrow, which made our march slow." Furthermore, he wrote, "my men were mostly old veterans and were inured to that kind of work, and I am proud to say that they were generally as steady in a retreat as they were during a fight, where they had half a chance. The rear guard simply took advantage of any topographical defense and if they could practice a ruse they invariably did it."[14]

The pace of the withdrawal meant that Pickett's entire force was not at Five Forks until after midmorning. Fitz Lee recollected that the last Confederate reached the crossroads between 8:00 and 9:00. There, sometime early on April 1, Pickett supposedly received a telegram from Robert E. Lee, ordering him to hold the strategic position "at all hazards"—so, at any rate, reported the general's widow thirty years later. No copy of the communiqué has been unearthed; moreover, La Salle Corbell Pickett, whose forté was fiction, had a tendency to exaggerate, distort, and falsify when writing about her husband's career. Even so, many historians concede the existence of such an order, although when he mentioned it in his report of the campaign, Pickett commented only that Lee directed him to hold his position "so as to protect the road to Ford's Depot." That station on the all-important South Side Railroad lay only seven miles from Five Forks. Pickett claimed he replied by requesting Lee to make a diversion of some sort so that his men would not be isolated and vulnerable.[15]

Pickett later asserted that he did not consider it wise to try to hold Five Forks with the troops he had on hand. This view was shared by his adjutant, Maj. Walter Harrison, who declared that "Five Forks was not a point to be protected, except by a very large force." By the standards of the campaign, Pickett's command was of moderate size. Pickett would have preferred to place a major geographical barrier between his position and the enemy— Hatcher's Run, which meandered about a mile north of Five Forks. Lee's order to hold the crossroads, however, was imperative. Pickett consoled himself with the belief, which he claimed to have derived from Lee's order, that he would not have to defend his post alone: "I supposed the commanding General intended sending up reinforcements."[16]

Pickett's reluctance to confront Warren and Sheridan in his current position, combined with his erroneous belief that help was on the way, may have affected his determination to hold his position. Over the next three hours or so, his men added to the breastworks previously thrown up along the White Oak Road, while digging additional rifle pits in rear of the barricades. The result was less than impressive. Major Harrison described the finished product as a shallow ditch fronted by a loose fence of pine logs, "hastily thrown up." To hold this line, which ran for about a mile and three-quarters parallel to the road, with the crossroads in the approximate center, Pickett had stationed, from west to east, Corse's brigade—its right flank covered by Rooney Lee's troopers—then the brigades of Terry, Steuart, Wallace, and Ransom. Pegram's cannons had been dispersed so that three, including the single operational section of Graham's Petersburg Battery of horse artillery, were on the right of Corse's infantry. Three other batteries were grouped near Five Forks, while McGregor's four-gun battery had been stationed to support Ransom's brigade on the far left.[17]

The ground between Ransom's flank and a meandering creek, a tributary of Hatcher's Run, Fitz Lee filled with Munford's troopers. Munford dismounted the majority and placed them on either side of a woods road in Ransom's left rear. The road was so narrow, and the foliage around it so thick, that it could accommodate only a couple of horsemen riding abreast. Munford's men were deployed diagonally because they had to conform to the shape of the flank, which ran east and then north at a sixty-degree angle, or "return."[18]

Fitz Lee's positioning of Rooney Lee and Munford was unexceptional. Both flanks needed to be held by horsemen, and these commands were the logical choices for the job. Fitz made less effective use of Rosser's men. At its commander's request, the division was permitted to take a position on the north side of Hatcher's Run. There, in the approximate center of the Confederate rear, it guarded Pickett's ordnance wagons and ambulances. Rosser later claimed he had requested the location because the terrain below the stream was so densely wooded there was no place for him on the front line. He also claimed that Dearing's and McCausland's animals were sore-backed and in need of rest. Once in place above Hatcher's Run, he had his men unsaddle and feed their mounts. By seeking this post, Rosser implied that his division had seen more arduous service than those of Rooney Lee and Munford. By granting his request, Fitz Lee appeared to agree.[19]

Yet another mounted force theoretically available to the defenders of Five Forks was a small brigade (one regiment and one large battalion) of North Carolinians under Brig. Gen. William P. Roberts, at twenty-three the youngest general officer in Confederate service. Although it answered to General Anderson, whose right flank, at the intersection of the White Oak and Claiborne Roads, it guarded, the little command was also charged with patrolling as far west as Pickett's left, a distance of nearly four miles. Tom Munford recalled that his 8th Virginia attempted to keep in communication with Roberts's men via videttes who would "ride backwards and forwards" over the intervening ground. As a means of covering such a wide and critical gap, this arrangement left much to be desired. In truth, Roberts's task was an impossible one, as the cavalry of the Army of the James would soon demonstrate.[20]

When he wrote his memoirs, Ulysses S. Grant described Ranald Mackenzie as "the most promising young officer in the army." Young he was—twenty-four—but by the spring of 1865, he had seen extensive service in both staff and line and had made a sterling record in a succession of demanding assignments. Much had been expected of the native New Yorker since he was graduated first in the West Point class of June 1862. Mackenzie had begun his war service as a lieutenant of topographical engineers, the army's elite corps. He spent two years as a staff officer in the Army of the Potomac, winning commendation from every commander he served, as well as several brevets for gallantry.

In July 1864, following conspicuous service at Cold Harbor, Mackenzie became the colonel of a Connecticut heavy artillery regiment that had been retrained as infantry. He led his "heavies" with conspicuous ability during Jubal Early's raid on Washington, then under Sheridan in the Shenandoah Valley. By the fall of 1864, he had moved up to brigade command in the VI Corps, in which position he was wounded while leading a charge at Cedar Creek. By the time his recuperation was complete, he was a brigadier general of volunteers.[21]

When Ord replaced Butler as commander of the Army of the James in January 1865, he entered into a series of disputes with his predecessor's chief of cavalry, August Kautz. Ord considered Kautz lazy and barely competent, and his troopers undisciplined and underachieving. He was not Kautz's only critic; James H. Wilson, who had served alongside the German-American during a raid south and west of Petersburg in June 1864, called his command "about 2000 of the wildest rag-tag and bob-tail cavalry I ever saw." For his part, Kautz became increasingly disenchanted with Ord's "exceptional orders" and "eccentric character." A break was inevitable; it occurred when, early in March 1865, Kautz went on leave with Grant's approval but without Ord's. When the brigadier returned from his furlough, he found Mackenzie in his place and he himself in command of a division of U.S. Colored Troops.[22]

Although he took over on the eve of a major campaign, Mackenzie quickly exerted his influence on the small, two-brigade division he had inherited. Described as "very active, somewhat nervous, often impetuous and exacting," the youngster tightened up discipline, upgraded training, and remounted units whose horses had seen hard service over the winter. Corporate morale soared; even Kautz, who had resented Mackenzie's coming, came to view him as "a very zealous officer" who communicated to officers and men his energy, vision, and thirst to succeed.[23]

Mackenzie viewed the coming movement against Lee's right flank as a showcase for the talent he saw in his new command. Thus he was chagrined that his participation should begin in the rear of his army. When Ord marched the infantry of Foster, Turner, and Birney south of the Richmond siege lines, Mackenzie's troopers guided them to the north bank of the James. At that point, the cavalry was pulled off the road and sent to the rear, where Ord's long train of supply wagons and ambulances had been halted by rough roads and high water. Mackenzie spent the next two days escorting the lumbering vehicles over the James via the pontoons at Aiken's Landing and then on to Petersburg, a job he accomplished without the loss of a wagon.

By morning of March 30, having delivered their charge into the hands of Meade's quartermasters at Humphreys's Station on the military railroad, the 1,700 officers, troopers, and horse artillerymen who had made the march from the Northside were ready to start the campaign anew. They remained, however, in that relatively quiet sector, doing picket duty, until shortly after midnight on April 1, when Grant relayed to Mackenzie orders to report at once to Phil Sheridan at Dinwiddie Court House. At 3:30 A.M., Mackenzie set out to comply.[24]

He reached Sheridan just after daylight, about an hour after Little Phil's men had tumbled out of their bivouacs to the bugle call of "Boots and Saddles." He met the local commander not at Dinwiddie, but within rifle range of Five Forks. By that hour, the lead elements of the V Corps were at last coming into view to the east of Sheridan's field headquarters. As yet, however, not enough foot soldiers were on hand to mount an offensive against Pickett. By now Warren was six hours late, and counting.

Little Phil was a study in nervous energy, shouting orders to his officers, riding to and fro to oversee dispositions, sending waves of staff officers to urge Warren forward. When finally able to give his undivided attention to the new arrival, he instructed Mackenzie to move, via a byroad, to the edge of the swamp that gave the White Oak Road its name. The winding trail struck the road at a point about two miles east of Pickett's left flank. Mackenzie was to seize and hold that section of the road until further orders reached him.[25]

Sheridan's visitor moved out promptly, determined to carry out his orders to the letter. His column passed through the trees with maximum stealth, its point riders scanning the terrain ahead for signs of the Confederate cavalry known to be in the area. About 1:00, when within a half mile of its destination, Mackenzie's advance guard made contact with Roberts's pickets. After a brief exchange, the graybacks turned and fled. Minutes later, Mackenzie's vanguard emerged into a broad clearing, on the far side of which, astride the White Oak Road, stretched a line of rifle pits protected in front by fieldworks and occupied by a substantial number of dismounted cavalrymen.

Col. Samuel P. Spear of the 11th Pennsylvania, commander of Mackenzie's 2nd Brigade, responded to his superior's order by advancing his old regiment. Spear posted one squadron, mounted, on either side of the woods road, supported by dismounted portions of a third squadron, with the remainder of the regiment farther to the rear. Then, at Spear's order, Maj. Robert S. Monroe prepared to charge the works at the head of four companies of the 11th. Before the troopers went forward, Lt. Dorman Noggle's 4th Wisconsin Battery, supported by the troopers of Col. Robert M. West's 1st Brigade, softened up the position with shot and shell.

Just before Monroe's men spurred into action, Mackenzie and Spear placed themselves at the head of the column and led the charge. Following their example, the squadrons galloped toward the left flank of the breastworks. Under a rattling fire from the defenders, they topped the barriers, lashing out with sabers and pistols. Those Confederates not felled by the onslaught clambered out of the pits and ran for their lives through the pines. They were pursued by a majority of the charging men, backed by the dismounted skirmishers on their flanks and in the rear. Lt. Col. Franklin Stratton of the 11th reported: "The rebels were completely dispersed at every point. Their number, as afterward ascertained, was 600, double the number of my regiment."[26]

The success thus gained was dearly bought. Major Monroe had been killed in the charge, along with two of his subordinates and several enlisted men; another officer had been taken prisoner. Of those at the forefront of the attack, Mackenzie had emerged unhurt (and having, in the words of the historian of the 11th, "won his spurs"), while Spear had taken a disabling wound, requiring his replacement by Col. Andrew W. Evans of the 1st Maryland. At this cost, the attackers had seized the White Oak Road, effectively cutting off the main body of Roberts's brigade from the Petersburg fortifications. The victors needed only to hold their ground until Warren's infantry came up, something Sheridan had assured Mackenzie would occur in a couple of hours, if not sooner (it was now about 2:00 P.M.). Then the final, decisive push toward Five Forks could begin.[27]

While Mackenzie was breaking through on the right, Sheridan's main body, two miles farther west, remained a few hundred yards below the White Oak Road. Even so, it had made good progress toward the enemy line. By 2:00 P.M., its dismounted men had crept far enough forward through trees and underbrush—Custer's division on the left, Devin's on the right—to force all elements of Pickett's force into their entrenchments.

This was as far as they could safely push without infantry support. Once his forward progress ceased, Sheridan began to formulate the plan he would put into effect as soon as Warren's entire command was up. He intended to attack the length of Pickett's line with his cavalry alone. Custer's men would feign a strike against the Rebel right and center, while Devin, in close cooperation with the V Corps, would assail the left, hoping to break through at or near the return. When the infantry struck, Mackenzie's cavalry would cover its right flank and then attack in the same general direction as Warren.

By now the V Corps was only a mile or two from Sheridan's field headquarters. Warren himself had reported at about 11:00. His meeting with Sheridan must have been icily formal. If the corps leader had attempted to explain his delay, Sheridan would have listened in angry silence, if he did not berate him for having the temerity to dredge up fanciful excuses.[28]

In truth, although Sheridan never would have admitted it, Warren had a legitimate reason, or body of reasons, for his late arrival. He had received the initial order to augment Sheridan—with a single division, Griffin's, via the Boydton Plank Road—shortly after 9:00 the previous night. But since Griffin's men had been heavily engaged that day and were still in contact with the enemy, Warren had made preparations to move his other two divisions, under Brevet Major Generals Romeyn B. Ayres and Samuel W. Crawford, first. Yet no one could get far via the plank road until a bridge over Gravelly Run, destroyed by the enemy, was replaced.

Warren immediately put his engineers on the job, but it was 2:00 A.M. on the first before a makeshift bridge was up. It took another four hours for Ayres's troops to cross it and proceed down the road to J. Boisseau's. Warren's plans having been revamped yet again, the other two divisions were forced to march to their meeting place with Sheridan via the Crump Road, a more roundabout route. Griffin did not arrive, midway between Dinwiddie Court House and Five Forks, until about 8:00 A.M., Crawford some time later. Neither would be in position to support Sheridan's horsemen for some hours.[29]

By then Warren's career was in jeopardy. At about 10:00 A.M., Sheridan had complained bitterly of his subordinate's tardiness to Horace Porter, whom Grant had assigned to remain with the cavalry throughout the day, sending him, "every half-hour or so," reports of its operations. In one of these, Porter relayed Sheridan's criticism, which had an immediate effect. Shortly before noon, Col. Orville Babcock of Grant's staff rode up to Sheridan with a message from the commanding general: "If in your judgment the Fifth Corps would do better under one of the division commanders, you are authorized to relieve General Warren and order him to report to General Grant, at headquarters."[30]

Porter heard Sheridan reply to the effect that he hoped he would not have to make use of such authority. But he did not say he regretted being entrusted with it.

By 1:00, Sheridan's men were in close contact with many sectors of Pickett's line, but they had not begun to exert heavy pressure on any point. In Tom Rosser's bivouacs above Hatcher's Run, all was serene; the sounds of carbine fire failed to penetrate that far. As though the war were a distant memory, the cavalryman began to think about dinner. Pangs of hunger made him recall the shad waiting in his ice-cooled ambulance. Presently he set his staff to unpacking and deboning the fish.

The mess was large enough that Rosser considered sharing it with a couple of his superiors. The division commander was a master of public relations and self-promotion. Gift giving had been a habit of his at least since January 1862, when, as a lowly captain of artillery, he had presented Brig. Gen. Jeb Stuart with an expensive, gilt-encrusted kepi. Stuart was gratified by the act of generosity. A few months later, when one of his Virginia regiments needed a colonel, Stuart put in a call to Rosser, giving him entry into the arm in which he would make his reputation.[31]

While the meal was being prepared, couriers splashed across the stream to the field headquarters of Pickett and Fitzhugh Lee. They inquired whether the gentlemen would do General Rosser the honor of their presence at a shad bake prepared by his commissary officer. Both men readily accepted and promised to join Rosser forthwith. By 2:00, both were on hand to help Rosser polish off the fish, as well as bottles of choice spirits that their subordinate kept in stock even during active campaigning.

Why the commander and the second in command of an expeditionary force in close contact with an aggressive enemy would abandon their posts appears to defy rational analysis. A clue to their behavior, however, is offered by Fitz Lee's postwar comment that as of early afternoon on April 1, neither believed an attack, either by cavalry or infantry, was imminent. Early the previous day, Pickett, Lee, and their subordinates had been alert to rumors, probably spread by Union prisoners, of a coming offensive. When none materialized over the next twenty hours, the generals supposed it had been preempted. Fitz Lee's uncle had told him that by attacking the Yankees south of Five Forks, Pickett would disarrange their formations and disrupt their plans. "After we made our attack on March 31," Fitz wrote, "I considered that the movement had been broken up, temporarily at least."[32]

Their confidence was badly misplaced: The offensive had not been forestalled, merely delayed by Warren's long, roundabout march. Even so, the absence of a timely attack does not excuse Pickett's and Lee's dereliction, which includes their failure to alert Rooney Lee, the ranking officer at Five Forks, that they were heading north to lunch and that in their absence, he was in command. Nor does it explain how the generals could ignore the warning signs that had begun to mount before 2:00 P.M. These included the increasing volume of carbine fire along the length of Pickett's less-than-impregnable defenses; the detectable presence of Yankee infantry at J. Boisseau's and at other points; and the success the cavalry of the Army of the James had gained to the east. Just before 2:00, in fact, Munford had personally informed Fitz Lee of Mackenzie's breakthrough, word of which had come from the displaced pickets of the 8th Virginia. Instead of riding to the threatened sector, Fitz asked Munford to investigate, adding, "If necessary, order up your Division and let me hear from you." Then, as if without a care, he rode off to join Pickett and Rosser—without informing Munford of his destination.[33]

Munford ran the errand his superior had assigned him, passing in rear of the infantry. As he rode, he noted that the Union troopers to the south had dug in, many having fortified their positions with felled trees and handfuls of sand. From their shelters, they were delivering a fire that Munford described as "quite brisk." The "sharp whistle" of their carbine rounds "was audible at every few rods."[34]

By making a wide circuit around the refused left, Munford eventually reached the point at which the White Oak Road met the road from Gravelly Run Church. There and nearby, the 8th Virginia, along with some of Roberts's North Carolinians, had rallied after being driven from their defenses by Mackenzie. Peering eastward, Munford spied in the distance a phalanx of mounted men in blue. It was a disconcerting sight, but it paled in comparison to what caught his eye when a member of the 8th Virginia directed his attention south and east: the head of a long column of Union infantry, forming lines of battle in a field on the left side of the Gravelly Run Church Road.

Recovering from the shock of his discovery, Munford "instantly dispatched [couriers] to General Fitz Lee and General Pickett, giving them what information [he] had acquired by observation, and ordered up the Division, to come through the woods over a very narrow country road." Munford remained at the strategic intersection until the head of his leading brigade appeared. But although "courier after courier was dispatched" to Pickett and Lee, "neither of these officers were at their headquarters." One of the colonel's aides rode the length of the White Oak Road without finding Pickett or learning his whereabouts. The last place this man, or anyone else, would have thought to look was a peaceful glade north of Hatcher's Run, where three general officers were eating and imbibing, oblivious to the cataclysmic events unfolding all around them.[35]

Even when Warren's troops, in midafternoon, moved within attack range of the Confederate left, their commander took his time deploying. By now Sheridan, his patience nearly gone, had instructed Merritt to begin feinting against the other flank. Even after Custer's division went forward, however, Warren was not in the proper position from which to launch his assault, nor had he followed precisely Sheridan's orders governing the placement of his troops. When Sheridan complained that if Warren delayed much longer the cavalry would exhaust its ammunition and be forced to break contact with the enemy, the corps commander, as Sheridan put it, "exhibited decided apathy, and he remarked with indifference that 'Bobby Lee was always getting people into trouble.'" Warren's superior believed that "with unconcern such as this, it is no wonder that fully three hours' time was consumed in marching his corps from J. Boisseau's to Gravelly Run Church, though the distance was but two miles."[36]

Finally, at 4:00 P.M., with the sun lowering, Warren reported himself ready to go forward. At Sheridan's signal, the long-deferred assault began. All along the line, dismounted cavalrymen left their works and rushed the defenses, furiously working their carbines. They could not cover all of the intervening ground, however, until Warren's attack hit home at the designated point, the refused left flank defended by Ransom's infantry and McGregor's battery. Yet for perhaps a half hour after the assault began, the V Corps did not strike the angle. Faulty reconnaissance on Sheridan's part had placed the return 1,200 yards east of its true position, ensuring that when they advanced, Warren's leading ranks went too far to the right. In fact, Crawford's division failed to veer left even after it reached the White Oak Road. Instead, its men continued north, effectively removing one-third of Warren's force from the field of battle. Warren's other division commanders, however, discovered their colleague's mistake, located the return, and struck it diagonally from the southeast.[37]

Until Ayres and Griffin corrected the attack path, the Rebel left—and, for that matter, Pickett's entire line—remained intact. The lack of pressure on the east side enabled Pickett's leaderless men to concentrate against the attacking cavalry. A converging fire ripped into Custer's and Devin's outfits, breaking up their formations and prodding dozens of men into retreat. After only a few minutes of such battering, the 20th Pennsylvania, a large, inexperienced regiment in Fitzhugh's brigade, turned about and ran for the rear, its colonel in the lead. By contrast, some veteran regiments, including at least a couple that contained no more than 100 officers and men, withstood the storm of bullets and shells with exemplary fortitude.[38]

Once Warren's people sorted themselves out and hit their objective, everything changed. After several minutes of the most desperate hand-to-hand fighting, involving not only point-blank discharge of firearms but also the use of clubbed muskets and bare fists, Pickett's left flank collapsed under the weight of blue bodies. When their infantry comrades began to mount the works on the Rebel left, Devin and Custer covered the remaining distance to the defenses in their front. While a band thumped and tootled way from the rear, most of Devin's men attacked afoot, as did Pennington's brigade of Custer's division, while Custer's remaining brigades, Wells's and Capehart's, launched mounted charges.

At the outset of his offensive, Custer's flag bearer fell, and the division colors hit the ground. An Ohio trooper saw the young general retrieve them

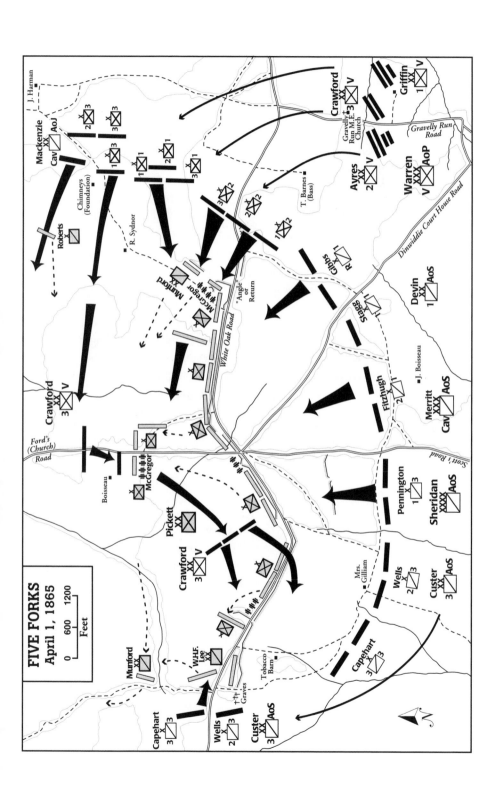

FIVE FORKS
April 1, 1865

0   600   1200
Feet

without breaking stride: "Swinging down on the side of his horse, he caught up the flag, and waving it over his head, stuck spurs to his horse and went over the works, the men following." As horses and riders topped the log and fence-rail barricades, the Ohioan observed that "about half of the men behind the works, ran, the rest we captured and many of those who got away left their guns." Soon the length of Pickett's works was enveloped in powder smoke and near-deafening sound, and teetering on collapse.[39]

Crawford's errant march had short- and long-term effects. In the short run, it delayed the strike against the return, while forcing the men of Ayres and Griffin into some awkward maneuvering that caused temporary confusion. It also complicated Mackenzie's ability to cooperate with the infantry. As he moved north, seeking Pickett's line but encountering only Munford's videttes, Crawford extended his right flank into the woods that Mackenzie occupied. He did so primarily because no one in the V Corps trusted the flank coverage that the "rag-tag and bob-tail" cavalry of the Army of the James had been assigned to provide. As another division leader told one of his subordinates, "Don't be too sure about Mackenzie, keep a sharp look-out for your own right."[40]

The result was that the horsemen of the Army of the James were blocked from turning west and attacking down the White Oak Road. The traffic jam spared Munford's division a stunning blow. As the colonel himself recalled in characteristic prose:

> We could see in the distance, McKenzie's [*sic*] mounted men with their fluttering colors and their gleaming sabers, and as we looked upon the yellow facing and trimmings to their blue coats, the hues of which were brought out by the rays of the descending sun, they had the appearance of the "Avenging Cavalry," but, fortunately for us, they had been thrown out of the fight by their infantry.[41]

As it turned out, Mackenzie's blow may not have been necessary. By the time his people circled around the roadblock and into the rear of Pickett's works, they found "the enemy giving away without much resistance." Mackenzie spent the balance of the day rounding up demoralized Confederates fleeing the clutches of the infantry. He found the opportunity to launch a couple of charges, but they merely hastened along Confederates who had made up their minds to quit the fight. When it grew dark Mackenzie halted and placed his men in camp on the battlefield.[42]

The long-term consequence of Crawford's error was the abrupt ending of G. K. Warren's career as a field commander in the Army of the Potomac. Long before the V Corps finally attacked, Sheridan's regard for his subordinate had reached its nadir. When the assault went awry, his temper boiled over. And when he sought out Warren, he could not find him; the corps leader had gone forward personally to straighten out the attack. For Sheridan, this was the final straw. He located Griffin, the senior division leader, and ordered him to take command of the corps. Then he sent his chief of staff to inform Warren that he had been relieved of command and should report to Grant's headquarters for further orders.

By the time Warren, aghast at the shocking news, reached Sheridan, darkness had come and the battle had been won. Since the V Corps had made the difference in the victory, the report of his firing seemed like a bad joke. But when the incredulous officer asked for confirmation, Sheridan gave it curtly. Warren then begged his superior to reconsider his action. "Reconsider, hell!" snapped Sheridan. "I never reconsider my decisions! Obey the order!"[43]

Minutes later, a devastated Warren was riding to the rear, and oblivion.

Later, Pickett tried to shift from himself and his infantry blame for the disaster that befell his command. In his official report, he repeated a criticism first lodged by General Ransom—that at the height of the battle, Munford's horsemen were "not in position" to oppose Warren. In fact, of all the troops engaged in the defense of Five Forks, the cavalry gave perhaps the strongest account of itself. Rather, defeat was due to Pickett's imperfectly constructed works, his failure to shore up his vulnerable flank, his unrealistic belief that R. E. Lee would reinforce him before the Yankees attacked, and his willingness to leave his troops leaderless—and his subordinates ignorant of his whereabouts—at a critical juncture. Above all, Pickett's command was too small to withstand a force as powerful as Sheridan's.[44]

Of Pickett's mounted forces, only Rosser's division failed to contribute materially to Confederate fortunes on April 1. Like Pickett and Fitz Lee, Rosser remained unaware of the threat posed by Sheridan's infantry until it was too late to do anything about it. The division leader claimed that the sound of heavy fighting failed to penetrate to the picnic nook he shared with his superiors. Not until about 4:30 did Pickett become sufficiently alert to events to send a messenger across the stream—a messenger who returned at a gallop with a tale of disaster.

At that point, Rosser remained with his command while Pickett and Lee mounted and galloped south. Pickett crossed the run and on the other side ran a gauntlet of enemy fire to reach the scene of disaster. He refused to halt short of Five Forks, shouting to one of Rooney Lee's aides who sought his attention: "Don't talk to me, my lines are broken!" When Pickett saw that he had no hope of salvaging the situation, or of withdrawing his men before they were shot down or taken prisoner, he wheeled to the rear, barely escaping with his life. For his part, Fitz Lee cited an inability to cross the run, the road to the ford having been blocked by the enemy by the time he reached it. Fitz claimed to have galloped back to Rosser's division, which he led west along the upper bank of the run, looking fruitlessly for a point at which to cross.[45]

After the battle was lost, Rosser's men finally earned their pay by countering a Union attempt, just before sundown, to cross the run and seize the railroad. Rosser received an arm wound in the fighting, his second of the campaign. Fitz Lee, who, having been cut off from the rest of his command, remained with Rosser throughout the rest of the day, ordered the brigades of McCausland and Dearing to take position in the road they had initially guarded, which led to Church Run Crossing on the South Side. There, beyond immediate danger of being gobbled up by Sheridan, Griffin, or Mackenzie, Rosser's men spent the night shooting at Federals on the south bank. Although their fear was groundless, some troopers worried they would fall prey to a Yankee offensive after dark. A diarist in the 35th Virginia Battalion wailed: "We are trying to hold Hatcher's Run, but My God the enemy are too strong for us, we check them at one point and they break out at another and still force us back. I wonder when it will end and how."[46]

If Rosser contributed little when the battle hung in the balance, Tom Munford and Rooney Lee fought hard even after they ought to have been overwhelmed. Munford, after returning from his excursion to the far left where he observed Warren's buildup, tried to prepare his command to meet the coming onslaught. Earlier, he had placed one of his regiments, Lt. Col. Cary Breckinridge's 2nd Virginia, along the edge of a clearing east of the refused flank, while keeping the remainder of the division in the woods to the rear. Just before Warren attacked, Munford moved his main body down the narrow trail to the front, dismounted most of it, and had it construct a "temporary work" of fence rails on Ransom's immediate left. When Crawford's division attacked, passing north toward the White Oak Road, Munford ordered his men to "fire on them as soon as they emerged" from the woods to the south. He had the troopers concentrate against a depression the attackers had to cross, an obstacle that Munford was "determined to take advantage of."[47]

Munford's dismounted troopers lashed the head of the infantry column with a fire that, for a time at least, did much damage. By lying prone behind their hastily constructed works, the Virginians minimized the casualties they took in return. Munford might have inflicted even greater damage had he been closely supported by McGregor's battery, but General Ransom, to whom Pickett had assigned the horse artillery, refused to share it. Afterward, Munford claimed that had McGregor been ordered to assist him, he could have caused absolute havoc in Crawford's ranks. As it was, "We did a great deal of execution . . . and the [Union] losses were very heavy. They were entirely exposed to our fire."[48]

Reacting to this threat, the infantry gradually shifted in Munford's direction and began a series of flanking movements. Out of sheer necessity, the colonel ordered his front line to disengage and fall back to its led horses. "My men," he later wrote, "had endured too many fights and engagements not to know when to retire and when to come forth and strike again." Despite having to cross "a rough broken country . . . in places exceedingly boggy," the division fell back stubbornly and in good order, firing as it went. The retrograde speeded up after Crawford's rear ranks began to concentrate against the 2nd Virginia. As Colonel Breckinridge recalled, the Federals "returned our fire at the rate of about one thousand shots to [our] one and soon swept us out of the way."[49]

By about 5:00 P.M., almost an hour after Warren's attack had begun, Munford had withdrawn to a point close to Hatcher's Run. There he met a distraught Pickett, who had just crossed the stream. The expeditionary commander begged Munford to hold back the oncoming enemy until he could reach Five Forks. As Pickett galloped off, Capt. James Breckinridge of the 2nd Virginia, brother of the regiment's commander and leader of the sharpshooters of Wooldridge's brigade, put his men in an exposed position beside a wood-fringed stream and had them fire into the head of a blue column trying to interpose between Pickett and his destination. Turning on the sharpshooters, the Federals decimated them and cut down their captain at point-blank range.[50]

Abandoning hope of further resistance, Munford collected as many of his men as he could, pointed them west, and led them across the rear of Pickett's works. Their withdrawal coincided with the complete collapse of the Confederate left—the timing of which probably prompted Ransom's criticism of the cavalry. On the far right, however, Rooney Lee's horsemen, most of them fighting afoot outside Pickett's breastworks, held on longer, keeping Custer's men at arm's length and preventing them from destroying the flank until many of the infantrymen in that sector, members of Corse's and Terry's brigades, could flee to safety.

The fighting on Rooney Lee's front began in the forenoon and lasted until well after 5:00 P.M. For the better part of that period, the hulking, heavily bearded Lee fought with Beale's troopers up front, dismounted ("something we did not like to do," he admitted, "but as they requested it I yielded"), and with Barringer's brigade, most of its men mounted, farther to the rear. Lee's division had one advantage that Munford lacked: the close support of Pegram's guns—at least until near sundown, when the young artillerist was felled by a Yankee bullet. But Rooney Lee's hastily constructed works appear to have been poorer than Munford's. One of Pegram's gunners described them as no more than three feet tall, "just high enough to insure them [the defenders] a death wound." Even so, the division continued to pour forth what one of Custer's men called "the most infernal fire it was ever my lot to be under."[51]

It seems not to have occurred to Lee that he was waging a doomed fight. One of his staff officers recalled that by about 5:00, the right flank was the scene of "a general melee and mix-up, with Pickett's men retreating in confusion behind us." Oblivious to the chaos, Lee did not realize that things were going badly until Pickett himself rode up to announce that his left flank had gone under. Lee took news calmly, but when General Beale galloped up minutes later to report that some Federals had gotten 100 yards in the division's rear, "that made an impression upon me."[52]

When Custer's cavalry tried to complete the encirclement by enveloping the embattled flank, Lee had Beale fall back "by degrees to his horses." As Beale disengaged, his superior fashioned Barringer's brigade into a rear guard, its men firing northward and westward at the same time. Lee then led a body of North Carolinians in an attack across swampy ground that drove back numerous would-be flankers. He even tried to rally his infantry comrades; a horse artilleryman recalled that he "took a flag and rode among them [the foot soldiers] begging them to rally, but no sir, they would not—they went on their way." As a diarist in the 9th Virginia observed, Lee's actions even "saved a good many of our . . . wagons ambulances & Artillery." After dark, pressure on the right flank began to abate. As Lee himself recalled, thereafter "nothing of any serious importance [occurred]; skirmishing maybe along the line, or a squadron charge here and there, but no serious attack." Still, many of his men appeared "very anxious" over reports from the left that "the day was lost."[53]

In due course, the reports were confirmed. Only then did Rooney Lee concede that his army had been beaten and that the defense line southwest of Petersburg had been demolished. By early evening of April 1, 1865, the end had truly begun for the Army of Northern Virginia.

SIX

"Our Men Are Scattered to the Four Winds"

THE VICTORY AT FIVE FORKS HAD BEEN OVERWHELMING. IN ADDITION TO INflicting an untold number of dead and wounded, Sheridan reported taking more than 5,000 prisoners (the actual number was closer to 2,500—still an impressive figure). The great majority of the captives were infantrymen; the cavalry's mobility enabled it to escape without devastating loss. Even so, both flanks of Pickett's now-shattered line lay covered with the bodies of cavalrymen, especially in Munford's sector, where Crawford's men and later Ayres's and Griffin's had taken a brutal toll of the dismounted troopers holding the makeshift works east of the return. Moreover, the ground on either side of Pickett's works was littered with the corpses of Union horsemen and the carcasses of their mounts. Some horses remained impaled on the defenses they had been trying to scale when shot. The time-worn adage that no one ever saw a dead cavalryman did not apply to this field, on this day.

If the attackers had paid a high price, their 1,100 casualties paled in comparison to those of the enemy, and the profits had been substantial. By isolating Pickett from the works at Petersburg, they had opened the South Side Railroad to seizure, a move sure to cause the evacuation, if not the surrender, of the forces defending the two most important cities in the Confederacy. Sheridan appreciated the magnitude of this achievement, much of the credit for which he gave to the horsemen who had spearheaded his offensive. In his postaction report, he commended Warren's three division commanders while omitting mention of Warren himself except to excoriate his conduct throughout the fight and to justify his relief. Yet he saved a large helping of praise for his mounted leaders: "To Generals Merritt, Custer, Devin, and Mackenzie, of

97

the cavalry, great credit is due, and to their subordinate commanders they will undoubtedly award the praise which is due to them for the hearty co-opera- tion, bravery, and ability which were everywhere displayed." Officers and troopers had fought so hard, for so long, because all "appeared to realize that the success of the campaign and fate of Lee's army depended upon it. They merit the thanks of the country and reward of the Government."[1]

Many of these sentiments were echoed, both in private and in official dis- patches, by Grant, who received word of Sheridan's victory at his Dabney's Mills headquarters sometime after 7:30 P.M. The news was conveyed to him by Horace Porter, who to reach headquarters braved a stream of moving vehi- cles, marching men, and the myriad obstructions that accumulate in an army's rear. The staff officer recalled that "ammunition trains and ambulances were still struggling forward for miles; teamsters, prisoners, stragglers, and wounded were choking the roadway. The coffee-boilers had kindled their fires. Cheers were resounding on all sides, and everybody was riotous over the victory." Reaching the Boydton Plank Road, Porter encountered troops who had yet to hear of Sheridan's success. When the lieutenant colonel's orderly shouted out the news, "the only response he got was from one of them who raised his open hand to his face, put his thumb to his nose, and yelled: No, you don't—April fool!' I then realized that it was the 1st of April."[2]

They found Grant outside his tent, seated around a campfire with mem- bers of the staff. Even before dismounting, Porter began shouting tidings of victory. The effect was electric: "For some minutes there was a bewildering state of excitement, grasping of hands, tossing up of hats, and clapping of each other on the back. . . . Dignity was thrown to the winds." Only the com- manding general failed to join in the merriment, even to the restrained degree expected of him, until Porter, in answer to the first question asked of him, stated that Sheridan had taken thousands of prisoners. "This was," said Porter, "the only part of my recital that seemed to call forth a responsive expression from his usually impassive features."[3]

Grant listened intently to the aide's detailed account of the battle, then:

With scarcely a word, [he] walked into his tent, and by the light of a flickering candle took up his "manifold writer," a small book which retained a copy of the matter written, and after finishing several dis- patches handed them to an orderly to be sent over the field wires, came out and joined our group at the campfire, and said as coolly as if remarking upon the state of the weather: "I have ordered an imme- diate assault along the line." This was about 9 o'clock.[4]

If Grant's reaction to the news of Sheridan's breakthrough was stoic, Robert E. Lee received it with even greater restraint. Like his opponent, Lee was not given to outbursts of emotion, much less to displays of fear and panic. Even so, the import of Pickett's overthrow alarmed him. The right flank gone, the remainder of the defensive line around Petersburg was susceptible to attack at almost every point. Moreover, Lee could no longer rely on an open supply line, the fragile ribbon that linked Petersburg's garrison to the outside world and transported the supplies that sustained it. He saw no alternative to abandoning Petersburg and Richmond. Yet he had not anticipated such a sudden and overwhelming defeat as Pickett had suffered. Thus he was unprepared to withdraw either garrison for at least twenty-four hours. Even so, he began to plan in earnest for that eventuality.

He had to prepare the government for the worst. Late on April 1, he wired news of the disaster to Secretary of War Breckinridge, adding that the location of Pickett's survivors was not known. He also reported that, based on prisoner interrogation, Ord's troops had joined Meade's southwest of Petersburg, no doubt to take part in a movement against the city's works. In an accompanying telegram to Jefferson Davis, Lee indicated his desire to meet with the president as well as with Breckinridge, but he pleaded an inability to leave his headquarters. He did not have to specify the topic he wished to discuss.[5]

Once the last prisoner had been rounded up, burial details had set to work, and medical attention had been given to as many of the wounded on both sides as could be reached, Sheridan stationed inside the captured works enough men to hold them through the night. He had Griffin place one of his divisions astride the road to the ford opposite Rosser's position. While these troops kept up a desultory fire, Griffin marched the rest of the V Corps back to Gravelly Run Church. There, at Sheridan's direction, he positioned the troops at right angles to the White Oak Road, facing Petersburg. The cavalry under Merritt—less Crook's division, which remained at and near Dinwiddie Court House—went into bivouac on a spacious plantation on the western flank of the battlefield near where Rooney Lee had stymied Custer. Mackenzie's troopers bedded down within supporting distance of the foot soldiers on the Ford Road.[6]

Dispositions complete, Sheridan perused a communiqué from Grant, notifying him that an attack on Petersburg's exterior defenses had been ordered for 4:00 the next morning. The assault would cover a vast front, from the Appomattox River to Hatcher's Run. Grant added: "From your isolated position I can give you no specific directions, but leave you to act according to circumstances. I would like you, however, to get something done to the South Side road even if they [Sheridan's men] do not tear up a mile of it." In this work, Sheridan would be supported by a division of the II Corps, which by morning would be located on the White Oak Road off his right flank.[7]

Studying Grant's dispatch, Sheridan determined that come morning, he would indeed "get something done" in the direction of the South Side Railroad, with or without infantry help. On the other hand, if the leader of the force to be assigned him proved to be more conscientious and less dilatory than the last one, Sheridan was confident that before sundown on April 2, Lee's last lifeline would be smoldering iron and splintered wood.

Driven from Five Forks by the hammering of Sheridan's cavalry and infantry, Pickett's survivors streamed across Hatcher's Run. They retreated in a manner so haphazard it drew comment from even the most exhausted survivors. "I have never seen an Army so demoralized," wrote an enlisted man in the 14th Virginia Cavalry. "Our men are scattered to the four winds." On the north side of Hatcher's Run, they trudged dejectedly up Ford's Road until reaching the railroad at Church Road Crossing, west of Sutherland's Station. There Pickett met Bushrod Johnson, with the two remaining brigades of his infantry division plus Brig. Gen. Eppa Hunton's brigade, the only element of Pickett's command that had not accompanied him to Five Forks. General Anderson had sent these troops to Pickett's assistance the previous day, but too late. By the time the would-be supports reached the railroad north of Hatcher's Run, the battle had been lost.[8]

Pickett and Johnson spent the balance of the night in track-side woods. While their comrades grabbed fitfully at sleep, Fitz Lee's horsemen, who appeared to have done a better job of maintaining unit cohesion, also reached Church Road Crossing. Even so, some regiments were in disorder. The 5th Virginia, for one, was in "a disorganized condition, being mixed up with other commands that had been stampeded the night before." With the troopers came McGregor's battery, which had barely escaped capture at Five Forks (the section of Graham's Petersburg Battery had not been so fortunate). Finally, sometime before morning, the remnants of Roberts's brigade straggled up from the far left to add their limited weight to Pickett's force. Fitz Lee promptly assigned them to Rooney Lee's division.[9]

During the night, Pickett determined to move north with the survivors of Five Forks, putting the Appomattox River between him and any pursuers. Before sunrise on April 2, he started up Brown's Road toward Exeter Mills, on the south bank of the river. While most of the men who had escaped the battlefield followed him, dozens of others slipped away in the darkness, heading for their homes and families. In their minds, the war was over, and to think it could be extended in hopes of salvaging a lost cause was an exercise in self-deception.

The march north was undertaken in a spirit of anxiety and foreboding, feelings heightened by the sounds of the preattack bombardment that Grant, Meade, and Ord had unleashed on the two cities. "All hearts and thoughts," Thomas Munford remembered, "were turned towards Petersburg and Richmond. All night we were anxious and uncertain about the effect of the result of the previous day. The very heavens were illuminated by the pyrotechnics of each contending Army. The din and roar of cannon and mortars and the sharper rattle and echo of musketry, was eternal."[10]

When he reached Exeter Mills early on the second, Pickett crossed Ransom's brigade to the far side of the river by ferryboat. Hoping to find a bridge to accommodate the rest of his command, the general moved upriver via the Namozine Road, on which he was met by a staff officer from General Anderson, directing him to return south and report to the corps commander at Sutherland's Station. A weary Pickett set out to comply, but before progressing far, he found the road clogged with stragglers from the Petersburg defenses. They brought word of two events that materially altered his plans. One was that Anderson had left his recent headquarters and was moving northwestward toward Amelia Court House on the Richmond & Danville Railroad.

Pickett shrugged, faced his column about, and moved west on Namozine Road. By now his men were in an even grimmer mood than before, and not only because of their arduous marching and countermarching. The second piece of news the Petersburg stragglers had brought them was that the city's exterior defenses had fallen to the Yankees and that preparations to evacuate the inner works were well under way.[11]

By 4:00 A.M. on the second, the guns and mortars that had pounded the Petersburg defenses for several hours almost without cessation fell silent. When Grant's headquarters gave the signal, large portions of the VI and IX Corps assaulted the city's exterior works from the east and south. Two hours later, two of General Ord's three divisions, which since the twenty-ninth had been occupying breastworks and rifle pits on the north side of Hatcher's Run, left their defenses and charged the works opposite them. In so doing, they released pent-up energy: For more than forty-eight hours, they had been awaiting the word to go forward.

In confirmation of their commander's belief, the men carried everything in front of them in one sweeping movement that not even marshy ground or a full-fledged swamp could stop. By sunrise, they had overrun rifle pits and surmounted abatis and slashings of felled trees. Most of the former occupants were fleeing at high speed to the city's intermediate works, leaving behind hundreds of dead, wounded, and captured. As Grant later phrased it, "The outer works of Petersburg were in the hands of the National troops, never to be wrenched from them."[12]

That did not mean that the enemy would not try. By 8:00, the victors were laboring to reverse the captured works in expectation of a counterattack. At that hour they learned that an even wider breakthrough had taken place in the VI and IX Corps' sectors. During these attacks, many of General Wright's troops had veered westward to become intermingled with Ord's. When General Gibbon learned that his next assignment was to move up the Boydton Plank Road and strike the second line of fortifications, he won permission to augment his force with the wanderers from the VI Corps. Soon the combined force was abandoning the outer works of Petersburg and moving north, arms at the ready.

At about 1:00 P.M., having reached his new objective, Gibbon formed a storming party. At his word, Foster's and Turner's men, covered in rear by Birney's division and on either flank by General Wright's troops, charged the key points on Petersburg's intermediate defense line, Forts Gregg and Whitworth. Foster's brigade attacked obliquely to the northwest against the larger and more heavily defended Gregg, while most of Turner's troops struck Whitworth, 100 yards farther west.

Both redoubts fell to the attackers, but only after some of the most savage close-quarters fighting of the war. Four assaults were necessary to carry Gregg, whose eleven-foot-high parapets and ten-foot-deep ditch were defended by 300 Mississippi riflemen. When the defenders had been overcome, and most of them killed, one Yankee compared the interior of the work to "nothing but a slaughter-pen." Another visitor found himself wading through "a pool of blood, a sight which can never be shut from memory." The loss of Fort Gregg, which had commanded the approaches to Whitworth, effectively doomed the smaller redoubt. When Turner's men scaled its uncompleted parapet, they found the fort abandoned, its demoralized garrison having fled inside Petersburg.[13]

The fall of Gregg, Whitworth, and other major works farther east meant that Petersburg's evacuation was a matter of hours. Grant, who wanted the city occupied by nightfall, had intended to follow up the initial assaults with an all-out offensive on Petersburg's interior line. But the high cost in casualties with which Ord, Wright, and Parke had purchased victory gave him pause. The wounded-panther ferocity with which the intermediate line had been defended told him that immeasurably heavier losses would follow. In the end, he suspended operations until the artillery could again soften up the defenders, this time from close-in positions.

If Lee did not evacuate, Grant would launch a new wave of assaults at 6:00 A.M., April 3. If Lee pulled out, Grant would run him to earth, if he had to put every bluecoat in Petersburg on his trail. No matter which direction Lee turned, he would find no resting place this side of heaven.[14]

━━━━━◦◦◦◦━━━━━

By midmorning on Sunday, April 2, the commander of the Army of Northern Virginia realized that Petersburg could not be held for more than a few hours. Its right flank was verging on collapse, and although defenders under Maj. Gen. John Brown Gordon had repulsed waves of IX Corps attackers, preventing a breakthrough below the line of the Appomattox, the Yankees would attack again and again, in ever greater numbers. The time had come to withdraw and take to the roads leading west.

Early that afternoon, from his headquarters one mile west of Petersburg, Lee sent Secretary of War Breckinridge a telegram that began: "I see no prospect of doing more than holding our position here till night. I am not certain that I can do that. If I can I shall withdraw to-night north of the Appomattox, and, if possible, it will be better to withdraw the whole line to-night from [the] James River." The enemy having interposed between the forces along Hatcher's Run and those at Petersburg, "our only chance, then, of concentrating our forces, is to do so near [the] Danville railroad, which I shall endeavor to do at once. I advise that all preparations be made for leaving Richmond to-night."[15]

The War Office had seen the evacuation coming; before he received Lee's fateful telegram, Breckinridge had begun packing up documents and valuables to be spirited out of the capital by wagon. The war secretary sent a copy of the wire by courier to St. Paul's Episcopal Church, where Jefferson Davis was attending Sabbath services. The ashen-faced president immediately left the church and repaired to his offices, where he announced the pending evacuation to his staff. As the packing resumed, Davis made plans to accompany most of his cabinet members to Danville via a train scheduled to leave the city at 8:00 P.M. The department archives would be stored aboard the same train, along with a half million dollars in gold and silver, the remnants of the Confederate Treasury. The train's limited cargo space would not accommodate other items worth bringing off, including some 350,000 reserve rations in the Confederate commissariat. These, it was decided, would be shipped by wagon to Lee's troops via Amelia Court House.[16]

The Richmond garrison was not lucky enough to be carried to safety by train. Before nightfall, its men would start on foot across the bridges over the James, which they would burn behind them in a futile attempt to prevent the capital's occupation.

On the morning of the second, as Grant had promised, Bvt. Maj. Gen. Nelson A. Miles's division, having come up in the night via the White Oak Road from the II Corps' position farther east, reported to Sheridan. At 7:30, Little Phil sent the command, followed by the divisions of Ayres and Crawford, back the way it had come to breach what remained of the works along the Claiborne Road. Miles did so without help from the V Corps, but before he could engage those Rebels he had chased to the north side of Hatcher's Run, his division, by request of Meade, was returned to the control of General Humphreys. Their direct support no longer needed, the troops of Ayres and Crawford, Sheridan at their head, crossed Hatcher's Run on the II Corps' left and angled toward Sutherland's Station. Sheridan hoped to come in on the rear of the force driven by Miles, but by the time he moved into action, he found the Rebels gone from his front.[17]

While Sheridan had been consorting with the infantry, his cavalry had been more than a little active. As per his orders, Merritt had led his two divisions across Hatcher's Run to engage Pickett and/or Johnson. Gregg's brigade of Crook's division accompanied him on this outing. The rest of the 2nd Division remained near Dinwiddie Court House for the better part of the day, guarding the cavalry's trains. That evening, it conducted the wagons out the White Oak Road to the scene of Miles's action, then moved up the Claiborne Road to its crossing of Hatcher's Run, where it spent the night. Another addition to Merritt's column was Ranald Mackenzie, whose men had spent the morning driving Rebels from the north side of Hatcher's Run opposite Gravelly Run Ford.[18]

After Merritt, Gregg, and Mackenzie crossed the run onto Ford's Road, Sheridan overtook their mounted column, having left the V Corps in the rear. He led the enlarged command to and across the South Side. Devin's division, followed by two of Custer's brigades and Mackenzie's men, crossed the tracks between Sutherland's Station and Ford's Station, nine miles farther west, while Custer's third brigade, accompanied by Irvin Gregg's brigade, crossed at Ford's.[19]

When the larger column reached the railroad, it encountered a part of Rooney Lee's division, which had been guarding the left flank of Pickett's and Johnson's infantry on the Namozine Road. Devin challenged the Rebels with a line of skirmishers, backed by two guns of Capt. Marcus P. Miller's combined Batteries C and E, 4th U.S. Artillery. Devin reported that he had everyone "placed in readiness for a fight, but a few rounds from Miller's section of battery were sufficient to induce the enemy to retire with precipitation." The way clear, Sheridan set the 1st Division to tearing up the railroad as a further means of isolating Petersburg. For about half a mile, as Devin reported, the tracks were levered up, "ties burnt, and rails heated and bent."[20]

At that point, abruptly, Sheridan ordered the work halted. Men wielding axes and crowbars looked quizzically at each other until staff officers galloped up to make a public announcement. A member of the 1st New York Dragoons described the "glorious news" that had made further demolition unnecessary: "Grant took Petersburg and Richmond this morning about 5:00 with a large amount of prisoners and artillery." While the bulletin was at best half-truth, Sheridan's troopers greeted it as they had the intelligence that Five Forks had fallen to them and their infantry comrades. Men threw back their heads and cheered; others tossed caps and hats into the air; more than one danced an impromptu jig.[21]

The demonstration had a wider audience than anyone realized. Scouts from the 2nd Virginia had crept up to the north side of the railroad, concealing themselves atop a brush-covered hill about 200 yards from the nearest Federal. They were treated to what their colonel called "the greatest jubilation we ever heard. The men . . . huzzared [*sic*] and cheered, and their bands played the most stirring airs. This great demonstration . . . was the announcement to us of the general break up of the Confederate lines." The scouts promptly rejoined their comrades to report the disheartening news.[22]

Once the head of Griffin's corps had come up to secure Sheridan's hold on the railroad, Little Phil sent Merritt and his jubilant troopers westward on the Cox Road, which paralleled the railroad. Sheridan himself remained behind with the infantry. His instructions to Merritt moved the cavalry in the same direction as Pickett's and Johnson's troops, although well south of them.

Rooney Lee's troopers, however, continued to operate off the left flank of the retreat column, intent on delaying the pursuers. After some minutes of travel, Devin's advance struck Lee's rear. This time Devin dismounted the majority of Fitzhugh's brigade and advanced it cross-country against the Rebel line.

That line proved to be a moving target. As Devin wrote, Fitzhugh's men "rapidly drove the enemy from one position to another" in the direction of the Namozine Road. The running battle continued into late afternoon. At about 5:00, Fitzhugh's scouts discovered that the rear guard of Pickett's column—infantry and artillery as well as cavalry—had taken position behind breastworks near a crossroads known as Scott's Corners, with Rooney Lee's skirmishers in front.[23]

As soon as their pursuers were within range, the Confederates showered them with musketry and artillery. Fitzhugh's men pulled back to escape the torrent, and Devin ordered up Stagg's brigade, also afoot, as a support force. He then advanced Miller's two pieces on the Namozine Road, their flanks protected by Gibbs's still-saddled Reserves. Devin noted with satisfaction that Miller's guns generated a "rapid and effective fire," under which the carbineers approached the enemy position from several directions.[24]

The guns could not, however, guarantee success. Devin threw three lines of attackers at the barricades, but he succeeded only in driving Lee's skirmishers inside them. By the time the third effort failed, it was close to 8:00 P.M., and Devin called it quits. His only consolation was that his men had turned back several attempted counterattacks. Only infantry support would have enabled them to carry the position, which had been strengthened to the point of impregnability during the time purchased by Rooney Lee's delaying tactics. Although General Griffin had sent Crawford's division to Sheridan's assistance in advance of the rest of the V Corps, it was fully a mile from the field of action when the shooting stopped.

After suspending his offensive, Devin moved his command half a mile to the south and bivouacked beyond range of the Rebel artillery. Unless Sheridan had other plans, Devin would have another go of it in the morning. Sooner or later, he and his comrades would find the Confederates out in the open, and that would be the end of their retreat.[25]

Robert E. Lee's last dispatch to the Confederate War Department, sent early on the evening of the second, announced that the evacuation of Petersburg had begun. As he wrote, the city's defenders were leaving their works and forming columns that would cross the Appomattox to the north side. At some point upriver, they would recross to the south bank, the side Amelia Court House was on. Securing the garrison's escape would be "a difficult operation," Lee realized, "but I hope not impracticable."[26]

As it happened, the evacuation proceeded with relative precision. From 8:00 P.M. until well after midnight, 12,000 troops of all arms, along with an indeterminate number of civilians, departed the besieged city via bridges over the Appomattox that were detonated as soon as the last soldier reached the other side. When the marching columns had closed up, and no stragglers appeared to remain, Lee joined the retreat astride his warhorse Traveller, accompanied by his staff and a small escort. Capt. John Esten Cooke, a longtime aide to Jeb Stuart, who saw and heard the army commander on this emotional occasion, marveled at his imperturbability: "His bearing still remained entirely composed, and his voice had lost none of its grave strength of intonation."[27]

Lee's impassiveness masked a mind and heart in tumult. The major emotion thus concealed was a pervasive sadness that, unless carefully controlled, might verge on despair. For Lee and his men, a long, costly struggle was coming to a bitter close. The future raised innumerable questions, chief among them, whether the remnants of his once-powerful command, bereft of its heavy defenses, could keep up the fight against a mighty enemy energized by approaching triumph.

Lee realized that his options were almost fatally limited. His only chance to keep the contest alive appeared to rest in moving along the Richmond & Danville from Amelia Court House into North Carolina, where Joseph Johnston, although heavily outnumbered by Sherman's legions, continued to fight on despite the odds. If Lee could link with the remnants of the Army of Tennessee, he and Johnston might strike Sherman an unexpected blow. Then, while one Union force was on the recoil, they might turn about and lash out at the forces under Grant, Meade, and Ord, who were certain to follow from Virginia. Lee, the realist, knew the chances of pulling off one victory, let alone two, were small, perhaps minuscule. But for the sake of the soldiers who still looked to him for guidance and strength, as well as to meet the demands of soldierly honor, he had to do his utmost to keep hope alive.[28]

Fully a day before he ordered Petersburg's abandonment, Lee took steps to strip the Richmond works of their defenders. On the afternoon of the first, while Pickett tried to hold off Sheridan and Warren, he had ordered Longstreet, with Maj. Gen. Charles W. Field's division, to move to Petersburg as rapidly as transportation could be furnished. Longstreet responded with alacrity, leaving behind only Maj. Gen. Joseph B. Kershaw's infantry division and the cavalry of Martin Gary. As Field departed, his position inside the capital's three lines of defense had been filled by the reserve forces of Ewell's Department of Richmond. Ewell's was a truly heterogeneous command. Division-sized, it consisted of Regular infantry and artillery, the garrisons of Chaffin's and Drewry's Bluffs, and miscellaneous units including Confederate seamen and marines, all under Lee's eldest son, Maj. Gen. George Washington Custis Lee, formerly Jefferson Davis's military aide.

By the time Custis Lee's father sent his last message to the War Department, the reserves were preparing to decamp, as were the remaining components of Longstreet's command. Ewell, Kershaw, and Gary had been directed to evacuate by way of the several bridges over the James, some of which were to be fired after their passage. Once on the south side, they were to march to Chesterfield Court House, about fifteen miles below the capital. Also heading for Chesterfield County were the troops, under Maj. Gen. William Mahone, who had been holding the lines at Bermuda Hundred following Pickett's departure. The evacuees of Richmond would constitute one column of retreat, while Mahone's men would make contact with the defenders of Petersburg, including the new arrivals under Longstreet, to form a second column. Both would converge at Amelia Court House, to which point the troops under Anderson, Pickett, and Fitz Lee would also be directed.[29]

The evacuation of Richmond proved to be more confused and chaotic, less suggestive of careful planning, than the emptying of Petersburg. Rumors of the garrison's pending departure had been afloat throughout the day, stirring concern among the city's population and, in some quarters, panic. Early that day, Col. William T. Robins of the 24th Virginia Cavalry, a component of Gary's brigade, had left his camp, four miles east of the capital, to attend Sunday services in the city. Upon the recessional, Robins found himself mobbed in the streets by civilians seeking confirmation of the rumors and asking his advice on what they should do. The colonel advised the people to "remain where they were" and "proceeded at once" to his regiment.[30]

Reaching camp, he found that the brigade's wagon train had been withdrawn into the city. It had become a part of the general supply train of the Richmond garrison, which was awaiting evacuation by Custis Lee in advance of the other troops. Robins also discovered that in his absence, his outfit had been moved to a point just behind the city's outer line of defense. The action suggested that the 24th, and probably Gary's entire command, was to replace the infantry who normally manned that sector.

He was correct: As soon as darkness fell, the foot troops were pulled to the rear, where they were formed into columns and led into the city. By 9:00,

Robins's regiment, along with the 7th South Carolina, the Hampton (South Carolina) Legion, and a detachment of the 7th Georgia, was filing into place behind the fortifications. Within an hour, the defenses in closest proximity to the enemy were manned entirely by dismounted cavalrymen.[31]

Gary's troopers must have realized that if General Weitzel's Yankees advanced against them, their organization would quickly go out of existence. Their nerves understandably on edge, the quasi-infantrymen found that they would have to remain in the works until early the next morning. Then they would withdraw through the city, bringing up the rear of the evacuating forces. When they had crossed the James, Gary's men would set fire to the last major bridge, Mayo's, which connected the foot of 14th Street with the suburb of Manchester.

A few troopers and horse artillerymen departed in advance of Gary's men, in company with the infantry units and the garrison's wagon train. These got to see, firsthand, the fear that swept the city in the wake of the evacuation—fear that bred disorder, including rioting, looting, vandalism, and other acts of lawlessness.

The resulting loss of public and private property—much of it, at any rate—could have been avoided. When the evacuation began, General Ewell, the highest-ranking officer in the city, rejected the advice of local officials and ordered the burning of government stores, including thousands of bales of cotton, to prevent their confiscation by the enemy. The ensuing blaze was spread far and wide by an unexpectedly strong southeast wind. Out-of-control flames engulfed almost a thousand structures: homes, stores, public buildings, and government property including warehouses, arsenals, and ordnance depots. Detonating ammunition spread the flames still farther. The final toll would approach $30 million worth of damage.[32]

By the time the evacuation was under way, it was dark. Flames were spreading through the capital and its suburbs to the south. An officer in Chew's horse artillery, in the capital on official business, observed people rushing madly through downtown Richmond and Manchester to escape the flames. The evacuation, which "fell like a death knell on the ears of the people," had been enough to instill fear in everyone; the fires turned fear into panic. Citizens stopped careening through the streets only long enough to beg passing troops to stay and fight the flames. For his part, the horse artilleryman rebuffed all such entreaties; he continued on foot, amid a throng of refugees in and out of uniform, to Mayo's Bridge. On the south side of the James, he paused to look back at "poor doomed Richmond," then turned and trudged on through the night to Chesterfield County, where he hoped to locate his unit.[33]

When at last ordered to relinquish their newly assumed posts on the front lines, Gary's brigade beheld similar sights and sounds even before they passed through the city. One of Robins's men recalled that the signal to move to the rear was the deliberate detonation of magazines stored inside the works: "The explosions that came at the appointed hour are ever to be remembered by those who heard them, reinforced as they were in their awe-producing effect by the explosions from the gun-boats in the James River and the magazines at Chapin's [Chaffin's] and Drewry's Bluff." These resources, too, had been set afire to foil their capture and use by the enemy.[34]

Once relieved, Gary's troopers filed to the rear and remounted—all, that is, except the 7th Georgia, nine of whose ten companies had lost their horses months before as part of a brigade reorganization. Then the little command, in column of fours, trotted out the River Road and into the city by way of Rocketts Landing. Officers and men alike expressed shock and disgust at the sights they saw in that lower-class suburb. Col. Alexander Cheves Haskell of the 7th South Carolina was surprised by the number of civilians abroad at that hour: "Skulks, deserters, thieves, starving families and hangers-on, and many [others] besides. Casks of whiskey and rum, burst open in hundreds or thousands, made a stream of liquor in the gutter on each side of the street. The mob was drinking, yelling, screaming and robbing."[35]

In his diary, Trooper Cornelius Carlton of the 24th Virginia, a native of the capital, recorded similar scenes as his regiment neared Mayo's Bridge:

> What [a] terrible morning—Richmond burning, gunboats burning and their magazines exploding. . . . The government stores . . . are thrown open to the populace who divide the goods. What a scramble. . . . Ladies labor under their burdens of a chest of tea, a roll of cloth or a huge bundle of something. One man with a hand cart bears away half [a] hogshead [of] sugar, another rolls a barrel of flour, another has a bucket of brandy. What a crowd! I can hardly get through them.

By patient exertion, Carlton and his comrades eventually reached the bridge. Minutes later, he reported, "I have crossed the Ja[me]s and am leaving my home and dear, dear friends behind me, maybe I will never see them more. If I never see you in this world I hope to meet you in heaven."[36]

Some of Gary's troopers left the city with a sarcastic farewell ringing in their ears. Edward Boykin of the 7th South Carolina never forgot the Irish washerwoman who shouted out her tenement window at the passing troops: "Yes, afther fighting them for four years ye're running like dawgs!"[37]

Occupation troops moved into Petersburg and Richmond within hours of their garrisons' exodus. Into the morning hours of April 3, Mayor W. W. Townes and a delegation from the city council walked the avenues of Petersburg, while "Lee's soldiers, in large bodies, in squads, and singly, passed along through the streets towards the bridges over the Appomattox." By daybreak, the last garrison member appeared to have departed; the only soldiers left in the city were hospital patients and surgeons, members of the Quartermaster's and Ordnance Departments, and the ubiquitous straggler.[38]

Shortly after daybreak, the mayor, accompanied by council member Charles F. Collier, walked out to the now-abandoned works on the southern outskirts. Near the point at which, two days before, Ord's troops had wrested Fort Gregg from its defenders, they hoped to arrange the peaceful surrender of the city, while securing the safety of its inhabitants. They had not waited long before, as Collier recalled, "there sprang forth, as from the bowels of the earth . . . a mighty host of Federal soldiers, and then followed such a shout of victory as seemed to shake the very ground on which we stood."[39]

Within minutes, hundreds of Yankees were surging past the city fathers. The mayor and he, Collier wrote, "attempted to state our mission, but the officers would not take time to stop to hear what we had to say, the men rushing ahead to enter the city, but bade us come along with them, they (the officers) promising to protect us and to protect our people." Upon returning to the city proper, the two men found that the Yankees had already taken full possession: "Reaching the court-house, we found the whole building, steeple and all, festooned with small Federal flags. Our mission, however, was now accomplished."[40]

The cavalry played a larger role in the occupation of Richmond, although the first units to approach the city were infantrymen posted just outside the now-abandoned defenses. For days, Godfrey Weitzel had been hoping against hope for word of the city's abandonment. The alternative, which he considered more likely, was that Longstreet or Ewell would notice that the lines opposite them had been stripped to the point of easy capture. The Union commander's anxiety had increased when Grant ordered him, at daybreak on the third, to probe the nearest defenses and determine the accuracy of rumors that all or some of Longstreet's men had gone south.

Weitzel's mind began to ease only after reports came in, early on the second, of the successful assault on Petersburg. These were closely followed by word from the pickets and scouts of Col. David M. Evans's 20th New York Cavalry that troop movements appeared to be in progress inside the capital.

Then came a report from Weitzel's signal officers of "great excitement" in the city's streets. But only after dark, when Richmond caught on fire and parts of it exploded, did Weitzel believe the city was on the verge of evacuation. He remained cautiously optimistic, but immobile, for several hours more until, sometime after dawn on the third, the troops on the advance line went forward and found the works in front of them empty. Then and only then did Weitzel order columns of foot soldiers to go forward along two nearly parallel thoroughfares, the New Market Road and the Osborne Pike.[41]

When Weitzel and his headquarters entourage moved toward the city at about 6:00 A.M., they were halted on the outskirts by Mayor Joseph Mayo, who was on the same errand that Mayor Townes had run at Petersburg. Realizing that he could not enter Richmond until he formally accepted its surrender, the general ordered one of his aides, Maj. Thomas Thatcher Graves, escorted by Major Stevens's squadron of the 4th Massachusetts Cavalry, to reach the city by the most direct route and claim it for the U.S. Army.[42]

When they started out, Graves and Stevens found that thousands of foot soldiers had preceded them. Unwilling to go around, the mounted party rode through the marching troops, shoving them off the road, oblivious to their shouts and curses. The horsemen clattered into Richmond in advance of everyone else, arriving at about 7:15; at once they made for the center of town. A female resident, a staunch secessionist, reacted angrily as the troopers "swept by" her. "As they turned the street corner," she said, "they drew their sabres with savage shouts, and the blood mounted even in my woman's heart with quick throbs of defiance."[43]

When the horsemen reached their destination, the principal public building of the city, another lady of Richmond looked on in shock and dismay: "I did not move—I could not—but watched the blue horseman ride to the City Hall, enter with his sword knocking the ground at every step, & throw the great doors open, & take possession of our beautiful city; watched two blue figures . . . unfurl a tiny flag [the pennant-size guidon of the 4th Massachusetts], & then I sank on my knees, & the bitter, bitter tears came in a torrent." The guidon, the first U.S. flag to fly over the city since early 1861, replaced the state flag of Virginia, which was hauled down and confiscated. From its lofty perch, the banner, despite its compact size, could be seen throughout Richmond.[44]

Long after Weitzel's command had taken up occupation duty in the city, where it restored order and extinguished most of the fires, another, larger body of horsemen trotted through the streets. It did so after dark, for the 5th Massachusetts Cavalry was composed of African-American enlisted men, and the Yankee conquerors—for all their mean-spirited treatment of the populace, at least in the minds of many residents—did not wish to offend local sensibilities by parading black soldiers through the city in broad daylight. Even so, the officers and men of the 5th, especially its commander, Col. Charles F. Adams, Jr., grandson and great-grandson of presidents, reveled in the symbolism inherent in the outfit's passage. Still, it took the colonel's father, the American minister to the Court of St. James, to put the event into historical perspective:

> It was a singular circumstance that you, in the fourth generation of our family, under the Union and the constitution, should have been the first [Adams] to put your foot in the capital of the Ancient Dominion, and that, too, at the head of a corps which prefigured the downfall of the policy which had ruled in that capital during the whole period now closely approaching a century. How full of significance is this history, which all of us are now helping to make! It is literally the third and fourth generation which is paying the bitter penalty for what must now be admitted were the shortcomings of the original founders of the Union.[45]

SEVEN

"This Delay Was Fatal, and Could Not Be Retrieved"

MUNFORD'S CAVALRY HAD SEEN ITS SHARE OF REAR-GUARD SERVICE, WHICH tended to be not only arduous, but also frustrating. For sheer vexation, however, the duty the command shouldered on April 2 took the prize. As Munford himself observed, to cover the rear of Johnson's foot soldiers as they marched up the south bank of the Appomattox, his men had to secure a countryside "cut up with interminable roads and byroads and paths, leading into each other in every direction, which made it very difficult to guard them when followed, as we were, by an elated and victorious enemy." In addition to covering so many potential routes of pursuit, Munford's men had to halt and erect works every time a major geographical obstacle such as a swamp or creek brought the main column to a standstill. Watching them at work during one such halt, a member of Fitz Lee's staff marveled at "the miraculous way our troops put up breastworks[;] in five minutes there was a breastwork about two miles long."[1]

Munford's only consolation was that throughout their stint in the rear, his men—formed into parallel columns, one following the Namozine Road, the other a byroad closer to the river—were not hard-pressed at any point. Sheridan's horsemen seemed to be "feeling for us with velvet gloves,'" as if intent on ascertaining their enemy's size before committing themselves to a strike. Well into the afternoon of the third, he said, the Federal advance "annoyed us considerably, causing us very frequently to <u>dismount</u> and prepare for action. These preparations, however, did not often result in the firing of a gun." And yet the work was so taxing and so fraught with danger that

Munford was happy to relinquish it to Rosser's division, which took over early on the third.[2]

Apparently Rosser's assignment lasted no more than a couple of hours, although it included holding the rear as the column, just before 2:00 A.M. on the third, crossed the wagon bridge that spanned fifty-foot-wide Namozine Creek. As the infantry, artillery, and wagons lumbered across, Roberts's brigade, supported by some infantry, built a heavy line of defenses on the west bank. As soon as the column had crossed, Roberts's men would fall in as the rear guard.[3]

Covering the rear of a retreat column in close contact with thousands of fast-moving pursuers would appear to have required a larger command than Roberts's. Even a destroyed bridge would not stymie those eager Yankees for long. The issue of rear-guard strength became critical late that morning, when Merritt's vanguard appeared on the east side of Namozine Creek. The Yankees promptly dismounted and poured carbine fire across the water at Roberts's men. Then horse artillery trundled up to add heft to the assault. Looking about and seeing their comrades moving off in the distance, the North Carolinians must have felt very much alone.[4]

At 10:20 on the morning of April 3, Grant informed Sheridan that although Petersburg had been captured, the garrison had escaped via the Appomattox and Cox Roads. Grant was forming a pursuit column, which he expected to lead west by noon. He now assigned his subordinate—the only commander in a position to head off the Rebels—two objectives: "It is understood that the enemy will make a stand at Amelia Court-House, with the expectation of holding the road between Danville and Lynchburg. The first object of [the] present movement will be to intercept Lee's army, and the second to secure Burkeville." Sheridan was to make his every move "according to this programme."[5]

Although he realized that the evacuees of Petersburg and Richmond would eventually become his targets, Sheridan continued to focus on running to earth the forces under Anderson. He continued to accompany Griffin's corps, which by hard marching had kept pace with the stop-and-start cavalry column. He was pushing the corps along in a manner new to it—in fact, much like a hard-riding cavalry column. Col. Charles S. Wainwright, Griffin's artillery chief, half marveled, half complained that Sheridan's "Irish blood shone out today in the haphazard way he drove ahead, first on one road, then on another, seeming to think that infantry and artillery could go wherever his own horse did, and a whole corps turn in an equally small space." However unorthodox Sheridan's methods appeared to the infantry and artillery, they achieved results. Little Phil recalled that throughout April 3, "hundreds and hundreds of prisoners, armed and unarmed, fell into our hands, together with many wagons and five pieces of artillery."[6]

From his post in the rear of the cavalry, Sheridan kept in touch by courier with Wesley Merritt, whom he urged to press the Rebels at every turn. He had entrusted to the brevet major general not only the troopers of the Army of the Shenandoah—Custer's were in the vanguard today, giving Devin's men a rest—but also the few dozen hand-picked scouts who since September 1864 had been risking their lives, virtually on a daily basis, to bring Sheridan up-to-date intelligence on enemy movements.

This band of resourceful secret service operatives, which at its peak during the Shenandoah Valley campaign had numbered sixty officers and men, had been depleted over the months, several of its members, captured in Confederate disguise, having been shot or hanged as spies. The scouts—adventurous fellows in their late teens and early twenties, savvy and hardened beyond their years—were led by an officer in whom Sheridan had implicit confidence. Endowed with a rare combination of daredevil recklessness and hard horse sense, twenty-six-year-old Maj. Henry H. Young of Rhode Island would come to be regarded in some circles as the Union's answer to the "Gray Ghost," the famous partisan leader John Singleton Mosby.[7]

The only elements of Sheridan's mounted arm not with Merritt this day were the men of Crook and Mackenzie. Crook's division had been left in the rear, where it was drawing rations and forage. Mackenzie was on detached service, Sheridan having assigned him duties well to the north of the main column.[8]

That morning, the horsemen of the Army of the James had set out for the lower bank of the Appomattox, where they hoped to locate bands of retreating Rebels compact enough to capture whole. Mackenzie marched north in two columns, both of which reached the river in early afternoon. Near Leonard's Mills, the lower column discovered, tracked, and surrounded 300 Confederates, accompanied by four pieces of artillery and a small supply train. Isolated from both Anderson's men and the fugitives from Petersburg, the enemy force surrendered as soon as it found itself under fire from the Henry rifle–wielding troopers of Maj. J. Stannard Baker's 1st District of Columbia Cavalry. Mackenzie's upper column failed to achieve such dramatic results, but it bagged its share of Rebels, mainly stragglers in groups of two and three.[9]

While Mackenzie captured and confiscated, Merritt, with Custer and Devin, proceeded, shortly after daylight on the third, to Namozine Creek.

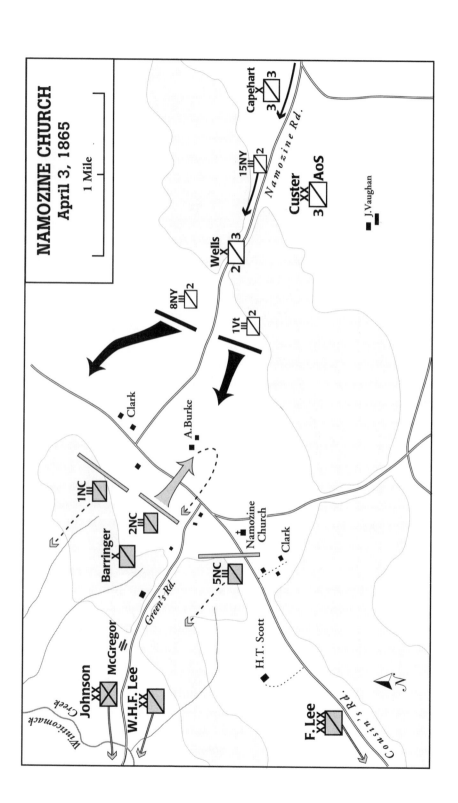

NAMOZINE CHURCH
April 3, 1865

1 Mile

Capehart

3 | 3

Namozine Rd.

15NY | 2

Custer
AoS

3

J.Vaughan

Wells

2 | 3

8NY | 2

1Vt | 2

Clark

A.Burke

1NC

2NC

Barringer

Namozine
Church

Clark

5NC

Green's Rd.

H.T. Scott

Johnson

McGregor

W.H.F. Lee

F. Lee

Cousin's Rd.

Whinomack Creek

N

Drawing up on the east bank sometime before noon, the generals discovered their quarry had crossed and had torched the bridge, also barricading nearby fords with felled trees and other obstructions. While his skirmishers exchanged shots with Roberts's troopers, Custer sent back for a cannon, part of a horse artillery unit on loan from Crook's division, Lt. James H. Lord's Battery A, 2nd United States. As soon as Lord unlimbered, he dosed the Rebels with rounds of canister—tin cans full of iron balls packed in sawdust, the deadliest kind of short-range ammunition. The men of Battery A manned their guns with proficiency and pride born of a long tradition. Their unit was arguably the most illustrious horse battery in Union service; its history stretched back to the Mexican War, and beyond. Lord's predecessors included such celebrated cannoneers as James Duncan, Henry Jackson Hunt (now artillery commander of the Army of the Potomac), John C. Tidball, and John Calef.[10]

While Lord held the North Carolinians in place, Custer had William Wells, leader of his advance brigade, dismount the 1st Vermont, send it across the river at a lower ford, and advance it toward Roberts's right flank. When the Vermonters waded the stream and came on, repeaters blazing, their enemy, already demoralized by Lord's shelling, edged toward panic. Their young general rushed forward and, by the most strenuous efforts, restored order, then supervised a smooth withdrawal. The historian of the 4th North Carolina gave Roberts full credit for extricating the little command from trouble, claiming that only his "marked gallantry and obstinate courage" had averted "what gave indication of a general stampede."[11]

Once the Tarheels fell back, Custer's men, followed by Devin's, forded the stream. On the enemy side, they marched west along Namozine Road, then south on Cousins's Road to Namozine Church. When they drew rein near that country chapel, Custer's men found themselves again confronting North Carolinians behind fieldworks. These were not Roberts's troopers, but members of Barringer's brigade, Wade Hampton's original command. The brigade was nothing like its old self: It had been depleted by battle casualties, and perhaps also by desertions, to no more than 800 officers and men—no more of a match for the thousands of Yankees it hoped to delay than Roberts's men had been.[12]

With only three of his four regiments available to him (the 3rd North Carolina was guarding Anderson's supply train), Barringer took what steps he could to slow the enemy. He later claimed that retreat was not an option; by order of a superior he did not identify, his men were to "fight to the last." Praying that the command could accomplish its mission without being annihilated, the brigadier placed the 5th North Carolina at the church, the 2nd North Carolina on the 5th's left flank along Green's Road, and the 1st North

Carolina on the left of the 2nd. The troopers were covered by a single cannon of McGregor's battery.

Again Wells's brigade sprang to the attack, this time concentrating against the enemy's left. The 1st Vermont advanced straight ahead, while the 8th New York curved to the right and attempted to outflank the 1st North Carolina. The New Yorkers achieved quick success; their objective broke apart almost at first contact. His line suddenly askew, Barringer ordered the 2nd North Carolina to countercharge. The regiment started out in good order, but when the 8th New York turned in its direction and charged in turn, the 2nd lost cohesion and its men whirled to the rear. As they fled, dismounted members of the 1st Vermont pelted them with carbine fire. With two-thirds of his position now dislodged, Barringer ordered the 5th North Carolina to fall back before it, too, could be broken.[13]

Hoping to turn defeat into disaster, Custer had Wells commit his last regiment to the fight. When the 15th New York galloped up to join the offensive, the entire Rebel line gave way. One North Carolinian's regiment, sent forward to stem the blue tide, found itself facing "Custer's full division." He recalled, "We drove them back once, but they kept coming. We began to run out of ammunition. It all happened so quickly that we were somewhat dazed. We slipped back into the woods while we had a few cartridges left, firing as we went."[14]

Most of Barringer's troopers were overtaken before they could escape. In fact, nearly half the brigade was surrounded and captured; the rest, as Custer exulted, "were driven at the gallop before a vastly inferior force. Prisoners, guns, and battle flags were captured all along the line of retreat." One banner, the property of the 2nd North Carolina, was wrested from its bearer by Custer's younger brother, Tom. For his bravery and boldness, the staff officer would be awarded the Medal of Honor.[15]

Of those North Carolinians who escaped death or capture, many galloped down Cousins's Road and into the rear of Fitz Lee's main body. As Colonel Breckinridge of the 2nd Virginia recalled, much of Wooldridge's brigade was "thrown into a panic and a stampede resulted. The panic spread rapidly towards the point and soon we were in a perfect jam of fleeing horsemen," from which horses and riders extricated themselves only by great exertion.[16]

Those retreating down Cousins's Road included General Barringer and members of his staff. For a time, it appeared that the little band had outdistanced its pursuers. Near Poplar Hill Church, the brigadier and his party finally drew rein. Nearby he happened upon a group of grayclad riders who claimed to be members of the 9th Virginia, Beale's brigade, Rooney Lee's division. They proposed to join the new arrivals in trying to locate Fitz Lee, but soon after the search began, they suddenly dropped their disguises, trained their pistols on Barringer and company, and identified themselves as Sheridan's scouts. One of the group revealed himself to be "Harry" Young.[17]

Once the shock of his predicament wore off, Barringer found his captors to be men of honor, especially their commander, whom he described as "a pleasant, entertaining and considerate gentleman." Young not only treated his prisoner with respect, but also went to great lengths to spare him embarrassment. When, the next day, he escorted Barringer to the rear past a Union regiment, he saw to it that the general's headquarters flag, a trophy that attracted "loud and repeated cheers" from the passing troops, was borne some distance in advance of the prisoner. "Listen to those fools," Young told him. "I knew they would do that, and I thought it would be mortifying to you, so I sent your flag on ahead." Barringer appreciated the major's "delicate consideration of my feelings."[18]

Considerate treatment continued after Barringer was turned over to Sheridan's provost marshals. The next morning, along with other officers captured on the third, he joined Little Phil for a breakfast of coffee and biscuits. Later he conversed pleasantly with Generals Meade and Wright, before being sent off to prison at City Point. There he had a brief audience with Abraham Lincoln, who, following the war council of the previous week, had remained at Grant's former headquarters, where he could receive news from the front by telegraph. Lincoln, who had served in Congress with the general's brother, provided Barringer with a note directing that he be made "as comfortable as possible under the circumstances during his confinement."[19]

⸺⸺≫❖≪⸺⸺

While Rebel stragglers were being rounded up at Namozine Church, Merritt had Custer push on after the fugitives. All three of the boy general's brigades would play major roles on the next leg of the pursuit. Custer accompanied Wells's men down Cousins's Road to harass Fitz Lee, Munford, and Rosser. Meanwhile, Capehart's West Virginians and New Yorkers, accompanied by Merritt, pursued Anderson's infantry and Beale's and Roberts's horsemen along Green's Road. After leaving a portion of his brigade near the church to guard the rear, Alexander Pennington stood ready to support Wells or Capehart as needed.[20]

Custer kept in contact with the Rebel rear, which was now manned almost exclusively by infantry, as far as the crossings of Deep Creek. By now Anderson had learned that the Green's Road Bridge over the stream had been rendered impassable by inundated approaches. Thus he led the main column, by a side road, back to Cousins's Road to reunite with Fitz Lee. The combined force continued south on Cousins's until regaining the Namozine Road at Poplar Hill Church. Then the column angled north along Cralle's Road to Brown's Bridge over Deep Creek. The pursuit force headed by Merritt, however, continued up Green's Road toward the unusable bridge, unaware of its condition.

At Mann's, a farm along Cralle's Road a mile or so below the still-passable Brown's Bridge, the infantry in rear of Anderson's column halted and threw up fieldworks to hold back Capehart's men until the main body and the wagons could pass Deep Creek. The foot soldiers did a better job than their cavalry compatriots had an hour or so before. Despite strenuous efforts, the Federals were unable to move them out of the way and halt the crossing. Late in the day, after the rear guard had gotten over, the Rebels set Brown's Bridge afire, temporarily ending the pursuit. Custer decided to desist until morning, although he allowed Pennington's men to probe the Rebels at long distance. That night, the division camped on Sweat House Creek, perhaps two miles from the ruined bridge.[21]

Once across Deep Creek, Anderson also called a halt, placing his weary troops in bivouac near the intersection of Cralle's Road and the road from Bevill's Bridge over the Appomattox. Bevill's was one of three bridges via which Robert E. Lee had hoped to recross the evacuees of Petersburg before moving to Amelia Court House. As it turned out, the approaches to Bevill's had been flooded by the same rains that made the Green's Road Bridge inaccessible. Lee had been forced to lead the troops to Goode's Bridge, eight miles farther upstream. Meanwhile, the remnants of Pickett's division, after returning from Exeter Mills that morning, had marched up the south bank of the Appomattox to the Cralle's Road-Bevill's Bridge Road intersection. There, in midafternoon, they joined Anderson, Johnson, and Fitz Lee.[22]

Merritt realized that the troops in his front had been, or were about to be, reinforced. En route to the Green's Road Bridge, his outriders had observed the troops from Petersburg moving along the north bank of the Appomattox toward a linkup with Anderson. The usually aggressive Merritt hesitated to confront such a large force until he heard from his superior. By courier, Sheridan directed him to bivouac in his present position and in the morning rejoin Custer at Brown's Bridge. As Sheridan later observed, "Darkness had again come to protect the Confederates, and we had to be content with meager results at that point."[23]

Not everyone considered it a lost day. After all, the Federals had compelled their enemy to abandon a succession of positions, while at Namozine Church, they had stampeded and captured one-fourth of Fitz Lee's cavalry. The bugler of 1st New York Dragoons ended his diary entry for April 3 with a simple observation: "It has been a fine day."[24]

One of his counterparts in gray, an enlisted man in the 14th Virginia, recorded in his diary different sentiments: "I have never had such a time as I have had to-day. The Yanks have run me nearly to death." This man turned in while mulling over the news of Petersburg's fall, news that made him feel "so very sad tonight."[25]

Early on April 4, Phil Sheridan moved to fulfill, via a single operation, both of the missions Grant had assigned him. He determined to push his cavalry from Deep Creek to the R & D depot of Jetersville, roughly midway between Burkeville and Lee's assumed destination, Amelia Court House. Such a move would effectively block the path Lee must take if he wished to hunt up Joe Johnston.[26]

This day the pursuers moved toward the railroad in five columns, two of them composed exclusively of infantry. On the Namozine Road came Sheridan, Griffin, and the V Corps, followed closely by Humphreys's II Corps, with the VI Corps, which had left Petersburg late on the third, farther to the rear. Meanwhile, on the Cox Road, the white troops of Ord's XXIV Corps were moving parallel to, and several miles south of, their comrades. Ord had left Birney's African-Americans behind to repair the South Side Railroad, which Sheridan's men and other Union troops had torn up west of Sutherland's Station and by which Grant wished to ship supplies to the rapidly moving front. Birney, a zealous abolitionist, believed that Ord, who had a reputation as something of a racist, had given his command this task as a means of denying it a role in overtaking and cutting off Lee. Birney planned to quit the job as soon as possible; then he would double-quick his troops to the front in hopes of getting in on the kill.[27]

The three columns of cavalry began as two. Wesley Merritt, having temporarily added Mackenzie's troopers, just back from Leonard's Mills, to his command, began the day by seeking to cross Deep Creek north of Brown's Bridge. Mackenzie, leading the march, managed to pass over at a ford that Merritt afterward determined was too deep and muddy to admit the passage of artillery and supply vehicles. He redirected the men of Devin and Custer until they were able to cross the headwaters of the creek. The long detour prevented Merritt from overtaking his quarry until late in the day, when, near Beaver Pond Creek, his men sparred at long range with a newly entrenched rear guard, which included artillery. By now Merritt knew that the troops under Robert E. Lee had crossed the Appomattox at Goode's Bridge and had reached the outskirts of Amelia Court House. Having fixed the enemy's positions, Sheridan's lieutenant put his troopers in camp early that evening.[28]

In the meantime, Mackenzie, after crossing Deep Creek, had veered north and west around the rear guard that confronted Merritt and proceeded to within a mile of Amelia Court House. Late in the afternoon, near a country crossroads with the familiar name of Five Forks, Lieutenant Colonel Stratton's 11th Pennsylvania and Major Baker's 1st District of Columbia Cavalry skirmished at long range with another rear guard. This belonged to Lee's main force, a fact Mackenzie had gleaned from "many and different sources." When the enemy advanced against him in force, the brigadier fell back but did not break contact. That night, Mackenzie was met by a courier from Sheridan with orders to remain in the Five Forks vicinity, "to be watchful and demonstrate, but not push the enemy."[29]

During the night, Merritt also received an order from Sheridan, one that turned the troopers of Devin and Custer and the cannoneers of Lord in a new direction. Merritt was to head for Jetersville and Sheridan's side. With Lee known to be in force at or near Amelia Court House, Sheridan intended to prevent him from moving south, even if cavalry alone had to do the job. Less than half an hour after receiving the dispatch, Merritt was on the road to Jetersville, about seven and a half miles below Amelia.[30]

Crook's division constituted the third mounted column hastening westward on April 4. Sheridan, aware that the 2nd Division was in position to reach the railroad before any other horsemen, that morning directed it to Jennings's Ordinary, a water stop about midway between Sheridan's headquarters and Burkeville Junction. There Crook would build yet another roadblock across the tracks of the R & D.

Crook, whose men had recovered from the drubbing they had absorbed at Dinwiddie Court House and were tired of bringing up the rear, galloped west at the head of Davies's and Smith's brigades. Gregg's men he left behind to protect the flanks of the infantry. At Dennisville, where the II and V Corps turned north toward Jetersville, the two brigades under Crook curved southwestward, passing through Fergusonville and crossing Barebone Creek, until, around midafternoon, they struck the railroad at the point assigned them. They expected to remain there for some time, but word soon reached them that Sheridan wanted both brigades to move up the tracks to Jetersville. Crook's men began to wonder if Little Phil was under pressure from the Rebels at Amelia Court House. If so, hard fighting awaited them at Jetersville.[31]

Sheridan had arrived at Jetersville Station not long before Crook's people reached Jennings's Ordinary. Major Tremain of the staff would describe the adjoining village as "scarcely a dozen dwellings, a store or two, blacksmith shop, post-office, and small railroad depot, where there were found a few cars, and, though otherwise barren of any signs of thrift and enterprise, the little place bore an air of comfort and respectability."[32]

Nervous energy had driven Sheridan to depart the head of the infantry column with which he had been traveling and, accompanied only by his escort, a detachment of the 1st U.S. Cavalry, to hasten to what was thought to be Lee's next destination. No Rebels were in sight when Sheridan reached the place of comfort and respectability, but that did not mean they would not soon appear.

"Having nothing else at hand," Sheridan, while waiting for Crook and Griffin, decided that his escort should assume a defensive posture. It proved to be a wise move. Barely had he placed pickets on the roads leading north when they brought to him a tall, lanky civilian riding a mule, who had blundered into their lines and had been behaving suspiciously ever since. The man proved to be a Rebel scout: When searched, he was found to be carrying, concealed in his boots, two copies of a telegram written by Lee and intended for delivery to the supply depots at Danville and Lynchburg, ordering 200,000 rations to be dispatched, as quickly as possible, to Burkeville Junction.[33]

Sheridan immediately realized the significance of the captured order, which he assumed had been sent by messenger because Crook's troopers had cut the telegraph wires at Jennings's Ordinary. "There was thus revealed," he later wrote, "not only the important fact that Lee was concentrating at Amelia Court House, but also a trustworthy basis for estimating his troops." It is not known how Sheridan determined from the number of rations how many soldiers Lee had with him, but it is easy to understand his conclusion that the Confederate commander was planning to escape into North Carolina—in which case he might soon be heading for Jetersville. For this reason, Sheridan sent word to Merritt and Crook to rush to his side. Now he also sent gallopers to speed up the V Corps. In response to his request, Griffin's weary marchers "redoubled their strides."[34]

As the infantry hastened onward, Sheridan devised a mission for Harry Young's scouts, with whom he remained in contact via courier. He wished the spies to find a way both to deny Lee the rations he had ordered and to make them available to Sheridan's own troops, who were themselves eager for a square meal. Thus he ordered Young to send four of his most resourceful operatives down the tracks to Burkeville. Two each were to carry a copy of Lee's message to telegraph stations outside Danville and Lynchburg. The ruse should be easy to pull off: What telegrapher or commissary officer would ignore a directive in Lee's hand, carried by couriers in Confederate gray?[35]

Sheridan's instincts were sound, but his troops failed to profit from the deception he set in motion. As soon as Lee's orders were sent over the wires, rations were hastened from both of the designated points toward Burkeville. Before the trains carrying them could be intercepted, however, Confederate officials learned that Burkeville was, or soon would be, in enemy hands and recalled the cars. In the end, 80,000 rations would find their way to the A.N.V., but one day late. The delay would prove detrimental, and perhaps fatal, to Lee's plans.

By early evening, Sheridan had been joined at Jetersville by Crook's division, as well as by the vanguard of Griffin's column. At daylight on the fifth, with the early arrivals dug in around the depot, Merritt, Devin, and Custer joined the growing crowd. The concentration relieved Little Phil's concern that Lee would hasten south and break his grip on the railroad.[36]

By morning of the fifth, the Confederates at Amelia Court House were probing Sheridan's lines, but they appeared disinclined to fight. Sheridan wondered why Lee had not advanced earlier with his entire force. A breakthrough to Burkeville was his only logical move under the circumstances, "the only chance the Army of Northern Virginia had to save itself." Why delay that effort until Jetersville had been secured? If Lee had given up the idea of trying to reach North Carolina and instead hoped to outrun his pursuers, why did every sign indicate that he remained immobile? Sheridan may not have been the second coming of Napoleon, but it did not take a military genius to see that the enemy had blundered.[37]

The several columns of Confederates came together at or within a few miles of Amelia Court House beginning on the morning of April 4. These included not only the main body (under Lee and Longstreet, including William Mahone's division), but also Anderson's column (Johnson's and Pickett's infantry and the horsemen of Fitz Lee); various commands from the Petersburg fortifications, including the remnants of the divisions of Major Generals Henry Heth and Cadmus Wilcox; and, the next day, the troops from Richmond under Dick Ewell and Custis Lee. Combined, the columns numbered almost 38,000 officers and men, about half the size of the forces tracking them.

Despite the odds, the arriving troops were in good spirits. By keeping a few steps ahead of their pursuers, they had fulfilled the first of their commander's major objectives—they had reached their initial destination reasonably intact. Now they were in a position to turn south and, before their enemy could mass to prevent it, head for Danville and North Carolina. The only problem facing Lee's men was an acute shortage of marching rations, which had not been issued at any time since the evacuation of the besieged cities.

Boxcars supposedly filled with foodstuffs were waiting for the men at Amelia Court House, but when they were opened, they were found to contain only ammunition. What had happened to the 350,000 rations that had started overland from Richmond on the night the government fled the city? Contemporary observers and latter-day historians would offer several theories, including the possibility that Harry Young's men had deliberately misdirected the wagons. A more plausible explanation involves miscommunication and conflicting orders in the wake of Richmond's fall, which had resulted in the train being sent to points unknown.[38]

The error was as critical as any mistake in war can be, for Lee's men were so desperately hungry they could not be expected to march, and possibly fight, unless quickly and thoroughly fed. With no food on hand, Lee felt constrained to delay his march south until his commissary officers could scour the surrounding area for edibles. He published an appeal, disseminated among local farmers, enlisting their help in meeting his desperate need for "meat, beef, cattle, sheep, hogs, flour, meal, corn, and provender in any quantity that can be spared," all of which would be paid for in Confederate scrip. To make up for any shortfalls in the quantity furnished by the locals, Lee sent the telegram drawing upon the supply officers of Danville and Lynchburg in the amount of 200,000 rations.[39]

By the following morning, the fifth, the situation had not improved. The wagons his staff had driven into the countryside returned empty, or nearly so. As it happened, not only was the neighborhood sparsely settled, but as a direct or indirect result of the war, its few farms provided their owners with a bare subsistence.

Lee had no recourse but to order his famished soldiers to resume the march. By the time they started down the R & D for Jetersville and Burkeville, it was 1:00 P.M.—the army had lost almost twenty-four hours at Amelia Court House. The delay had enabled Sheridan to firm up his hold on the railroad and close the most direct route to North Carolina. Looking back on his predicament, Lee decided that "this delay was fatal, and could not be retrieved."[40]

EIGHT

"Old Bob Lee Is in a Pretty Tight Place"

FOR THE OFFICERS AND MEN OF THE ARMY OF NORTHERN VIRGINIA, THE TRIP south from Amelia Court House began in pain and suffering and ended in a decision equally painful. After their long layover at Amelia, the Confederates—with the possible exception of Ewell's and Custis Lee's slow-moving troops, who had joined the rest of the fugitives only that morning—were no longer bone-tired. They were, however, ravenous. The Army of Northern Virginia had been used to campaigning on half rations and even quarter rations, but going for days without any rations at all, and almost no forage for their horses, was a new and wholly unpleasant experience. One of Rooney Lee's staff officers noted that April 5 was "[my] third day of total abstinence from food of any kind and very little water, for lack of which I suffered most." His distress continued even when he slept, for he was tortured throughout the night by "dreams of feasting."[1]

The absence of rations was bound to affect the ability of the army to keep ahead of the enemy and thereby remain alive. As John Esten Cooke observed: "The tendency of military life is to make man an animal, and to subject his mind in a great measure to his body. Feed a soldier well, and let him sleep sufficiently, and he will fight gaily. Starve him, and break him down . . . and he will despond. He will fight still, but not gaily."[2]

In contrast to Lee's troops, their enemy ate well, and often. Especially was this the case in the cavalry, whose mobility facilitated dropping out of the march and raiding local chicken coops and springhouses. Maj. Robert Bell of the 21st Pennsylvania informed his wife that everyone in his regiment had more provisions "than he gets time to cook." He explained that "there is no meat issued to our men, nothing but hard tack[,] coffee and sugar but they get any amount of beef, hogs, turkies [sic], chicken, geese, ducks." Largely as a result, "I never enjoyed better health in my life than since we started on this raid and now it is going on the eighth day."[3]

Fitz Lee's cavalry, riding immediately in front of Longstreet's corps, arguably suffered more than the infantry, for its motive power was declining. Horses were dropping along the road; many had simply starved to death. The cavalry's plight was worsened because of the operational demands that continued to be made on it. One such demand, which Robert E. Lee levied on his horsemen soon after they left Amelia, would, ironically, unite them with a wagon train, one that carried, among other things, enough provisions to sustain man and beast for days to come.

The wagons were those that had accompanied Custis Lee's reserves from the Richmond front; in addition to rations, they carried ordnance and baggage. The train had crossed the Appomattox on a bridge well above that which most of the retreat force had used. Lee, in preparation for moving on from Amelia Court House, had sent the train northwestward via the crossroads hamlet of Paineville. In that vicinity, roving Yankees had attacked the wagons, which were guarded by white soldiers and driven by African-American teamsters.[4]

Martin Gary's brigade of cavalry, which Fitz Lee had deployed along the western flank of the army, had spied the Yankees just before they overtook the train and had reported their presence to Amelia Court House. Fitz set out to overtake the enemy with the few thousand troopers remaining with Rosser and Munford. Their departure left the mobile support of the army in the hands of Rooney Lee.[5]

After Fitz and company rode off, the main column continued down the R & D. About three miles south of Amelia, Rooney Lee's scouts sent back word that Yankee cavalry, in strength unknown, had occupied Jetersville. Of greater concern was an accompanying report of large bodies of Union infantry moving in the cavalry's rear. Soon it was learned that the foot soldiers had reached the depot and were entrenching astride the railroad.

The news placed Robert E. Lee in a quandary, while raising several questions. Should he continue on and try to clear the unexpected roadblock, or should he bypass it? If he challenged the enemy, would his famished troops be strong enough to put up a fight? If he opted to detour, could he put enough distance between his men and their pursuers to reach the R & D by another route?

After conferring with Longstreet, his "Old War Horse," as well as with his cavalryman son and other subordinates, Lee decided not to risk everything by attacking blindly toward Jetersville. Instead, he heeded the warning of Rooney's scouts, who reported (prematurely, as it turned out) that two full corps of infantry had reached the railroad. Instead of stopping to fight, the army would side-step toward Farmville, twenty-some miles west of Amelia Court House. From that village, which abutted two meandering landmarks, the Appomattox River and the South Side Railroad, the army could turn south and, by passing through Prince Edward Court House, return to the R & D. It could, that is, if able to keep ahead of Grant, Meade, and Ord. If Sheridan's horsemen alone barred the new path, Lee felt confident of breaking through to North Carolina. But if the road from Farmville was blocked by as many foot soldiers as now appeared to be flooding into the Jetersville vicinity, the game would be up for the Army of Northern Virginia.[6]

Aware of how dearly Lee's layover at Amelia Court House had cost him, Sheridan was more eager than ever to confront the Confederates and put an end to the frustrating and costly chase. Once the V Corps began to arrive at Jetersville, Little Phil importuned both Grant (who was riding with Ord's column on the Cox Road) and Meade (who was accompanying Humphreys's II Corps, five miles in rear of Griffin's men) to hasten to his side. Adding weight to the V Corps would produce a roadblock too heavy for Lee to move. "We can capture the Army of Northern Virginia," Sheridan assured Grant, "if force enough can be thrown to this point, and then advance upon it. . . . Lee is at Amelia Court House in person. They are out, or nearly out, of rations."[7]

Sheridan would show the enemy no mercy in this, their hour of greatest trial—mercy had no place in either his personal or his professional lexicon. His attitude perfectly suited the men who had congregated around Jetersville. That morning, Major Bell of Crook's division wrote of the cavalry's success and its prospects for the future: "We think that old Bob Lee is in a pretty tight place as at this time we are on his front and flank with three divisions of cavalry and the fifth Corps while the 2nd and 6th Corps with one division of cavalry [Mackenzie's] will be in his rear by this evening."[8]

Sheridan's unwillingness to ease up on his enemy led him, early on the morning of the fifth, to place a large detachment of the 2nd Cavalry Division off Lee's right flank, west of Amelia Springs. Crook assigned the task to Davies's brigade, which broke camp before daylight and rode due north. After reaching the Springs, about seven miles from Lee's position, Davies continued up the road toward Paineville. Crossing Flat Creek on Burton's Bridge, he turned right, passed through Paineville and, a few miles farther north, encountered the head of Custis Lee's wagon train, trundling away from the Amelia Court House vicinity.[9]

The sight of a supply column ripe for seizure fired the imagination of every red-blooded cavalryman. As Major Tremain put it, "The prospect of capture, plunder, or destruction of a large train of army wagons induces inspirations appreciated only by veterans, while . . . it renders a body of men impetuous, resolute, and invincible." But when about to pounce on the slow-moving vehicles, Davies saw that the train was protected not only by guards, but also by artillery. He deferred his strike until in a position to neutralize the cannons. The enemy, detecting his presence, brought up one of the guns, but before it could be loaded, Davies ordered a charge on its flank by the six companies of Maj. Hampton S. Thomas's 1st Pennsylvania. Thomas formed his understrength regiment, led it up the road at a gallop, and overran the battery. Then he and his men turned on the train guards and, with slashing sabers and spitting pistols, scattered them "in all directions."[10]

Virtually immobile, its protection gone, the train was now Davies's for the taking. At his order, Lt. Col. Melzer Richards's 24th New York joined Thomas's men in racing along the length of the train. Tremain saw riders "dashing up and down the road, now shooting the drivers, now charging their guards; now unceremoniously overhauling the contents of a heavily laden wagon, or attempting to drive off mules, drivers, wagons and all. Scared contrabands grinned and impudent teamsters looked gloomy as the miscellaneous paraphernalia of an army baggage train was hurriedly turned inside out."[11]

When the vehicles had been emptied and decisions had been made as to the disposition of their contents, Davies's staff officers distributed sulfur matches among the men, who methodically set fire to 200 wagons, ambulances, caissons, and limbers. Up in smoke went small-arms ammunition, which exploded harmlessly when the fire touched it off, as well as medical stores, infantry and cavalry equipment, and provisions including as many rations as could not be carted off. Numerous items were confiscated rather than destroyed. Tremain called those articles brought off by the soldiers "a curious index of personal taste. With some, money, jewelry, and wearing apparel, when desirable, seemed to be the favorite choice; while one eager party was obliged to disperse and desist in their interesting endeavors to force [open] a salamander safe."[12]

As the wagons blazed, Davies turned his men eastward and led them, along with their captures—more than 600 prisoners of both races, as well as several battle flags—toward Flat Creek. En route, they added to their haul by overtaking and capturing an artillery unit that had been cut off from Lee's army. The new prizes included several Coehorn mortars and at least four Whitworth rifles, breech-loading cannons made in England and purchased by Confederate agents early in the war.[13]

Because their plundering was a serious blow to enemy resources and pride, Davies's men were not permitted to reach home base scot-free. Soon after they departed Paineville, Gary's brigade began to snipe at them. The South Carolinians were too few to inflict real damage, but then the Federals were set upon by Fitz Lee, with Rosser's division and the better part of Munford's. A fight broke out near Amelia Springs that piled high the casualties on both sides. Fitz seemed intent on delivering a painful message, perhaps because the ruined vehicles included the headquarters wagon he had left behind in Richmond. One of his staff officers lamented that he himself had "lost everything" except what he had on. "Desks, papers &c all burnt."[14]

Once he saw that the foe had him outnumbered as well as outpositioned, Davies, who had not been in such a tight spot since the Buckland Races, made a run for it. He led his 1,200 troopers on a wild ride through Amelia Springs and across Flat Creek. Though weary and hungry, the Confederates were exhilarated by their adversaries' predicament; they pursued with a vengeance. Spearheaded by Dearing's Laurel Brigade, with Munford's men, many of them dismounted, in close support, the pursuers flayed Davies's flanks and rear guard with sabers, pistols, and carbines. Dearing led an especially effective charge in response to the order of his superior, Rosser, to "ride over 'em!" As the division commander recalled, "The words were scarcely out of my mouth before he waved his hat over his head and commanded 'Forward! Gallop! March!' And in a moment he had closed with the enemy, broke his line and sent him thundering on through Amelia Springs, Dearing and his gallant riders close on their heels."[15]

The pressure did not abate until the antagonists were within a mile of Jetersville, and then only because Irvin Gregg's people rushed up to support their comrades. The impetuous Gregg piled into the pursuers, mixed with them in a particularly violent sword and pistol duel, and eventually forced them to draw off. For a time, however, the rescuers had appeared to be in greater peril than their comrades. At one point, Gregg led a portion of his command so far in front of the rest that he escaped by the narrowest of margins. Two days hence, he would not be so fortunate.[16]

The casualty toll was remarkably high, especially in the commissioned ranks. Notable fatalities included Capt. James Rutherford, a brilliant young member of Dearing's staff who had left his studies in Europe to fight, only to fall in his first battle; and Capt. Hugh McGuire of the 11th Virginia, mortally wounded when leading a party of his regiment against six times as many assailants. On the Union side, the seemingly charmed life of Hugh Janeway had been ended by a pistol ball in the skull ("No better or braver officer," Davies wrote, "has ever fallen on the field of battle"). Lieutenant Colonel Richards had been mortally wounded, and Major Thomas, during Gregg's counterattack, had fallen from the saddle with a wound that would cost him a leg.[17]

Having visited sufficient retribution on the foe, the Confederates withdrew to Amelia Springs, where they spent the night. There Fitz Lee totaled up the balance sheet. He concluded that thirty of the enemy had been killed in the fighting, "principally with the saber"—a tactical rarity, given the Confederates' preference for firearms in close-quarter fighting—"and 150 wounded and captured." Although Fitz did not enumerate his own losses, they appeared "not very heavy."[18]

The disparity conjured up memories of the good old days, when every encounter with the Yankees ended one-sidedly. For the first time in what seemed like decades, "we whipt them handsomely," an officer in the 4th Virginia informed his wife. That night, visions of banquet food may again have disturbed the sleep of Fitz Lee's troopers, but presumably the men also dreamed of unstoppable saber charges and frightened, fleeing Yankees.[19]

About two hours after Lee started down the tracks from Amelia Court House, George Meade, riding in the van of Humphreys's corps, arrived at Jetersville. Now Sheridan was backed by elements of two infantry corps, while 80 percent of the cavalry available to him was also on hand. The aggregate strength was sufficient to ease any lingering concern that Lee would bull his way through to Burkeville. If he tried that now—and increasingly it looked as though he would not—he would be thrown back with heavy loss.[20]

For his part, Little Phil was ready to take on the Rebels at Amelia and get the climactic confrontation over with. The trouble was that not everyone in authority shared his enthusiasm for combat. Meade had no desire to take the offensive until the rest of Humphreys's troops were in place, preferably augmented by the VI Corps, which was still strung out on the road from Deep Creek. Cautious, conservative Meade was also under the weather, suffering from an undiagnosed illness that sapped his strength to such a degree that he could not deploy his own troops. Upon reaching Jetersville, he asked Sheridan to put the II Corps in position—something he never would have done, especially given his attitude toward Little Phil, had he been well.[21]

Sheridan took on the job without complaint, moving two of Humphreys's three divisions to the left of the V Corps, the sector that seemed most likely to come under assault if Lee regained the fighting spirit he seemed to have lost. The 3rd Division, II Corps, he massed on Griffin's right. About an hour before sundown, the advance of Wright's column reached the depot, reuniting the VI Corps and Sheridan for the first time since the Valley campaign. Sheridan placed these troops, too, on Griffin's right flank, where, like Humphreys's men, they erected breastworks and spent considerable time strengthening them.[22]

With so much manpower available to him, Sheridan wished to use it as soon as possible. His objective would be the head of Lee's column, not its rear. The earliest he could attack—if Meade would consent to it—would be the morning of the sixth. But by then, Sheridan feared, only the end of Lee's column would be in sight. By now it was too late for Lee to strike south from Amelia; his only course was to turn west and continue his retreat. Davies's reconnaissance to Paineville, which had discovered wagons moving northwestward, suggested as much.

If Lee turned toward Farmville, as Sheridan believed he would, the Federals would have to outmarch him before they outfought him. From talking to the indisposed general's staff officers, however, Sheridan got the impression that in the morning, Meade intended to advance up the railroad toward Amelia, as if Lee would remain to receive his thrust. Little Phil was certain that the Confederate leader was too smart to do that.

Thus at 3:00 P.M., even before the VI Corps had reached him, Sheridan sat down to write Grant a message, which one of Young's scouts would deliver to the lieutenant general's new headquarters on the South Side Railroad. Ostensibly to keep Grant posted on the cavalry's operations, Sheridan summarized Davies's attack on the enemy train (without mentioning the brigade's rough handling on the way back) and enclosed a piece of captured correspondence that he believed would please its unintended recipient. The letter, apparently written that morning by one of Lee's colonels, began, "Dear Mamma: Our army is ruined, I fear." Then, without explaining why, Sheridan told Grant: "I wish you were here yourself. I feel confident of capturing the Army of Northern Virginia if we exert ourselves. I see no escape for Lee."[23]

Grant was about four miles west of Nottoway Court House on the railroad when, at about 6:30 P.M., he received Sheridan's message. It was handed to him by a gray-clad soldier whose disguise was so complete it must have given the commanding general and his staff a start. Grant was then—as he had been

since leaving Petersburg early on the afternoon of the third—traveling with
Ord. The latter's column continued to consist of Gibbon's white troops, Birney's African-Americans being in the rear, where they were dividing their time
between marching and repairing sections of a railroad now important as a
route of Union supply. That work was especially arduous, for Birney's men
had to re-lay one side of the rails to reduce the road's five-foot gauge to accommodate the smaller-gauge trains of the U.S. Military Railroad.[24]

Freed of hard labor, Ord had concentrated on making the best possible
time on the march. Each day, the pace had increased in response to Grant's
concern that Lee might forge ahead of Meade and Sheridan or slip past them
into North Carolina. The men of the XXIV Corps had made fifteen miles the
first day out and close to twenty the following day; on April 3, they would
march twenty-eight miles, a distance that would leave everyone "jaded and
completely worn out." That night, however, the head of Ord's column would
reach Burkeville Junction, enabling Grant to throw a second blocking force
across the R & D. Even so, Grant continued to worry that his opponent
would surmount every roadblock and reach Joe Johnston. That morning, in a
dispatch to Sherman, he had suggested that his old subordinate strike not for
Greensboro, as originally intended, but for Danville, there to join Meade's
and Ord's people in pincering the Army of Northern Virginia, which Grant
estimated to consist of about 20,000 officers and men.[25]

New concerns beset Grant after he perused Sheridan's 3:00 P.M. dispatch.
After a brief consultation with Ord, he decided to relocate to Jetersville. Accompanied by his staff and a fourteen-man detail from his headquarters escort, Capt. Julius W. Mason's 5th U.S. Cavalry, the lieutenant general struck
cross-country on his powerful steed, Cincinnati. The jaunt ended at Sheridan's headquarters sometime after 10:00 that night. In the kitchen of a mod-
est farmhouse, the two generals talked strategy over a late supper, then called
on General Meade. The army leader, still suffering from his debilitating illness, assured Grant that he would be well enough to advance on Amelia
Court House in the morning. At Sheridan's urging, Grant stressed that Meade
must get in front of the Army of Northern Virginia, which might already be
moving west, not merely trail it. Meade forcefully stated his belief that Lee
had been run to earth and would stay at Amelia until made to leave.

Sheridan, who upon Meade's arrival had returned to cavalry command,
remained unconvinced that Lee would consent to be attacked. Therefore, he
secured Grant's permission to lead Merritt's horsemen toward Deatonville at
an early hour on the sixth. Grant took the additional step of notifying Ord to
move in the same direction from his more southerly position.

To comply, Ord would require mobile reconnaissance, the only horsemen accompanying him being his five-company escort from the 4th Massachusetts. To augment that unit, Grant took steps to return Mackenzie to Ord's side. Then the planning conference that had begun at Sheridan's headquarters broke up, and the principals retired for the night. All needed their sleep; they knew that April 6 would be a busy, and perhaps a critical, day in the effort to overtake the enemy and end a war too long, too costly, and far too cruel.[26]

On the fourth, while the troopers under Merritt concentrated on overhauling Anderson, Johnson, and Fitz Lee, Mackenzie's cavalry had remained in the Five Forks vicinity, keeping watch over the graybacks at Amelia Court House. Unaware that Lee was going to linger, Mackenzie considered it his mission to keep the enemy immobile until Sheridan could secure Jetersville. Thus on April 5, he ordered his 2nd Brigade, now led by Col. Andrew W. Evans, to raid the R & D about four miles below Amelia, where two bridges carried the railroad over timber-fringed Nibbs Creek. In response, a dismounted detachment of Evans's 1st Maryland (Union) Cavalry, later reinforced, seized that point and held it until attacked by a body of Rebels large enough, in Evans's opinion, to constitute a brigade. Most of the Marylanders had time to remount and race to safety, but a party of the regiment was cut off and lost several men to capture. During the affair, a row broke out between Evans and Mackenzie when the latter reversed several of his subordinate's tactical decisions—conduct that Evans not only resented, but also declared responsible for the captures. When the Confederates advanced menacingly toward Evans's men, Mackenzie ordered them to withdraw.[27]

Mackenzie later compounded his less-than-sterling performance by misconstruing his enemy's actions. Unaware that Lee was searching desperately for provisions, Mackenzie cited the pressure applied by his troopers as the reason the enemy remained at Amelia throughout the day. He likewise misinterpreted Lee's destruction of almost 100 fully loaded caissons. Mackenzie attributed the action to Lee's fear that as soon as his army was in motion, Mackenzie would attack and capture the ordnance. In reality, Lee had the ammunition destroyed because he considered it unstable and dangerous, as well as unneeded. It had been exposed to the effects of time and weather since the previous winter, when stored in that out-of-the-way place, beyond the enemy's reach.[28]

Mackenzie's men spent a second night in the Five Forks–Amelia Court House vicinity before being recalled, early on April 6, to Jetersville. By a wide circuit to the south, they joined Sheridan, who at once ordered them returned to Ord at Burkeville. About 4:00 P.M., the troopers reached the rail junction, where they joined their army for the first time in four days. Mackenzie learned that Ord was about to leave Burkeville for Prince Edward Court House. He also discovered that he had arrived twelve hours too late to join in a daring mission designed to curtail Lee's retreat.[29]

Early that morning, Ord had formed an expeditionary force in response to an order from Grant that he destroy any bridges west of Burkeville that Lee might use after leaving Amelia. Ord had focused on the Farmville vicinity. Two days before, the Federals had captured an engineer on the South Side Railroad, who under interrogation had revealed that two trains carrying supplies for Lee's troops had been sent to Farmville. Grant, and now Ord, believed Lee was heading to that town preparatory to heading south to Danville.

Four miles east of Farmville, the 125-foot-tall High Bridge, a railroad span, crossed the Appomattox River, flanked by a less lofty wagon bridge. Believing Lee would cross one structure or the other, Ord determined to reach them first and render both unusable. For the assignment, to be executed prior to the army's departure from Burkeville, he made some rather unorthodox selections: two regiments of infantry, the 54th Pennsylvania and the 123rd Ohio, plus the better part of his escort, three of the five companies of Colonel Washburn's regiment of Massachusetts horsemen. As senior participant, Washburn would command the combined force.[30]

Apparently Ord believed that because High Bridge had to be held long enough to complete its destruction, the staying power of infantry was critical to the success of the enterprise. His orders to Washburn were "to push as rapidly as the exhausted condition of men and horses would permit, for the bridge, make a reconnaissance when near there, and, if not too well guarded, to burn it, returning at once with great caution."[31]

The idea behind the mission was a good one, but the planning that went into it, as well as the composition of Washburn's column, left much to be desired. Ord's willingness to push an isolated force deep into unknown territory meant the project carried more than its fair share of risk. This became vividly clear when, about 10:00 A.M. on the sixth, eight hours after the cavalry and infantry set out, the army leader received a dispatch from Sheridan reporting that Lee's army had left Amelia and was moving in Ord's direction. Ord wrote that his "command was immediately put in position to meet them, but it seems they turned off and took the road toward Farmville."[32]

Ord appears to have anticipated trouble, for he had already dispatched his chief of staff, Bvt. Brig. Gen. Theodore Read ("the most gallant and reliable officer I had at hand"), with a small escort, to overtake and then supervise

Washburn's force, with orders to reconnoiter High Bridge thoroughly before trying to seize it from the numerous Confederates known to be guarding it. Only after receiving Sheridan's message, however, did Ord appreciate the danger facing Read and Washburn. At that point, he sent yet another emissary to High Bridge. This officer was to inform Washburn and Read that Lee was moving in their direction and to order them to abort the mission and return to Ord's headquarters. For the rescue force, the trick was to reach Farmville before the enemy did.[33]

After dark on the fifth, Lee diverged from the railroad and moved west via Rice's Station on the South Side Railroad. His troops could not have looked forward to another long march on an empty stomach. Beyond the additional hardships it would cause, any movement by night through unfamiliar territory entailed risks. One hazard materialized at the outset, when Mahone's division took a wrong road out of Amelia Court House and became separated from Longstreet's command at the forefront of the marching column. The mistake was rectified, but Mahone had to fight his way past some Union troopers roving far from Sheridan's and Mackenzie's forces.[34]

Once the Confederates crossed Flat Creek and passed through Amelia Springs, their spirits rose. Rumors spread along the column that provisions awaited them just up ahead. The reports were true: At Amelia Springs, Lee had been contacted by Commissary General Isaac M. St. John, who informed him that 80,000 rations—the contents of the train that had been directed to Burkeville and then recalled by alert dispatchers—were now at Farmville, beyond enemy reach. At Lee's order, the commissary officer decamped for the village on the Appomattox, to ready the rations for issuance as soon as Lee's men marched in.

Lee received a second piece of welcome news as his men trudged on through the night. Outriders from Fitz Lee's division, which led the march, turned the tables on Sheridan's scouts by capturing two of Harry Young's men and confiscating a message they had been carrying from Grant at Jetersville to Ord at Burkeville. The dispatch, dated 10:10 the previous evening, directed the commander of the Army of the James to assume a position from which to observe the roads toward Farmville. From the contents of the message, Lee was able not only to determine the relative positions of the Union forces, but also to discover that his enemy believed him heading for Farmville. That meant if he expected to continue to evade his pursuers, he would have to put maximum distance between them before morning revealed his leave-taking.[35]

By dawn on April 6, Lee's troops were still several miles from Farmville and a full meal. At about that time, Longstreet learned from Gary's scouts, as well as from local residents, that a body of Union infantry, possibly with mounted support, had passed his flank, heading in the direction of Farmville. Longstreet did not have to think hard to discern the purpose of this movement. Without taking the time to notify Fitz Lee, who, in response to an order from his uncle, was explaining "the situation of things" to infantry commanders at the rear of the column, Longstreet notified Tom Rosser of the Yankees running loose in his front. The fiery Rosser put himself at the head of 700 members of his division and started off, at the fastest pace that tired horses could tolerate, for High Bridge.[36]

The Army of the Potomac took to the road, heading north and slightly east from Jetersville, shortly after dawn on the sixth. It was strictly an infantry operation: The II Corps led out, followed by the VI (the IX Corps remained well to the rear, picketing the Cox Road). By that hour, Sheridan had already left Jetersville, leading Merritt and Crook on a westward track parallel to Lee's left flank. General Meade, in personal command of the troops marching up the R & D, was feeling better this morning. His temper, however, continued to flare, and his nerves were on edge. To some extent, these were manifestations of the risk inherent in the coming confrontation with Lee. They were also by-products of his latest dispute with Sheridan.

It rankled Meade sorely not only that Sheridan occasionally treated him with contempt, but also that Sheridan's mentor, Grant, allowed him to get away with it. Sheridan's latest offense was his almost sneering insistence that he alone knew what Lee was going to do this day. To display his superiority, he had ridden out of Jetersville in advance of the infantry's movement. Worse than Sheridan's insolence was the fact that he had won Grant's permission to run off with the army's cavalry force. As he had almost a year ago, when starting out on the mission that resulted in Jeb Stuart's death, the Irishman had left the army sightless, without the power to determine, at distance, the enemy's numbers and dispositions. Meade seethed inwardly, reflecting that, as much as anything Sheridan had done, this latest act perfectly captured the man's selfishness and conceit.[37]

It had begun to rain, and the accompanying fog, which limited the visibility of Meade's scouts, aggravated the column's lack of mobile intelligence. Not until almost 9:00 A.M. did the mist begin to lift, granting the men of Miles's division a good view of the countryside ahead. Suddenly, the advance guard sent back word that the road was empty of Rebels. Turning to the left and peering through the rain, the lookouts saw what appeared to be the rear of a column of horsemen trotting westward. A minute later, the riders were lost to view beyond a ridge.

The men in the advance realized what had happened. Lee was no longer at Amelia Court House; he was making a run for Farmville. To keep the pursuit going, the Army of the Potomac would have to change direction. Officers immediately gave the order to do so, and the shift was accomplished without notable difficulty. But by the time it was complete, a several-mile gap separated Humphreys's advance and the rear of that cavalry force. The gap would take extremely hard marching to close. From his position well down the moving column, George Meade could be heard cursing like a high-stakes gambler who had been cleaned out.[38]

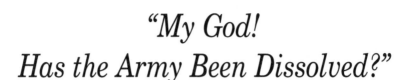

NINE

"My God!
Has the Army Been Dissolved?"

THEODORE READ OVERTOOK WASHBURN'S COMMAND JUST BEFORE IT COM-
pleted its eighteen-mile journey to High Bridge. However, the captain sent to
recall Read, Washburn, and everyone else on the ill-conceived expedition was
cut off and forced to backtrack to Ord's column, his mission unaccom-
plished. His retreat doomed the infantry and cavalry sent to seize and destroy
the mammoth span over the Appomattox.[1]

With Read on the scene, Washburn's cavalry and the two infantry outfits,
under the direct command of Lt. Col. Horace Kellogg of the 123rd Ohio,
advanced to a point about a mile from High Bridge, then halted. At about
8:00 A.M., while Read and the foot soldiers waited, Washburn's horsemen
crossed Sandy River and advanced on the regiment of Virginia Reserves, 356
strong, found to be guarding the span. The guards were ensconced inside
four earthen redoubts, defended by a total of twenty-one cannons. The little
forts were protected in front by a morass that could be crossed only by a now-
broken access bridge.

Although only eighty strong, Washburn's force advanced boldly against
the main defensive work, whose position commanded the approaches to the
others. In less than an hour, the troopers had replanked the bridge, crossed
the swamp, charged the fort, and chased out its occupants, who retreated toward Farmville. Apparently none of the enemy's guns was in working condition, or all lacked ammunition, for no account of the affair mentions their
use against Washburn.

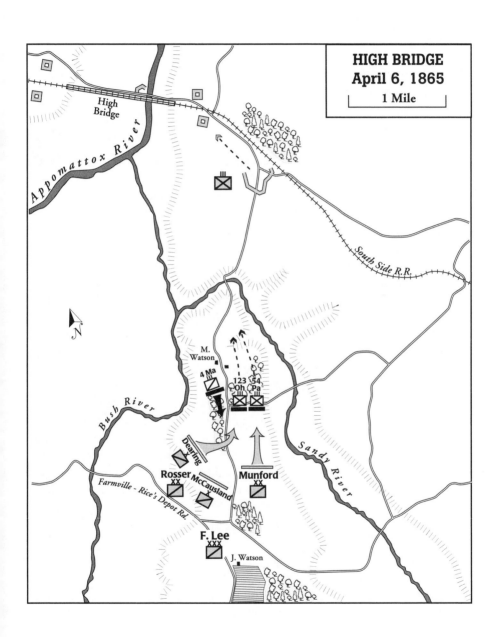

HIGH BRIDGE
April 6, 1865

1 Mile

High
Bridge

Appomattox River

South Side R.R.

N

M.
Watson

4 Ma

123
Oh

54
Pa

Bush River

Sandy River

Dearing

Rosser

McCausland

Munford

Farmville - Rice's Depot Rd.

F. Lee

J. Watson

The victorious Federals galloped up the tracks of the South Side Railroad to confront defenders who had rallied in front of the bridge. These proved too few to pose much of a threat; Washburn dispersed them, then hunted up combustible materials to pile on the wooden sections of the bridge. By noon, he was ready to use them, but he had run out of time— Confederate cavalry was on the scene in force.[2]

Colonel Munford, at the head of his division, had reached Rice's Station, four miles south of High Bridge and seven miles from Farmville, a little before 11:00 that morning. He found infantry on the scene, and it was busily erecting earthworks along the railroad. Its commander, Longstreet, who had reached the depot in advance of R. E. Lee and the main body, initially ordered the colonel to guard his men's right flank as they worked. A little later, however, Longstreet recalled Munford and revealed that he had just dispatched Rosser to overhaul an enemy detachment observed heading for High Bridge with the evident intention of burning it or blowing it up. He had enjoined Munford's colleague to "capture or destroy the detachment, *if it took the last man of his command to do it.*" Now, worried that he had underestimated the size of the enemy force, Longstreet directed Munford to follow rapidly and assist Rosser in neutralizing the Yankees.[3]

Munford moved out quickly enough, but perhaps amid some concern. He had no qualms about supporting Rosser, although he doubted the man would give him any credit, published or otherwise, for assisting him. While Munford was confident that his officers and men would comport themselves honorably in any fight, hunger pangs notwithstanding, he feared that their winded, half-starved animals might not hold up under the demands of the mission. And although he knew them to be soldiers of ability and versatility, Munford may have worried about the maiden outing of two artillery officers, Lt. Col. R. Preston Chew and Maj. James Breathed, in command of cavalry.

That morning, Fitz Lee had sought to assist a couple of regiments in Munford's brigade deficient in field officers. He had "temporarily assigned" Chew to command the 3rd Virginia of Wooldridge's brigade and Breathed to lead the 8th Virginia, Boston's brigade. The appointments had been based on the theory that the talents of these officers, whose positions in the horse artillery had been effectively abolished by the dearth of serviceable batteries, were too valuable to go untapped, especially when officer expertise was in short supply. Munford thought Lee's reasoning sound, and he was happy to have the two officers in his command. A third stalwart of the old Stuart Horse Artillery, Capt. James Thomson, Chew's successor as commander of the battery that bore the lieutenant colonel's name, was likewise making the journey at Munford's side, having volunteered his services, although not in any official capacity.[4]

Close to noon, as Munford's hard-riding column neared High Bridge, the sounds of gunfire drifted up from beyond the right flank. At its commander's order, the division turned onto a byway that Rosser appeared to have taken in an attempt to outflank the enemy. Munford moved his men through a dense woods toward the sound of the fighting. On the far edge of the trees, he dismounted Wooldridge's brigade and ordered it to advance as skirmishers. Boston's men, who remained mounted, he moved to the far right, ready to charge the Yankees if necessary.

Clearing the woods, Wooldridge's men, as Munford wrote, "came to quite a broad field, across which, in a piece of woods opposite us, the enemy's Infantry were distinctly seen. Our skirmishers soon opened as they advanced, and the enemy responded, vigorously. We could see Rosser's mounted men charging and we pushed on, losing some valuable officers and men" to the rifle fire of Kellogg's foot soldiers. Despite a steady stream of minié balls, Wooldridge's line kept moving, firing as it went. It suffered several casualties before it reached the other side of the field, but it felled at least as many, especially once the Yankees were distracted by a saber charge by Boston's troopers.[5]

Munford was gratified, but not surprised, to observe Chew urging onward the men of his new outfit. He was even more impressed when Major Breathed led his regiment at an extended gallop toward the point where the enemy's fire was the thickest. When he reached the Union line, however, Breathed was challenged by two saber-wielding officers. Because he was not a trained cavalryman, the major wielded only a pistol, with which he managed to parry the blows of both assailants. When one rammed his horse into Breathed's, the artilleryman was unceremoniously dumped from the saddle. For a few seconds, until his boot came loose, he was dragged along the ground, his foot caught in the stirrups. Then, when lying flat on the ground, the major killed one of his adversaries with a pistol shot. The second Yankee was gunned down by one of Breathed's couriers, who came to the officer's aid just in time. Rosser, who witnessed the entire confrontation, was impressed by the artilleryman's bearing: "In a moment Breathed was back in the saddle again, with only one boot, and again joined in the fight."[6]

By charging frontally against the infantry while Dearing's and McCausland's brigades attacked their flanks, Munford pried the Yankee infantry from the woods and sent it scrambling toward the bridge it intended to destroy. Just as the foot soldiers broke and ran, however, Washburn's troopers charged down the road from the bridge and slammed into Rosser's rear and flank. The Confederate leader wrote of the intervention: "I never witnessed a more handsome attack." After the fight, a Virginian asked a member of Washburn's regiment: "Was your colonel drunk or crazy this morning[?] . . . . We have seen hard fighting, but we never heard of anything like this [charge] before!"[7]

Surprised to take so heavy a blow from such a small force, Rosser's division milled about in disorder before the men recovered and followed their commander in a series of devastating counterattacks. They forced the Yankees into retreat, then chased them down, shooting and slashing them until they surrendered. By then a score had fallen, including Washburn himself. Having suffered a severe wound in the throat, the colonel had then been knocked senseless by a low-hanging tree limb. While lying helpless on the ground, he had taken a saber blow to the head, which fractured his skull ("underlined murdered . . . long after the fight," in the words of one of his men). He would die of his wounds sixteen days later.

Another who took a mortal wound in this "most savage hand-to-hand fight" was General Read. Some accounts identify the staff officer's killer as James Dearing, who, with what Rosser called "undaunted, determined pluck," led one of the charges against Washburn and himself fell mortally wounded. Ord deeply regretted the loss of his favorite staff officer, but the highly popular Dearing was mourned throughout the cavalry, A.N.V.[8]

After Washburn's band disintegrated, Rosser and Munford turned back to the foot soldiers who had fled toward High Bridge. Boston's brigade, still in the saddle, took up the chase, followed by McCausland's. Working in tandem, the commands pinned Kellogg's people to the south side of the bridge. When the Federals tried to make a stand, the cavalry charged them from several angles. The foot soldiers were quickly decimated; most of those not cut down in the melee were captured. A few, including Kellogg, took refuge in neighboring woods, where they hid out overnight. When Ord's main body occupied the area late the following day, it found the fugitives wandering about, dazed and weak from hunger and exposure.[9]

Two more high-ranking Confederates suffered fatal wounds in the attacks that overthrew Kellogg's men. Colonel Boston was shot through the skull, while Captain Thomson, who had cheated death a few months before when Chew's Battery was overrun by charging Federals, took a rifle ball in the spine. Tom Rosser, who seemed to attract bullets, was again shot in the arm. His latest injury may have resulted from his inability to defend himself with the saber—the result, in turn, of the wound he had received at Five Forks.[10]

In payment for their many scars, the Confederates killed forty-two of the enemy, took almost 800 prisoners, and saved an escape route of critical importance to their army. By any measurement, these were major accomplishments. Union officers later attempted to invest Read's and Washburn's mission

Gen. Robert E. Lee

LIBRARY OF CONGRESS

Lt. Gen. James Longstreet

NATIONAL ARCHIVES

Maj. Gen. George E. Pickett
MUSEUM OF THE CONFEDERACY

Maj. Gen. Fitzhugh Lee
LIBRARY OF CONGRESS

Maj. Gen. William H. F. Lee
LIBRARY OF CONGRESS

Maj. Gen. Thomas L. Rosser
PHOTOGRAPHIC HISTORY OF THE CIVIL WAR

Brig. Gen. Thomas T. Munford
LIBRARY OF CONGRESS

Brig. Gen. Martin W. Gary
LIBRARY OF CONGRESS

Brig. Gen. James Dearing
LIBRARY OF CONGRESS

Col. Elijah V. White
LIBRARY OF CONGRESS

Lt. Col. R. Preston Chew
V.M.I. ARCHIVES

Maj. James Breathed
NATIONAL ARCHIVES

Lt. Gen. Ulysses S. Grant

Maj. Gens. Gouverneur K. Warren (far left), George G. Meade (third from left), Andrew A. Humphreys (second from right) LIBRARY OF CONGRESS

Maj. Gen. Edward O. C. Ord

Maj. Gen. Philip H. Sheridan
LIBRARY OF CONGRESS

Maj. Gen. George Crook
LIBRARY OF CONGRESS

Brevet Maj. Gen. Wesley Merritt
LIBRARY OF CONGRESS

Brevet Maj. Gen. George A. Custer

Brevet Maj. Gen.
Henry E. Davies

Brig. Gen. Thomas C. Devin

LIBRARY OF CONGRESS

Brig. Gen. Alfred Gibbs

U.S. ARMY MILITARY HISTORY INSTITUTE

Brig. Gen. Ranald S. Mackenzie

LIBRARY OF CONGRESS

Brevet Brig. Gen. J. Irvin Gregg

Brevet Brig. Gen. Charles H. Smith

Brevet Brig. Gen. William Wells

Col. Charles E. Capehart

Col. Alexander C. M. Pennington (far right)

Col. Alanson M. Randol
LIBRARY OF CONGRESS

Sheridan's Arrival at Dinwiddie Court House
ROSSITER JOHNSON, CAMPFIRES AND BATTLEFIELDS

Entry of U. S. Forces into Richmond

LIBRARY OF CONGRESS

Attack of the V Corps at Five Forks

LIBRARY OF CONGRESS

Attack on Confederate Wagon Trains at Paineville

BATTLES AND LEADERS OF THE CIVIL WAR

Surrender of Ewell's Troops at Little Sailor's Creek

BATTLES AND LEADERS OF THE CIVIL WAR

High Bridge

Appomattox Station

with strategic value, claiming it had forced Lee to halt his retreat until the situation at High Bridge was under control, thus losing critical time on the march to Farmville. The record fails to support this contention, reducing the attempt to burn High Bridge to a heroic failure. Still, the episode is notable for the desperate quality of the fighting, which, as one historian put it, "resounded with echoes of medieval combat," and it did prevent the Confederate cavalry from taking part in the battle of Sailor's Creek.[11]

Chivalric or not, the struggle had taken the lives of many good men on both sides. Looking back years later, an unusually contemplative Tom Rosser lamented: "It would have been better to have allowed the enemy to capture us all and burn all the bridges in the country rather than to have thrown away such lives as Dearing's, Boston's, Thompson's [sic], and Knott's [Capt. John L. Knott of the 12th Virginia, a prominent member of the Laurel Brigade], for they died for no purpose . . . the cause was already lost!"[12]

But the cause still conferred benefits on those who served it faithfully and well, even those whose contributions had long been overlooked. Minutes after the shooting ceased, Tom Munford sent his adjutant and inspector general, Capt. Henry C. Lee, to make a verbal report of the day's action to the cavalry's commander, who happened to be the captain's older brother. When the aide returned, he informed Munford that Fitz Lee would see to it the colonel received his promotion forthwith. That night, just before Munford turned in, a courier from cavalry headquarters handed him a copy of an order, in Fitz's handwriting, announcing Munford's appointment as brigadier general. The action would have to win the consent of the Confederate Congress, which had fled Richmond, never to readjourn. Fitz nevertheless assured his long-suffering subordinate that official confirmation would come in due time.[13]

Phil Sheridan had told them so. Although he did not learn until late in the morning of the sixth that Lee had slipped Meade's trap, Little Phil had been right to regard the Rebels' flight as a *fait accompli*. When he wrote his memoirs, he took great satisfaction in recalling his own prescience and Meade's gullibility: "Satisfied that this [Lee's escape] would be the case, I did not permit the cavalry to participate in Meade's useless advance, but shifted it out toward the left to the road running from Deatonville to Rice's Station, Crook leading and Merritt close up." In the cavalry's rear came the VI Corps; General Wright's route of march lay roughly two miles below Robert E. Lee's. Meanwhile, the V Corps had followed Humphreys's troops to and then west of Amelia, directly in the fugitives' rear. Finally, Ord's and Gibbon's troops had left Burkeville at last and were moving toward Prince Edward Court House along a route four to five miles south of Sheridan's.[14]

Their mobility enabled the troopers to close with their prey more quickly than the infantry, but they lacked the power to force the Rebels to halt, except briefly. When the roads on which the opposing columns marched began to converge toward Deatonville, detachments from Crook's division ranged north to stab at the enemy's lower flank. They concentrated on discomfiting the troops guarding Anderson's supply train, near the shank of the enemy column (only Ewell's and Gordon's men were in line behind Anderson). Just before noon, Sheridan directed Crook to overhaul those vehicles. The brigades of Gregg and Smith forged ahead of the main body, continuing west until, at Pride's Church, they turned right and headed toward Deatonville. At Atkinson's place, about a mile and a half up the Pride's Church Road, Smith angled westward and soon encountered Anderson's supply train.

Reconnoitering, Gregg and Smith discovered that the enemy had observed their approach. They had built breastworks across the road, occupied by elements of Pickett's and Johnson's divisions. Smith deployed his command by placing the 1st Maine and 6th Ohio on the right of the road on which the train was traveling, the 13th Ohio on the left, and the 2nd New York Mounted Rifles in column in the rear. The dispositions were barely complete when Gregg showed his impulsiveness by launching a direct attack on Anderson's position, only to be repulsed, as Smith reported with evident satisfaction, "amidst considerable confusion."[15]

Smith advanced part of his line in support of his retreating comrades. After Lt. Col. Jonathan P. Cilley's 1st Maine passed through a thicket, "almost impassable to mounted men," two of its companies broke through to the train itself. Under the unexpected onslaught, the guards fell back in panic. But before the wagons could be captured, reinforcements hastened up and drove back the squadron with, as Smith admitted, "heavy loss." Smith was about to launch a second advance, in greater depth, when Crook ordered both brigades back to the column.[16]

Lee's train had been saved, if only temporarily. After the Federals rode off, Anderson got back on the road and hastened to overtake the command ahead of him, Mahone's division. This was a frustrating experience, since Anderson's pace was tied to that of the wagons. Then too, the distance he had to travel seemed constantly to be lengthening. Because Mahone had kept moving during Crook's attack, a gap of almost two miles had opened in the retreat column. If the enemy discovered and exploited the breach, the train would soon be under siege yet again.[17]

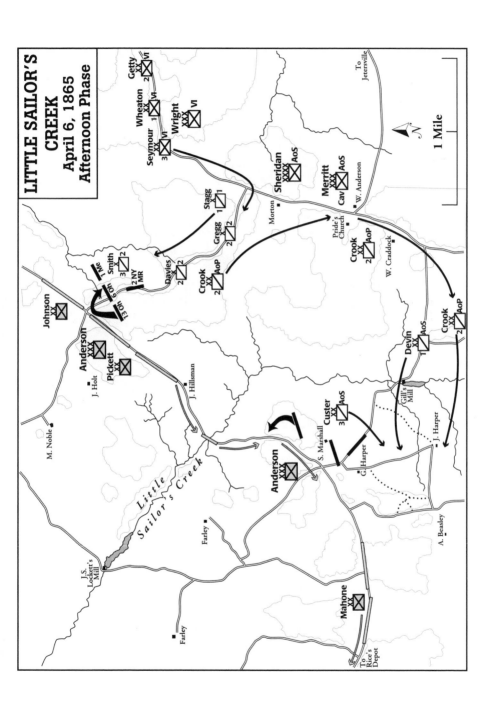

LITTLE SAILOR'S
CREEK
April 6, 1865
Afternoon Phase

Getty
2 ☒ VI

Wheaton
XX
Seymour 1 ☐ VI
3 ☒ VI Wright
XXX ☐ VI

Stagg
1 ☐

Gregg
2 ☐
2

Smith
X
3 ☐ 2
7 Me
1 ☐
Davies 6 Oh
2 ☐ 2 NY
MR
13 Oh

Sheridan
XXX AoS

Merritt
Cav ☒ AoS
W. Anderson

Johnson
XX ☒

Anderson
XX ☒

Pickett
XX ☒

Crook
XX
2 ☐ AoP

Morton

Pride's
Church

Crook
XX
2 ☐ AoP
W. Craddock

Crook
XX
2 ☐ AoP

Devin
1 ☒ AoS
Gill's
Mill

J. Holt

J. Hillsman

M. Noble

Custer
XX
3 ☒ AoS
S. Marshall
G. Harper

J. Harper

Anderson
XXX ☒

Little
Sailor's
Creek

Farley

J.S.
Lockett's
Mill

A. Beasley

Mahone
XX ☒
To
Rice's
Depot

Farley

To
Jetersville

1 Mile

When Gregg and Smith turned north at Pride's Church, Sheridan—who was about to leave the cavalry column to ride at the head of the VI Corps—had ordered Crook to continue west with Davies's brigade, followed closely by Merritt, Custer, and Devin. Past Pride's, the road jogged briefly to the south before angling west once again. It led the cavalry across Little Sailor's Creek at Gill's Mill, and toward Marshall's Crossroads. At Marshall's, the head of the mounted column was less than a mile from Lee's troops on the road to Rice's Station. Custer, who moved up to assume a position on the right flank, could clearly see the great expanse of open road between Mahone and Anderson. The division leader realized that he only needed to go forward to interpose between major segments of the enemy column.

Before Custer could exploit the opening, his scouts observed a Confederate artillery unit—it proved to be the slow-moving battalion of artillery attached to Longstreet's corps—try desperately to fill the void. Cannons in motion were an even more inviting target than supply wagons. With an Indian-style whoop, Custer's men charged down a ridge and into a little valley where the Rebel guns stood helpless. Before the pieces could be aimed or even loaded, the Yankees were in among them, cutting down their crews and the battery teams.

In mere minutes, Custer had seized ten guns. Soon, however, enough foot soldiers double-quicked from the rear to plug the gap and force Custer back. The boy general retreated in good spirits, not only because his men had taken so many coveted prizes, but also because he knew that with the rest of the Army of the Potomac coming up, a large portion of Lee's army might well be brought to bay. When that happened, Custer would be there.[18]

⸻⸻

Early in the afternoon, Fitz Lee ended his liaison duties and prepared to ride to High Bridge to rejoin Rosser and Munford. He had barely started out in company of his staff and escort, when he found he was going nowhere. Crossing Little Sailor's Creek in the general vicinity of Anderson's infantry, Fitz suddenly heard the sharp, slapping sound of carbine fire and realized that Sheridan's horsemen had struck at or near the head of the Confederate column.

Looking southward, Fitz witnessed the approach of Custer's division, its attack on Longstreet's artillery, and its repulse by Anderson. Then he saw numerous other troopers come up in Custer's rear and press Anderson's line as if cavalry attacking a major gathering of infantry were standard procedure. Fitz was impressed, but he waited impatiently for Anderson to clear the upstarts away. "I was detained there some time," he complained, "hoping an attack would be made to reopen the way." Eventually Anderson's men launched a countermovement, but then, for reasons beyond Fitz's imagination, they stopped, or were stopped.[19]

The nonplussed cavalryman turned about and, scanning the fields to the north, spied Ewell's vanguard coming down the road toward the creek. It occurred to him that the corps commander remained ignorant of the situation in his front, which, while apparently under control, would become a major problem if Union infantry came up behind the cavalry. Thus he rode to Ewell's side and informed him of Anderson's predicament and the gap that separated him from Mahone. Ewell, whose command preceded the larger supply train that served Lee's army, immediately shunted the wagons off to the north, via the Jamestown Road, where they appeared to be beyond the reach of the oncoming Yankees.[20]

Perhaps deliberately, or perhaps because Ewell failed to inform him of the change of route, John Brown Gordon, whose corps constituted Lee's rear guard, trailed the wagons up the Jamestown Road instead of halting to support Ewell. For much of the day, Gordon, his rear and flanks guarded by Rooney Lee's horsemen, had been fending off the slow but steady Federals of Andrew Humphreys. Recently it had begun to look as if Gordon had outrun his pursuers, but soon after turning onto the Jamestown Road, he was again hit in the rear, this time by Stagg's cavalry, which Sheridan had temporarily attached to the VI Corps. Until called south later in the afternoon, the Wolverines posed such a threat to the supply train and so discomfited Gordon that Sheridan erroneously assumed they were responsible for Gordon's divergence from the route followed by his comrades.[21]

Even when finally free of cavalry harassment, Gordon found that his troubles were not over. Well into evening, Humphreys's II Corps pressed the Confederate rear guard. Time and again Gordon's infantry and Rooney Lee's dismounted horsemen deployed behind whatever cover they could find and lashed the head of the pursuit force with musketry and carbine fire. While the Federals formed to meet each threat, the supply wagons kept moving westward. Successful stands were made at Vaughan's house, further west near Deatonville, and then along Sandy Creek.

As Gordon and Lee must have foreseen, any advantage they gained would be temporary. As evening approached, Humphreys shifted direction, reached the Jamestown Road, and began a more direct pursuit of the wagon train. The increased pace enabled the Yankees to overtake the wagons near Lockett's farm. Not far away, the supply vehicles had attempted to cross the double bridges near the confluence of Big and Little Sailor's Creeks, but the wagons had become bogged down in the muddy approach to the spans, "out of which," Gordon recalled, "the starved teams were unable to drag them." By now, as the corps commander reported, Lee's troopers "had been withdrawn to another portion of the line of march." Lacking mounted support, Gordon's men attempted to cover the wagons while their guards and drovers extricated them from the morass. Gordon maintained that his men repulsed two frontal assaults, but a third attack, which struck not only his front but also both of his flanks, drove the rear guard across the water in "considerable confusion."[22]

On the far bank, the Confederates were protected by carefully placed artillery. By now, however, they had suffered critical losses. Before the sun went down, Humphreys's men captured upwards of 1,700 Rebels as well as three cannons and as many as 300 of the wagons Gordon and, for a time, Rooney Lee had so desperately tried to protect.[23]

After sending the wagons on their way, Ewell, accompanied by Fitz Lee, moved his command across Little Sailor's Creek. On the north side, he deployed a small guard, including a detachment of "Company Q," the mythical unit to which all dismounted cavalry belonged. After crossing, Ewell left Fitz and conferred with Anderson as to how or whether they should team to oppose those feisty troopers near Marshall's Crossroads.

As the infantry generals conferred, Fitz Lee saw a new and more serious threat materialize to the northeast: "The enemy made his appearance in the rear of Ewell's column, necessitating the formation of another line of battle on Sailor's Creek." The newcomers, he quickly learned, were members of the VI Corps. Their approach forced the Confederates south of the stream to face in nearly opposite directions. Anderson's men, the wagon train in their rear, continued to face east against the Union horsemen. Ewell's men, meanwhile, turned about to confront the approach of Sheridan and Wright. When Merritt's horsemen, soon afterward, sidled southward onto terrain more favorable to mounted operations, the soldiers of Anderson and Ewell found themselves fighting back-to-back.[24]

<hr />

By the time the VI Corps advanced toward Ewell's position, it was almost 5:00. Sheridan and Wright spent another hour forming battle lines and running cannons forward to soften up the enemy position. With daylight fading, Sheridan decided to attack with the two divisions that had reached the field—those of Bvt. Maj. Gen. Frank Wheaton and Brig. Gen. Truman Seymour. He would not wait until Bvt. Maj. Gen. George W. Getty's division came on the field. The motley appearance of Ewell's command, and the lack of depth in its formation, told Little Phil that Getty would not be needed.

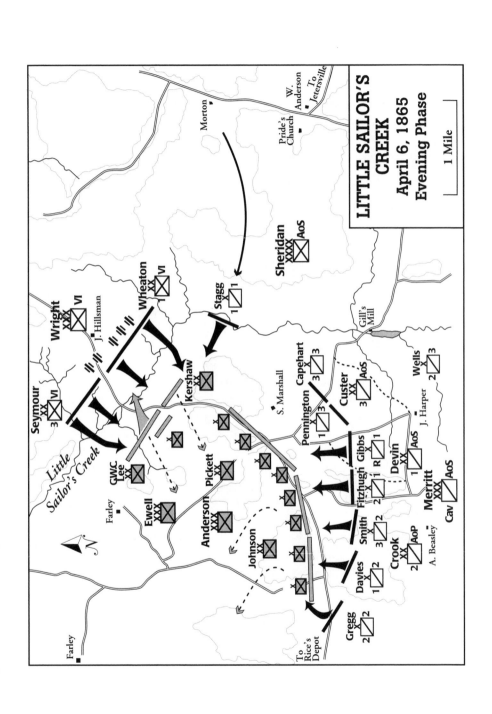

LITTLE SAILOR'S
CREEK
April 6, 1865
Evening Phase

1 Mile

W.
Anderson
To
Jetersville

Morton

Pride's
Church

Sheridan
XXX AoS

Stagg
1

Gill's
Mill

Wright
XXX VI

Wheaton
XX VI
1 VI

J. Hillsman

Seymour
XX 3 VI

Kershaw
XX

Capehart
X 3
3 3

Custer
XXX 3 AoS
3

Wells
X 3
2 3

Pennington
X 3
1 3

J. Harper

S. Marshall

Little
Sailor's Creek

GWC
Lee
XX

Pickett
XX

Fitzhugh
X
2

Gibbs
X 1 R 1
2 1

Devin
XX
1 AoS

Merritt
XXX AoS
Cav

Farley

Ewell
XXX

Anderson
XXX

Johnson
XX

Smith
X
2 3

Crook
XX
2 AoP

A. Beasley

Davies
X
1 2

Farley

To
Rice's
Depot

Gregg
X
2 2

While Sheridan readied his assault, Merritt, who, although more than a mile south of the VI Corps, kept in touch with his superior by courier, readied the cavalry, including (apparently by special arrangement) Crook's men, for an advance on Anderson's troops and wagons. Merritt deployed his line, facing north, with Crook's division on the left, two-thirds of Devin's in the center (Stagg remained detached), and two of Custer's brigades on the right. The only mounted force not on the field was Wells's brigade, which was reconnoitering near Amelia Court House.[25]

Wright's infantry, who finally went forward shortly after 6:00 P.M., rushed through the farmland north of Little Sailor's Creek, then splashed across the rain-swollen stream. The high water slowed the attack; by the time Seymour's and Wheaton's men reached the enemy's side, momentum appeared to have been lost. Seeing an opening, troops along Ewell's right, including heavy artillery units serving as infantry, counterattacked with surprising verve, forcing many of Wheaton's men back across the stream. Small wonder that Sheridan later called the day's fighting "one of the severest conflicts of the war, for the enemy fought with desperation to escape capture, and we, bent on his destruction, were no less eager and determined."[26]

Among the most eager and determined were the gun crews attached to the VI Corps. At a critical moment, they wheeled forward and laid a devastating fire on the Rebels, reducing Ewell's right to human kindling. Seymour's troops then struck the enemy's left, and Wheaton's, their stamina renewed, crushed the already-splintered right. Completing the double envelopment, Wheaton's men surged toward the center, surrounding their foe and cutting the retreat route toward Rice's Station. Ewell's defenders, fearful and frustrated, threw down their weapons and put up their hands. Some continued to hold their rifles high but by the barrel, a historic gesture of surrender. The impulse to capitulate became almost universal: Before the sun went down, almost 3,500 members of Ewell's corps had given up and been taken prisoner. The captives included Ewell, Custis Lee, Kershaw, and three other general officers.[27]

When Sheridan and the infantry went forward, so did the horsemen of the Armies of the Potomac and the Shenandoah. Like their comrades to the north, the troopers had to cross open ground—in this case, a field almost 1,000 yards long—to reach their objective. An attack of this depth, especially in the face of an entrenched force of veteran infantry, would have been beyond the capabilities—in fact, beyond the wildest dreams—of the Union cavalry of 1861–63. At this late date, however, it was simply another tactical exercise that must be executed if the war were to be won.

But it would have to be a cooperative effort between Custer's troopers on the right and Crook's farther west. Although precise timing was required, the advance began prematurely, to the detriment of Crook's 1st New Jersey. The culprit appears to have been General Davies, who placed the mounted regiment on open ground along Custer's left flank, while posting the rest of his brigade, unsaddled, in heavy underbrush farther to the left. At the outset, the Jerseymen suffered no casualties, for they deployed beyond effective rifle range of the enemy. Not long after they took up their position, however, Davies rode up to their commander, Major Robbins, and notified him to stand ready to move forward. As Robbins later recalled,

> I was informed by General Davies that the whole corps was to charge, so, when the bugle sounded, I moved my regiment forward on a walk, then gave the order to trot. Fortunately, however, noticing that Custer's command on my right had not moved, I looked and saw that the other regiments of our brigade had not stirred. The thought flashed across my mind that there must be a blunder somewhere; two lieutenants and many men were wounded, and horses were dropping fast. Forced to retire, I moved to the right and placed the regiment under an elevation of ground. Subsequently, we returned to our first position.[28]

There indeed had been a blunder; as Robbins later learned, Davies's order had been "rather premature." It was not the first time that the brigade leader had been guilty of a costly error. Robbins vividly remembered the mounted assault Davies had ordered the previous December against an artillery-studded fortification south of Petersburg, which had resulted in a severe repulse and numerous casualties in the ranks of the 1st Massachusetts. It appears that Robbins also blamed Davies for the April 5 death of the major's superior and friend, Hugh Janeway, whose detachment of the 1st New Jersey had been permitted to fight unsupported against larger numbers of the enemy at Paineville.[29]

Some time after Robbins's men aborted their attack, a properly coordinated assault got underway. The troopers of Crook and Custer struck with a power and spirit that carried everything in their path. Attacking dismounted against the Confederate right, Gregg's and Smith's brigades moved slowly but implacably forward, supported by elements of Davies's command that had not accompanied the 1st New Jersey on its errant advance. Looking on from the rear, Major Tremain described the result in breathless prose:

> A bugle sounded, and as bugle after bugle echoed "the charge" along that line of cavalry, there was one grand jump to conflict. All was dust and confusion; horses and men fell dead across the rebel works. Every firearm might have been discharged, but on one side all was

desperation, horror, and dismay, while on the other, confidence, enthusiasm, and victory. The rebel line was gone, and squads, companies, and regiments were flying over the hills. Horsemen were among them, and turned them back with empty arms as prisoners. Others more quickly sought for safety, by waving the white flag of surrender. Troopers in blue rode fearlessly and carelessly among a motley mob in gray, and received their unceremonious surrender.[30]

General Davies called the combined assault, which gained his men a foothold on the strategic road to Rice's Station, "one of the finest charges of the war, [the men] riding over and capturing their works and its defenders." According to Davies, the attack resulted in the capture of scores of prisoners and 300 to 400 supply wagons. He brought off the haul without "losing one prisoner, animal, or gun, in spite of the desperate efforts of the enemy to retake them."[31]

On the other side of the field, Pennington's brigade of Custer's division attacked on horseback, breaking though to another section of Anderson's train, but only after overcoming several repulses. Sergeant Hannaford of the 2nd Ohio recalled that the division's first efforts melted away under the fire of Anderson's artillery:

The main road we had been moving on & the road the train was on was [were] about a mile apart[,] having two deep ravines between them. . . . Before we reached the 2nd ravine the shell was flying over our head. . . . By this time [those at] the head of the column were in a terrible confusion jamming, turning twisting & trying to get out. . . . If at this time the enemy had had only a good Co. of Cav. to dash at us, we would have been back with our artillery in two minutes.[32]

But Anderson had no cavalry support, and Custer's subordinates managed to halt the charging troops before the division could be decimated. They ordered the men to shift toward a more lightly guarded portion of the train. Hannaford noted:

This was done & our Regt. took off thro the fields on our left on the gallop gradually making for the train, yelling like Indians. This was the salvation of the whole movement . . . for we soon flanked the train guard who had been hastily drawn up in line to oppose us. This done we came on the wagon train where there was not a single guard.

. . . Most of the drivers jumped off and ran away on our approach, or ran toward us swinging their hats in token of surrender.[33]

Custer's success was abetted by a series of hard-hitting attacks against Kershaw's brigade, on the far Confederate left, by Stagg's Wolverines, who, supported by Miller's Battery C/E, 4th Artillery, had gone into position between Custer and Wheaton. The critical blow against the Confederate left was delivered, however, by the unflinching West Virginians of Capehart's brigade, who advanced on horseback against a more heavily defended sector than Pennington had struck. Sergeant Hannaford stared in awe as Capehart's men "came on in double line . . . at right angles to the rebel line[,] lapping far in their rear. The fire [they received] as they neared the rebel line was terrific[,] opening gaps in their lines but if a horse was shot & the rider unhurt he would jump up . . . firing as he went."[34]

At first the Southern unionists advanced at "a slow walk," their celebrated horses maintaining near-perfect alignment despite the rifle balls and shell fragments whipping past them:

Forward they move[,] never once checking, not even wavering, pouring in their deadly fire as they go. At last when almost to the enemy's line, the word is given to charge & like a bullet . . . they are away & into & over the rebel breastwork with a rousing cheer, in which [fight] we now join for the first [time], for we had been spell bound with admiration at their coolness & bravery & splendid discipline.[35]

Devin, leapfrogging around Custer's left flank, also provided substantial assistance to the 3rd Division. In fact, Devin claimed to have twice rescued Custer's men from danger brought on by their leader's habit of attacking without first testing the opposition. By riding over sections of the enemy's works, as they had at Five Forks, Devin's men helped Custer's crush the left and left center of the enemy line. In the end, most of Pickett's and Johnson's men emulated the comrades in their immediate rear, discarding their weapons and either running for the woods along the creek or remaining in place, arms raised. Fewer Rebels surrendered to Merritt's men than to Wright's, but they included two of Pickett's most capable subordinates, Generals Corse and Hunton. All told, 6,000 Confederates fell into the hands of their enemy this day, perhaps the darkest in the annals of the Army of Northern Virginia.[36]

So it appeared, at least, to the man at the top. Toward the close of the fighting, as Anderson's beaten troops fled across Big Sailor's Creek, Robert E. Lee, in company with William Mahone, rode up from Rice's Station to survey the damage from a hill beside the stream. The scenes that met his eyes—scenes not only of defeat, but of wholesale demoralization—shook his mind and heart. As the mob of refugees raced past him, none showing the least inclination to rally and fight again, Lee could not stop himself from exclaiming: "My God! Has the army been dissolved?"[37]

His fighting blood up, Wesley Merritt wished to follow the victory with a devastating pursuit of what remained of the foe. Leaving Custer and Crook to gather up spoils and corral prisoners, the corps commander led Devin's division out the road to Rice's Station, which now teemed with Rebel stragglers, many of them eager to be taken captive and be treated to their first full meal in what seemed like months. Under the moonlight, the Federals pressed on toward the tracks of the South Side Railroad until, some miles from the battlefield, they struck Mahone's division. The Rebel infantry had hunkered down to turn back any pursuers. In addition to well-prepared fieldworks, they had artillery to sweep the road on which the cavalry was advancing.

Merritt, unwilling to be cowed, and determined to avoid looking as if he were, made a vigorous attempt to cross the stream despite the opposition. The predictable result, as reported by Devin, was "a heavy fire of musketry, shell, and canister at short range." The effort made, his honor upheld, Merritt decided to desist until dawn's early light.[38]

Another reason for his fall-back was the lack of cooperation he received from the Army of the James, which late in the day reached the outskirts of Rice's Station to challenge Longstreet's troops. Had General Ord put sufficient pressure on the entrenched enemy, he might have forced Mahone's recall from Merritt's front. So, at any rate, Merritt argued in his post-campaign report, complaining that "the Army of the James was not operating with vigor against the enemy." He may have had a point, for in his own report, Ord could not explain why he had failed to press Longstreet, commenting only that his "column was developed, skirmishers moving up when night came on. That night they [Longstreet's men] again broke for Lynchburg." Instead of mounting a strong pursuit, Ord made plans to continue the fight the following day after his army reached Farmville. Lacking support, Merritt broke contact with Mahone and withdrew a mile to the east, where, at about midnight, he put Devin's tired but exhilarated troopers into bivouac.[39]

As the sun went down over High Bridge, burial details combed the littered plain, while surgeons worked by lamplight to minister to the wounded on both sides, and chaplains tried to comfort the dying. Meanwhile, Munford's cavalry—principally the men of Wooldridge's brigade—occupied the local defenses, those the Virginia Reserves had built months earlier as well as those the Yankees had thrown up that afternoon. Members of Beale's brigade continued to round up prisoners, while comrades prepared to escort those already in tow to prison in Lynchburg, forty-five miles away. Some of Rosser's troopers, aware that Meade's and Ord's commands were not far off, picketed the roads that came in from the east and south. With the better part of his division, Rosser started back to Rice's Station to assist Longstreet against Ord. Before the horsemen reached the depot, however, the Army of the James had ended its operations for the night.[40]

Lee, at Rice's, refused to wait for the Yankees to renew their assault in the morning, especially since Meade might also be up by then. He ordered Longstreet, with the divisions of Mahone (which now included the remnants of Anderson's broken command), Heth, Wilcox, and Field, to move in the dark up the railroad to Farmville, where the lure of waiting rations continued to energize tired soldiers. Robert E. Lee's energy, however, must have flagged when he reflected that these commands, plus the three divisions of John B. Gordon, which had assimilated what remained of Ewell's troops, were all that remained of his infantry. One-fifth of the army had been left on the field of Sailor's Creek, either as captives or corpses.[41]

Not everyone under Lee was privy to the grim details of Anderson's and Ewell's defeat. In fact, many soldiers heard nothing about Sailor's Creek until late that evening. One who remained ignorant for several hours after the battle was Edward Boykin of the 7th South Carolina, who knew only "that there was heavy fighting, and that being a matter of course, excited no surprise."[42]

Boykin was one of 300 troopers under Martin Gary whom Longstreet had belatedly dispatched to join Munford and Rosser at High Bridge. They had not arrived in time to take part in the fighting, due not only to the lateness of their departure, but also to the condition of their mounts. "We had been having a very tiresome march on our worn-out horses," Boykin recalled, "through the fields on the side of the road, giving up the road proper to the wagon trains and [foot] troops, sometimes dismounting and leading our horses, to relieve them as much as possible."[43]

When Gary's men finally reached High Bridge, they kept moving, crossing the imposing structure and on the far side taking the road to Farmville. They reached that village with the self-descriptive name after dark, although apparently they did not partake of the rations waiting there. They did, however, overtake a broken-down commissary wagon, which, although picked over, still contained some edibles. The troopers filled their haversacks "with whatever they could find; and whatever they got, either in this way or at the country houses, was liberally shared with their friends and officers."[44]

Gary's men may not have been hungry when they bedded down that night, but they knew other discomforts. They were now in Virginia's hill country, where nights were cold and fires a necessity. Whenever the wind-blown flames died out, as they did several times that night, Boykin, who had bedded down beside Colonel Haskell, had to build up the fire. "At one of these movements," he recalled, "we were surprised to find . . . two men, who, attracted by the fire, cold and tired, had crept to its friendly warmth, making a needless apology for their presence. We found one to be a colonel of Pickett's division, the other a lieutenant." The uninvited guests, especially the colonel, made Boykin and his superior realize fully "how complete the destruction of that famous fighting division must have been as an organization, that we should find a regimental commander who did not know where to look for its standard." That told Boykin all he needed to know about the outcome of the fighting along Sailor's Creek.[45]

Back on that sanguinary battlefield, Phil Sheridan scrawled a message to be delivered to Grant, again traveling with Ord's column. Little Phil briefly described the great victory, enumerated some of his captures ("several thousand prisoners, 14 pieces of artillery, with caissons, and a large number of wagons"), and stressed that his men continued to hunt down those few Rebels who had escaped. He closed with a plea for better support by Meade and Ord and for an energetic pursuit toward Farmville: "If the thing is pressed I think that Lee will surrender."[46]

Grant forwarded a copy of Sheridan's message to City Point, where he knew it would be received as favorably as it had at his headquarters. The next morning, Abraham Lincoln replied by telegraph: "Let the thing be pressed."[47]

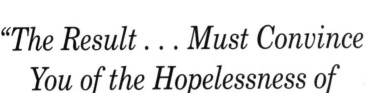

TEN

"The Result ... Must Convince You of the Hopelessness of Further Resistance"

THE HEAD OF LONGSTREET'S DIVISION REACHED THE OUTSKIRTS OF FARM-ville at about 9:00 A.M. on the seventh. At once the men were marched to the north side of the Appomattox, and there, on the ridges overlooking the town, they partook of a full meal for the first time since leaving Petersburg and Bermuda Hundred. Longstreet's column, preceded by Rooney Lee's horse-men, passed in turn before the commissary wagons, where each soldier re-ceived a small helping of meat and an equally small ration of hard bread.[1]

While officers and men quieted their week-long hunger pangs, Lee con-ferred with his ranking subordinates and made plans to continue the retreat. By now he had come to doubt the efficacy of striking south toward the R & D, a movement likely to be intercepted by the hard-marching troops of Meade and Ord. Instead, he would follow the South Side Railroad toward Campbell Court House, near Lynchburg. In that town were stored major quantities of the resources his troops needed, not the least important being another 180,000 prepared rations. But because Lee intended to turn south be-fore reaching Lynchburg, the rations would have to be sent to him elsewhere.

One of the factors on which the army's escape appeared to depend was the destruction of several bridges once the rear guard had crossed them. Their de-molition would force Grant to rebuild the structures or replace them with a pontoon train that may not have kept up with the fast-moving Federals. Either result would double or treble the distance between Lee and his pursuers. Lee assigned a trusted lieutenant, Billy Mahone, to burn both the railroad span and the adjacent wagon deck. Once the army had departed Farmville, it would burn two other bridges—one a railroad trestle, the other a foot and wagon span—that crossed the Appomattox north of town.[2]

Despite the precise instructions Lee issued before departing Farmville early in the afternoon of the seventh, only High Bridge was fired correctly. Through a mix-up between Mahone and the army's engineers, the wagon span was set afire too late to prevent the nearest pursuers, Bvt. Maj. Gen. Francis C. Barlow's division of Humphreys's corps, from extinguishing the flames while simultaneously exchanging rifle fire with the Confederates who had just crossed. The II Corps then prevented Mahone's men from retaking the bridge and again trying to destroy it. Humphreys's troops crossed upon the charred but intact structure and proceeded toward Farmville. On the way, they confiscated a huge cache of ordnance that had been stored in forts on the southeast side of the river.[3]

Barlow's success at firefighting opened the way for the rest of the corps, as well as Wright's men, to cross the Appomattox. Some of these troops got over by way of the wagon span, others via a pontoon bridge that, despite Lee's hopes, was quickly laid adjacent to the burned structure. Their crossing deprived the Confederates of the rest they sorely needed, which they had hoped to enjoy in Farmville. It forced them to depart hastily over roads leading north to Cumberland Church, then west toward Concord Church and New Store. The abruptness of their leave-taking dealt a particularly cruel blow to the troops at the rear of the column. Only the vision of ample rations had kept them moving to Farmville; now they found the meat and bread virtually snatched from their mouths. Before being able to feed everyone, General St. John had to move the trains west of Farmville to prevent their capture.[4]

Whereas the wagon bridge had been fired too late, the bridges north of Farmville were set ablaze prematurely. The flames stymied the Yankees but also cut off most of Munford's and Rosser's troopers and exposed them to capture en masse. Munford's men had been moving toward Farmville by marching up the line of the South Side Railroad. On their right, Rosser's division, the other half of the rear guard, was moving up a parallel road. The rear guards of both columns were exchanging fire with the horsemen of George Crook, who had been pressing them in flank and rear since daylight.

According to Munford, as soon as he and Rosser crossed the bridges north of town, the inflammable materials that had been piled on them were to have been ignited by the commander of Munford's rear echelon, Maj. Daniel A. Grimsley of the 6th Virginia, a member of what had been Payne's brigade, then Boston's, and now Col. William A. Morgan's (the colonel, commander of the 1st Virginia, had been transferred from Wooldridge's brigade). Munford also claimed that after the leading brigade of his division crossed the span, one of Wooldridge's subordinates usurped Grimsley's authority by lighting the combustibles. Apparently the officer mistook Rosser's approaching troopers for the Yankees known to be vigorously pressing the army's rear.

The fire spread rapidly, preventing not only Rosser but also Morgan from using either the railroad or the wagon bridge. Both forces were obliged to seek crossing points farther upstream. Rosser managed to find a ford about two miles above the blazing span, where he crossed the high-rising river with some difficulty. Munford led Morgan's men to a bridge still standing above the town, which overlooked the road to Cumberland Court House. Morgan's crossing was "somewhat sheltered" by the guns of Lt. Col. William T. Poague's battery, which unlimbered on the far side of the Appomattox and shelled Crook's approaching troopers. Even with artillery support, the crossing, especially in Rosser's sector, was a hazardous operation. And when men and mounts struggled onto dry ground, they found their ordeal far from over.[5]

All morning long, Munford recalled, "General Crook's Cavalry were closely upon our trail. We were compelled to dismount and be on the <u>qui vive</u>." Now, when Munford's men ascended the north bank of the Appomattox, "we saw the 21st Va. Cavalry, of Rosser's command (Colonel W. E. Peters) fighting with Crook's cavalry in the town of Farmville." By some stratagem, the Yankees had gotten ahead of them. From that position, they might bring the retreat to a screeching halt—something that Munford and his colleagues would have to fight vigorously, if not desperately, to prevent.[6]

When Longstreet left Rice's Station for Farmville after dark on the sixth, Sheridan sent Crook's division, followed by the VI Corps, to tail him. Grant had now divided his forces into three columns. The northernmost consisted of Humphreys's infantry corps, which operated off the enemy's right flank via the High Bridge Road. Crook, trailed not only by Wright's infantrymen but also by Ord's, took the middle route, directly in Lee's rear. Merritt's horsemen, Sheridan again at their head, had been sent to operate farther south, via Prince Edward Court House, with the V Corps in their rear. In their new position off Lee's left flank, the troopers of Devin and Custer would end any lingering possibility that Lee might turn south and make a break for North Carolina.[7]

Crook's horsemen responded to Grant's instructions with a close, aggressive pursuit, striking the end of Longstreet's column, especially the cavalry guarding it, at every opportunity. Apparently the blows fell hardest on Munford's division, for years later its commander vividly recalled the pain they caused. For his part, Rosser remembered only that "the enemy pursued us slowly and nothing more than skirmishing at long range was engaged in . . . until we reached Farmville."[8]

Crook's men were spurred on by the sights they witnessed on the road to Farmville, sights that revealed an enemy on the verge of dissolution. The historian of the 1st Maine beheld

> all sorts of munitions of war laying around in loose profusion,—a dead rebel soldier lying on the road where he halted his last time, with every appearance of having died from hunger and exhaustion,— dead horses, the infallible army guideboards, lying where they dropped, and others abandoned because unable longer to carry their riders,—all informed the men that the men ahead of them were in a great hurry. . . . [this] had an exhilarating effect upon their spirits.[9]

Another welcome sight was the abundance of provisions available on all sides. Like their enemy, the Federals had outdistanced their commissary wagons, and as Crook himself recalled, they "had to subsist chiefly on the country." Unlike the pursued, the pursuers were not pushed along from place to place so rapidly that they lacked the time to forage; nor did they share their enemy's reluctance to empty the corncribs and chicken coops of Virginians. Crook's men rode with "provisions tied to their saddles. Some would have a ham, others chickens, ducks, geese, turkeys . . . fowls with their legs tied, and sticking their heads up, struggling to get loose. The whole presented a most ludicrous spectacle."[10]

The heaviest skirmishing during the morning occurred when the Confederates crossed Bush River (the Yankees called it "Briery Creek"), just east of Farmville. There, although the men of Munford and Rosser offered "considerable resistance," Smith's brigade, the 13th Ohio in the lead, pushed across the water. Under a covering fire from the Henry rifles of the 1st Maine, the Ohioans shoved the Rebels down the road toward town. But not every Confederate took off running. When Smith dispatched a courier with orders to stop the Ohioans and have them fall back and regroup, the man rode up to what he supposed was the regiment and "presented the compliments of the general commanding, with orders to halt." The troopers who halted—more from astonishment than anything else—turned out to be members of Rosser's division; the uniforms of both cavalries had become so begrimed they were unidentifiable beyond close range. Smith noted gravely that the messenger "did not report the execution of this order" until released by the enemy two days later.[11]

From Bush River, Smith's men, leading Crook's column, pushed on and entered what one member of the division called "the flourishing little village of Farmville." At this time, Lee's army had massed on Cumberland Heights, north of the town, preparatory to starting westward along the north bank of the Appomattox. Smith's troopers secured the town, in which they lingered until the brigades of Davies and Gregg came up to join them. Everyone was on the scene by 1:00 P.M.; soon afterward, Crook led them to the now-bridgeless river. His scouts had located a ford northwest of town, where the horsemen sloshed their way across. When the operation ended, the re-formed column, Irvin Gregg's men now in the lead, passed up the plank road that led to Buckingham Court House.[12]

By moving north, Crook's men encountered Barlow's division of the II Corps on its northern track. Humphreys's men were also closing in on Lee's rear, the infantry portion of which was concentrating near Cumberland Church, where Lee planned to make a stand. At about 1:00 P.M., the II Corps came up to challenge the enemy, and a general fight broke out. The fighting was heaviest toward the Confederate left, held by Mahone's division with the support of Rooney Lee's troopers, augmented by the 2nd Virginia of Munford's division. The troopers were under overall command of Fitz Lee, one of only four corps and division commanders to have escaped capture at Sailor's Creek (the others being Anderson, Johnson, and Pickett, each of whom, his command broken up, would be stripped of his position before the campaign ended).

Humphreys, unaware that the bridges north of Farmville had been destroyed, believed that other elements of Meade's army had crossed there and were now in position to strike the Rebel rear while he attacked from the other side. When the corps commander heard heavy firing coming from the general direction of the Rebel rear, he supposed it the work of Wright's corps, attacking in concert with him. Accordingly, Humphreys struck the left, only to be thrown back with heavy loss.[13]

Historians believe that the firing Humphreys took as a signal to attack had been generated not by Wright's foot soldiers, but by Crook's cavalry, which had attacked a wagon train on the Buckingham Court House Road. Late that afternoon, Gregg's brigade, still leading Crook's column, spied a large body of horsemen—members of Rosser's command—near an intersection beside a colliery southwest of Cumberland Church. The Rebels appeared to be loping along, as if unaware of Crook's proximity. This was enough to spur Gregg into action, but then his scouts spied a section of R. E. Lee's supply train moving in Rosser's midst—the wagons would account for the cavalry's slowness. Gregg placed himself at the head of Col. Samuel B. M. Young's

4th Pennsylvania, and without waiting for the rest of the brigade to form behind him, started the 4th toward the wagons at an extended gallop. Young's
men began whooping and hollering, as if a fearsome noise would stop the
train in its tracks.[14]

Unbeknownst to Gregg, he was being led into a trap. This was not, however, the culmination of careful planning on the enemy's part. In later years,
Munford and Rosser offered contradictory versions of how the trap had been
set. Munford recalled that after Gregg attacked Rosser, Munford's men came
to the rescue in such a way as to pincer the 4th Pennsylvania. Rosser, of
course, argued that he, not Munford, had saved the day by attacking Gregg in
flank. Munford's claim appears to have more validity, and there is more than a
hint of truth in his lament that Rosser's version of events was another example
of a "chronic" propensity to warp truth and rewrite history.[15]

The facts of the case are fairly straightforward. Just before Gregg, at about
4:30 P.M., spurred his Pennsylvanians forward, Munford's division had again
been marching parallel to Rosser's. Just before the Yankees came on the scene,
however, the command had turned southward, where shielded from view by a
ridge. There Munford was in an excellent position to strike the enemy's left as
they charged past, and he did not let the opportunity go by. With a shout at
least as loud and as sustained as their opponents', Munford's men galloped
back up the road. As they passed, they spied, alongside the road, Robert E. Lee
astride Traveller. "We cheered him," one trooper recalled, "and he gravely lifted
his hat in acknowledgment of our greeting. I believe, if Grant's whole army had
been there then, they could not have reached or harmed that grey head as long
as one of those cavalry boys lived to raise a sabre or handle a pistol."[16]

Munford's riders were still accelerating when they crashed into the flank
and rear of Young's regiment. The bone-jarring impact lifted men on both
sides out of the saddle and bowled over horses. When the chaos subsided, a
shooting and hacking contest broke out along the length of the narrow, fence-
lined road. The fences served as a net for bagging Yankees, almost thirty of
whom were hemmed in and taken prisoner. Eleven others were killed, more
than thirty wounded. Most of the remainder, including Young, managed to
cut a path to safety. Not so fortunate was Gregg, who, with at least one member of his staff, was captured. According to some accounts, the general was
bagged by Lt. Col. "Lige" White of the 35th Virginia Battalion, Rosser's division, who had succeeded to command of the Laurel Brigade upon Dearing's
wounding at High Bridge.[17]

Another who claimed the honor of capturing Gregg was an officer in the
Washington Artillery of New Orleans, a member of the train guard. This man,
who interviewed the brevet brigadier, described him as "quite chagrined" and

quoted him as saying "he had thought he would have had an easy time of it destroying our moving trains, and had not expected to run into the jaws of a whole park of artillery." The cannoneer surmised that "it was fortunate that we were there just in the nick of time, for had Gregg obtained possession of the road, he stood a good chance of cutting off Gen. Lee and staff and capturing them."[18]

Young's repulse and Gregg's capture marked the last fighting Rosser and Munford saw this day; in fact, as Rosser observed, they "were not further annoyed by the enemy" over the next two days. One reason was that shortly after the 4th Pennsylvania's repulse, Fitz Lee came down from Cumberland Church at the head of his cousin's division to build a formidable line of works across the road on which the wagons continued to roll. Most of the army's cavalry occupied those defenses throughout the night.[19]

As if brought up short by this display, Crook prepared to withdraw rather than try to liberate his captured subordinate. His action surprised the enemy; as one of Rosser's men remarked sarcastically, "We presumed that [the rest of] Gregg's men, supposed to be thrice our number, would have returned to the rescue of their gallant commander, who refused to run away from about 400 half-starved, worn-out Confederates, but they decided to look after their supper."[20]

In fact, Crook withdrew in response to an order from Sheridan, who had decided that their quarry should be stalked from the flank, not from the rear. Thus, when the last of Young's fugitives had safely rejoined him, Crook led the entire division back to Farmville. On the village outskirts, he turned sharply west and rode eight miles along the South Side Railroad, halting for the night near Prospect Station. His men had had a hard day, culminating in what Major Bell called a "bad old fight." That fight had left a rancid taste in the mouth of every member of the division, one they took to bed with them. It is doubtful that Crook and his troopers would have felt any less disheartened had they known their opponents' success this day would be the last they would ever savor.[21]

Munford's and Rosser's triumph had left their highest-ranking spectator in an enthusiastic mood. When Rooney Lee's division reached the field at the close of the fracas, Robert E. Lee conversed briefly with his second son. Among other things, he praised the pluck and fighting spirit of his horsemen, which, especially in light of the army's recent trials, he found most gratifying. Then the elder Lee added a comment that jarred the ears of the eavesdropping John

Esten Cooke: "Keep your command together and in good spirits. Don't let them think of surrender. I will get you out of this."[22]

Cooke reflected that it was the first time he had heard anyone in authority refer to surrendering. And it had come from Marse Robert himself.

Lee was not the only one of high station to consider his army's capitulation, however indirectly. Grant, who late that morning had entered Farmville in the company of Ord and Gibbon, believed that, Lee having failed to prevent his pursuers from crossing the Appomattox, there was no escape for the Army of Northern Virginia. Early that evening, he opened communication with his adversary, sending through the lines a letter calling on Lee to acknowledge that "the result of the last week must convince you of the hopelessness of further resistance."[23]

The Confederate commander returned a polite refusal of Grant's request, which was received the following morning. But although he did not share Grant's appraisal of his army's situation, Lee did inquire of the terms the Union general would offer "on condition of its surrender." Grant replied with a single stipulation: that every member of Lee's command be "disqualified for taking up arms against the Government of the United States until properly exchanged." Grant further offered to meet Lee or his emissary, "at any point agreeable" to the Confederate commander for the purpose of arranging surrender terms.[24]

Into the afternoon of the seventh, while Crook pressed the rear of Lee's column and was pressed by it, the cavalry riding with Phil Sheridan and Wesley Merritt—the divisions of Devin and Custer—rode rather than fought. Through much of the day, as they trotted westward from Big Sailor's Creek, Sheridan believed they were fulfilling a mission integral to the success of Grant's strategy: the blocking of Lee's escape route to the south. By midday, however, he had begun to suspect that the action was moving away from him, that he should be somewhere else than where he was. Thus when, at about 4:00 P.M., he reached Prince Edward Court House and found Mackenzie's troopers there, he sent the horsemen of the Army of the James across Buffalo Creek, then north to Prospect Station to join Crook in hunting for the enemy in that locality.[25]

Sheridan was not the only cavalryman who feared that he was being misused or misdirected. After reporting to Ord's headquarters at Burkeville Junction on the sixth, Mackenzie and his men had accompanied their army to High Bridge on the heels of Read and Washburn. En route, the division engaged in nothing beyond scouting, foraging, and accepting the surrender of Confederate stragglers. Only after Grant's headquarters ordered Mackenzie to Prince Edward Court House did the pace of events pick up. Reaching the village at about 3:00 P.M., Mackenzie found a sizable force of gray cavalry loitering nearby. The enemy was "promptly charged, and driven through the town, leaving behind thirty-eight prisoners." Then Mackenzie awaited Sheridan's arrival. As soon as Little Phil appeared and gave him his orders, Mackenzie was off again at high speed, this time to Prospect Station.[26]

After he rode off, Sheridan conferred with Merritt, Custer, and Devin as to their future course. During the confab, a courier from Crook rode up with word that the Rebels had left Farmville and had crossed to the north side of the Appomattox. The news made the pursuers wonder if Lee was no longer considering an end run into North Carolina, but was heading for Lynchburg. At once Sheridan returned Merritt's men to the saddle and had them follow Mackenzie to Buffalo Creek. The two columns would unite, at or in advance of Prospect Station. At the depot, they would join Crook's division for a movement west in full force.

Sheridan would receive a certain amount of criticism for having so long pursued a path far removed from Lee's route of march; yet he had good reasons for doing so. Ever attuned to the thinking of the commanding general, he was aware of Grant's concern that even at this late date Lee might turn toward Danville, giving his pursuers the slip, just as Longstreet "had slipped away already from General Ord's troops at Rice's Station." The lieutenant general was trying to sift through conflicting intelligence from scouts and local Unionists on Lee's heading and intentions. Some of Grant's informants had the Rebels moving directly or by a roundabout route to Danville. Major Tremain later speculated that these observers had misidentified hordes of stragglers moving south as members of Lee's column. In any case, Grant advised Sheridan of the many reports that Lee "will strive [to head] south by roads farther up river" from Farmville. It was only natural that Little Phil not only gave these rumors credence, but also acted upon them.[27]

Even those who criticized Sheridan for being out of position admitted that it turned out for the best. By pursuing the route he did, he placed the cavalry in the right location—south of the Appomattox—to prevent Lee from turning toward North Carolina. Below the river, not only did Sheridan have

the shorter route to Appomattox Station, Lee's probable near-term destination, but his horsemen could also operate free from hindrance by slow-moving infantry. Only Ord's and Griffin's commands now marched south of the
Appomattox; they would remain in the cavalry's rear until Sheridan needed
them.

According to Tremain, Mackenzie's men reached Prospect Station not
only before Merritt, Devin, and Custer, but also before Crook. The little division rode in sometime after midnight on the eighth. When Crook's men arrived half an hour later, the horsemen of the Army of the James were already
reconnoitering up the railroad, a reflection of the energetic, get-things-done
attitude of their leader. A nighttime reconnaissance was not the *modus
operandi* of the Union cavalry, but it was a necessary response to Lee's decision
to pull out of Cumberland Church under cover of darkness. In a desperate attempt to push ahead of his enemy, the Confederate commander was forcing
his troops to make their third night march in a row. Mackenzie encountered
none of these troops, however, on his scouting mission. Meanwhile, Merritt
got only as far as Buffalo Creek, four miles from Prospect Station, before
Sheridan halted him for the night. The next morning, the eighth, he joined
Crook at the depot.[28]

In their recent travels, neither Crook nor Mackenzie had turned up signs
that Lee planned to recross the Appomattox. The Confederates appeared to
be hugging the north bank near the point at which the river branched off into
numerous tributaries, most of which were easily fordable. If it continued
along this route, Lee's army would strike the meandering South Side in the
vicinity of Appomattox Station, three miles southwest of Appomattox Court
House. Accordingly, the Federals turned in that direction. On the way west,
Sheridan attached Mackenzie's men to Crook's command. Crook took a close
look at Mackenzie's small division and pronounced it a large brigade. It would
remain so for the duration of the campaign.[29]

The consolidated command had barely left Prospect Station, Merritt's
men moving west by north toward Walker's Church, Crook's toward Pamplin's Depot on the railroad, when a horseman galloped up to the head of the
column and asked for Sheridan. The point riders were startled by the newcomer's gray uniform, but Little Phil immediately recognized him as Sgt.
James White, one of Major Young's scouts. White reined in his foam-flecked
horse, saluted in haste, and even as he tried to catch his breath, delivered some
startling news.

The sergeant had come from deep inside enemy territory, where he had
spent the morning. Some miles beyond Appomattox Station, he had seen several trains packed with Confederate rations "feeling their way" up the South

Side line. It was obvious to White that the train crew was seeking Lee's army, or what remained of it, but had no firm idea of its location. The sergeant still carried a copy of the captured telegram that Lee had addressed to the commissary officers at Danville and Lynchburg. With the document in hand, he flagged down the lead train and, by impersonating a member of General St. John's staff (White affected a more than passable Southern accent), he persuaded its crew to proceed to Appomattox Station, where, he insisted, Lee's famished troops were heading. White believed that depot to be far from Lee's line of march, but within reach of Sheridan's horsemen. Fearing that the trainmen would discover his ruse if no one was at the depot to claim the provisions, White, as soon as he was out of sight of the train, had galloped off, looking for Sheridan.[30]

Sheridan knew that Harry Young trusted the sergeant's veracity and judgment, and he was prepared to do the same. But he did not have to, for minutes after White reached him, Young's chief scout, who had observed the arrival of two of the supply trains at Appomattox Station, rode up to confirm the sergeant's story. Minutes later, everyone in the mounted column was racing toward the station, fourteen miles away, Custer's men on the main road, Devin's and Crook's on the flanks. Their leader urged them on in exultant tones. As long as he had a hand in its demise, Little Phil did not care if Lee's army died of starvation instead of combat casualties.[31]

For the infantry of the Army of the James, thus far this campaign, like so many that had gone before, had been a vast disappointment. Its officers and men had been gratified and even honored to be included in Grant's plans to bring to heel the Confederacy's main army. They had begun the movement in fine style, wresting from their defenders the breastworks that lined Hatcher's Run, then, at great cost, capturing the forts that anchored Petersburg's intermediate defenses, a feat that effectively doomed the city. In succeeding days, however, they had been given precious little to do, at least nothing of evident value.

Changes in Grant's strategy had deprived the army of a chance to capture the interior of Petersburg via a climactic assault. When the pursuit of Lee commenced, the command had been left in a mostly inactive sector. While the II, V, and VI Corps and Sheridan's horsemen had dogged Lee's heels, lashed his flanks, forced him to abandon position after position, and denied him rest and food, the men of the XXIV and XXV Corps had been reduced to sealing off an escape route that Lee had not availed himself of. Not counting the suicide mission on which Read and Washburn had been sent, only once did Ord's troops come in sustained contact with the enemy. But on the sixth, delays in launching an assault and Longstreet's unwillingness to linger a few more hours may have cost the army a chance to end the chase at Rice's Station.

Its lack of opportunity to reap glory had combined with the grueling pace the army had kept up ever since leaving Petersburg—a pace no other infantry column had equaled—to threaten morale throughout the ranks. The situation seemed unlikely to change: When other troops overhauled Lee, Ord's men would be left to applaud from the sidelines. And if by some miracle the army was placed in a position to strike a blow before the end came, would it be too exhausted, too footsore, to take full advantage? It was a disheartening situation, but one that dovetailed perfectly with the Army of the James's long history of opportunities squandered and battles lost through ill luck, poor timing, the obtuseness of its former leaders—Ben Butler headed a long list of names—or a combination of these factors.

Then, however, came Sheridan's sprint for Appomattox Station. When word filtered back to the troops in the cavalry's rear that errant trains, and perhaps Lee's army itself, might be a few miles up the road, waiting to be intercepted, Ord's officers and men felt a new sense of purpose, an urge to push ahead to a place where, despite all the odds, it might taste victory while it was still warm. Suddenly the marching pace picked up—it would remain at a remarkable level throughout the day. Ord, in fact, would march the men almost continuously for the next twenty hours, an accomplishment that, as one participant claimed, had "no parallel in the history of the Rebellion, or any war in Europe."[32]

The most notable feature of the day's travel would not be the distance covered or the pace maintained, but the uncomplaining attitude—in fact, the downright enthusiasm—of the marchers. Urged on by their commander, his subordinates, and their fellow soldiers, men who had fallen out of the column to rest or boil coffee abruptly returned to the road, while those who had limped along on blistered feet began to vie with their comrades for first place in the ranks.

No one strove to go longer or farther than the African-Americans of Birney's division. Sensing the approach of a long-held dream, the Colored Troops of the XXV Corps displayed extraordinary endurance and fortitude. Before the march ended, these soldiers, who at the outset had been held farthest to the rear, would accomplish feats that no other participant in this campaign—not even the suddenly light-footed troops of Gibbon, Foster, and Turner—would match. Like their white comrades, the African-Americans asked only one thing of the gods of war——that in the end, their effort would be worth the physical and emotional stress it inflicted on everyone involved.[33]

⸺⸻≫●◦◦≪⸻⸺

Custer's division, moving up the railroad via Evergreen Station, was the first of Sheridan's forces to approach the depot where the supply trains were believed to be waiting. At about 2:00 P.M., Pennington's brigade, at the head of Custer's column, advanced gingerly toward Appomattox Station from the southeast, expecting opposition from a heavy guard. Instead, the riders found on the siding of the depot—exactly as Sheridan's scouts had reported—four trainloads of rations and matériel sent from Lynchburg. The boxcars were crammed with everything from canteens to canned goods, crackers to quinine. The precious cargo was guarded not by battalions of infantry but by small detachments of Martin Gary's cavalry. Most of the horsemen were some distance north and west of the station, patrolling the commodious Richmond-Lynchburg Stage Road in the direction of Appomattox Court House.[34]

Intent on securing the spoils before they could be spirited away, Custer ordered the lead regiment of Pennington's brigade, Col. Alanson M. Randol's 2nd New York, to take the train crews by surprise. The New Yorkers approached their objective with as much stealth as hundreds of shod hooves would allow, a detachment of four of the outfit's most enterprising enlisted men in the lead. The advance guard did its job well; the engineers aboard three of the trains knew nothing of the enemy's presence until they found themselves staring at the business end of drawn pistols, whose owners shouted for them to surrender. Behind the advance men came the rest of their regiment, followed by the balance of Pennington's brigade.[35]

Pennington dismounted enough men to secure the depot and the surrounding area. Meanwhile, two regiments from another brigade galloped westward to tear up track toward Lynchburg, thus preventing belated attempts to escape. This effort fell short, for soon after the Yankees' arrival, a portion of the fourth train—one locomotive and one or two cars—got up steam, backed out of the station, and headed for Lynchburg at full throttle. Although pursued by shouting, shooting Federals, the train made good its escape.

Noting the proximity of Gary's men and wary that other Confederates might not be far off, Randol determined to relocate the captured trains to a less exposed position. Thus he put out a call for troopers who had been engineers in civilian life. At least two men, members of the 2nd West Virginia of Capehart's recently arrived brigade, stepped forward and climbed aboard the locomotives. It was noted that the volunteers "were in a jubilant mood, play-

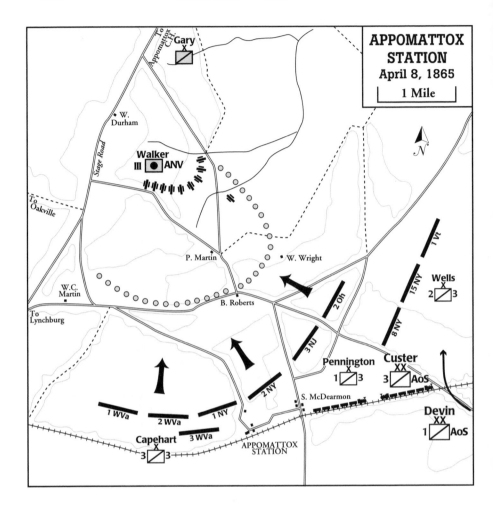

fully running the woodburning trains back and forth, with bells ringing and whistles screaming." They were still making merry when, at about eight o'clock, Phil Sheridan reached the station. The major general recalled that the erstwhile engineers "were delighted evidently to get back at their old calling. They amused themselves by running the trains to and fro, creating much confusion, and keeping up such an unearthly screeching with the whistles that I was on the point of ordering the cars burned [later one did go up in flames]. They finally tired of their fun, however, and ran the trains off to the east toward General Ord's column."[36]

The merriment at Appomattox Station halted abruptly when shot and shell began to rain down upon the depot and its occupants. Although few casualities resulted, the barrage created chaos and consternation in the Union ranks. It took several minutes before the source of the opposition could be located. Only then did Custer's men realize they had overtaken the quarry they had pursued for the past six days.

Unbeknownst to the majority of Custer's command, part of the advance guard of Robert E. Lee's retreat column, Brig. Gen. R. Lindsay Walker's reserve artillery and wagon train, had encamped in the muddy fields two miles north of the station. Perhaps an hour before Custer's arrival to the south, Walker, at the close of a grueling day's march, had placed his train in park and allowed his cannoneers and the wagon guards, including the main body of Martin Gary's brigade, to fall out and eat. This was the first day in more than a week—not counting the all-too-brief interval outside Farmville—that the men had been allowed to consume rations at their leisure. The rest stop was especially appreciated because, for Walker's artillerists, the going had been not only slow but also fraught with hard labor. As one officer remembered, the column had had to "stop often both night and day to prize our wagons out of the mud." No one in the command, including its leader, suspected that any Yankees were within ten miles of their bivouac, much less just over the next rise.[37]

Their complacency had been shattered at about 4:00 P.M., when a party of blue-clad horsemen topped the hill and charged down upon them. Suddenly the cry went up: "Yankees! Sheridan!" and everyone scrambled for his firearms, then for whatever cover the open fields provided. Lt. W. F. Robinson of the Ringgold Battery, formerly a part of the Petersburg defenses, recalled that "the enemy's cavalry, under General Custer, rode right into our camp, shooting as they came, and took possession of our wagons containing all our baggage."[38]

At first, the Federals' appearance provoked what one Confederate officer called a "disgraceful panic." Then Walker's men realized they had plenty of formidable weapons to use against the newcomers. Gunners made a dash for their cannons, which had been placed in a circle facing south, and hauled them about. Without noticing that Robinson and his men stood between them and their targets, the artillerymen began flinging canister at the Yankees. Only after several comrades fell dead or wounded did the gunners repent of their hastiness and shift their plane of fire.[39]

In addition to endangering their own men, Walker's gunners fired just above the heads of Gary's troopers, who were falling back from the charging Federals to the presumed safety of the artillery park. As soon as they reached Walker's camp, the cavalrymen were pressed into service as defenders. The scene quickly became frenetic in the extreme; as the 7th South Carolina's Edward Boykin recalled, "amid the flashing, and the roaring, and the shouting,

rose the wild yell of a railroad whistle, as a train rushed up almost among us
. . . sounding on the night air as if the devil himself had just come up and was
about to join in what was going on."[40]

Walker's initial volley dispersed most of the Yankees who had barged into
his camp, but they were quickly replaced by a long, deep line of skirmishers,
some mounted, some afoot. In front of them rode Colonel Pennington,
followed closely by Custer, who, although making a conspicuous target, sat
his charger as if oblivious to the rain of shells and musketry that he attracted.
Lieutenant Robinson observed him "on a white horse in the center of a
long line of cavalry . . . urging his men to charge, telling them that there
was only a handful of Confederates opposing them. I urged my men to take
good aim and shoot at General Custer, and I shot at him a number of
times myself."[41]

Although the Union commander remained unscathed, for hours he was
unable to push aside the "handful of Confederates" opposing his veteran
troopers. Robinson speculated that the Yankees were cowed by shouts of
"Bring up the Second Brigade!" and "Hurry up the division," commands designed to make the attackers believe they were facing foot soldiers. In fact, the
only infantry within reach of the battlefield was John Gordon's corps, which
had halted for the night a few miles to the northeast, outside Appomattox
Court House. Gordon's command, despite having been broken down by
"hunger and want of sleep . . . [and] a march rarely surpassed in its severe trials," might have been of substantial assistance to Walker in his contest with
Custer, but no one in the corps appeared willing to help. Gordon's second-in-
command, Maj. Gen. Bryan Grimes, recalled that at about 9:00 P.M. his division marched in the direction of the firing but halted beyond reach of Custer's
carbines and remained there for the balance of the contest.[42]

Even without infantry support, Walker's men made a far better showing
than their enemy—and probably Walker himself—expected. Their ability to
resist owed not only to their advantage in heavy ordnance and the support of
Gary's troopers, but also to the assistance they received from Col. T. M. R. Talcott's 1st and 2nd Confederate Engineer Regiments, another element of the
Confederate advance guard. Thus reinforced, the artillerists and wagon guards
fought, as Robinson said, "with the greatest enthusiasm, keeping Custer's cavalry back until dark, and then we continued the fight by shooting at the enemy
by the flash of their guns." Edward Boykin considered the engagement "one of
the closest artillery fights, for the numbers engaged" in the war: "The guns
were fought literally up to the muzzles. It was dark by this time, and at every
discharge the cannon was ablaze from touch-hole to mouth, and there must

have been six to eight pieces at work, and the small arms of some three or four hundred men packed in among the guns in a very confined space."[43]

Boykin claimed that the Federals "made three distinct charges, preluding always with the bugle, on the right, left, and centre. . . . They would get within thirty or forty yards of the guns and then roll back, under the deadly fire that was poured upon them from the artillery and small arms." In fact, Boykin's estimate of the number of assaults was probably too low; time after time, Custer threw forces of various sizes at the enemy camp. Most of the attackers dismounted to pepper away at the cannoneers and their supports; when the Rebel gunners got their range, they would hastily retire. Many, however, regrouped and came on again as later opportunities developed. Assessing the Union effort, one historian makes the point that "Custer, having no definite information as to how many men and cannon Walker had at his disposal, would make scattered attacks on the Confederates as his men arrived on the field. There was a partial necessity for this because of the nature of the battlefield, being heavily wooded and traversed by various wagon paths." The terrain had a tendency to disorder attack formations by slowing or halting portions of every battle line. Left unsupported, other units drew such a concentrated fire that they had to make a quick retreat.[44]

Piecemeal or not, Custer's assaults eventually wore down his opponents. Some time between 8:00 and 9:00, with the main body of Wells's and Capehart's brigades on the field in support of Pennington, and with Devin's division having gone into position on Custer's right, the boy general launched a climactic assault. By now, the enemy's strength had ebbed away, not only due to casualties, but also because men and cannons had begun to disperse almost from the outset of the fighting. Some had withdrawn in the direction of Lynchburg, others northward toward the hamlet of Oakville, while still others retreated to the safety of Lee's main body outside Appomattox Court House. When Custer led his strengthened and realigned ranks down the hill and over the enemy's camp, he found that many, if not most, of its occupants, including the troopers of Gary and the engineers under Talcott, had departed. Those who remained and fought on were systematically decimated.[45]

Carried away by the momentum of the attack, a portion of Wells's brigade shot past the enemy's left flank in the darkness and soon found itself on the stage road from Lynchburg. On that crowded thoroughfare the detachment encountered supply vehicles, wagon guards, and miscellaneous bodies of Confederate infantry. The troopers exchanged gunfire with their dimly visible opponents, and even managed to take some of them prisoner. Then they ran into dismounted members of Gary's brigade, double-quicking from the recent battlefield toward Appomattox Court House. The gray troopers assembled in a wooded area just off the stage road and threw out a skirmish line with the intent of ambushing their adversaries. When the Federals approached, they fired into the column, emptying many saddles.[46]

Temporarily halted but undeterred, Wells's troopers regrouped, tended to their injured, corralled their prisoners, and pushed ahead through the darkness, hoping to fix the position of Lee's main body. They promptly struck the vanguard of that body, a skirmish line from Brig. Gen. William Henry Wallace's infantry brigade, which had gone into bivouac just east of the village. Alerted to the cavalry's coming, the foot soldiers waited patiently as the head of the Union column—about a dozen members of the 15th New York Cavalry, under Lt. Col. Augustus Root—entered the town from the west and charged noisily through the streets. About fifteen rods from the courthouse, near the point at which Main Street and the stage road branched out to intersect the Prince Edward Court House Road, Wallace's skirmishers unleashed a volley that killed Root and at least one of his men and wounded an unknown number of others. Capt. Albert Skiff of Root's regiment, who escaped harm on this occasion only to fall severely wounded on the following day, recalled that

> we charged immediately in front of the Court House; there receiving a volley of rebel bullets, we were instantly driven backward. In a moment all was confusion, and after exchanging several shots we were obliged to retreat. I was just at the point of turning about when a riderless horse [Root's] sprang to my side . . . [and] I realized that another true and noble life had been sacrificed at the shrine of our suffering country.

The survivors galloped back to the safety of Custer's position, leaving Root's body in the moonlit road. It was still there two days later, "although having been stripped of all outer garments."[47]

Because Walker could not bring off his heaviest pieces, Custer claimed as trophies two dozen or more guns, along with upwards of 200 wagons and hundreds of prisoners. The spoils suggested that the recent fight had ended successfully for the Federals, but Custer's men did not feel like victors. Walker's gunners and guards had hauled perhaps seventy-five cannons to safety, thus denying major spoils to their opponents. They made good their escape because time and again the Federals had faltered when they should have overwhelmed their opposition with machine-like precision. Custer's men vowed to redeem themselves, once they caught up with the rest of Lee's army and engaged more traditional opponents.[48]

They would get the opportunity—their leader was certain of it. From the reports of his scouts, Sheridan had confirmed that he had gotten ahead of Lee's column, whose retreat he was now in a position to cut off. By advancing a short distance to the northeast along the Richmond-Lynchburg Stage Road, his troopers would be squarely athwart the enemy's path. That done, all that was needed was for Grant to arrive with enough infantry and artillery to maintain the roadblock.

Even before the last of Walker's escapees faded into the shadows, Little Phil made preparations to follow. Between nine and ten o'clock he sent dispatches to Grant, Ord, and Griffin, urging them to hasten to his side, emphasizing that if they pressed on, there was no means of escape for the enemy, who had reached "the last ditch."[49]

For Sheridan, the route to that mythical excavation lay across the fields and pastures of Appomattox County, where thousands of enemy campfires glowed in the night, as far as a tiny cluster of private dwellings and public buildings surrounding a country courthouse. The road to victory was now only two and a half miles long.

ELEVEN

"The Sun Went Down, and with It the Hopes of a People"

FOR THE HORSEMEN OF FITZHUGH LEE, APRIL 8 HAD BEEN UNUSUALLY UN-
eventful. A captain in the 1st Virginia pronounced the day "the first we
passed without fighting" since Dinwiddie Court House. For much of afternoon, Breckinridge's 2nd Virginia occupied the normally dangerous position
in the extreme rear of Lee's column. "We naturally looked for much trouble,"
the colonel recalled, "and we were mystified as time passed without the least
pressure from the rear." Although, at several points, Humphreys's infantry
prodded the weary Confederates on their way, the day passed without the
crack of a carbine or the sighting of one blue-jacketed horseman on the road
behind.[1]

After days of sometimes frantic activity, the quiet was rather unsettling.
Tom Rosser, whose division also pulled rear-guard duty for part of the day,
adopted an almost complaining tone when he reported to Fitz Lee that Sheridan's men "had all left the rear." Apparently out of boredom, Rosser asked his
superior's permission to cut loose from the column and go in search of the
enemy's supply train, which he intended to burn in retaliation for the hundreds of wagons the Yankees had waylaid over the past week. It was a foolhardy idea, and Fitz rejected it out of hand, although Rosser professed not to
know why.[2]

As the march progressed, the quiet became even more disconcerting, for
Fitz Lee and some of his subordinates began to suspect what was happening.
If the Yankees were no longer pressing them from the rear, they must be trying to pass their flank and get in front of them. By late in the day, the same
suspicion had begun to filter down to the rank and file. The feeling intensi-
fied when reports came in that enemy horsemen had been observed off the
left flank, straining toward some point on the railroad. Then came word that

Federal infantry had been sighted at New Store, near the right front of the column. The Yankees appeared to be closing in from all sides.[3]

By late afternoon, after the column came to an unusually early halt a mile or so from Appomattox Court House and the cavalry dismounted to bivouac in surrounding fields, the army had begun to experience a crisis of morale. Typical of the state of affairs within the cavalry was the experience of Trooper William B. F. Leech and his comrades in Company H, 14th Virginia, Beale's Brigade, Rooney Lee's Division:

> Tired and hungry, Co. H, now numbering less than 20 men, with no commissioned officers present, gathered around a small fire, with no rations of supper and nothing in store for a morning meal. Yet these wants were barely spoken of; the question under discussion was of a more serious character. Our march to[ward] Lynchburg had been intercepted by Gen. Grant's forces. We were nearly surrounded. The enemy were in front, left flank and rear. We were fast being encircled and unless we could force a way through the lines in front at an early hour the next morning, then all would be lost.[4]

In gathering darkness, Leech's company convened to discuss "whether we should abandon the idea of fighting our way through on the following day or not." A yes vote meant surrender or dispersal. Every member of the remnant had his say; the vote appeared to be about evenly divided between giving up and going on. Then the regimental color bearer, James Wilson, made an emotional plea that they all stay together and fight through the following day. As Wilson spoke, the implications of surrender suddenly became very real. Leech asked himself: "Was the cause, so dear to every Southern heart, to fail at last after all the privations and suffering of our people? What would become of our homes and the dear ones around our firesides?"[5]

These and similar thoughts prompted every member of Company H to adopt the course that Wilson advocated. They would go on, come what may, and fight through to the finish. On the morrow, even if their regiment went under, each survivor would strive to keep the cause alive, if it meant journeying to North Carolina to join Johnston's army. The issue resolved, each man settled down to sleep despite the complaining of his stomach and the nervous pounding of his heart. For Leech and many of his comrades, however, it could not be done: "A thousand thoughts," ranging from the terrible to the pathetic, "drove sleep from our eyes."[6]

Another who slept not a wink that night was Phil Sheridan, kept awake by caffeine, nervous excitement, the press of myriad duties, and the feverish activity all around him. The insomniac had a lot of company; as a member of his entourage observed, "no one slept that night. Generals Merritt, Crook, Devin, Custer, and other prominent officers were frequently at Sheridan's headquarters. There were all sorts of rumors that General Lee was about to surrender and everybody was jubilant."[7]

Yet no one could be certain of the enemy leader's intentions, and until they became evident the fighting would go on. Sheridan's next move was to take up a position as close as possible to Lee's troops outside Appomattox Court House and hold them there until the better part of two Union armies reached him. It was a dicey job, considering the weight the tired, hungry, yet feisty Confederates could bring to bear on the Union horsemen. Still, it had to be done, and done well, if what remained of the Army of Northern Virginia was to be kept from reaching North Carolina.

First came the task of selecting the force to take position in the enemy's immediate front. After its exertions at Appomattox Station, Custer's division deserved a rest, as did Devin's, which had supported Custer closely during the latter stages of the fighting. A fresher force, however, was available for the assignment: the 2nd Cavalry Division, Army of the Potomac. Over the past twenty-four hours, Crook's command, now enlarged by the addition of Mackenzie's division-turned-brigade, had done little more than march and confiscate spoils of war.

It had spent the eighth moving between Prospect Station on the South Side Railroad (where, as one of its men wrote, "we found neither station nor prospect") and points west. From Prospect it had proceeded along the tracks to Pamplin's Depot, where it discovered the rations and supplies that had been dispatched the previous day from Farmville to Lee's presumed location. Crook's advance guard promptly seized the train and appropriated its cargo, which included boxes of Springfield rifle-muskets. Late in the day the division resumed its trek in response to a report from Sheridan that other supply trains earmarked for the Army of Northern Virginia were sitting at Appomattox Station, ripe for capture. Sheridan himself, accompanied by the men of Merritt, Devin, and Custer, was already heading there via the more direct road from Prospect Station.[8]

By the time the 2nd Division reached the depot and the site of Custer's engagement with Walker, Gary, and Talcott, the fighting had all but ceased. At Sheridan's direction, two brigades assumed a reserve position in Custer's rear, while a third moved up to link with his left flank. The fourth component of the newly arrived command, Mackenzie's troopers of the Army of the James, went into bivouac at Plain Run, about a mile closer to Appomattox

Court House. For a time it looked as if the respite from combat that the 2nd Division had recently enjoyed was going to continue.

But appearances deceived. At about 9:00 P.M., cavalry headquarters ordered Smith's brigade—that part of the 2nd Division that had moved up on Custer's left—to proceed to the stage road and relieve Custer's videttes on the outskirts of Appomattox Court House. It was a critical assignment, for by all indications the road from Richmond to Lynchburg constituted Lee's only escape route, one the Confederate leader would surely seek to use come morning. Dutifully but warily, Smith went forward, his 6th Ohio in advance of the column. Within minutes his men were crossing the recent field of action, which lay awash in the debris of battle. The command passed "burning wagons, scattered munitions of war of every kind, muskets, caissons, clothing, blankets, and all sorts of stores, strewed in every direction, some partially destroyed.[9]

Reaching the stage road, the column turned northeast and marched to a point about a half-mile from the village. It halted a few hundred yards in front of the stage road's intersection with the Oakville (or Bent Creek) Road. While details trotted a quarter-mile farther east to build a picket line almost within rifle-range of the Rebels, Smith dismounted the main body and staked out a defensive perimeter that straddled the stage road. The 6th Ohio, which took position on the south side of the road, formed the right flank of this line, with the 1st Maine on its left, and the 2nd New York to the left of the Mainers. Smith's fourth regiment, the 13th Ohio, was kept in the saddle and so distributed to cover each flank. In front, Smith positioned his only support, two 3-inch ordnance rifles of Lord's battery.[10]

Most of the men began to build a breastwork of such "fence rails and dirt as could be dug up with pointed sticks and sharp ended rails." This makeshift position they would have to hold as long as possible come morning, buying time for Ord's and Griffin's infantry to reach the field. Their commander was fully aware of how difficult the job would be. Until relieved, 2,000 troopers would be attempting to hold back 30,000 Rebels of all arms. But there was no help for it—on the defense of the ground that Smith's men had begun to dig up rested both the expectations and the hopes of their army.[11]

That evening, at his field headquarters on the edge of a woods about a mile east of Appomattox, Robert E. Lee met with his senior lieutenants, Longstreet, Gordon, and Fitz Lee. The four men attempted to plan the next day's operations. Since these would be tailored to the strength of the enemy force that had been observed west of town, there was much discussion as to the composition of that force. The army leader believed it was made up strictly of cavalry, in which case the army would probably clear the road to Lynchburg rapidly and without serious difficulty.[12]

Longstreet and Gordon appear to have concurred with their superior, but the commander's nephew was convinced that enemy infantry as well as horsemen were in their front—a much tougher nut to crack. When the planning session broke up after midnight, Fitz continued to argue the point with Gordon. The cavalry leader insisted that Gordon should attack the enemy in the morning, while Gordon was equally adamant that the horsemen should strike first. In the end, both were assigned a major role in the action to come. Infantry and horsemen would form on the western edge of the village and at daylight would go forward side by side to open the stage road. As soon as the way was clear, the infantry would hold it while the army's wagons proceeded toward Lynchburg under cavalry escort.

Robert E. Lee, who had been advised by at least one subordinate whose opinion he valued that the army's situation was hopeless, had inserted a contingency clause into the plan of operations. If Union infantry in sufficient strength to secure the road was discovered to be in front of them, he would be compelled to accept Grant's terms for surrendering the army. For a time, Longstreet, Gordon, and Fitz Lee silently mulled over that possibility. Finally, Fitz spoke up: In the event of a cease-fire pending a surrender, he wished to lead as many of his men as he could gather through the lines to Lynchburg. He feared that Grant would require the cavalry not only to lay down its arms, but also to surrender its horses. This would cause hardship to his men, who owned their mounts, as well as to their families. Although no record exists of Robert E. Lee's response, he appears to have approved Fitz's proposal.[13]

After the meeting broke up, Fitz called Thomas Munford to the army's open-air headquarters. As Munford recounted the brief meeting, Lee "informed me of the status of affairs, and gave me orders to be ready at daylight to move out with the Division, when we would attack the enemy, and if successful in clearing the Lynchburg Road, the Infantry would follow." Munford listened intently, then brought up the fact that he and numerous officers and men of his command hailed from the Lynchburg area. All were determined to get home by the shortest route—through the enemy's lines. If he could go into position on the far right of the battle line facing the stage road, Munford vowed "I would stake my life . . . that we would go to Lynchburg." He quoted Fitz Lee as replying: "Bully for you, Munford; you shall have the right of the line." Then Fitz reiterated his intention that Munford's appointment as brigadier general be duly confirmed. Neither he nor his subordinate foresaw that the imminent collapse of the Confederate government would deal a final blow to Munford's hopes of promotion.[14]

Apparently Munford accepted without comment the necessity of surrender if his attempt to break through to Lynchburg failed. Others, including his colleague Rosser, refused even to consider that alternative. Rosser's division had not relinquished its rear-guard duties till late in the day; its commander had ridden into the village a few hours after darkness descended. Down the lane from the courthouse, he pulled up at the home of an acquaintance, Maj. Wilmer McLean. Rosser recalled, "[We] spent the night talking over our war experiences." Although the general's war career had been more active than his host's, McLean had seen exciting times as well: The first major land battle of the war had been fought near his wife's former home near Manassas Junction. He had moved to Appomattox Court House, as he told Rosser, to escape the fighting, but the effort had failed. In fact, McLean had moved south strictly for reasons of employment.[15]

About 2:00 A.M. on Sunday, the ninth, the pair was interrupted by a knock on McLean's front door. Inside stepped John Gordon and Fitz Lee, mournful expressions on their faces. According to Rosser, "[I saw] by the dim light of several tallow candles, which were burning in the room, that something terrible had happened and I at once demanded the news." By his recollection, one or the other visitor informed him that Robert E. Lee had decided that come morning, he would either surrender or disperse the army.[16]

Rosser's memory was hazy, for the army leader had not ruled out the possibility of fighting on. Still, the mention of surrender set him off, and he shot to his feet. "General Lee [will] not surrender me in the morning!" he declared. "My scouts had informed me that the Lynchburg Road was clear [this was manifestly untrue, given the conspicuous presence of Smith's brigade] and I began making arrangements to move before daylight." He calmed down only after being assured by General Gordon: "If I would wait until daylight . . . he would go with me, and with this understanding I got everything ready and waited."[17]

Still driven by the vision of approaching victory and the prospect of having a hand in it, the infantry and artillery of the Army of the James outdid themselves throughout April 8 and into the morning of the ninth. On the eighth, they marched, with the briefest of rest stops, from Farmville to Evergreen Station on the South Side, a distance of thirty-two miles. Add to that accomplishment the marching they had done since leaving Burkeville on the fifth, and they had come 110 miles in four days. Here was a milestone long to be cherished, but only if it helped bring about the surrender of Lee's army.[18]

At 11:00 P.M. on the eighth, when within four miles of Appomattox Station, the marching column shuddered at last to a halt. Bone-weary, footsore troops were permitted to fall out, catch their breath, and grab some sleep. Those not too tired to eat enjoyed an almost sumptuous supper, for they were near enough to the boxcars Custer's men had broken into that they could add to their regular fare such tidbits as bacon and molasses.[19]

The men enjoyed no more than four hours' rest before their equally weary officers woke them and broke up their bivouacs. By 3:00 in the morning everyone was back on the road—everyone, that is, except General Gibbon, who slept so soundly that he failed to awaken until after four. Frantically rousing his still-slumbering aides, Gibbon learned to his immense relief that his leading division, Foster's, had hit the road on time and was on its way to Appomattox Station. Gibbon was a West Pointer with almost twenty years' service in the army, his subordinate a volunteer officer with no prewar military experience. Disgusted by his own frailty, the corps commander stalked through his bivouac, shouting for all the world to hear: "General Foster is a better soldier than I am!"[20]

———————

At first light on Palm Sunday morn, April 9, Lee marshaled what remained of his army for what he realized might be its last fight. His men ate a scant breakfast—coffee, a crust of bread, perhaps a few kernels of parched corn—and then formed ranks facing Smith's hilltop breastwork. Gordon's infantry and Fitz Lee's horsemen spread out into a discontinuous line that eventually stretched for nearly a mile, northwest to southeast of the courthouse town. Gordon's foot soldiers, 7,000 strong, made up three-quarters of that line; Fitz Lee's command, whose strength was probably fewer than 2,500, was concentrated along the right. Munford's men, as Fitz had promised, were on the far flank, with Rosser's division on their left. Farther south, Rooney Lee's troopers connected with the right flank of the infantry. Longstreet's command, the largest Confederate force on the field, lay four miles farther east near New Hope Church.[21]

According to the plan worked out among the corps commanders, Gordon's men would advance in echelon, obliquing to the left so as to sweep across, and then secure, the stage road. The cavalry was supposed to conform, as much as possible, to this movement, although it would appear that from

the outset, Munford and Rosser intended to move in a more direct line, passing above the stage road and around Smith's left. That route would lead them
to that stretch of road in the enemy's rear, where they would enjoy free passage to Lynchburg, thus relieving them of any obligation to surrender. Rooney
Lee's intentions are less easily discerned. Being in close contact with the infantry, his fortunes were closely tied to those of Gordon; if more Yankees than
anticipated were on the field and the Confederate infantry was stopped or driven back, Rooney would act accordingly. Because Robert E. Lee was the ar-
chitect of the day's strategy, his son may have felt duty bound to share the fate
of the main army rather than try to evade it.

Sometime after 6:30 on that foggy morning, bugles squalled and the thin
gray line moved forward, Gordon's men, as per the plan, making a quarter
turn to the southwest. Their heading placed them in a direct line with the
cavalrymen of Devin and Custer, whom Sheridan had begun to shift north to
cover Smith's right flank. As Gordon pivoted, his flank brushed Smith's position, but Rooney Lee's men, farther to the right, struck it squarely. As if by
careful calculation, cavalry took on cavalry, the natural order of things on any
battlefield.[22]

With momentum and desperation on their side, Lee's men, advancing in
column of squadrons, achieved early success. The demibrigade of William
Roberts, at last an organic part of the division from which it had so long been
detached, charged down a hill, thrashed through a creek bottom, topped another rise, and crossed a tree-bordered field in which Lord's cannons had unlimbered. "When we got within 200 yards of them," one of Roberts's men
wrote of the enemy, "they began to run. Some went into the woods, some
took shelter under the gun carriages, and all quit firing." The artillery, supported only by Smith's picket line, fell into Roberts's hands with surprising
ease. Just as surprisingly, the little command managed to haul both pieces to
the rear. Smith's men made strenuous efforts to recover them, but they were
now under assault by Beale's brigade and what remained of the troops that
Rufus Barringer had commanded prior to April 3. Smith's pickets were
quickly killed, captured, or dispersed. Then the attackers thudded into the
main line of the Union brigade, and the fighting truly began.[23]

Smith's men had been instructed to hold their position for as long as humanly
possible, giving Ord's troops, and Griffin's in their rear, time to reach the field
and secure the stage road. If overwhelmed, the troopers were to fall back
slowly by the right flank. Crook had relayed these instructions to Smith just

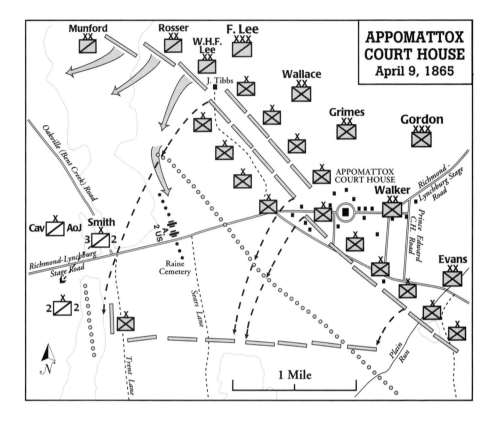

Munford
Rosser
F. Lee
W.H.F. Lee
J. Tibbs
Wallace
Grimes
Gordon

**APPOMATTOX
COURT HOUSE**
April 9, 1865

Oakville (Bent Creek) Road

APPOMATTOX
COURT HOUSE
Walker

Richmond-Lynchburg Stage Road

Cav   AoJ   Smith
3   2

A. 2 US

Richmond-Lynchburg
Stage Road

Raine
Cemetery

Prince Edward C.H. Road

Evans

2   2

Sears Lane

Plain Run

Trent Lane

N

1 Mile

before dawn, adding, "Of course, we cannot defeat the [enemy] force, but want to gain as much time as possible."[24]

Smith followed his orders to the letter. Although by 7:00 A.M. he was under attack from all sides, he urged his men by words and gestures to hang on, to hunker down behind their works and fire through them, aiming not so much at the oncoming riders as at their horses. In response, the men of Ohio, Maine, and New York held on to the last—perhaps as long as a half hour or ninety minutes. Their stationary position, while it made them an easy target, enabled them to squeeze off good shots, and the volume of fire from their seven-shot Spencer carbines and sixteen-round Henry rifles took a heavy toll of the attackers. In the end, however, by force of numbers, Rooney Lee crushed both of Smith's flanks and began to collapse the center as well. At their commander's order, those who could disengage did so, withdrawing to their led horses. Remounting under fire, most managed to gallop to safety.[25]

By now General Crook had had time to build additional lines of defense. On a ridge in Smith's left rear, he had positioned the newly attached troopers of the Army of the James, supported by a section of Lt. E. W. Olcott's Battery

M, 1st United States, a unit on loan from the artillery brigade of the XXV Corps. Crook had Mackenzie deploy his 11th Pennsylvania on the far left flank, where it remained mounted. Mackenzie then dismounted the 1st District of Columbia, the 1st Maryland, and the 5th Pennsylvania, and deployed them so as to cover the intersection of the Oakville Road and the road to Lynchburg, where Smith had been positioned.

The newcomers would make only a brief stand, but one long enough to cover Smith's retreat. En route to the rear, dozens of Smith's men joined Mackenzie's in an attempt to hold the intersection. But Mackenzie knew he could not remain in position for long. One of Crook's aides had informed him just before his men were committed that he should "withdraw slowly when it became necessary," adding that it would become necessary "very soon."[26]

Mackenzie's task was made difficult by the nature and strength of his opposition: He faced not only Rooney Lee's horsemen, but also the foot soldiers on Gordon's right flank. Then, too, Mackenzie had been forced to deploy on the run, a Herculean effort under the circumstances. The brigadier later claimed, "There would have been no trouble in repulsing the enemy from our immediate front, but the attack came so soon after our arrival that the connection which I had commenced establishing between my right and General Crook's left could not be made." To worsen his situation, some "unauthorized person," never identified, not only placed Mackenzie's led horses so far to the rear that their riders could not quickly remount, but also sent one of Olcott's guns into an exposed position, where it was attacked and captured. The result of this unhappy combination of events was a fighting retreat, which Mackenzie's men made in remarkably good order.[27]

As the Army of the James withdrew, Crook cobbled together yet another line of resistance in the form of Irvin Gregg's old brigade. That morning, Rosser, into whose hands the brigade leader and many of his men had fallen on the seventh, had released his prisoners en masse, but not before relieving them of their boots and other belongings. It would be days, however, before Gregg would retake the field; in his absence, Samuel B. M. Young continued to direct his command, as he had for the past two days.[28]

For Young, April 9 appeared to bear an unhappy resemblance to the "bad old fight" near Cumberland Church. When his four regiments hustled up from the south to cover the Lynchburg Road, they found Smith's troopers "retiring by the right and Mackenzie by the left oblique, and the enemy, taking advantage, charged one regiment of cavalry through the interval, and came up on [Young's] rear." In this moment of crisis, Young turned to his lead regiment, his own 4th Pennsylvania, which had been entrapped and routed on the seventh. The 4th responded splendidly, charging into the head of the Confederate outfit, slicing through its ranks, and eventually forcing its retreat.[29]

By then, however, the Rebel regiment had taken a heavy toll of the enemy in its front, especially in captures—a remarkable feat considering its small size. This was the 14th Virginia, Beale's brigade, the outfit that included the pitiful remnant that had been Company H. Commanded today by Capt. Edwin E. Bouldin, a veteran of Gettysburg and dozens of lesser actions, the 14th had bounded forward in response to a volley of orders from Rooney Lee: "Mount your horses! Form fours! Forward, March!" Off it had gone, over terrain alternately rough and rolling, aiming not only at the Union cavalry astride the stage road but also at the remaining section of artillery—Olcott's—that supported them.[30]

A member of the plucky outfit recalled its dash toward the Yankee line:

> After going about a quarter of a mile we came to an open field, on the opposite side of which, up a gradual slope in the edge of a pine forest, was posted a Yankee battery, supported by infantry [dismounted cavalry] behind temporary breastworks of logs, rails, and trees. . . . Capt. E. E. Bouldin [cried out] "Forward, charge! Boys, follow me!" Just as our colors were planted on one of the guns, out of the woods on our left flank came a regiment of Yankee cavalry in fine style . . . [we] capturing quite a number of prisoners.[31]

The Federals who counterattacked may have suffered some losses but they inflicted many more. The 4th Pennsylvania struck the Virginians' flanks with such force that the 14th disintegrated into small detachments that were easily deflected from Young's main body. Although they could not prevent the Rebels from hauling off Olcott's gun (the section's other piece managed to evade capture), the Federals made them pay dearly for their coup.[32]

The most notable casualty in the 14th was its color-bearer, James Wilson, he who had so eloquently persuaded William Leech and other comrades to resist disbanding and fight one more day. Wilson fell, "dying almost instantly," while attempting to plant his banner in the barrel of the captured cannon. The flag that fell from his hands was quickly seized by Sgt. John Donaldson of the 4th Pennsylvania, who so stoutly prevented its recapture that he would be awarded the Medal of Honor. Of the hundreds of battle flags, Union and Confederate, that had been lost in combat since mid-1861, Wilson's would be the last. Wilson himself would win recognition as one of the last horse soldiers to yield up his life in this long and bitter struggle.[33]

Young's counterattack, although highly effective, meant only a temporary reprieve for his brigade. The 8th and 16th Pennsylvania deployed, dismounted, in rear of the positions abandoned by Smith and Mackenzie and tried to block further penetration. They did so with marked success. The 8th blunted a drive against the left of the line, while the 16th double-quicked to the rear and drove a body of Confederates from a wood along the other flank.[34]

Impressed by the brigade's exertions, Wesley Merritt, who was now on the field directing operations, gathered supports for the embattled Pennsylvanians. At his command, Devin placed Fitzhugh's brigade, backed by a section of Miller's battery, on the right of Young's line and some distance in front of it. Fitzhugh's men had been patrolling the LeGrand Road, which ran below and roughly parallel to the Richmond-Lynchburg Stage Road along a ridge south of Appomattox Court House. In that area the Yankees were not only in contact with the Confederate left flank outside the village, but also in a position to help take some of the pressure off their comrades farther north.[35]

Soon enough, Fitzhugh found a certain amount of pressure being exerted against him. Detecting the cavalry's presence, Gordon's infantry corps, when moving forward to the morning's attack, turned in its direction with the intention of scattering its members and forcing the withdrawal of the nearby artillery section of Lt. Frederick Fuger. As he neared the Union line, however, Gordon encountered resistance not only from Fitzhugh and Fuger but also from Stagg's Wolverine Brigade, which had hurried into formation on Fitzhugh's left. The enlarged defense force held the line for several minutes against the oncoming horde, thus diverting pressure from Young. Finally, but grudgingly, Fitzhugh and Stagg retired under a hail of musketry. Fuger's artillerymen displayed even more stubbornness, refusing to limber up until the attackers were within 100 yards of their position.[36]

The dislodged troopers retreated on foot to the edge of the hilltop they occupied south of the LeGrand Road. There they made another, longer, stand, building a bulwark against further enemy advance, one immeasurably strengthened by the arrival of Gibbs's Reserve Brigade. Later the Federals boasted that "the steady and rapid firing of our spencers" brought the Rebel infantry to a dead halt.[37]

Another factor in the enemy's deceleration was the arrival of additional Union reinforcements. As Gordon pressed the new line, one of Stagg's regimental commanders, Col. George G. Briggs, rode to an elevation along his outfit's flank, where "I was enabled to see what I took to be the entire Confederate army. It was going into position in a sort of valley with higher land upon either side." Ordinarily, such a sight might have inspired a foreboding, but Briggs noticed that "there seemed to be great confusion" in the enemy's ranks: "Squads of men were running in various directions, and artillery, foot, and horse appeared badly mixed up in their effort to form a line of battle." Turning to his left and rear, the colonel saw a possible reason for the chaos: "General Custer's approaching column."[38]

To be sure, the 3rd Cavalry Division was coming into action belatedly. Aware that the command had fought long and hard the night before, Sheridan had refused to commit it until he felt compelled to. Roger Hannaford of the 2nd Ohio recalled that after he and his comrades breakfasted at dawn, "no movement was made for an hour or two after. We curried & fed our horses . . . [and] chatted together over the events of the previous evening as we washed ourselves" from a stream bordering their bivouac.[39]

Recalling his division's inability to overwhelm and crush its enemy the previous night, Hannaford observed that the corporate morale remained pretty low. Yet when bugles finally called Custer's people to saddle up and get in motion, "we saw a sight that revived our drooping spirits wonderfully. The main road was full of colored troops . . . almost ready to drop from fatigue." These were members of the all-black XXV Corps, part of the advance contingent of Ord's Army of the James. The cavalry's continued ability to hold Lee's people at bay depended on these men and their white comrades reaching the front in substantial numbers.

Although few of Hannaford's comrades were ardent Negrophiles, "we gave them a hearty cheer, which brought forth a quick response & seemed to infuse new life for a moment in the poor, footsore, weary fellows." The cheering continued as the cavalry trotted past the African-Americans, the two columns heading toward the same destination—the cockpit of battle—by different routes.[40]

Custer's path led his men in rear of Devin's position along the LeGrand Road. Reaching the hill occupied by Brigg's regiment, Custer dismounted and went forward until he shared the colonel's panoramic view of the enemy line. Then, remounting, he led the column farther to the right in hopes of gaining a better position from which to launch an attack in concert with the now-arriving infantry—not only the head of Ord's column but also the vanguard of Griffin's V Corps.

To reach the desired spot, Custer's men passed through a broad, open field where they were exposed to the fire of a dozen or more Rebel cannons southwest of Appomattox Court House. Fortunately, few casualties resulted, and soon the column was sheltered by a thick woods. Turning abruptly north, the line of riders struck the LeGrand Road at a point beyond Devin's right flank. "Down this we went," one rider recalled, "part of the time on a brisk trot, then a lope." The men's spirits kept pace with the faster gait, elevated by prevalent rumors that Lee had sent a flag of truce through the lines, seeking a peace parley with Grant.[41]

When the column came to a sudden halt and Generals Sheridan and Merritt spurred past, the men's enthusiasm took the form of sustained cheering. The noise subsided, however, when, off to the east, Custer's point riders suddenly spied Rebel horsemen—members of Gary's brigade—heading their way. In short order, Pennington's brigade, which had the advance, was careening up the road, its men shouting their lungs out. They came on with such verve that their startled enemy turned and raced off. Their advance may have been a ruse, for they were heading toward the safety of a concealed artillery position. Heedless of the danger ahead, Pennington's men pursued for a quarter of a mile or more before skidding to a halt. "Here we were confronted by twelve pieces of artillery," one trooper recalled, "12 pounders, ranged on the brow of the hill, in the bushes, but the gunners forebore to fire . . . and, having re-formed our line, [we] moved back into the woods about a hundred paces, and dismounting, stood at horse for an hour or two."[42]

At least one Federal refused to give up the chase. Fortified by heavy doses of whiskey, Sgt. Benjamin F. Weary of the 2nd Ohio continued to charge even after his comrades fell back and took shelter. Perhaps encouraged by the artillery crew's unwillingness to discharge its pieces, he rode through its ranks shouting "Surrender, you damned rebels!" This was provocative enough, but then the sergeant intruded upon the adjacent bivouac of Colonel Talcott's engineer command. Although well-armed, the engineers at first laughed at Weary's drunken bravado. But when he reached down from the saddle, grabbed the unit's battle flag, and began to ride off, Weary toppled to the ground, his body riddled with bullets and spouting "a dozen streams of blood."[43]

Although the dead man's comrades remained in their wooded sanctuary, Custer sent other elements of the command into action against Gary's troopers and their artillery supports. One of Wells's regiments, the 8th New York, formed a skirmish line and was soon blasting away across an open field; the Rebels on the other side quickly reciprocated. After ten minutes given to such diversion, General Gary mounted a portion of his brigade and led it against the skirmishers, who scrambled back to their main body. Then Col. John J. Coppinger's 15th New York, the outfit whose executive officer had been cut down in the streets of Appomattox Court House the night before, charged in turn, forcing the South Carolinians and Virginians into a retreat just as hasty as the 8th New York's. With that, the fighting on this part of the line took on a desultory quality, as if participants on both sides preferred to wait for momentous events to unfold.[44]

Despite the strong support of Custer and Devin, the men under George Crook continued to be hard-pressed as they strove to deny the Richmond-Lynchburg Stage Road to the enemy. By nine A.M., their roadblock was coming apart at the seams. Smith's and Mackenzie's men were too far from the scene to offer effective resistance to the gray tide building on the northern reaches of the thoroughfare. Davies's brigade had been sent to reconnoiter the enemy's right flank and was thus in no position to oppose the Rebel advance. Young's Pennsylvanians, the only troopers left on the field, were holding on by their fingertips, minutes away from being overwhelmed and dispersed. Wesley Merritt would liken their situation to "opposing the force of a cyclone with a wall of straw."[45]

Some minutes past nine, the last dismounted Federal was pushed to the side of the road. When they became fully aware of this fact, Lee's soldiers raised a shout of triumph. The cry swelled into a chorus that swept the length of the contested field. The path to Lynchburg lay open; the Yankees that had blocked it were gone from view; and the Army of Northern Virginia would live to fight—if only to retreat—another day.

Then, quite abruptly, the shouting died down. Men in gray and butternut uniforms, who minutes before had beheld the pathway to salvation, now recoiled at the sight of dozens—hundreds—of blue-clad infantrymen racing up from the southwest to take position in rear of Crook's displaced battle line. The Army of the James had reached the field at last, and in intimidating strength.[46]

It took only minutes for the new arrivals to undo everything the cavalry's opponents had achieved since sunrise. The once-jubilant Rebels stared wordlessly as the leading element of Ord's column— Col. Thomas Osborn's brigade of Foster's division—took position on a ridge to the south side of the stage road. Then Col. George Dandy's brigade of the same division rushed up to occupy the high ground on Osborn's left. Minutes later, the men of Col. Harrison Fairchild's brigade, backed by Battery B, 1st Artillery, arrived to extend Dandy's line farther to the north.

Like the comrades who had preceded them, Fairchild's men began erecting breastworks atop the hills they occupied. As they labored, their battery opened fire on the head of the nearest gray column. Disheartened by the display of might, the Confederates eventually moved forward, but wearily and tentatively. They launched a limited attack, but before they could strike a heavy blow, the advance elements of Turner's division clambered up to prolong and protect Foster's right. Turner's ranks included many African-Americans of the XXV Corps, whose determination to contribute to the climactic battle of the war had been exceeded only by their unprecedented marching ability.[47]

Its extraordinary endurance had enabled the Army of the James to arrive in time to choke off Lee's retreat. That endurance had been activated and fortified by the unflagging efforts of its officers to urge the command forward. The primary motivator had been the army's commander. Since leaving Farmville, Edward Ord had ridden up and down his columns, exhorting the marchers to ever greater speed, reminding them of the prize waiting just up the road, and promising they would never have to make another forced march after today's work was done.

Ord's ability to prod and inspire, combined with the men's knowledge that they controlled the outcome of the day, so strengthened their will to fight that when they topped the last stretch of high ground south of the battlefield, they broke ranks in a frenzy to confront the enemy as quickly as possible. All semblance of unit formation, of marching order, was lost in the wild scramble across the fields toward the stage road. Soldiers hustled up in groups large and small, each vying with his comrades for a good place on the firing lines.

To the cavalry, across whose rear the foot soldiers charged, it was a novel as well as a most welcome sight. One of Custer's officers recalled, "Here, for the first time during the war, I saw men straggling ahead of their colors to get into a fight!" Behind the stragglers came Ord himself, galloping along on his big charger, waving his hat above his head and shouting in exultation: "Your legs have done it, my men! Your legs have done it!"[48]

With Ord's men in front of him, with Griffin's off his southeastern flank and coming fast, and with the II Corps, followed by the VI, prodding his army's rear near New Hope Church, Robert E. Lee understood that the time had come to activate his contingency plan. Sometime after 10:00, he authorized his staff to run up a white flag, the prelude to a long, mournful trip through the lines to meet General Grant.

A number of truce flags went forward from Lee's position, some borne by individual officers, others by parties of officers and men. Intended to halt the fighting as quickly as possible, they instead caused confusion, especially in the ranks of units slow to get the word to cease firing. This became a problem after several generals crossed the lines to discuss details of the truce with their nearest counterparts. Most of these meetings, including one between Phil Sheridan and John Brown Gordon, were cordial, but two led to angry confrontations and nearly to physical violence. Both occurred after flag bearers rode into Sheridan's lines near the intersection of the LeGrand and Prince Edward Court House Roads, south of the village.

One of the truce parties was referred to George Custer, who responded with bellicosity instead of jubilation. The division leader told the flag bearer: "We will listen to no terms but that of unconditional surrender. We are behind your army now and it is at our mercy." When the party returned to its own lines, Custer followed it under a truce flag of his own. Encountering General Longstreet, he briefly continued his blustering, going so far as to demand that Longstreet's troops lay down their weapons on pain of annihilation. Longstreet bristled at the message and the tone in which it was delivered; he angrily replied that if the truce should lapse, it would be Custer's cavalry that faced destruction. Custer, looking about at the infantrymen and cannons now surrounding him, was suddenly chastened. Taking a deep breath, he saluted Longstreet and rather sheepishly returned to his command.[49]

The second contretemps involved the fiery commander of Gary's brigade, which confronted Custer's division southeast of the courthouse. William Blackford, Stuart's former staff officer, now a lieutenant colonel of engineers, was on hand for Sheridan's parley with Gordon. When Little Phil's party, which had ridden in under a white flag, was fired on by a Confederate unit—it turned out to be Blackford's own regiment—Gordon sent the lieutenant colonel, accompanied by Lt. Vanderbilt Allen of Sheridan's staff, to arrange a cease-fire.

En route, the pair came upon Gary's men, who had continued to fire at the Federals opposite them even though the latter had stopped shooting. When Allen reported the purpose of his errand, the brigade's commander roundly cursed him and threatened, despite Allen's status as a flag bearer, to take him prisoner. When Blackford explained that General Lee had begun preparations to surrender the army, Gary "quivered as if he had been shot, and sat still in his saddle a moment, and then, returning his sabre, which he held still drawn in his hand, he said, 'Then I will be damned if I surrender!'" Edward Boykin maintained that Gary added: "We are South Carolinians, and don't surrender!" Turning to Allen, the red-faced general exclaimed: "Besides, sir, I take commands from no officers but my own, and I do not recognize you or any of your cloth as such!"[50]

The acrimony continued until another member of the party, a Union captain, assumed a conciliatory tone and showed Gary enough deference to soothe his pride. Minutes later, the Federals were permitted to return to their lines. After Blackford rejoined General Gordon, Boykin recalled, "We drew back to the artillery and infantry that were just behind us, and formed our battered fragments into regiments."[51]

As the guns fell silent all along the line, the Confederates attempted to assimilate and understand everything that had happened. And yet, Boykin noted:

> The idea of a complete surrender, which we began now to see was inevitable, came as an awful shock. Men came to their officers with tears streaming from their eyes, and asked what it all meant, and would, at that moment, I know, have rather died the night before than see the sun rise on such a day as this. And so the day wore on, and the sun went down, and with it the hopes of a people who, with prayers, and tears, and blood, had striven to uphold that falling flag.[52]

Not every Confederate cavalryman laid down his sword this day. As Munford had predicted, by diverging to the right instead of moving in the direction the infantry had taken, the brigades of Wooldridge and Morgan were able to pass around the Federals opposite them. Colonel Breckinridge of Munford's old regiment observed: "We made a detour to the right through fields, woods[,] over hill and valley, bearing to the left after going perhaps a mile and reached the Lynchburg road at the top of a considerable hill a few miles west of the C[ourt] H[ouse]."[53]

It appears that Munford's route—suggested to him by a civilian guide intimately familiar with the local countryside—led northwestward along the Oakville Road, across the main branch of the Appomattox River, then cross-country to the southwest. Crossing the road from Appomattox Station to Oakville, the vanguard of his column struck the Richmond-Lynchburg Stage Road well in rear of the Federals opposing Rooney Lee, Rosser, and their infantry comrades.

Although this stretch of highway held no dismounted opponents dug in behind breastworks, Munford was not yet home free. Roving parties of Davies's brigade were not far off; moreover, they were spoiling for a fight, believing that the rest of their division, so heavily engaged farther south, would benefit from a diversion. This they attempted to provide by striking at the head and flanks of Munford's column. Subsequently, Davies was assisted by a portion of Young's brigade, whose men had re-formed after being dislodged from the eastward stretches of the same road. Later still, elements of Mackenzie's brigade joined Davies, although it cannot be determined how many added their weight to the fight against Munford.[54]

Munford may not have welcomed any encounter. Evidence suggests that the new brigadier left Appomattox Court House even before his comrades farther south made contact with Smith's vedettes. Perhaps he hoped not only to escape the fate of the troops on his left but to avoid fighting altogether. If so, he was disappointed. Shortly before his advance unit, the 4th Virginia, topped the hill that overlooked the stage road, it encountered one of Davies's skirmish lines. Munford promptly threw out skirmishers of his own, mostly from the vaunted 1st Virginia, and the fighting began to heat up. As they arrived, Munford formed the rest of his regiments along both sides of the road. Most of the men remained in the saddle, although some dismounted to oppose an equal number of Union pickets advancing on them afoot.[55]

As the last regiment in Munford's column, the 2nd Virginia, reached the highway, it took an unexpected blow from the rear. Wheeling about, its commander, Col. Cary Breckinridge, charged the assailants with a couple of squadrons; the Yankees fled in the general direction of Appomattox Court House. A few minutes later, Davies's men struck again, this time, apparently, in greater strength. One Union officer later claimed that the entire brigade charged Munford's column—an unlikely occurence given the size of the force that met and repulsed the effort: a single squadron of the 1st Maryland Battalion under Col. Gus Dorsey and Capt. W. I. Rasin. As always, success came at a price—in this case, Pvt. William C. Price, perhaps the last Confederate to die in action, although that distinction was claimed for many another unfortunate soldier. Shortly before Price fell, Rasin also took a fatal wound.[56]

Members of the force that Dorsey and Rasin opposed later claimed that orders from their own army, not the opposition of the 1st Maryland, had prompted them to break contact and fall back. Capt. Samuel Cormany of the 16th Pennsylvania insisted that just as the second attack got under way, staff officers came galloping up from the south, shouting, "For Gods sake Stop that Charge!" Within minutes, Cormany wrote, "the Rebels show the white flag, and Their Bugle blows 'Cease firing' and Ours blows the HALT! and all is quiet [in] an instant."[57]

At some point a white flag did appear along the stage road, but questions about its point of origin would spark much debate. Munford, for one, averred that a truce party advanced from the Union line with word that Lee and Grant had called a halt to the fighting pending negotiations to surrender the A. N. V. In response, offensive operations on the stage road ceased and Munford drew up his regiments in column, as if on parade. To glean details of the cease-fire, the division commander, accompanied by a few subordinates, entered the lines opposite his headquarters, where he was soon conferring with a bevy of high-ranking opponents including Davies, Young, and Mackenzie. Munford found the behavior of all three "very civil." Cordial feelings began to flow, as did, presently, peach brandy from the canteen of Colonel Breckinridge's chief quartermaster. Several Federal officers (Munford did not name them) availed themselves of his invitation to sample the beverage.[58]

The pleasantries abruptly ended when Mackenzie tried to persuade Munford to surrender his command. Politely refusing, the Confederate immediately returned to his own lines. He discovered that in his absence, some of his subordinates had held a meeting of their own, trying to decide whether to continue to Lynchburg or surrender in place. Munford brought the balloting to a close by announcing that everyone was going to Lynchburg whether he liked it or not. Without further discussion, he led the column up the stage road, while the Federals across the way, bound by the rules of truce parties, looked on helplessly.[59]

Later in the day, Tom Rosser, accompanied by Fitz Lee, fulfilled the promise he had made in his superior's presence by following his colleague's lead. Rosser's division had seen more action this day than Munford's, having closely supported both Rooney Lee and Gordon at several points in the morning's fighting. Gordon's foot soldiers had been even more heavily engaged, but when the truce flags went up, they were too far from Rosser's side to accompany him to Lynchburg. Late that day, when Lee and Grant met in Wilmer McLean's parlor to work out surrender arrangements, Gordon's men found themselves bound by their terms.[60]

So, too, did Rooney Lee's horsemen. Cut off by Ord's troops from Munford and Rosser, they shared the fate of Gordon's men rather than that of their cavalry comrades. Their leader regretted his inability to escape the formal process of laying down his command's arms. For the cavalry this ceremony took place on the tenth, two days before the main body of Lee's army surrendered their weapons, ammunition, and battle-scarred flags.[61]

Humiliating as this experience might have seemed, however, Rooney Lee was the scion of a family that lived by the same code of honor upon which they believed their dying nation had been built. By taking part in the surrender ritual, he and his men paid final respects to an army that had gone down fighting. Somehow this course seemed preferable to turning one's back on that army in the moment of its greatest trial and leaving it to its fate.

Flight to Lynchburg proved ineffective, especially after Joe Johnston surrendered to Sherman late in April and Gen. Richard Taylor laid down his arms in early May, thus ending hostilities east of the Mississippi River. The troopers who escaped from Appomattox eventually faced up to their responsibilities by disbanding their units, surrendering themselves to the Federal authorities, and accepting paroles or, in a few isolated cases, serving a brief confinement before being released to their homes and families. There they could reflect on four years of service marked by tremendous hardships and near-crippling handicaps, but also by triumphs and accomplishments unsurpassed in the annals of the American cavalry.[62]

For their part, in the weeks following Lee's surrender, the troopers of the Armies of the Shenandoah, the Potomac, and the James were kept busy guarding prisoners and supplies, confiscating weapons, occupying outlying portions of middle and eastern Virginia, and overawing those few Confederates who refused to accept defeat. Their last sustained military operation as a body began two weeks after Lee's capitulation, when the War Department rejected the terms Sherman had proposed for the surrender of Johnston's army. Given the prospect of renewed fighting in that theater, on the twenty-second Sheridan was ordered to lead his entire command, as well as the VI Corps, to Greensboro, there to unite with Sherman's armies. The Federal troopers, by then encamped around Petersburg, started south two days later. They got only as far as Danville, the so-called Last Capital of the Confederacy, before word reached them that a second round of negotiations between Sherman and his opponent had produced a surrender document acceptable to the government authorities. For the horsemen of the armies of the United States, their war was over.[63]

It was at the outset of the Danville Expedition that Thomas C. Devin sat down in his tent on the outskirts of Petersburg to write a letter to his brother, John, in New York City. In addition to including the usual elements of personal correspondence—inquiring about family members, passing along the latest camp gossip—the newly minted major general of volunteers attempted to evaluate what the Union cavalry had contributed to the campaign just ended, and to suggest how the outcome might have been different absent that contribution. Although neither a renowned theorist nor a polished writer, the general achieved his purpose quite nicely:

> We do not claim you can tell the people that Sheridan and his cavalry alone annihilated Lees Army but we <u>do claim</u> that Sheridan put on the Army of the Potomac the "legs" they never before possessed[,] without which legs Lees Army would today have been intact and in connection with Johnston. . . . And we claim that Sheridans Cavalry fighting by day and marching by night were eternally in front of Lees Army and holding them by the throat until said legs could come up and finish the job.[64]

NOTES

ABBREVIATIONS USED IN NOTES:
ACHNHP   Appomattox Court House National Historical Park
B&L   *Battles and Leaders of the Civil War*
CV   *Confederate Veteran*
CWTI   *Civil War Times Illustrated*
DU   William R. Perkins Library, Duke University
LC   Library of Congress
MB   *Maine Bugle*
MC   Eleanor S. Brockenbrough Library, Museum of the
       Confederacy
MOLLUS   Military Order of the Loyal Legion of the United States
MSS   Correspondence or papers
NA   National Archives
OR   *The War of the Rebellion: A Compilation of the Official*
       Records of the Union and Confederate Armies
SHSP   *Southern Historical Society Papers*
UNC   Wilson Library, University of North Carolina
USAMHI   U. S. Army Military History Institute
UV   Alderman Library, University of Virginia
VHS   Virginia Historical Society

CHAPTER 1

1. A. Wilson Greene, *Breaking the Backbone of the Rebellion: The Final Battles of the Petersburg Campaign* (Mason City, Iowa, 2000), 1–40.

2. George E. Pickett to La Salle Corbell Pickett, Aug. ——, 1864, Arthur Crew Inman MSS, John Hay Lib., Brown Univ., Providence, R. I.; *OR,* I, 42, pt. 2: 299, 576, 1271–72; pt. 3: 1213; 46, pt. 2: 576; pt. 3: 1332, 1353; David E. Johnston, *The Story of a Confederate Boy in the Civil War* (Portland, Ore., 1914), 283; James I. Robertson, Jr., *18th Virginia Infantry* (Lynchburg, Va., 1984), 29–30; Robert K. Krick, *30th Virginia Infantry* (Lynchburg, Va., 1983), 58–60; Lee A. Wallace, Jr., *3rd Virginia Infantry* (Lynchburg, Va., 1986), 53.

3. Thomas Horne to "My Dear Mollie," Feb. 27, 1865, Horne MSS, Ablah Lib., Wichita State Univ., Wichita, Kans.

4. Robert T. Hubard memoirs, 117, DU.

5. William W. Blackford, *War Years with Jeb Stuart* (New York, 1945), 280–81.

6. Robert K. Krick, *9th Virginia Cavalry* (Lynchburg, Va., 1982), 43; Henry R. Pollard, *Memoirs and Sketches of the Life of Henry Robinson Pollard: An Autobiography* (Richmond, 1923), 117; Cadwallader J. Iredell to his wife, March 8, 10, 1865, Iredell MSS, UNC.

7. Edward M. Boykin, *The Falling Flag: Evacuation of Richmond, Retreat and Surrender at Appomattox, by an Officer of the Rear-Guard* (New York, 1874), 61; Thomas T. Munford, "The Last Days of Fitz Lee's Division of Cavalry, Army of Northern Virginia, 1865," 4–5, VHS.

8. Robert J. Driver, Jr., *1st Virginia Cavalry* (Lynchburg, Va., 1991), 54; Robert J. Driver, Jr., and H. E. Howard, *2nd Virginia Cavalry* (Lynchburg, Va., 1995), 69; Thomas P. Nanzig, *3rd Virginia Cavalry* (Lynchburg, Va., 1989), 27; Kenneth L. Stiles, *4th Virgnia Cavalry* (Lynchburg, Va., 1985), 23; Krick, *9th Virginia Cavalry,* 32; Robert J. Driver, Jr., *10th Virginia Cavalry* (Lynchburg, Va., 1992), 31–32; Daniel T. Balfour, *13th Virginia Cavalry* (Lynchburg, Va., 1986), 12; John Fortier, *15th Virginia Cavalry* (Lynchburg, Va., 1993), 56, 59; Robert T. Hubard memoirs, 65; Robert E. Lee, *Lee's Dispatches: Unpublished Letters of General Robert E. Lee, C.S.A., to Jefferson Davis and the War Department of the Confederate States of America, 1862–65,* ed. by Douglas Southall Freeman and Grady McWhiney (New York, 1957), 71 and n.-73 and n.; William D. Hardin to "Dear Sister," Mar. 27, 1865, DU.

9. Robert E. Lee, *The Wartime Papers of R. E. Lee,* ed. by Clifford Dowdey and Louis H. Manarin (Boston, 1961), 890.

10. Edward G. Longacre, *Lee's Cavalrymen: A History of the Mounted Forces of the Army of Northern Virginia, 1861–1865* (Mechanicsburg, Pa., 2002), 42–44.

11. Edward G. Longacre, *Lincoln's Cavalrymen: A History of the Mounted Forces of the Army of the Potomac, 1861–1865* (Mechanicsburg, Pa., 2000), 46–49; Robert J. Driver, Jr., *5th Virginia Cavalry* (Lynchburg, Va., 1997), 71.

12. Michael P. Musick, *6th Virginia Cavalry* (Lynchburg, Va., 1990), 75–76.

13. Edwin H. Claybrook to "My darling 'Little Sis,'" Feb. 26, 1863, Claybrook MSS, MC; Andrew H. Kay to "Dear Brother," Jan. 17, 1865, Kay MSS, VHS.

14. The following summary of operations by the cavalry of the Army of Northern Virginia, 1861–64, is based on too many sources to include in a single citation. For a more complete list of references on this topic, please refer to the author's *Lee's Cavalrymen*.

15. Driver, *1st Virginia Cavalry*, 108–9; *OR*, I, 46, pt. 1: 477–82, 486–88; pt. 2: 793, 1296.

16. *OR*, I, 46, pt. 1: 480, 503; pt. 2: 994, 1281–82, 1290–91, 1308–13; pt. 3: 14–15, 38, 41, 43; James Longstreet, *From Manassas to Appomattox: Memoirs of the Civil War in America* (Philadelphia, 1896), 591; Mottrom D. Ball to Thomas L. Rosser, Mar. 19, 1865, Rosser MSS, UV; Rawleigh W. Downman to his wife, Mar. 18, 1865, Downman MSS, VHS; Cornelius H. Carlton diary, Mar. 10–17, 1865, VHS.

17. *OR*, I, 42, pt. 2: 1219–20, 1310–11.

18. Ibid., 43, pt. 2: 874–75, 914; Thomas L. Rosser, *Riding with Rosser*, ed. by S. Roger Keller (Shippensburg, Pa., 1997), 43–44.

19. *OR*, I, 46, pt. 1: 384, 386–87, 390.

20. Robert E. Lee to Wade Hampton, Aug. 1, 1865, Edward L. Wells MSS, Charleston Lib. Soc., Charleston, S.C.; Lee, *Lee's Dispatches*, 315.

21. *OR*, I, 46, pt. 1: 390, 1275–76; Janet Hewett et al., eds., *Supplement to the Official Records of the Union and Confederate Armies*, (Wilmington, N.C., 1994–2001), I, 8: 613; Edwin H. Claybrook to "My Dear 'Little Sis,'" Mar. 1, 1865, Claybrook MSS; Richard L. Armstrong, *7th Virginia Cavalry* (Lynchburg, Va., 1992), 84–85; Jack L. Dickinson, *16th Virginia Cavalry* (Lynchburg, Va., 1989), 65–67; John Harper Dawson, *Wildcat Cavalry: A Synoptic History of the Seventeenth Virginia Cavalry . . .* (Dayton, 1982), 73–74.

22. Nanzig, *3rd Virginia Cavalry*, 69.

CHAPTER 2

1. Stewart W. McIlwraith to "Dear Father and Brother," Mar. 24, 1865, USAMHI.

2. Frederick Whittaker, *Volunteer Cavalry—The Lessons of a Decade, by a Volunteer Cavalryman* (New York, 1871), 5; Wesley Merritt, "The Appomattox Campaign," in *War Papers and Personal Reminiscences, 1861–1865: Read before the Commandery of the State of Missouri, MOLLUS* (St. Louis, 1892), 110.

3. Longacre, *Lincoln's Cavalrymen*, 6–11, 40–42; Longacre, *Lee's Cavalrymen*, 44–48.

4. Charles S. Wainwright, *A Diary of Battle: The Personal Journals of Colonel Charles S. Wainwright, 1861–1865*, ed. by Allan Nevins (New York, 1962), 515.

5. Allen C. Redwood, "Following Stuart's Feather," *Journal of the Military Service Institution of the United States* 49 (1911): 116–17.

6. For complete source citations on cavalry operations in the Army of the Potomac, 1861–65, please refer to the author's *Lincoln's Cavalrymen*.

7. Ezra J. Warner, *Generals in Blue: Lives of the Union Commanders* (Baton Rouge, La., 1964), 123–24; Edward P. McKinney, *Life in Tent and Field, 1861–1865* (Boston, 1922), 144; Henry E. Tremain, *Last Hours of Sheridan's Cavalry: A Reprint of War Memoranda* (New York, 1904), 37–39.

8. Francis B. Heitman, comp., *Historical Register and Dictionary of the United States Army* . . . (Washington, D.C., 1903), 1: 423; Warner, *Generals in Blue*, 172–73; Joseph Flint, *Regimental History of the First New York Dragoons* . . . (Washington, D.C., 1865), 7.

9. *OR*, I, 43, pt. 1: 519; pt. 2: 218, 220, 249; Edward G. Longacre, *Custer and His Wolverines: The Michigan Cavalry Brigade, 1861–1865* (Conshohocken, Pa., 1997), 201, 251–52.

10. DeWitt Crumb, *22d Regiment N.Y. Vol. Cav.: Historical Address* . . . (South Otselic, N.Y., 1887), 12.

11. Heitman, *Historical Register and Dictionary*, 782; Longacre, *Custer and His Wolverines*, 130, 141, 147, 152, 230, 232.

12. Warner, *Generals in Blue*, 549–50. See also Elliott Wheelock Hoffman, "Vermont General: The Military Development of William Wells, 1861–1865," Masters thesis, Univ. of Vermont, 1974.

13. Roger Hannaford, Memoir of the Appomattox Campaign, 11, ACHNHP.

14. *OR*, I, 46, pt. 1: 1101; Philip H. Sheridan, *Personal Memoirs of P. H. Sheridan* (New York, 1888), 2: 125.

15. *OR,* I, 46, pt. 1: 365–37; Theodore Lyman, *Meade's Headquarters, 1863–1865: Letters of Colonel Theodore Lyman from the Wilderness to Appomattox,* ed. by George R. Agassiz (Boston, 1922), 310; Alphonso Rockwell, *Rambling Recollections: An Autobiography* (New York, 1920), 164.

16. George Crook, *George Crook: His Autobiography,* ed. by Martin F. Schmitt (Norman, Okla., 1960), 136; M. J. Darley to Philip H. Sheridan, Mar. 1, 1865, Sheridan MSS, LC.

17. George Crook to R. B. Hayes, Mar. 28, 1865, Crook MSS, Rutherford B. Hayes Presidential Center, Fremont, Ohio.

18. Tremain, *Last Hours of Sheridan's Cavalry,* 124.

19. Heitman, *Historical Register and Dictionary,* 477, 895.

CHAPTER 3

1. *OR,* I, 46, pt. 2: 1289–91, 1294, 1301–4, 1306–15, 1317; pt. 3: 1317–18, 1324, 1357–58.

2. Edwin C. Bearss and Chris M. Calkins, *The Battle of Five Forks* (Lynchburg, Va., 1985), 10.

3. *OR,* I, 36, pt. 1: 388; pt. 3: 1357, 1360.

4. Edward G. Longacre, *Pickett, Leader of the Charge: A Biography of General George E. Pickett, C.S.A.* (Shippensburg, Pa., 1995), 60–152.

5. Jeffry Wert, *General James Longstreet, the Confederacy's Most Controversial Soldier: A Biography* (New York, 1993), 394–95.

6. *OR,* I, 46, pt. 3: 1371; Walter Harrison, *Pickett's Men: A Fragment of War History* (New York, 1870), 142–43; Douglas Southall Freeman, *Lee's Lieutenants: A Study in Command* (New York, 1942–44), 3: 656–57.

7. *OR,* I, 46, pt. 3: 1358–59, 1362.

8. Ibid., pt. 1: 52; Horace Porter, "Five Forks and the Pursuit of Lee," in *B&L* 4: 708.

9. *OR,* I, 46, pt. 3: 86, 173; Greene, *Breaking the Backbone of the Rebellion,* 206–07.

10. *OR,* I, 47, pt. 1: 27–28; pt. 3: 33, 42.

11. Ibid., 46, pt. 1: 48–50; George Gordon Meade to Margaret Sargent Meade, Apr. 12, 1865, Meade MSS, Historical Soc. of Pennsylvania, Philadelphia; Lyman, *Meade's Headquarters,* 351.

12. Sheridan, *Personal Memoirs,* 2: 125–29.

13. Ibid., 131–32; *OR,* I, 46, pt. 3: 215.

14. Sheridan, *Personal Memoirs,* 2: 132–35.

15. August V. Kautz memoirs, 103, USAMHI; *New York Herald*, Mar. 29, 1865; Horace Porter, *Campaigning with Grant*, ed. by Wayne C. Temple (Bloomington, Ind., 1961), 414; John S. Adams, "With Lincoln from Washington to Richmond in 1865," *Appleton's Magazine* 9 (1907): 523–24.

16. Bernarr Cresap, *Appomattox Commander: The Story of General E. O. C. Ord* (San Diego, 1981), 81–144.

17. *OR*, I, 46, pt. 1: 1160; pt. 3: 105, 188–89, 207, 210–11, 238–39.

18. Ibid., pt. 1: 1227; Godfrey Weitzel, "Entry of United States Forces into Richmond, Virginia, April 3, 1865 . . .," 1, Cincinnati Historical Soc.; August Kautz memoirs, 104.

19. *OR*, I, 46, pt. 1: 555–56.

20. Ibid., 1160.

21. Ibid., 1227, 1244.

22. Ibid., 1160; Edward G. Longacre, *Army of Amateurs: General Benjamin F. Butler and the Army of the James, 1863–1865* (Mechanicsburg, Pa., 1997), 284.

23. *OR*, I, 46, pt. 3: 208, 211, 236; Joel C. Baker, *The Fall of Richmond: War Papers No. 2, Vermont Commandery of the Loyal Legion* (Burlington, Vt., 1892), 5.

24. *OR*, I, 46, pt. 1: 1160, 1173, 1179, 1185, 1192, 1234–35; pt. 3: 236; *New York Tribune*, Mar. 31, 1865; *New York Herald*, Apr. 3, 1865; William H. Wharf, "From Chapin's Farm to Appomattox," *MB* n.s. 3 (1896): 232.

25. Porter, *Campaigning with Grant*, 444.

26. Bearss and Calkins, *Battle of Five Forks*, 11–12.

27. *OR*, I, 46, pt. 3: 1360.

28. Ibid., pt. 1: 1298–99; pt. 3: 1358; Hewett et al., eds., *Supplement to the OR*, I, 8: 467.

29. *OR*, I, 46, pt. 3: 1361; Munford, "Last Days of Fitz Lee's Division," 5.

30. *OR*, I, 46, pt. 3: 1358–59; Robert A. Driver, Jr., *First & Second Maryland Cavalry, C.S.A.* (Charlottesville, Va., 1999), 114.

31. *OR*, I, 46, pt. 3: 1327–28; Robert J. Trout, "Galloping Thunder: The Stuart Horse Artillery Battalion . . .," *North & South* 3 (September 2000): 83.

32. *OR*, I, 46, pt. 1: 1299; Hewett et al, eds., *Supplement to the OR*, I, 8: 467.

33. Hewett et al., eds., *Supplement to the OR*, I, 8: 467. Italics have been added to Lee's quote.

34. Ibid., I, 7: 779.

35. Longacre, *Pickett, Leader of the Charge,* 160–61, 179–80.

36. Ibid., 19, 60, 63, 92; Wert, *General James Longstreet,* 45, 97, 105.

37. *OR,* I, 46, pt. 1: 1101, 1116; Sheridan, *Personal Memoirs,* 2: 135–38; Walter H. Jackson diary, Mar. 29, 1865, Bentley Historical Lib., Univ. of Michigan, Ann Arbor.

38. *OR,* I, 46, pt. 1: 1101, 1116, 1129, 1134, 1141; pt. 3: 267; Sheridan, *Personal Memoirs,* 2: 138–39; Frederick C. Newhall, "With Sheridan in Lee's Last Campaign," *MB* 1 (1894): 301; Andrew A. Humphreys, *The Virginia Campaign of '64 and '65: The Army of the Potomac and the Army of the James* (New York, 1883), 325; Robert Bell to his wife, Mar. 31, 1864 [1865], Bell MSS, ACHNHP.

39. *OR,* I, 46, pt. 1: 1101–2, 1143–44; Sheridan, *Personal Memoirs,* 2: 139.

40. *OR,* I, 46, pt. 1: 1102; pt. 3: 266; Sheridan, *Personal Memoirs,* 2: 140–41.

41. W. H. F. Lee, Report of W. H. F. Lee's Division, Cavalry Corps, Army of Northern Virginia, March 29–April 9, 1865, 1, VHS; William F. Lewis diary, Mar. 29–30, 1865, MC; John B. Moseley diary, Mar. 29–30, 1865, VHS; Driver, *1st Virginia Cavalry,* 110.

42. Rosser, *Riding with Rosser,* 64; Munford, "Last Days of Fitz Lee's Division," 53–56; Burke Davis, *To Appomattox: Nine April Days, 1865* (New York, 1959), 43.

CHAPTER 4

1. *OR,* I, 46, pt. 1: 675–76, 797–802, 845–48, 853–54, 892, 898–99, 1160, 1173, 1214; pt. 3: 242–45, 249–58, 268–70; Bearss and Calkins, *Battle of Five Forks,* 14–31.

2. *OR,* I, 46, pt. 3: 266.

3. Ibid., 323; Sheridan, *Personal Memoirs,* 2: 141–42.

4. Sheridan, *Personal Memoirs,* 2: 142–44; *OR,* I, 46, pt. 3: 325.

5. Porter, "Five Forks and the Pursuit of Lee," 710.

6. Sheridan, *Personal Memoirs,* 2: 144–45.

7. Ibid., 145.

8. Ibid., 145–46.

9. David M. Jordan, *"Happiness Is Not My Companion": The Life of General G. K. Warren* (Bloomington, Ind., 2001), 140–41, 159–61; Edward G. Longacre, "Gouverneur K. Warren: A Profile," *CWTI* 10 (Jan. 1972): 16–18.

10. Hewett et al., eds., *Supplement to the OR,* I, 7: 779–80.

11. Ibid., I, 7, 779; 8: 440, 467; *OR,* I, 46, pt. 1: 1299.

12. *OR,* I, 46, pt. 1: 390; Hewett et al., eds., *Supplement to the OR,* I, 8: 474, 530–32, 620–21.

13. *OR,* I, 46, pt. 1: 1299; Hewett et al., eds., *Supplement to the OR,* I, 8: 467.

14. William H. F. Payne to Joseph R. Anderson, Dec. 13, 1903, Payne MSS, MC; Ezra J. Warner, *Generals in Gray: Lives of the Confederate Commanders* (Baton Rouge, La., 1959), 230–31; Stiles, *4th Virginia Cavalry,* 11; OR, I, 46, pt. 1: 1299.

15. Munford, "Last Days of Fitz Lee's Division," 9; Hewett et al., eds., *Supplement to the OR,* I, 8: 440; Francis W. Dawson, *Reminiscences of Confederate Service, 1861–1865* (Charleston, S. C., 1882), 142; OR, I, 46, pt. 1: 1299.

16. Jeffry Wert, "His Unhonored Service," *CWTI* 24 (June 1985): 29–34.

17. *OR,* I, 27, pt. 2: 737–38.

18. J. E. B. Stuart to Thomas L. Rosser, Sept. 30, 1863, Rosser MSS, UV; Driver and Howard, *2nd Virginia Cavalry,* 95.

19. Sheridan, *Personal Memoirs,* 2: 141–42; *OR,* I, 46, pt. 1: 1116, 1122, 1128.

20. *OR,* I, 46, pt. 1: 1116, 1141, 1144.

21. Ibid., 1122, 1128.

22. Ibid., 1299; Hewett et al., eds., *Supplement to the OR,* I, 7: 780.

23. Rosser, *Riding with Rosser,* 63; Hiram W. Harding diary, Mar. 29–30, 1865, MC.

24. *OR,* I, 46, pt. 1: 1299; Hewett et al., eds., *Supplement to the OR,* I, 8: 467; Munford, "Last Days of Fitz Lee's Division," 10; Stiles, *4th Virginia Cavalry,* 80.

25. Munford, "Last Days of Fitz Lee's Division," 10–14.

26. *OR,* I, 36, pt. 3: 324.

27. Ibid., 324–25.

28. Ibid., 380.

29. Ibid., I, 46, pt. 1: 1102, 1116, 1122, 1128; Sheridan, *Personal Memoirs,* 2: 149; Walter H. Jackson diary, Mar. 31, 1865; Munford, "Last Days of Fitz Lee's Division," 14; Bearss and Calkins, *Battle of Five Forks,* 32–47. This last source, the most detailed modern account of the fighting on March 31, 1865, forms the basis for the battle narrative that follows.

30. *OR,* I, 46, pt. 1: 1102, 1110, 1117, 1141, 1144, 1148, 1154; pt. 3: 339; Sheridan, *Personal Memoirs,* 2: 149; Walter R. Robbins, *War Record and Personal Experiences of Walter Raleigh Robbins from April 22, 1861, to August 4, 1865,* ed. by Lilian Rea (Chicago, 1923), 112; Edward G.

Longacre, *Jersey Cavaliers: A History of the First New Jersey Volunteer Cavalry, 1861–1865* (Hightstown, N.J., 1992), 235–36.

31. *OR*, I, 46, pt. 1: 1299; Munford, "Last Days of Fitz Lee's Division," 14–15; Hewett et al., eds., *Supplement to the OR*, I, 7: 780; 8: 440–41.

32. *OR*, I, 46, pt. 1: 1141, 1156–57, 1299; Sheridan, *Personal Memoirs*, 2: 150; Hewett et al., eds., *Supplement to the OR*, I, 7: 780, 829–30; 8: 467, 474–75, 533, 614, 620–21; Lee, Report of W. H. F. Lee's Division, 1; Hiram W. Harding diary, Mar. 31, 1865; James McClure Scott memoirs, 14, VHS; Rosser, *Riding with Rosser*, 63; Daniel B. Coltrane, *The Memoirs of Daniel Branson Coltrane, Co. I, 63rd Reg., N.C. Cavalry, C.S.A.* (Raleigh, N. C., 1956), 39–40; David Cardwell, "The Battle of Five Forks," *CV* 22 (1914): 117; Walter Clark, ed., *Histories of the Several Regiments and Battalions from North Carolina in the Great War, 1861–'65* (Goldsboro and Raleigh, N.C., 1901), 1: 439; Robert H. Moore, II, *The 1st and 2nd Stuart Horse Artillery* (Lynchburg, Va., 1985), 138.

33. *OR*, I, 46, pt. 1: 1156–57; pt. 3: 339, 381–82.

34. Ibid., pt. 1: 1102, 1141–42, 1144, 1148, 1157; pt. 3: 381; Sheridan, *Personal Memoirs*, 2: 150; Hewett et al., eds., *Supplement to the OR*, I, 7: 780–81; Lee, Report of W. H. F. Lee's Division, 1; Robbins, *War Record and Personal Experiences*, 114–16; Rufus Barringer diary, Apr. 1, 1865 [covering events of Mar. 31], UNC.

35. *OR*, I, 46, pt. 2: 1122–23, 1144, 1148–49; Longacre, *Jersey Cavaliers*, 236–37; Tremain, *Last Hours of Sheridan's Cavalry*, 43.

36. *OR*, I, 46, pt. 2: 1123.

37. Munford, "Last Days of Fitz Lee's Division," 16.

38. *OR*, I, 46, pt. 1: 1102, 1110, 1129–30; Sheridan, *Personal Memoirs*, 2: 151–52; James Bradley diary, Mar. 31, 1865, Connecticut Historical Soc., Hartford; Stephen Z. Starr, ed., "Dinwiddie Court House and Five Forks: Reminiscences of Roger Hannaford, Second Ohio Volunteer Cavalry," *Virginia Magazine of History and Biography* 73 (1965): 419–20.

39. *OR*, I, 46, pt. 1: 1102, 1110, 1117, 1123, 1144; Hewett et al., eds., *Supplement to the OR*, I, 7: 781; Hiram Rix, Jr., diary, Mar. 31, 1865, Clarke Historical Lib., Central Michigan Univ., Mount Pleasant; Newhall, "With Sheridan in Lee's Last Campaign," 1: 307; Munford, "Last Days of Fitz Lee's Division," 16–17.

40. Thomas C. Devin, "Didn't We Fight Splendid," *CWTI* 17 (Dec. 1987): 39.

41. *OR*, I, 46, pt. 1: 1123, 1128, 1154–55, 1157; pt. 3: 381; Sheridan, *Personal Memoirs*, 2: 151; Rosser, *Riding with Rosser*, 63–64; Robert Bell to

his wife, Mar. 31, 1864 [1865], Bell MSS; Caroline B. Sherman, ed., "A New England Boy in the Civil War," *New England Quarterly* 5 (1932): 337.

42. Tremain, *Last Hours of Sheridan's Cavalry,* 50.

43. *OR,* I, 46, pt. 1: 1102–3, 1117, 1130, 1144; Newhall, "With Sheridan in Lee's Last Campaign," 1: 311; Robert T. Hubard memoirs, 118.

44. Sheridan, *Personal Memoirs,* 2: 153; Newhall, "With Sheridan in Lee's Last Campaign," 1: 312.

45. *OR,* I, 46, pt. 1: 1134–35; Sheridan, *Personal Memoirs,* 2: 151–53; Starr, ed., "Dinwiddie Court House and Five Forks," 420–23.

46. *OR,* I, 46, pt. 1: 1103, 1157.

47. Clark, ed., *Histories of the Several Regiments and Battalions from North Carolina,* 1: 442; Devin, "Didn't We Fight Splendid," 39.

48. Hewett et al., eds., *Supplement to the OR,* I, 7: 781.

CHAPTER 5

1. Hewett et al., eds., *Supplement to the OR,* I, 7: 781.

2. Munford, "Last Days of Fitz Lee's Division," 19–22.

3. Porter, "Five Forks and the Pursuit of Lee," 711; *OR,* I, 46, pt. 3: 381.

4. Porter, "Five Forks and the Pursuit of Lee," 711.

5. *OR,* I, 46, pt. 1: 812–16, 846, 868–69, 883–86, 896–900.

6. Porter, "Five Forks and the Pursuit of Lee," 711.

7. *OR,* I, 46, pt. 3: 381; Sheridan, *Personal Memoirs,* 2: 155.

8. *OR,* I, 46, pt. 3: 381.

9. Hewett et al., eds., *Supplement to the OR,* I, 7: 781; Munford, "Last Days of Fitz Lee's Division," 23, 27.

10. *OR,* I, 46, pt. 1: 1299.

11. Ibid.; Hewett et al., eds., *Supplement to the OR,* I, 8: 469; Munford, "Last Days of Fitz Lee's Division," 23–24.

12. *OR,* I, 46, pt. 1: 1103–4, 1117, 1123, 1130; pt. 3: 435–37; Sheridan, *Personal Memoirs,* 2: 155–57.

13. Hewett et al., eds., *Supplement to the OR,* I, 8: 470.

14. Munford, "Last Days of Fitz Lee's Division," 24–25.

15. *OR,* I, 46, pt. 3: 1371; Harrison, *Pickett's Men,* 138; La Salle Corbell Pickett, *Pickett and His Men* (Atlanta, 1900), 86; Freeman, *Lee's Lieutenants* 3: 661 and n.; Hewett et al., eds., Supplement to the OR, I, 7: 781.

16. Harrison, *Pickett's Men,* 138–40; Hewett et al., eds., *Supplement to the OR,* I, 7: 781.

17. Harrison, *Pickett's Men,* 138; Bearss and Calkins, *Battle of Five Forks,* 77–78.
18. Munford, "Last Days of Fitz Lee's Division," 30, 33, 36; Hewett et al., eds., *Supplement to the OR,* I, 8: 441–43.
19. Rosser, *Riding with Rosser,* 64; Hewett et al., eds., *Supplement to the OR,* I, 8: 470; Dickinson, *16th Virginia Cavalry,* 67.
20. Hewett et al., eds., *Supplement to the OR,* I, 8: 441, 443, 470.
21. Ulysses S. Grant, *Personal Memoirs of U. S. Grant* (New York, 1885–86), 2: 541; Warner, *Generals in Blue,* 301–2; Heitman, *Historical Register and Dictionary,* 1: 672.
22. August V. Kautz diary, Feb. 28, Mar. 8, 11–24, 26, 28, 1865, Kautz MSS, LC; August V. Kautz memoirs, 101–4; *OR,* I, 46, pt. 2: 977; pt. 3: 55, 212–13; James Harrison Wilson, "The Cavalry of the Army of the Potomac," in *Papers of the Military Historical Society of Massachusetts, Volume XIII: Civil and Mexican Wars, 1861, 1846* (Boston, 1913), 59.
23. Theodore F. Vaill, *History of the Second Connecticut Volunteer Heavy Artillery . . .* (Winsted, Conn., 1868), 330–34; August V. Kautz diary, Mar. 24, 1865, Kautz MSS.
24. *OR,* I, 46, pt. 1: 1244, 1248; pt. 3: 211, 236, 238–39, 378; *History of the Eleventh Pennsylvania Volunteer Cavalry* (Philadelphia, 1902), 147–48.
25. *OR,* I, 46, pt. 1: 1244.
26. Ibid., 1244, 1248, 1254–55; *Eleventh Pennsylvania Cavalry,* 148–49.
27. *OR,* I, 46, pt. 1: 1244, 1255; *Eleventh Pennsylvania Cavalry,* 149.
28. Sheridan, *Personal Memoirs,* 2: 158–60; Porter, "Five Forks and the Pursuit of Lee," 711.
29. *OR,* I, 46, pt. 1: 819–26.
30. Porter, "Five Forks and the Pursuit of Lee," 711–12; Sheridan, *Personal Memoirs,* 2: 160.
31. Rosser, *Riding with Rosser,* 64; J. E. B. Stuart to Thomas L. Rosser, Jan. 22, 1862, Rosser MSS, UV.
32. Hewett et al., eds., *Supplement to the OR,* I: 467, 481.
33. Munford, "Last Days of Fitz Lee's Division," 34.
34. Ibid.
35. Ibid., 34–35.
36. *OR,* I, 46, pt. 1: 831; Sheridan, *Personal Memoirs,* 2: 160–61.
37. *OR,* I, 46, pt. 1: 831–35, 838–39, 869–70.
38. Whittaker, *Volunteer Cavalry,* 32; Merritt, "Appomattox Campaign," 115.

39. W. G. Cummings, "Six Months with the Third Cavalry Division under Custer," in *War Sketches and Incidents: As Related by Companions of the Iowa Commandery, MOLLUS* (Des Moines, 1893–98), 1: 304; Robert W. Hatton, ed., "Just a Little Bit of the Civil War, as Seen by W. J. Smith, Company M, 2nd Ohio Volunteer Cavalry," *Ohio History* 84 (1975): 226.

40. *OR,* I, 46, pt. 1: 869–70, 879–80; Joshua L. Chamberlain, *The Passing of the Armies: An Account of the Final Campaign of the Army of the Potomac . . .* (New York, 1915), 126–28; Joshua L. Chamberlain, "Five Forks," in *War Papers: Read before the Commandery of the State of Maine, MOLLUS* (Portland, 1898–1908), 2: 227.

41. Munford, "Last Days of Fitz Lee's Division," 39–40.

42. *OR,* I, 46, pt. 1: 1244–45, 1248, 1251, 1255; *Eleventh Pennsylvania Cavalry,* 149.

43. Chamberlain, *Passing of the Armies,* 114; Jordan, *"Happiness Is Not My Companion,"* 232.

44. Hewett et al., eds., *Supplement to the OR,* I, 7: 781–83.

45. Ibid., I, 8: 471–72; Robert J. Trout, *In the Saddle with Stuart* (Gettysburg, Pa., 1998), 105.

46. Trout, *In the Saddle with Stuart,* 105; *OR,* I, 46, pt. 1: 1299–1300; Rosser, *Riding with Rosser,* 64–65; John E. Divine, *35th Battalion Virginia Cavalry* (Lynchburg, Va., 1985), 66.

47. Munford, "Last Days of Fitz Lee's Division," 35–41; Hewett et al., eds., *Supplement to the OR,* I, 8: 441–44.

48. Munford, "Last Days of Fitz Lee's Division," 35–36; Hewett et al., eds., *Supplement to the OR,* I, 8: 443.

49. Munford, "Last Days of Fitz Lee's Division," 40–41; Cary Breckinridge, "The Second Virginia Cavalry Regt. from Five Forks to Appomattox," 1–2, VHS.

50. Munford, "Last Days of Fitz Lee's Division," 44–45; Breckinridge, "Second Virginia Cavalry Regt.," 2.

51. Lee, Report of W. H. F. Lee's Division, 1; Hewett et al., eds., *Supplement to the OR,* I, 8: 535; Cardwell, "Battle of Five Forks," 117; Moore, *1st and 2nd Stuart Horse Artillery,* 140; Starr, ed., "Dinwiddie Court House and Five Forks," 428.

52. Trout, *In the Saddle with Stuart,* 105; Hewett et al., eds., *Supplement to the OR,* I, 8: 535, 537.

53. Hewett et al., eds., *Supplement to the OR,* I, 8: 535; Moore, *1st and 2nd Stuart Horse Artillery, 142;* Hiram W. Harding diary, Apr. 1, 1865.

CHAPTER 6

1. *OR,* I, 46, pt. 1: 1106.
2. Porter, "Five Forks and the Pursuit of Lee," 714–15.
3. Ibid., 715.
4. Ibid.
5. Sheridan, *Personal Memoirs,* 2: 171; *OR,* I, 46, pt. 1: 1263–64; Lee, *Wartime Papers of R. E. Lee,* 922–24.
6. *OR,* I, 46, pt. 1: 839, 851, 1105–6.
7. Ibid., pt. 3: 434.
8. Ibid., pt. 1: 1263; Hewett et al., eds., *Supplement to the OR,* I, 7: 746; John B. Moseley diary, Apr. 2, 1865.
9. *OR,* I, 46, pt. 1: 1300; Hewett et al., eds., *Supplement to the OR,* I, 7: 783; Driver, *5th Virginia Cavalry,* 107.
10. Munford, "Last Days of Fitz Lee's Division," 65.
11. Hewett et al., eds., *Supplement to the OR,* I, 7: 783; Chris M. Calkins, *The Appomattox Campaign, March 29–April 9, 1865* (Conshohocken, Pa., 1997), 53–55.
12. *OR,* I, 46, pt. 1: 1160–61, 1174; Grant, *Personal Memoirs,* 2: 448.
13. *OR,* I, 46, pt. 1: 1161, 1174, 1179, 1214, 1221–22, 1235; John Gibbon, *Personal Recollections of the Civil War* (New York, 1928), 299–300; Humphreys, *Virginia Campaign of '64 and '65,* 369; Morris Schaff, *The Sunset of the Confederacy* (Boston, 1912), 27–28; Theodore Read to Edward O. C. Ord, Apr. 2, 1865, Ord MSS, Bancroft Lib., Univ. of California, Berkeley; Thomas M. Harris to C. H. Hurd, Apr. 5, 1865, Harris MSS, West Virginia Univ. Lib., Morgantown; Longacre, *Army of Amateurs,* 294–96.
14. Grant, *Personal Memoirs,* 2: 435.
15. *OR,* I, 46, pt. 3: 1378.
16. William C. Davis, *Breckinridge: Statesman, Soldier, Symbol* (Baton Rouge, La., 1974), 502–4.
17. *OR,* I, 46, pt. 1: 711–12, 715, 724–25, 734, 1106; Sheridan, *Personal Memoirs,* 2: 172–73.
18. *OR,* I, 46, pt. 1: 1106, 1118, 1124, 1131, 1144, 1149, 1155, 1157.
19. Ibid., 1124, 1131, 1245.
20. Ibid., 1124.
21. Walter H. Jackson diary, Apr. 2, 1865.
22. Breckinridge, "Second Virginia Cavalry Regt.," 2–3; Munford, "Last Days of Fitz Lee's Division," 67.
23. *OR,* I, 46, pt. 1: 1124; Sheridan, *Personal Memoirs,* 2: 173; Calkins, *Appomattox Campaign,* 54–55.

24. *OR*, I, 46, pt. 2: 1118–19, 1124; Sheridan, *Personal Memoirs,* 2: 173.
25. *OR*, I, 46, pt. 1: 1124–25.
26. Ibid., 839, 1119, 1125; pt. 3: 491.
27. Burke Davis, *To Appomattox: Nine April Days, 1865* (New York, 1959), 136–37.
28. Calkins, *Appomattox Campaign,* 9–13.
29. Ibid., 45–46, 58, 63; *OR*, I, 46, pt. 1: 1293, 1296; pt. 3: 1372–82; Hewett et al., eds., *Supplement to the OR,* I, 7: 775–76.
30. Darryl Holland, *24th Virginia Cavalry* (Lynchburg, Va., 1997), 88–89.
31. Ibid., 89–90.
32. *OR*, I, 46, pt. 1: 1292–94; George A. Bruce, *The Capture and Occupation of Richmond* (Boston, 1918), 5–6; John A. Campbell, *Recollections of the Evacuation of Richmond, April 2d, 1865* (Baltimore, 1880), 4–5; Rembert W. Patrick, *The Fall of Richmond* (Baton Rouge, La., 1960), 101–2; "Evacuation of Richmond: Reports of Gens. Ewell and Kershaw," *Transactions of the Southern Historical Society* 1 (1874): 102–3; Dallas D. Irvine, "The Fall of Richmond," *Journal of the American Military Institute* 3 (1939): 78–79; *New York Herald,* Apr. 12, 1865.
33. Lewis T. Nunnelee memoirs, 186–87, MC.
34. Henry R. Pollard, *Memoirs and Sketches,* 126.
35. Louise Porter Daley, *Alexander Cheves Haskell: The Portrait of a Man* (Norwood, Mass., 1934), 169.
36. Cornelius H. Carlton diary, Apr. 2, 1865.
37. Boykin, *Falling Flag,* 11.
38. Charles F. Collier, "War Recollections: Story of the Evacuation of Petersburg, by an Eye-Witness . . .," *SHSP* 22 (1894): 71.
39. Ibid., 71–72.
40. Ibid., 72.
41. *OR*, I, 46, pt. 1; 1170–73, 1227; pt. 3: 212, 237, 271, 384, 437–39, 495–96, 500–502; August V. Kautz memoirs, 103–4; August V. Kautz diary, Apr. 2–3, 1865, Kautz MSS; Weitzel, "Entry of United States Forces into Richmond," 2–6; Bruce, *Capture and Occupation of Richmond,* 5–7; George F. Shepley, "Incidents of the Capture of Richmond," *Atlantic Monthly* 46 (1880): 19–22; *New York Herald,* Apr. 5, 1865; Edward H. Ripley, "Final Scenes at the Capture and Occupation of Richmond, April 3, 1865," in *Personal Recollections of the War of the Rebellion: Addresses Delivered before the Commandery of the State of New York, MOLLUS,* ed. by A. Noel Blakeman (New York, 1891–1912), 3: 473; Royal B. Prescott, "The Capture of Richmond," in *Civil War Papers: Read before the Commandery of the State of Massachusetts, MOLLUS*

(Boston, 1900), 1: 64; *New York Tribune,* Apr. 8, 1865; Baker, *Fall of Richmond,* 9, 12.

42. Weitzel, "Entry of United States Forces into Richmond," 6–7; August V. Kautz memoirs, 104.

43. Thomas Thatcher Graves, "The Fall of Richmond, II: The Evacuation," in *B&L* 4: 726–28; "The First Federal to Enter Richmond . . . Major A. H. Stevens," *SHSP* 30 (1902): 152–53; William B. Arnold, *The Fourth Massachusetts Cavalry in the Closing Scenes of the War for the Maintenance of the Union, from Richmond to Appomattox* (Boston, n.d.), 27–28; Katharine M. Jones, *Ladies of Richmond, Confederate Capital* (Indianapolis, 1962), 281.

44. Arnold, *Fourth Massachusetts Cavalry,* 28–29; Philip Van Doren Stern, *An End to Valor: The Last Days of the Civil War* (Boston, 1958), 185.

45. Charles F. Adams et al., *A Cycle of Adams Letters, 1861–1865,* ed. by Worthington Chauncey Ford (Boston, 1920), 2: 264–65.

CHAPTER 7

1. Munford, "Last Days of Fitz Lee's Division," 66; Balfour, *13th Virginia Cavalry,* 44.

2. Munford, "Last Days of Fitz Lee's Division," 67; Rosser, *Riding with Rosser,* 65–66.

3. Calkins, *Appomattox Campaign,* 69–70.

4. *OR,* I, 46, pt. 1: 1119, 1131.

5. Ibid., pt. 3: 528.

6. Wainwright, *Diary of Battle,* 517; Sheridan, *Personal Memoirs,* 2: 174.

7. Tremain, *Last Hours of Sheridan's Cavalry,* 97–101; H. P. Moyer, comp., *History of the Seventeenth Regiment Pennsylvania Volunteer Cavalry* (Lebanon, Pa., 1911), 176–77, 222; Wainwright, *Diary of Battle,* 517; Richard P. Weinert, "Maj. Henry Young: A Profile," *CWTI* 3 (Apr. 1964): 38–42. For some fact and much romance about Young's career, see *The Campaign Life of Lt.-Col. Henry Harrison Young . . .* (Providence, R. I., 1882).

8. *OR,* I, 46, pt. 1: 1144–45, 1149, 1155, 1157, 1245.

9. Ibid., 1245, 1248, 1250–51.

10. Ibid., 1119, 1131.

11. Ibid., 1140; Clark, ed., *Regiments and Battalions from North Carolina,* 3: 470; Thomas B. Keys, *Tarheel Cossack: W. P. Roberts, Youngest Confederate General* (Orlando, Fla., 1983), 65–66.

12. Clark, ed., *Regiments and Battalions from North Carolina*, 1: 442. This account of the 1st North Carolina was reprinted as Rufus Barringer, *The First North Carolina: A Famous Cavalry Regiment* (n.p., n.d.).

13. *OR*, I, 46, pt. 1: 1131, 1138, 1140; Clark, ed., *Regiments and Battalions from North Carolina*, 1: 442–43.

14. *OR*, I, 46, pt. 1: 1131, 1139; Coltrane, *Memoirs of Daniel Branson Coltrane*, 41–42.

15. *OR*, I, 46, pt. 1: 1115, 1131–32, 1258.

16. Breckinridge, "Second Virginia Cavalry Regt.," 3–4.

17. Rufus Barringer diary, Apr. 3, 1865; Clark, ed., *Regiments and Battalions from North Carolina*, 1: 778–79; *OR*, I, 46, pt. 1: 1139; Lee, Report of W. H. F. Lee's Division, 2; Moyer, comp., *Seventeenth Pennsylvania Cavalry*, 176–77; Coltrane, *Memoirs of Daniel Branson Coltrane*, 42.

18. Rufus Barringer diary, Apr. 3, 1865; Clark, ed., *Regiments and Battalions from North Carolina*, 1: 780.

19. Clark, ed., *Regiments and Battalions from North Carolina*, 1: 780–82; Rufus Barringer diary, Apr. 3–22, 1865.

20. Calkins, *Appomattox Campaign*, 72.

21. *OR*, I, 46, pt. 1: 1132, 1136, 1138–40.

22. Hewett et al., eds., *Supplement to the OR*, I, 7: 746, 783; Calkins, *Appomattox Campaign*, 72–73.

23. *OR*, I, 46, pt. 1: 1119; Sheridan, *Personal Memoirs*, 2: 174.

24. Walter H. Jackson diary, Apr. 3, 1865.

25. John B. Moseley diary, Apr. 3, 1865.

26. *OR*, I, 46, pt. 1: 1106; Sheridan, *Personal Memoirs*, 2: 174.

27. *OR*, I, 46, pt. 1: 681, 839, 905, 1161, 1174, 1235, 1237; Longacre, *Army of Amateurs*, 284.

28. *OR*, I, 46, pt. 1: 1119, 1245.

29. Ibid., 1245, 1250, 1255; *Eleventh Pennsylvania Cavalry*, 151.

30. *OR*, I, 46, pt. 1: 1106–7, 1119.

31. Ibid., 1142, 1145, 1149, 1155, 1157–58; Robert Bell to his wife, Apr. 5, 1865, Bell MSS.

32. Tremain, *Last Hours of Sheridan's Cavalry*, 111–12.

33. Sheridan, *Personal Memoirs*, 2: 175.

34. Ibid.

35. Ibid., 175–76.

36. Ibid., 176; *OR*, I, 46, pt. 1: 1106–07, 1119; John Bakeless, "The Mystery of Appomattox," *CWTI* 9 (June 1970): 20–21.

37. *OR*, I, 46, pt. 1: 1107.

38. Ibid., 1265, 1294; Hewett et al., eds., *Supplement to the OR*, I, 7: 746, 776; Thomas G. Jones, "Last Days of the Army of Northern Virginia," *SHSP* 21 (1893): 79; Bakeless, "Mystery of Appomattox," 20–23; Clark, ed., *Regiments and Battalions from North Carolina*, 1: 781–82.

39. *OR*, I, 46, pt. 1: 1265; Jones, "Last Days of the Army of Northern Virginia," 79–80; Calkins, *Appomattox Campaign*, 76.

40. *OR*, I, 46, pt. 1: 1265.

CHAPTER 8

1. Trout, *In the Saddle with Stuart*, 106.

2. John Esten Cooke, *Wearing of the Gray: Being Personal Portraits, Scenes and Adventures of the War* (Baton Rouge, La., 1997), 557.

3. Robert Bell to his wife, Apr. 5, 1865, Bell MSS.

4. *OR*, I, 46, pt. 1: 1294, 1296; Calkins, *Appomattox Campaign*, 87.

5. Munford, "Last Days of Fitz Lee's Division," 72; Rosser, *Riding with Rosser*, 67.

6. Calkins, *Appomattox Campaign*, 91, 94–95; William Mahone, "On the Road to Appomattox," *CWTI* 9 (Jan. 1971): 8.

7. *OR*, I, 46, pt. 3: 573; Robert Bell to his wife, Apr. 5, 1865, Bell MSS.

8. *OR*, I, 46, pt. 1: 1107, 1142, 1145.

9. Ibid., 1145, 1149–50; Robbins, *War Record and Personal Experiences*, 117–18; George Crook to Rutherford B. Hayes, Apr. 12, 1865, Crook MSS.

10. *OR*, I, 46, pt. 1: 1145; Tremain, *Last Hours of Sheridan's Cavalry*, 125–26.

11. Tremain, *Last Hours of Sheridan's Cavalry*, 127.

12. *OR*, I, 46, pt. 1: 1145, 1150; Calkins, *Appomattox Campaign*, 88.

13. *OR*, I, 46, pt. 1: 1301; Henry C. Lee diary, Apr. 5, 1865, MC.

14. Rosser, *Riding with Rosser*, 67; Cornelius H. Carlton diary, Apr. 5, 1865; Breckinridge, "Second Virginia Cavalry Regt.," 5; Driver, *1st Virginia Cavalry*, 113; Stiles, *4th Virginia Cavalry*, 83–84; Driver, *5th Virginia Cavalry*, 108; Richard L. Armstrong, *11th Virginia Cavalry* (Lynchburg, Va., 1989), 99; Holland, *24th Virginia Cavalry*, 98–101; William L. Parker, *General James Dearing, C.S.A.* (Lynchburg, Va., 1990), 89–90.

15. *OR*, I, 46, pt. 1: 1145, 1150, 1155, 1158; Thomas M. Covert to his wife, Apr. 12, 1865, Covert MSS, USAMHI.

16. Henry E. Davies, *General Sheridan* (New York, 1899), 239–40.

17. *OR*, I, 46, pt. 1: 1143, 1146, 1150; Munford, "Last Days of Fitz Lee's Division," 72–73; Robbins, *War Record and Personal Experiences*, 119;

Hampton S. Thomas, *Some Personal Reminiscences of Service in the Cavalry of the Army of the Potomac* (Philadelphia, 1889), 25.

18. Rosser, *Riding with Rosser,* 67; *OR,* I, 46, pt. 1: 1301.
19. Rawleigh W. Downman to his wife, Apr. 6, 1865, Downman MSS.
20. *OR,* I, 46, pt. 1: 681, 840, 1106; Sheridan, *Personal Memoirs,* 2: 176.
21. Sheridan, *Personal Memoirs,* 2: 176–77.
22. Ibid., 176.
23. *OR,* I, 46, pt. 3: 582.
24. Calkins, *Appomattox Campaign,* 92–93; *OR,* I, 46, pt. 1: 1180; pt. 3: 532; John Gibbon to John W. Turner, Apr. 3, 1865, Turner MSS.
25. William S. Lincoln, *Life with the Thirty-fourth Mass. Infantry in the War of the Rebellion* (Worcester, Mass., 1879), 392–93; *OR,* I, 46, pt. 1: 55; pt. 3: 510.
26. Grant, *Personal Memoirs,* 2: 469; Sheridan, *Personal Memoirs,* 2: 178–79; Porter, "Five Forks and the Pursuit of Lee," 720.
27. *OR,* I, 46, pt. 1: 1245, 1251–52.
28. Ibid., 1245; Calkins, *Appomattox Campaign,* 85.
29. *OR,* I, 46, pt. 1: 1245, 1249, 1253; *Eleventh Pennsylvania Cavalry,* 151.
30. *OR,* I, 46, pt. 1: 1161; pt. 3: 557; Edward T. Bouvé, "The Battle of High Bridge," in *Civil War Papers: Read before the Commandery of the State of Massachusetts, MOLLUS* (Boston, 1900), 2: 404–6.
31. *OR,* I, 46, pt. 1: 1161.
32. Ibid.
33. Ibid., 1161–62; Bouvé, "Battle of High Bridge," 407; Porter, "Five Forks and the Pursuit of Lee," 720.
34. Mahone, "On the Road to Appomattox," 8.
35. Calkins, *Appomattox Campaign,* 91–92.
36. *OR,* I, 46, pt. 1: 1301–2; Hewett et al., eds., *Supplement to the OR,* I, 7: 776; Rosser, *Riding with Rosser,* 68.
37. Freeman Cleaves, *Meade of Gettysburg* (Norman, Okla., 1960), 325.
38. *OR,* I, 46, pt. 1: 604, 681–82.

CHAPTER 9

1. S. C. Lovell diary, Apr. 6, 1865, ACHNHP.
2. C. M. Keyes, ed., *The Military History of the 123rd Regiment Ohio Volunteer Infantry* (Sandusky, Ohio, 1874), 110–11; Bouvé, "Battle of High Bridge," 407.
3. Hewett et al., eds., *Supplement to the OR,* I, 7: 776; Longstreet, *From Manassas to Appomattox,* 612; Rosser, *Riding with Rosser,* 68; Munford, "Last Days of Fitz Lee's Division," 75–76.

4. Munford, "Last Days of Fitz Lee's Division," 77–78.

5. Ibid., 76.

6. Rosser, *Riding with Rosser,* 69; George A. Hundley, "Beginning and the Ending: Reminiscences of the First and Last Days of the War . . . ," *SHSP* 23 (1895): 309–10.

7. Henry Bruce Scott, *The Surrender of General Lee and the Army of Northern Virginia at Appomattox, Virginia, April 9, 1865* (Boston, ca. 1916), [4]; Bouvé, "Battle of High Bridge," 408–9, 412; Milton B. Steele diary, Apr. 6, 1865, MC.

8. P. C. Garvin to "My Dear Sir," June 11, 1865, 4th Massachusetts Cavalry Letterbook, 54, USAMHI; S. C. Lovell diary, Apr. 6, 1865; Arnold, *Fourth Massachusetts Cavalry,* 30–31; Scott, *Surrender of General Lee,* [3]-[4]; Bouvé, "Battle of High Bridge," 410; Burleigh Cushing Rodick, *Appomattox: The Last Campaign* (New York, 1965), 73; Driver, *1st Virginia Cavalry,* 114; Stiles, *4th Virginia Cavalry,* 84; Driver, *5th Virginia Cavalry,* 109.

9. Rosser, *Riding with Rosser,* 68–69; William N. McDonald, *A History of the Laurel Brigade, Originally the Ashby Cavalry of the Army of Northern Virginia, and Chew's Battery,* ed. by Bushrod C. Washington (Baltimore, 1907), 377; William L. Wilson, *A Borderland Confederate,* ed. by Festus P. Summers (Pittsburgh, 1962), 99; Driver, *5th Virginia Cavalry,* 109–10; Divine, *35th Battalion Virginia Cavalry,* 67; Parker, *General James Dearing,* 89.

10. Tremain, *Last Hours of Sheridan's Cavalry,* 175; Keyes, *123rd Ohio,* 110–11; Joseph W. Keifer, *Slavery and Four Years of War . . . A Narrative of the Campaigns and Battles of the Civil War in Which the Author Took Part, 1861–1865* (New York, 1900), 2: 216–19; Edwin Snyder, *Adventures and Misadventures, Civil and Military, of a Union Veteran of the Civil War* (Topeka, Kans., 1909), 40–42.

11. Bouvé, "Battle of High Bridge," 411; Rodick, *Appomattox,* 72.

12. *OR,* I, 46, pt. 1: 1302–3; Wilson, *Borderland Confederate,* 99; Henry C. Lee diary, Apr. 6, 1865; Driver, *5th Virginia Cavalry,* 109; Dennis E. Frye, *12th Virginia Cavalry* (Lynchburg, Va., 1988), 81; Rosser, *Riding with Rosser,* 70.

13. Munford, "Last Days of Fitz Lee's Division," 77–78, 84.

14. Sheridan, *Personal Memoirs,* 2: 179.

15. *OR,* I, 46, pt. 1: 1107, 1142, 1158.

16. Ibid., 1158.

17. Ibid., 165.

18. Ibid., 1132; Schaff, *Sunset of the Confederacy,* 110; Calkins, *Appomattox Campaign,* 105.

19. *OR,* I, 46, pt. 1: 1301–2.
20. Ibid., 1294, 1302.
21. Ibid., 682, 1107–8; Hewett et al., eds., *Supplement to the OR,* I, 7: 797; Sheridan, *Personal Memoirs,* 2: 179, 183; Newhall, "With Sheridan in Lee's Last Campaign," *MB* 2(1895): 251.
22. Hewett et al., eds., *Supplement to the OR,* I, 7: 797–98; John Brown Gordon, *Reminiscences of the Civil War* (New York, 1905), 429–30.
23. Calkins, *Appomattox Campaign,* 113–14.
24. *OR,* I, 46, pt. 1: 1294, 1297, 1302.
25. Ibid., 905–6, 1107–8, 1120, 1124, 1132, 1138–39.
26. Ibid., 906, 913–14, 979, 1108, 1265–66, 1294–95, 1297; Hewett et al., eds., *Supplement to the OR,* I, 7: 747; Sheridan, *Personal Memoirs,* 2: 180–82; Chris M. Calkins, *Thirty-six Hours before Appomattox: April 6 and 7, 1865* (Farmville, Va., 1980), 6–11.
27. *OR,* I, 46, pt. 1: 906, 914–15, 979, 1283–84, 1295, 1297; Newhall, "With Sheridan in Lee's Last Campaign," 2: 254–56.
28. Robbins, *War Record and Personal Experiences,* 120–21; *OR,* I, 46, pt. 1: 1151.
29. Robbins, *War Record and Personal Experiences,* 100–101, 118–19; Henry R. Pyne, *The History of the First New Jersey Cavalry* (Trenton, 1871), 300–2.
30. Tremain, *Last Hours of Sheridan's Cavalry,* 152–53.
31. *OR,* I, 46, pt. 1: 1142, 1145–46, 1151; Crook, *Autobiography,* 138; Sheridan, *Personal Memoirs,* 2: 181.
32. Luman F. Tenney, *War Diary of Luman Harris Tenney, 1861–1865,* ed. Frances Andrews Tenney (Cleveland, 1914), 155; Hannaford, Memoir of the Appomattox Campaign, 2.
33. *OR,* I, 46, pt. 1: 1132; Hannaford, Memoir of the Appomattox Campaign, 2.
34. *OR,* I, 46, pt. 1: 1108, 1120; Sheridan, *Personal Memoirs,* 2: 180, 183; Hannaford, Memoir of the Appomattox Campaign, 11.
35. Hannaford, Memoir of the Appomattox Campaign, 11.
36. *OR,* I, 46, pt. 1: 1120, 1124–25, 1129, 1132, 1136, 1289–90; James Bradley diary, Apr. 6, 1865; Hiram Rix, Jr., diary, Apr. 6, 1865; Walter H. Jackson diary, Apr. 6, 1865; Newhall, "With Sheridan in Lee's Last Campaign," 2: 291–92.
37. Mahone, "On the Road to Appomattox," 9.
38. *OR,* I, 46, pt. 1: 1120, 1125; Sheridan, *Personal Memoirs,* 2: 184.
39. *OR,* I, 46, pt. 1: 1120, 1162, 1174.
40. Driver, *5th Virginia Cavalry,* 111; Rosser, *Riding with Rosser,* 70.

41. *OR,* I, 46, pt. 1: 682, 1266; Hewett et al., eds., *Supplement to the OR,* I, 7: 776, 797.

42. Boykin, *Falling Flag,* 28.

43. Ibid., 27.

44. Ibid., 29.

45. Ibid.

46. *OR,* I, 46, pt. 3: 610.

47. Abraham Lincoln, *The Collected Works of Abraham Lincoln,* ed. by Roy P. Basler et al. (New Brunswick, N. J., 1953), 8: 392.

CHAPTER 10

1. *OR,* I, 46, pt. 1: 1266.

2. Mahone, "On the Road to Appomattox," 10–11.

3. Ibid., 11, 42; *OR,* I, 46, pt. 1: 683, 758–59.

4. *OR,* I, 46, pt. 1: 1266.

5. Munford, "Last Days of Fitz Lee's Division," 79; Rosser, *Riding with Rosser,* 70.

6. Munford, "Last Days of Fitz Lee's Division," 79.

7. *OR,* I, 46, pt. 1: 55–56, 1109, 1162.

8. Munford, "Last Days of Fitz Lee's Division," 79–80; Rosser, *Riding with Rosser,* 70.

9. Edward P. Tobie, *History of the First Maine Cavalry, 1861–1865* (Boston, 1887), 418.

10. Crook, *Autobiography,* 139.

11. *OR,* I, 46, pt. 1: 1158.

12. Ibid., 1158–59; Robert Bell to his wife, Apr. 7, 1865, Bell MSS.

13. *OR,* I, 46, pt. 1: 683–84, 713, 759–61, 768–69; Mahone, "On the Road to Appomattox," 42–43; Breckinridge, "Second Virginia Cavalry Regt.," 6–7.

14. Calkins, *Appomattox Campaign,* 133; Sheridan, *Personal Memoirs,* 2: 188; Newhall, "With Sheridan in Lee's Last Campaign," 2: 303.

15. Munford, "Last Days of Fitz Lee's Division," 80–81; Rosser, *Riding with Rosser,* 70–71.

16. Munford, "Last Days of Fitz Lee's Division," 81; Driver, *1st Virginia Cavalry,* 114; Nanzig, *3rd Virginia Cavalry,* 74; Divine, *35th Battalion Virginia Cavalry,* 69; Hundley, "Beginning and the Ending," 310.

17. *OR,* I, 46, pt. 1: 1109, 1142, 1151, 1303; Crook, *Autobiography,* 139; Hannaford, Memoir of the Appomattox Campaign, 24; Munford, "Last Days of Fitz Lee's Division," 81; Edward H. McDonald, "I Felt a Ball

Strike Me, I Could Not Tell Where," *CWTI* 7 (June 1968): 32; Milton B. Steele diary, Apr. 7, 1865.

18. William Miller Owen, *In Camp and Battle with the Washington Artillery of New Orleans . . .* (Boston, 1885), 378–79.

19. Rosser, *Riding with Rosser,* 71; *OR,* I, 46, pt. 1: 1303.

20. Marcellus French, "Second Dispatch from Grant to Lee," *CV* 8 (1900): 258.

21. *OR,* I, 46, pt. 1: 1109, 1142; Robert Bell to his wife, Apr. 7, 1865, Bell MSS.

22. Davis, *To Appomattox,* 289–90.

23. *OR,* I, 46, pt. 1: 56; pt. 3: 619; Porter, *Campaigning with Grant,* 453, 459; Horace Porter, "The Surrender at Appomattox Court House," in *B&L* 4: 729.

24. *OR,* I, 46, pt. 1: 56; pt. 3: 641, 664.

25. Ibid., pt. 1: 1109; Sheridan, *Personal Memoirs,* 2: 187–88.

26. *OR,* I, 46, pt. 1: 1245, 1249, 1255; *Eleventh Pennsylvania Cavalry,* 152.

27. *OR,* I, 46, pt. 1: 1109, 1142; pt. 3: 633, 653–54; Sheridan, *Personal Memoirs,* 2: 188; Tremain, *Last Hours of Sheridan's Cavalry,* 200–201.

28. *OR,* I, 46, pt. 1: 1109; Tremain, *Last Hours of Sheridan's Cavalry,* 199; Calkins, *Appomattox Campaign,* 138.

29. *OR,* I, 46, pt. 1: 1142; pt. 3: 653–54; Sheridan, *Personal Memoirs,* 2: 188–89; Stephen Tripp, "The Cavalry at Appomattox, April 9, 1865," *MB* n.s. 5 (1898: 212.

30. *OR,* I, 46, pt. 1: 1109; Sheridan, *Personal Memoirs,* 2: 188–89; Bakeless, "Mystery of Appomattox," 26–27.

31. *OR,* I, 46, pt. 1: 1109, 1120, 1126, 1132; Sheridan, *Personal Memoirs,* 2: 189–90.

32. *OR,* I, 46, pt. 1: 1162, 1181, 1187, 1215, 1235, 1243; *New York Herald,* Apr. 14, 1865; Longacre, *Army of Amateurs,* 306–7.

33. *OR,* I, 46, pt. 1: 1162, 1235–36, 1243; Gibbon, *Personal Recollections,* 307–8, 315; *New York Herald,* Apr. 14, 1865; John Gibbon to John W. Turner, Apr. 8, 1865, Turner MSS.

34. Chris M. Calkins, *The Batles of Appomattox Station and Appomattox Court House, April 8–9, 1865* (Lynchburg, Va. 1987), 28–29.

35. Alanson M. Randol, *Last Days of the Rebellion: The Second New York Cavalry (Harris Light) at Appomattox Station and Appomattox Court House, April 8 and 9, 1865* (San Francisco, 1883), 5–6.

36. *OR,* I, 46, pt. 1: 1109, 1120, 1132, 1136–37; pt. 3: 653–54; Calkins, *Battles of Appomattox,* 30–32; Hiram Rix, Jr., diary, Apr. 8, 1865; William Wells to his parents, Apr. 11, 1865, Wells MSS, Guy W. Bailey

Lib., Univ. of Vermont, Burlington; Walter H. Jackson diary, Apr. 8, 1865; Hannaford, Memoir of the Appomattox Campaign, 24–25; Randol, *Last Days of the Rebellion,* 5–6; Cummings, "Six Months with the Third Cavalry Division," 310; Schaff, *Sunset of the Confederacy,* 192; Hatton, ed., "Just a Little Bit of the Civil War," 227; Sheridan, *Personal Memoirs,* 2: 190.

37. Boykin, *Falling Flag,* 45–49; Calkins, *Appomattox Campaign,* 154.
38. W. F. Robinson, "Last Battle Before Surrender," *CV* 32 (1924): 470–71.
39. Ibid.; Calkins, *Battles of Appomattox,* 32–34.
40. Boykin, *Falling Flag,* 50–51.
41. Robinson, "Last Battle Before Surrender," 471.
42. Ibid.; *OR,* I, 46, pt. 1: 1109, 1120, 1132, 1140; Hannaford, Memoir of the Appomattox Campaign, 25; Randol, *Last Days of the Rebellion,* 7–8; Hewett et al., eds., *Supplement to the OR,* I, 7: 798, 800.
43. Robinson, "Last Battle Before Surrender," 471; Boykin, *Falling Flag,* 50–51.
44. Calkins, *Battles of Appomattox,* 35.
45. *OR,* I, 46, pt. 1: 1109, 1120, 1126, 1137, 1140; pt. 3: 653; William Wells to his parents, Apr. 11, 1865, Wells MSS.
46. Randol, *Last Days of the Rebellion,* 8; Chauncey S. Norton, *"The Red Neck Ties," or, History of the Fifteenth New York Volunteer Cavalry . . .* (Ithaca, N. Y., 1891), 93–96.
47. Norton, *"Red Neck Ties,"* 96.
48. *OR,* I, 46, pt. 1: 1109, 1120, 1126, 1137, 1140; pt. 3: 653; Calkins, *Battles of Appomattox,* 40.
49. *OR,* I, 46, pt. 1: 1109; pt. 3: 654; Sheridan, *Personal Memoirs,* 2: 191.

CHAPTER 11
1. Driver, *1st Virginia Cavalry,* 115; Breckinridge, "Second Virginia Cavalry Regt.," 7.
2. Rosser, *Riding with Rosser,* 71.
3. *OR,* I, 46, pt. 1: 684; Calkins, *Battles of Appomattox,* 9–19.
4. William B. F. Leech, Memoir of the Appomattox Campaign, [2], VHS.
5. Ibid.
6. Ibid.
7. Philip H. Sheridan, "Last Days of the Rebellion," in *Military Essays and Recollections: Papers Read before the Commandery of the State of Illinois, MOLLUS* (Chicago, 1891–1907), 1: 433; Moyer, comp., *Seventeenth Pennsylvania Cavalry,* 315–16.

8. Calkins, *Appomattox Campaign,* 150.

9. Calkins, *Battles of Appomattox,* 42–44.

10. C.H. Smith, "Incidents of Appomattox," *MB* 3 (1893): 42–43; *OR,* I, 46, pt. 1: 1159; Calkins, *Battles of Appomattox,* 42–44; 62–63.

11. Calkins, *Battles of Appomattox,* 42–43; Tobie, *First Maine Cavalry,* 422–24.

12. Hewett et al., eds., *Supplement to the OR,* I, 7: 793; *OR,* I, 46, pt. 1: 1303; Calkins, *Battles of Appomattox,* 55.

13. Hewett et al., eds., *Supplement to the OR,* I, 7: 793, 800; *OR,* I, 46, pt. 1: 1303.

14. Munford, "Last Days of Fitz Lee's Division," 83–84.

15. Rosser, *Riding with Rosser,* 72.

16. Ibid., 72–73.

17. Ibid., 73.

18. *OR,* I, 46, pt. 1: 1174, 1180, 1186–87, 1203, 1218; pt. 3: 611, 1389; Grant, *Personal Memoirs,* 2: 481; Porter, *Campaigning with Grant,* 124; Gibbon, *Personal Recollections,* 306; Lincoln, *Thirty-fourth Mass.,* 395; Rodick, *Appomattox,* 97; *New York Herald,* Apr. 14, 1865.

19. S. C. Lovell diary, Apr. 8, 1865; Gibbon, *Personal Recollections,* 311; William H. Wharff, "From Chapin's Farm to Appomattox," *MB* n.s. 3 (1896): 234; Calkins, *Battles of Appomattox,* 45.

20. Gibbon, *Personal Recollections,* 307–8, 315.

21. *OR,* I, 46, pt. 1: 1266, 1303; Hewett et al., eds., *Supplement to the OR,* I, 7: 777, 793, 798–801.

22. Calkins, *Battles of Appomattox,* 57–76.

23. Blackford, *War Years with Jeb Stuart,* 291; Clark, ed., *Regiments and Battalions from North Carolina,* 4: 96; Calkins, *Battles of Appomattox,* 62; Keys, *Tarheel Cossack,* 69.

24. *OR,* I, 46, pt. 1: 1142–43, 1159; Smith, "Incidents of Appomattox," 42–43; Calkins, *Battles of Appomattox,* 63.

25. *OR,* I, 46, pt. 1: 1159; Smith, "Incidents of Appomattox," 43–44.

26. *OR,* I, 46, pt. 1: 1143, 1245–46.

27. Ibid., 1246.

28. Calkins, *Appomattox Campaign,* 144–45.

29. *OR,* I, 46, pt. 1: 1155.

30. Ibid., 69; John E. Bouldin, "Our Last Charge," *CV* 22 (1914): 557.

31. Calkins, *Battles of Appomattox,* 69.

32. *OR,* I, 46, pt. 1: 1155.

33. Leech, Memoir of the Appomattox Campaign, [3]-[6]; Edwin E. Bouldin, "The Last Charge at Appomattox: The Fourteenth Virginia

Cavalry," *SHSP* 28 (1900): 251–53; W. L. Moffett, "The Last Charge of the 14th Virginia Cavalry at Appomattox C. H., Va., April 9, 1865," *SHSP* 36 (1908): 13–16; Bouldin, "Our Last Charge," 557.

34. *OR*, I, 46, pt. 1: 1155–56.
35. Ibid., 1126–29; Calkins, *Battles of Appomattox*, 73.
36. *OR*, I, 46, pt. 1: 1126.
37. Calkins, *Battles of Appomattox*, 73.
38. Ibid.
39. Hannaford, Memoir of the Appomattox Campaign, 28.
40. Ibid., 28–29.
41. Calkins, *Battles of Appomattox*, 109.
42. Ibid., 111–12.
43. Ibid., 113–14; Hannaford, Memoir of the Appomattox Campaign, 33.
44. *OR*, I, 46, pt. 1: 1138, 1140–41; Norton, *"Red Neck Ties,"* 98–99.
45. Merritt, "Appomattox Campaign," 125–27.
46. *OR*, I, 46, pt. 1: 1162–63, 1175; Longacre, *Army of Amateurs*, 308–9.
47. *OR*, I, 46, pt. 1: 1162–63, 1175, 1181, 1187, 1196, 1203–4, 1215, 1236, 1239, 1243; Calkins, *Battles of Appomattox*, 79–93.
48. Cummings, "Three Months in the Third Cavalry Division," 311; Joshua L. Chamberlain, "Appomattox," in *Personal Recollections of the War of the Rebellion: Addresses Delivered before the Commandery of the State of New York, MOLLUS*, ed. by A. Noel Blakeman (New York, 1891–1912), 3: 269; Calkins, *Battles of Appomattox*, 25–27.
49. Edward W. Whitaker to Joshua L. Chamberlain, Apr. 29, 1901, Whitaker MSS, ACHNHP; Cummings, "Six Months in the Third Cavalry Division," 312–13. The most thorough account of the truce flags is Harris S. Colt, "Flags at Appomattox," a copy of which is in ACHNHP.
50. Blackford, *War Years with Jeb Stuart*, 288–91; Boykin, *Falling Flag*, 59–60; Sheridan, *Personal Memoirs*, 2: 194, 196–97; W. G. Hinson, "Gen. Sheridan's Reference to Gen. M. C. [M. W.] Gary, of South Carolina," *CV* 2 (1894): 278; J. H. Doyle, "With Gary's Brigade at Appomattox," *CV* 29 (1921): 332.
51. Boykin, *Falling Flag*, 60.
52. Ibid., 61.
53. Munford, "Last Days of Fitz Lee's Division," 92–93; Breckinridge, "Second Virginia Cavalry Regt.," 8.
54. Calkins, *Battles of Appomattox*, 116.
55. Munford, "Last Days of Fitz Lee's Division," 88, 92–93.
56. Ibid.; Driver, *First & Second Maryland Cavalry*, 120–23.

57. Samuel E. Cormany and Rachel B. Cormany. *The Cormany Diaries: A Northern Family in the Civil War,* ed. by James C. Mohr and Richard E. Winslow, III (Pittsburgh, 1982), 539–40.

58. Munford, "Last Days of Fitz Lee's Division," 94–95.

59. Ibid., 96.

60. Rosser, *Riding with Rosser,* 73; Hewett et al., eds., *Supplement to the OR,* I, 7: 793, 798, 801–03.

61. Calkins, *Appomattox Campaign,* 187; Frank P. Cauble, "The Proceedings Connected with the Surrender of the Army of Northern Virginia, April, 1865" (typescript in ACHNHP), 156–57.

62. Thomas T. Munford to Ranald S. Mackenzie, Apr. 13, 17, 1865, Munford MSS, DU; John Gibbon to Thomas T. Munford, Apr. 21, 1865, Ibid.; Samuel W. Melton to Thomas L. Rosser, Apr. 10, 1865, Rosser MSS, UV; Breckinridge, "Second Virginia Cavalry Regt.," 10; Rawleigh W. Downman to his wife, Apr. 25, 1865, Downman MSS; Driver, *1st Virginia Cavalry,* 117; Armstrong, *11th Virginia Cavalry,* 98–99.

63. Mark K. Greenough, "Aftermath at Appomattox: Federal Military Occupation of Appomattox County, May-November 1865," *Civil War History* 31(1985): 5–23; Longacre, *Army of Amateurs,* 315–19; *OR,* I, 46, pt. 1: 1315–17; Calkins, *Appomattox Campaign,* 198–200.

64. Devin, "Didn't We Fight Splendid," 40.

BIBLIOGRAPHY

UNPUBLISHED MATERIALS

Adams, Charles F., Jr. Correspondence. Houghton Library, Harvard University, Cambridge, Mass.

Alberts, Don E. "General Wesley Merritt, Nineteenth Century Cavalryman." Ph.D. diss., University of New Mexico, 1975.

Alexander, Charles G. Diary, 1865. Alderman Library, University of Virginia, Charlottesville.

Alexander, E. Porter. Correspondence. Wilson Library, University of North Carolina, Chapel Hill.

Allen, John C. Diary, 1865. Virginia Historical Society, Richmond.

Allen, R. Alfred. Diary, 1865. William R. Perkins Library, Duke University, Durham, N.C.

Baker, Allen. Diary, 1865. U. S. Army Military History Institute, Carlisle Barracks, Pa.

Barnitz, Albert. Diary, 1865. Beinecke Rare Book and Manuscript Library, Yale University, New Haven, Conn.

Barringer, Rufus C. Correspondence and Diary, 1865. Wilson Library, University of North Carolina.

"The Battle of High Bridge, April 6, 1865." Appomattox Court House National Historical Park, Appomattox, Va.

"Battle of Sayler's Creek." Appomattox Court House National Historical Park.

Beale, Richard L. T. History of 9th Virginia Cavalry. Alderman Library, University of Virginia.

Beane, Thomas O. "Thomas Lafayette Rosser: Soldier, Railroad Builder, Politician, Businessman (1836–1910)." Master's thesis, University of Virginia, 1957.

Bell, Robert. Correspondence. Appomattox Court House National Historical Park.

Blackford, William W. "First and Last; or, Battles in Virginia." Library of Virginia, Richmond.

Bradley, James. Diary, 1865. Connecticut Historical Society, Hartford.

Breckinridge, Cary. "The Second Virginia Cavalry Regt. from Five Forks to Appomattox." Virginia Historical Society.

Carlton, Cornelius H. Diary, 1865. Virginia Historical Society.

———. History of the 24th Virginia Cavalry. J. Y. Joyner Library, East Carolina University, Greenville, N.C.

Carr, Henry C. Diary, 1865. U. S. Army Military History Institute.

Cauble, Frank P. "The Battle of Appomattox Station, April 8, 1865, and the Battle of Appomattox Court House, April 9, 1865: A Narrative Study to Accompany Troop Movement Maps." Appomattox Court House National Historical Park.

———. "The Proceedings Connected with the Surrender of the Army of Northern Virginia, April, 1865." Appomattox Court House National Historical Park.

Chewning, Charles R. Diary, 1865. Handley Regional Library, Winchester, Va.

Clarke, Garland H. Diary, 1865. Virginia Historical Society.

Claybrook, Edwin C. Correspondence. Eleanor S. Brockenbrough Library, Museum of the Confederacy, Richmond, Va.

Colt, Harris S. "Flags at Appomattox." In possession of the author, New York, N.Y.

Cooke, John Esten. Correspondence and Diary, 1865. Alderman Library, University of Virginia.

Covert, Thomas M. Correspondence. U.S. Army Military History Institute.

Crawford, J. Milton. Letter of May 18, 1865. U. S. Army Military History Institute.

Crook, George. Correspondence. Rutherford B. Hayes Presidential Center, Fremont, Ohio.

———. Correspondence. U.S. Army Military History Institute.

Custer, George Armstrong. Correspondence. Monroe County Historical Museum, Monroe, Mich.

———. Correspondence. New York Public Library, New York, N.Y.

————. Correspondence. United States Military Academy Library, West Point, N.Y.

Davis, Thomas J. Diary, 1865. Maryland Historical Society, Baltimore.

Dearing, James. Correspondence. Historical Society of Pennsylvania, Philadelphia.

Devin, Thomas C. Correspondence. In possession of Miss M. Catherine Devin, Midland Park, N.J.

Dickinson, Henry C. Diary, 1865. Virginia Historical Society.

Doherty, William. Letter of April 10, 1865. Clarke Historical Library, Central Michigan University, Mount Pleasant.

Donohoe, John C. Diary, 1865. Library of Virginia.

Downman, Rawleigh W. Correspondence. Virginia Historical Society.

Edwards, Thomas W. B. Correspondence and Diary, 1865. Library of Virginia.

Feamster, Thomas L. Diary, 1865. Library of Congress, Washington, D.C.

Follmer, John D. Diary, 1865. William L. Clements Library, University of Michigan, Ann Arbor.

Ford, Thomas J. Letter of January 4, 1865. Waldo Library, Western Michigan University, Kalamazoo.

Fortier, John B. "Story of a Regiment: The Campaigns and Personnel of the Fifteenth Virginia Cavalry, 1862–1865." Master's thesis, College of William and Mary, 1968.

4th Massachusetts Cavalry. Letterbook, 1864–65. U.S. Army Military History Institute.

Franklin, William. Letter of January 18, 1865. Bentley Historical Library, University of Michigan.

Freeman, Douglas Southall. Papers. Library of Congress.

Gatewood, Andrew C. L. Diary, 1865. Wise Library, West Virginia University, Morgantown.

Gary, Martin W. Correspondence. South Caroliniana Library, University of South Carolina, Columbia.

————. Correspondence. Virginia Historical Society.

Generals' Reports of Service, War of the Rebellion, 1863–65. Record Group 94, Entry 160, National Archives, Washington, D.C.

Gibson, John A. Diary, 1865. Virginia Historical Society.

Gordon, John W. Diary, 1865. Eleanor S. Brockenbrough Library, Museum of the Confederacy.

Gordon, W. H. "Operations from the Evacuation of Petersburg to Appomattox." U.S. Army War College Study, 1914. U.S. Army Military History Institute.

Grant, Ulysses S. Papers. Library of Congress.

Gregg, J. Irvin. Correspondence. Historical Society of Pennsylvania.

Grommon, Franklin P. Diary, 1865. Bentley Historical Library, University of Michigan.

Gross, Frank. Diary, 1865. Bentley Historical Library, University of Michigan.

Grussell, T. W. Diary, 1865. William R. Perkins Library, Duke University.

Hall, Rowland M. Correspondence. North Carolina State Department of Archives and History, Raleigh.

Hanmer, Herman D. Correspondence. In possession of Mr. Reginald Pettus, Keysville, Va.

Hanna, Stewart. Letter of March 21, 1865. U.S. Army Military History Institute.

Hannaford, Roger. Memoir of the Appomattox Campaign. Appomattox Court House National Historical Park.

Hardin, William D. Letter of March 27, 1865. William R. Perkins Library, Duke University.

Harding, Hiram W. Diary, 1865. Eleanor S. Brockenbrough Library, Museum of the Confederacy.

Harris, Thomas M. Correspondence. Wise Library, West Virginia University.

Hill, Charles S. "Siege of Petersburg from August 1, 1864, to the Surrender at Appomattox." U.S. Army War College Study, 1916. U.S. Army Military History Institute.

Hoffman, Elliott Wheelock. "Vermont General: The Military Development of William Wells, 1861–1865." Master's thesis, University of Vermont, 1974.

Horne, Thomas. Correspondence. Ablah Library, Wichita State University, Wichita, Kans.

Hubard, Robert T. Letter of January 9, 1865. Alderman Library, University of Virginia.

———. Memoirs. William R. Perkins Library, Duke University.

Huddleston, Peter L. Diary, 1865. Fredericksburg-Spotsylvania National Military Park, Fredericksburg, Va.

Iredell, Cadwallader J. Correspondence. Wilson Library, University of North Carolina.

Jackson, Walter H. Diary, 1865. Bentley Historical Library, University of Michigan.

Johnson, Elijah S. Diary, 1865. Virginia Historical Society.

Kautz, August V. Correspondence and Diaries, 1864–65. Library of Congress.

———. Memoirs. U.S. Army Military History Institute.

Kay, Andrew H. Correspondence. Virginia Historical Society.

Lambert, W. H. Letter of June 8, 1865. New Jersey Historical Society, Newark.

Lee, Fitzhugh. Correspondence. Earl Gregg Swem Library, College of William and Mary, Williamsburg, Va.

———. Correspondence. U.S. Army Military History Institute.

———. Correspondence. Virginia Historical Society.

———. Report of Cavalry Operations, Army of Northern Virginia, March 28–April 9, 1865. Gilder Lehrman Collection, New York, N.Y.

———. Report of Lee's Division, Cavalry Corps, Army of Northern Virginia, May 1864. Eleanor S. Brockenbrough Library, Museum of the Confederacy.

Lee, Henry C. Diary, 1865. Eleanor S. Brockenbrough Library, Museum of the Confederacy.

Lee, Robert E. Papers. Virginia Historical Society.

Lee, W. H. F. Correspondence. Alderman Library, University of Virginia.

———. Report of W. H. F. Lee's Division, Cavalry Corps, Army of Northern Virginia, March 29–April 9, 1865. Virginia Historical Society.

Leech, William B. F. Memoir of the Appomattox Campaign. Virginia Historical Society.

Lewis, William F. Diary, 1865. Eleanor S. Brockenbrough Library, Museum of the Confederacy.

Loveland, C. F. History of the 6th Ohio Cavalry. Ohio State Library, Columbus.

Lovell, S. C. Diary, 1865. Appomattox Court House National Historical Park.

Lyle, Henry. Correspondence. U.S. Army Military History Institute.

Mason, St. George T. Diary, 1865. Virginia Historical Society.

McIlwraith, Stewart W. Letter of March 24, 1865. U.S. Army Military History Institute.

McVicar, Charles W. Memoirs. Library of Congress.

Meade, George Gordon. Correspondence. Historical Society of Pennsylvania.

Merritt, Wesley. Correspondence. New York Public Library.

Miller, J. Wright. Letter of February 18, 1865. U.S. Army Military History Institute.

Monaghan, John W. Diary, 1865. Bentley Historical Library, University of Michigan.

Moore, John H. "Appomattox Court House: Community, Village, and Families, 1845–1870." Appomattox Court House National Historical Park.

Morey, William C. History of the 1st New York Dragoons. William R. Perkins Library, Duke University.

Moseley, John B. Diary, 1865. Virginia Historical Society.

Munford, Thomas T. Correspondence. Eleanor S. Brockenbrough Library, Museum of the Confederacy.

———. Correspondence. Library of Congress.

———. Correspondence. Library of Virginia.

———. Correspondence. Preston Library, Virginia Military Institute, Lexington.

———. Correspondence. William R. Perkins Library, Duke University.

———. "The Last Days of Fitz Lee's Division of Cavalry, Army of Northern Virginia, 1865." Virginia Historical Society.

Nunnelee, Lewis T. Memoirs. Eleanor S. Brockenbrough Library, Museum of the Confederacy.

Ord, Edward O. C. Correspondence. Bancroft Library, University of California, Berkeley.

———. Correspondence. C. H. Green Library, Stanford University, Palo Alto, Calif.

Patrick, Marsena R. Diary, 1865. Library of Congress.

Payne, Alexander D. Diary, 1865. Virginia Historical Society.

Payne, William H. F. Correspondence. Virginia Historical Society.

———. Correspondence and Memoirs. Eleanor S. Brockenbrough Library, Museum of the Confederacy.

———. Papers. Library of Virginia.

Perkins, Frederick. "A Historical Study on the Siege of Petersburg from August 1, 1864, to Surrender at Appomattox." U.S. Army War College Study, 1915. U.S. Army Military History Institute.

Pickett, George E. Papers. Arthur Crew Inman Collection, Brown University Library, Providence, R.I.

Porter, Horace. Correspondence. Library of Congress.

Prentiss, George H. Letter of February 26, 1865. U.S. Army Military History Institute.

Preston, Noble D. Memoirs. New York Public Library.

Pringle, John D. Letter of May 8, 1865. U.S. Army Military History Institute.

Rand, Arnold A. Memoirs. U.S. Army Military History Institute.

Rappalyea, Lewis C. Diary, 1865. New Jersey Historical Society.

Rawlins, John A. Papers. Library of Congress.

Readnor, Henry W. "General Fitzhugh Lee, 1835–1915." Ph.D. diss., University of Virginia, 1958.

Ressler, Isaac H. Diary, 1865. U.S. Army Military History Institute.

Rix, Hiram, Jr. Diary, 1865. Clarke Historical Library, Central Michigan University.

Rosser, Thomas L. Correspondence. Alderman Library, University of Virginia.

———. Correspondence. Eleanor S. Brockenbrough Library, Museum of the Confederacy.

———. Correspondence. Library of Congress.

———. Correspondence. Virginia Historical Society.

Scott, James McClure. Memoirs. Virginia Historical Society.

Sedinger, James D. Memoirs. Wise Library, West Virginia University.

Sexton, Hiram. Letter of January 30, 1865. U.S. Army Military History Institute.

Sharrah, John. Diary, 1865. Appomattox Court House National Historical Park.

Sheridan, Philip H. Correspondence. Henry E. Huntington Library, San Marino, Calif.

———. Correspondence. Library of Congress.

———. Correspondence. United States Military Academy Library.

Simonds, George W. Letter of August 1, 1865. Bentley Historical Library, University of Michigan.

Steele, Milton B. Diary, 1865. Eleanor S. Brockenbrough Library, Museum of the Confederacy.

Stevens, Atherton H. Correspondence. Massachusetts Historical Society, Boston.

Swift, Eben. "The Tactical Use of Cavalry in the Appomattox Campaign." U.S. Army War College Study, 1910. U.S. Army Military History Institute.

Thomas, Robert N. "Brigadier General Thomas T. Munford and the Confederacy." Master's thesis, Duke University, 1958.

Thompson, Stephen W. Diary, 1865. Clarke Historical Library, Central Michigan University.

Turner, John Wesley. Correspondence. U.S. Army Military History Institute.

Turrentine, James A. Diary, 1865. Virginia Historical Society.

Unidentified Enlisted Man, 2nd New York Cavalry. Diary, 1865. New York Public Library.

Veil, Charles H. Memoirs. War Library, National Commandery, Military Order of the Loyal Legion of the United States, Philadelphia, Pa.

Watkins, Richard H. Correspondence. Earl Gregg Swem Library, College of William and Mary.

———. Correspondence. Virginia Historical Society.

Weitzel, Godfrey. "Entry of United States Forces into Richmond, Virginia, April 3, 1865 . . ." Cincinnati Historical Society, Cincinnati, Ohio.

Wells, Edward L. Papers. Charleston Library Society, Charleston, S.C.

Wells, William. Correspondence. Guy W. Bailey Library, University of Vermont, Burlington.

Whitaker, Edward W. Correspondence. Appomattox National Historical Park.

Willis, Byrd C. Diary, 1865, and Memoirs. Library of Virginia.

Wilson, William L. Memoir of Appomattox Campaign. Gilder Lehrman Collection.

NEWSPAPERS

Daily Richmond Examiner
New York Herald
New York Times
New York Tribune
Petersburg Express
Petersburg Register
Philadelphia Weekly Times
Richmond Daily Dispatch
Richmond Daily Enquirer
Richmond Sentinel
Richmond Times-Dispatch
Richmond Whig

ARTICLES AND ESSAYS

Adams, John S. "With Lincoln from Washington to Richmond in 1865." *Appleton's Magazine* 9 (1907): 523–24.

Adams, Silas. "Capture of Richmond, Virginia, April 3, 1865." In *War Papers: Read before the Commandery of the State of Maine, Military Order of the Loyal Legion of the United States.* 3 vols. (Portland: various publishers, 1898–1908), 3: 251–62.

"Appomattox and the Last Man Killed." *Maine Bugle* n.s. 3 (1896): 35–36.

Bakeless, John. "The Mystery of Appomattox." *Civil War Times Illustrated* 9 (June 1970): 18–32.

Barnes, John S. "With Lincoln from Washington to Richmond in 1865." *Appleton's Magazine* 9 (1907): 515–24, 742–51.

Barringer, Rufus. "Cavalry Sketches." *The Land We Love* 4 (1867–68): 1–6.

Becker, Joseph. "Richmond." *Frank Leslie's Popular Monthly* 38 (1894): 358–67.

Blow, William M. "Sussex Light Dragoons: A Roll of This Gallant Organization [and] Something of Its History." *Southern Historical Society Papers* 25 (1897): 273–75.

Bouldin, Edwin E. "Charlotte Cavalry: A Brief History of the Gallant Command . . ." *Southern Historical Society Papers* 28 (1900): 71–81.

———. "The Last Charge at Appomattox: The Fourteenth Virginia Cavalry." *Southern Historical Society Papers* 28 (1900): 250–54.

Bouldin, John E. "Our Last Charge." *Confederate Veteran* 22 (1914): 557.

Bouvé, Edward T. "The Battle of High Bridge." In *Civil War Papers: Read before the Commandery of the State of Massachusetts, Military Order of the Loyal Legion of the United States.* 2 vols. (Boston: F. H. Gilson Co., 1900), 2: 403–12.

Bowyer, N. B. "Reminiscences of Appomattox." *Confederate Veteran* 10 (1902): 77–78.

Cardwell, David. "The Battle of Five Forks." *Confederate Veteran* 22 (1914): 117–20.

Catton, Bruce. "Sheridan at Five Forks." *Journal of Southern History* 21 (1955): 305–15.

Chamberlain, Joshua L. "Appomattox." In *Personal Recollections of the War of the Rebellion: Addresses Delivered before the Commandery of the State of New York, Military Order of the Loyal Legion of the United States,* edited by A. Noel Blakeman. 4 vols. (New York: G. P. Putnam's Sons, 1891–1912), 3: 260–80.

———. "Five Forks." In *War Papers: Read before the Commandery of the State of Maine, Military Order of the Loyal Legion of the United States.* 3 vols. (Portland: various publishers, 1898–1908), 2: 220–67.

———. "The Military Operations on the White Oak Road, Virginia, March 31, 1865." In *War Papers: Read before the Commandery of the State of Maine, Military Order of the Loyal Legion of the United States.* 3 vols. (Portland: various publishers, 1898–1908), 1: 207–53.

———. "Reminiscences of Petersburg and Appomattox." In *War Papers: Read before the Commandery of the State of Maine, Military Order of the Loyal Legion of the United States.* 3 vols. (Portland: various publishers, 1898–1908), 3: 161–82.

Cilley, Jonathan P. "The Dawn of the Morning at Appomattox." In *War Papers: Read before the Commandery of the State of Maine, Military Order of the Loyal Legion of the United States.* 3 vols. (Portland: various publishers, 1898–1908), 3: 263–78.

Collier, Charles F. "War Recollections: Story of the Evacuation of Petersburg, by an Eye-Witness . . ." *Southern Historical Society Papers* 22 (1894): 69–73.

Colston, Frederick M. "Recollections of the Last Months in the Army of Northern Virginia." *Southern Historical Society Papers* 38 (1910): 10–15.

"Company C, Ninth Virginia Cavalry, C. S. A.: Its Roster and Gallant Record." *Southern Historical Society Papers* 23 (1895): 330–32.

Conrad, Holmes. "The Cavalry Corps of the Army of Northern Virginia." In *The Photographic History of the Civil War,* edited by Francis Trevelyan Miller. 10 vols. (New York: Review of Reviews Co., 1911), 4: 76–114.

Coski, John, ed. "Forgotten Warrior: General William Henry Fitzhugh Payne." *North & South* 2 (September 1999): 76–89.

Cummings, W. G. "Six Months in the Third Cavalry Division under Custer." In *War Sketches and Incidents: As Related by Companions of the Iowa Commandery, Military Order of the Loyal Legion of the United States.* 2 vols. (Des Moines: P. C. Kenyon Press, 1893–98), 1: 296–315.

"Custer at the Surrender." *Southern Bivouac* n.s. 1 (1885–86): 76–77.

Day, W. A. "Life among Bullets: In the Rifle Pits." *Confederate Veteran* 29 (1921): 216–19.

Dent, Frederick T. "'I Think Lee Will Surrender Today': The Letters of Frederick Dent." *Civil War Times Illustrated* 17 (April 1978): 34–39.

Devin, Thomas C. "Didn't We Fight Splendid." *Civil War Times Illustrated* 17 (December 1978): 38–40.

Doyle, J. H. "When Richmond Was Evacuated." *Confederate Veteran* 39 (1931): 205–6.

———. "With Gary's Brigade at Appomattox." *Confederate Veteran* 29 (1921): 332.

"Evacuation of Richmond: Reports of Gens. Ewell and Kershaw." *Transactions of the Southern Historical Society* 1 (1874): 101–06.

"The Fall of Richmond." *Harper's New Monthly Magazine* 33 (1866): 92–96.

"The First Federal to Enter Richmond . . . Major A. H. Stevens." *Southern Historical Society Papers* 30 (1902): 152–53.

French, Marcellus. "Second Dispatch from Grant to Lee." *Confederate Veteran* 8 (1900): 258–59.

"Gen. Rufus Barringer." *Confederate Veteran* 9 (1901): 69–70.

Gibbon, John. "Personal Recollections of Appomattox." *Century* 63 (1902): 936–43.

Graves, Thomas Thatcher. "The Fall of Richmond: II. The Evacuation." In *Battles and Leaders of the Civil War,* edited by Robert Underwood Johnson and Clarence Clough Buel. 4 vols. (New York: Century Co., 1887–88), 4: 726–28.

Greenough, Mark K. "Aftermath at Appomattox: Federal Military Occupation of Appomattox County, May-November 1865," *Civil War History* 31 (1985): 5–23.

Hall, H. C. "Some Recollections of Appomattox." *Maine Bugle* n.s. 1 (1894): 133–40.

Harbord, J. G. "The History of the Cavalry of the Army of Northern Virginia." *Journal of the United States Cavalry Association* 14 (1904): 423–503.

Hatfield, C. A. P. "The Evolution of Cavalry." *Journal of the Military Service Institution of the United States* 15 (1894): 89–103.

Hatton, Robert W., ed. "Just a Little Bit of the Civil War, as Seen by W. J. Smith, Company M, 2nd Ohio Volunteer Cavalry." *Ohio History* 84 (1975): 101–26, 222–42.

Hawes, Percy G. "Last Days of the Army of Northern Virginia." *Confederate Veteran* 27 (1919): 341–44.

Hinson, W. G. "Gen. Sheridan's Reference to Gen. M. C. [M. W.] Gary, of South Carolina." *Confederate Veteran* 2 (1894): 278.

Hodges, J. D. "A Generous Enemy." *Confederate Veteran* 21 (1913): 495.

Howard, McHenry. "Retreat of Custis Lee's Division, and Battle of Sailor's Creek." *Southern Historical Society Transactions* 1 (1874): 61–72.

Hundley, George A. "Beginning and the Ending: Reminiscences of the First and Last Days of the War . . .," *Southern Historical Society Papers* 23 (1895): 294–313.

Irvine, Dallas D. "The Fall of Richmond." *Journal of the American Military Institute* 3 (1939): 67–79.

Johnston, Angus J. "Lee's Last Lifeline: The Richmond & Danville." *Civil War History* 7 (1961): 288–96.

Johnston, Nathaniel B. "What Confederate Battery Fired the Last Gun at Appomattox?" *Southern Historical Society Papers* 9 (1881): 430.

Jones, J. William. "Appomattox: The True Story of the Surrender." *Historical Magazine* 31 (1873): 235–39.

Jones, Thomas G. "Last Days of the Army of Northern Virginia." *Southern Historical Society Papers* 21 (1893): 57–103.

Jones, Walter. "The Flag of Truce at Appomattox." *Confederate Veteran* 39 (1931): 300–303.

Kaigler, William. "Concerning Last Charge at Appomattox." *Confederate Veteran* 6 (1898): 524; 7 (1899): 357.

Kurtz, Henry I. "Five Forks: The South's Waterloo." *Civil War Times Illustrated* 3 (October 1964): 5–11.

Lamb, John. "The Confederate Cavalry: Its Wants, Trials, and Heroism." *Southern Historical Society Papers* 26 (1898): 359–65.

Lay, John Fitzhugh. "Reminiscences of the Powhatan Troop of Cavalry." *Southern Historical Society Papers* 8 (1880): 418–26.

Lee, Fitzhugh. "Report of Major General Fitzhugh Lee of the Operations of the Cavalry Corps, A.N.V., from March 28th to April 9th, 1865." *Southern Historical Society Transactions* 2 (1875): 77–85.

Lee, George Washington Custis. "Report of General G. W. C. Lee, from 2d to 6th April, 1865." *Southern Historical Society Transactions* 1 (1874): 118–21.

Livermore, Thomas L. "The Generalship of the Appomattox Campaign." In *Papers of the Military Historical Society of Massachusetts, Volume VI: The Shenandoah Campaigns of 1862 and 1864 and the Appomattox Campaign, 1865* (Boston: The Society, 1907), 449–506.

London, H. A. "The Last Volley at Appomattox." *Confederate Veteran* 7 (1899): 557–58.

Longacre, Edward G. "Gouverneur K. Warren." *Civil War Times Illustrated* 10 (January 1972): 11–20.

Lord, Francis A. "Confederate Cavalrymen Found Revolvers Better Than Sabers or Rifles." *Civil War Times Illustrated* 1 (January 1963): 46–47.

Luvaas, Jay. "Cavalry Lessons of the Civil War." *Civil War Times Illustrated* 6 (January 1968): 20–31.

Mahone, William. "On the Road to Appomattox." *Civil War Times Illustrated* 9 (January 1971): 4–11, 42–47.

Marshall, Charles. "Appomattox Courthouse: Incidents of the Surrender . . ." *Southern Historical Society Papers* 21 (1893): 353–60.

McDonald, Edward H. "I Felt a Ball Strike Me, I Could Not Tell Where." *Civil War Times Illustrated* 7 (June 1968): 28–34.

McDonald, William N. "Lee's Retreat." *Southern Bivouac* 1 (1882–83): 28–34.

McGlashan, Peter A. S. "Our Last Retreat." In *Addresses Delivered Before the Confederate Veterans Association of Savannah, Ga.* 5 vols. (Savannah: Braid & Hutton, 1893–1902), 2: 57–65.

Merritt, Wesley. "The Appomattox Campaign." In *War Papers and Personal Reminiscences, 1861–1865: Read before the Commandery of the State of*

Missouri, Military Order of the Loyal Legion of the United States (Saint Louis: Becktold & Co., 1892), 108–31.

Metts, James I. "Last Shot Fired at Appomattox." *Confederate Veteran* 7 (1899): 52–53.

Mitchell, Joseph B. "Sayler's Creek." *Civil War Times Illustrated* 4 (October 1965): 9–16.

Moffett, W. L. "The Last Charge of the 14th Virginia Cavalry at Appomattox C. H., Va., April 9, 1865." *Southern Historical Society Papers* 36 (1908): 13–16.

Moore, J. Scott. "Rockbridge Second Dragoons: A Short History of the Company . . ." *Southern Historical Society Papers* 25 (1897): 177–80.

Moore, J. Staunton. "The Battle of Five Forks." *Confederate Veteran* 16 (1908): 403–4.

Morgan, Michael R. "Feeding General Lee's Army: A New Version of an Incident of the Surrender at Appomattox." *Southern Historical Society Papers* 21 (1893): 360–61.

———. "From City Point to Appomattox with General Grant." *Journal of the Military Service Institution of the United States* 41 (1907): 227–55.

Newhall, Frederic C. "With Sheridan in Lee's Last Campaign." *Maine Bugle* n.s. 1 (1894): 201–13, 297–317; 2 (1895): 1–7, 96–112, 236–56, 289–308; 3 (1896): 1–14.

Norvell, Guy S. "The Equipment and Tactics of Our Cavalry, 1861–1865, Compared with the Present." *Journal of the Military Service Institution of the United States* 49 (1911): 360–76.

Packard, Joseph. "The Retreat from Petersburg to Appomattox." *Maryland Historical Magazine* 12 (1915): 1–19.

Parker, James. "Mounted and Dismounted Action of Cavalry." *Journal of the Military Service Institution of the United States* 39 (1906): 381–87.

Perry, Herman H. "Appomattox Courthouse: Account of the Surrender of the Confederate States Army, April 9, 1865." *Southern Historical Society Papers* 20 (1892): 56–61.

Pollard, Edward A. "Recollections of Appomattox's Court-house." *Old and New* 4 (1871–72): 166–75.

Porter, Horace. "Five Forks and the Pursuit of Lee." In *Battles and Leaders of the Civil War,* edited by Robert Underwood Johnson and Clarence Clough Buel. 4 vols. (New York: Century Co., 1887–88), 4: 708–22.

———. "The Surrender at Appomattox Court House." In *Battles and Leaders of the Civil War,* edited by Robert Underwood Johnson and Clarence Clough Buel. 4 vols. (New York: Century Co., 1887–88), 4: 729–46.

Prescott, Royal B. "The Capture of Richmond." In *Civil War Papers: Read before the Commandery of the State of Massachusetts, Military Order of the Loyal Legion of the United States.* 2 vols. (Boston: F. H. Gilson Co., 1900), 1: 47–72.

Rachal, William M. E., ed. "The Occupation of Richmond, April 1865: The Memorandum of Events of Colonel Christopher Q. Tompkins." *Virginia Magazine of History and Biography* 73 (1965): 189–98.

Redwood, Allen C. "Following Stuart's Feather." *Journal of the Military Service Institution of the United States* 49 (1911): 111–21.

Reece, Frances R., ed. "The Final Push to Appomattox: Captain [John A.] Clark's Account of the Seventh Michigan Cavalry in Action." *Michigan History Magazine* 28 (1944): 456–64.

Ripley, Edward H. "Final Scenes at the Capture and Occupation of Richmond, April 3, 1865." In *Personal Recollections of the War of the Rebellion: Addresses Delivered before the Commandery of the State of New York, Military Order of the Loyal Legion of the United States,* edited by A. Noel Blakeman. 4 vols. (New York: G. P. Putnam's Sons, 1891–1912), 3: 472–502.

Robinson, W. F. "Last Battle before Surrender." *Confederate Veteran* 32 (1924): 470–71.

Rodenbough, Theophilus F. "Cavalry War Lessons." *Journal of the United States Cavalry Association* 2 (1889): 103–23.

"Roll of Company E, Thirteenth Virginia Cavalry, and . . . the Role of the Flag of the Regiment." *Southern Historical Society Papers* 34 (1906): 210–11.

Schwab, Julius L. "Some Closing Events at Appomattox." *Confederate Veteran* 8 (1900): 71.

"The Second Virginia Regiment of Cavalry, C. S. A.: Tribute to its Discipline and Efficiency . . ." *Southern Historical Society Papers* 16 (1888): 354–56.

Shepherd, Joseph D. "Company D, Clarke Cavalry: History and Roster of This Command . . ." *Southern Historical Society Papers* 24 (1896): 145–51.

Shepley, George F. "Incidents of the Capture of Richmond." *Atlantic Monthly* 46 (1880): 18–28.

Sheridan, Philip H. "Last Days of the Rebellion." In *Military Essays and Recollections: Papers Read before the Commandery of the State of Illinois, Military Order of the Loyal Legion of the United States.* 4 vols. (Chicago: various publishers, 1891–1907), 1: 427–39.

Sherman, Caroline B., ed. "A New England Boy in the Civil War." *New England Quarterly* 5 (1932): 310–44.

Smith, C. H. "Incidents of Appomattox." *Maine Bugle* 3 (1893): 41–45.

Spencer, Warren F., ed. "A French View of the Fall of Richmond: Alfred Paul's Report to Drouyn de Lhuys, April 11, 1865." *Virginia Magazine of History and Biography* 73 (1965): 178–88.

Starr, Stephen Z., ed. "Dinwiddie Court House and Five Forks: Reminiscences of Roger Hannaford, Second Ohio Volunteer Cavalry." *Virginia Magazine of History and Biography* 87 (1978): 417–37.

Stevens, Hazard. "The Battle of Sailor's Creek." In *Papers of the Military Historical Society of Massachusetts, Volume VI: The Shenandoah Campaigns of 1862 and 1864 and the Appomattox Campaign, 1865* (Boston: The Society, 1907), 437–48.

Stribling, Robert M. "Story of the Battle of Five Forks and Other Events of the Last Days of the Confederacy: The Appomattox Surrender." *Southern Historical Society Papers* 37 (1909): 172–78.

Sulivane, Clement. "The Fall of Richmond: I. The Evacuation." In *Battles and Leaders of the Civil War,* edited by Robert Underwood Johnson and Clarence Clough Buel. 4 vols. (New York: Century Co., 1887–88), 4: 725–26.

Swan, William W. "The Five Forks Campaign." In *Papers of the Military Historical Society of Massachusetts, Volume VI: The Shenandoah Campaigns of 1862 and 1864 and the Appomattox Campaign, 1865* (Boston: The Society, 1907), 257–408.

Swift, Eben. "The Tactical Use of Cavalry." *Journal of the Military Service Institution of the United States* 44 (1909): 359–69.

Thompson, Magnus S. "Col. Elijah V. White." *Confederate Veteran* 15 (1907): 158–60.

———. "From the Ranks to Brigade Commander." *Confederate Veteran* 29 (1921): 298–303.

Timberlake, W. L. "In the Siege of Richmond and After." *Confederate Veteran* 29 (1921): 412–14.

Tremain, Henry E. "The Last Days of Sheridan's Cavalry." *Maine Bugle* n.s. 5 (1898): 168–81, 245–75, 295–312.

Tripp, Stephen. "The Cavalry at Appomattox, April 9, 1865." *Maine Bugle* n.s. 5 (1898): 212–16.

Trout, Robert J. "Galloping Thunder: The Stuart Horse Artillery Battalion . . ." *North & South* 3 (September 2000): 75–84.

Watson, Walter C. "The Fighting at Sailor's Creek." *Confederate Veteran* 25 (1917): 448–52.

Weinert, Richard P. "Maj. Henry Young: A Profile." *Civil War Times Illustrated* 3 (April 1964): 38–42.

Wert, Jeffry. "His Unhonored Service." *Civil War Times Illustrated* 24 (June 1985): 29–34.

Wharff, William H. "From Chapin's Farm to Appomattox." *Maine Bugle* n.s. 3 (1896): 231–35.

White, P. J. "The Fifth Virginia Cavalry." *Confederate Veteran* 17 (1909): 72–75.

Wilson, James Harrison. "The Cavalry of the Army of the Potomac." In *Papers of the Military Historical Society of Massachusetts, Volume XIII: Civil and Mexican Wars, 1861, 1846* (Boston: The Society, 1913), 33–88.

Wooldridge, William B. "Itinerary of the Fourth Virginia Cavalry, March 27th-April 9th, 1865." *Southern Historical Society Papers* 17 (1889): 376–78.

Wright, J. E. M. "From Petersburg to Appomattox Court House." *Maine Bugle* n.s. 1 (1894): 115–23.

BOOKS AND PAMPHLETS

Adams, Charles F., et al. *A Cycle of Adams Letters, 1861–1865.* Edited by Worthington Chauncey Ford. 2 vols. Boston: Houghton Mifflin Co., 1920.

Address Delivered Before R. E. Lee Camp, C. V. . . . in the Acceptance of the Portrait of General William H. Payne, by Leigh Robinson. Richmond, Va.: Wm. Ellis Jones, 1909.

Alexander, Edward Porter. *Fighting for the Confederacy: The Personal Recollections of General Edward Porter Alexander.* Edited by Gary A. Gallagher. Chapel Hill: University of North Carolina Press, 1989.

———. *Military Memoirs of a Confederate: A Critical Narrative.* New York: Charles Scribner's Sons, 1907.

Allardice, Bruce S. *More Generals in Gray.* Baton Rouge: Louisiana State University Press, 1995.

Allen, Stanton P. *Down in Dixie: Life in a Cavalry Regiment . . . from the Wilderness to Appomattox.* Boston: D. Lothrop, 1888.

The Appomattox Campaign: Organization of the Union Forces (Commanded by Lieutenant-General U. S. Grant), March 28–April 9, 1865. Washington, D.C.: War Records Office, 1883.

Archibald, William C. *Home-Making and its Philosophy . . .* Boston: privately issued, 1910.

Armstrong, Richard L. *11th Virginia Cavalry.* Lynchburg, Va.: H. E. Howard, 1989.

———. *7th Virginia Cavalry.* Lynchburg, Va.: H. E. Howard, 1992.

Arnold, William B. *The Fourth Massachusetts Cavalry in the Closing Scenes of the War for the Maintenance of the Union, from Richmond to Appomattox.* Boston: privately issued, n.d.

Aston, Howard. *History and Roster of the . . . Thirteenth Regiment Ohio Cavalry Volunteers: Their Battles and Skirmishes, Roster of the Dead, Etc.* Columbus, Ohio: Fred J. Heer, 1902.

Backus, Samuel W. *Californians in the Field: Historical Sketch of the . . . 2d Massachusetts Cavalry: Paper Prepared and Read before the California Commandery of the Military Order of the Loyal Legion of the United States.* San Francisco: privately issued, 1889.

Badeau, Adam. *Military History of Ulysses S. Grant, from April, 1861, to April, 1865.* 3 vols. New York: D. Appleton & Co., 1881.

Baker, Joel C. *The Fall of Richmond: War Paper No. 2, Vermont Commandery of the Loyal Legion.* Burlington: privately issued, 1892.

Balfour, Daniel T. *13th Virginia Cavalry.* Lynchburg, Va.: H. E. Howard, 1986.

Barringer, Rufus. *The First North Carolina: A Famous Cavalry Regiment.* n.p.: privately issued, n.d.

Bartlett, A. M. *History of the Twelfth Regiment New Hampshire Volunteers in the War of the Rebellion.* Concord N.H.: Ira C. Evans, 1897.

Bates, Samuel P. *History of Pennsylvania Volunteers, 1861–5.* 5 vols. Harrisburg, Pa.: B. Singerly, 1869–71.

———. *Memoir of Oliver Blachly Knowles, Late Colonel of the 21st Pennsylvania Cavalry and Brevet-Brigadier General.* Philadelphia: privately issued, 1875.

Battles Fought by the Cavalry under the Command of Major General P. H. Sheridan, U. S. Army, from May 4, 1864, to April 9, 1865. n.p.: privately issued, 1865.

The Battles of "Gravelly Run," "Dinwiddie Court-House," and "Five Forks," Va., 1865: Argument on Behalf of Lieut. Gen. Philip H. Sheridan, U.S.A. . . . before the Court of Inquiry . . . in the Case of Lieut. Col. and Bvt. Major-General Gouverneur K. Warren . . . Delivered July 27th, 28th and 30th, 1881. Chicago: privately issued, 1881.

Baylor, George. *Bull Run to Bull Run, or Four Years in the Army of Northern Virginia . . . Company B, Twelfth Virginia Cavalry, C.S.A., with Leaves from My Scrap-book.* Richmond: B. F. Johnson Publishing Co., 1900.

Beach, William H. *The First New York (Lincoln) Cavalry from April 18, 1861 to July 7, 1865.* Milwaukee: Burdick & Allen, 1902.

Beale, George W. *A Lieutenant of Cavalry in Lee's Army.* Boston: Gorham Press, 1918.

Beale, Richard L. T. *History of the Ninth Virginia Cavalry in the War Between the States.* Richmond: B. F. Johnson Publishing Co., 1899.

Bean, Theodore W. *The Roll of Honor of the Seventeenth Pennsylvania Cavalry* . . . Philadelphia: James S. Claxton, 1865.

Bearss, Edwin C., and Chris M. Calkins. *The Battle of Five Forks.* Lynchburg, Va.: H. E. Howard, 1985.

Bernard, George S., ed. *War Talks of Confederate Veterans.* Petersburg, Va.: Penn & Owen, 1892.

Bill, Alfred Hoyt. *The Beleaguered City: Richmond, 1861–1865.* New York: Alfred A. Knopf, 1946.

Black, Robert C., III. *The Railroads of the Confederacy.* Chapel Hill: University of North Carolina Press, 1952.

Blackford, Charles Minor, and Susan Leigh Blackford. *Letters from Lee's Army; or, Memoirs of Life in and out of the Army in Virginia during the War Between the States.* Edited by Charles Minor Blackford III. New York: Charles Scribner's Sons, 1947.

———. *Memoirs of Life in and out of the Army in Virginia during the War Between the States.* 2 vols. Lynchburg, Va.: J. P. Bell Co., 1894–96.

Blackford, William W. *War Years with Jeb Stuart.* New York: Charles Scribner's Sons, 1945.

Boatner, Mark Mayo, III. *The Civil War Dictionary.* New York: David McKay Co., 1959.

Bolton, Horace W. *Personal Reminiscences of the Late War.* Chicago: privately issued, 1892.

Booth, George Wilson. *Personal Reminiscences of a Maryland Soldier in the War Between the States, 1861–85.* Baltimore: Fleet, McGinley & Co., 1898.

Bowen, James R. *Regimental History of the First New York Dragoons* . . . Lyons, Mich.: privately issued, 1900.

Boykin, Edward M. *The Falling Flag: Evacuation of Richmond, Retreat and Surrender at Appomattox, by an Officer of the Rear-Guard.* New York: E. J. Hale & Son, 1874.

A Brief History of the Fourth Pennsylvania Veteran Cavalry . . . Pittsburgh: Ewens & Eberle, 1891.

Browne, Frederick W. *My Service in the U.S. Colored Cavalry* . . . Cincinnati: privately issued, 1908.

Bruce, George A. *The Capture and Occupation of Richmond.* Boston: privately issued, 1918.

Bushong, Millard K., and Dean M. Bushong. *Fightin' Tom Rosser, C.S.A.* Shippensburg, Pa.: Beidel Printing House, 1983.

Calkins, Chris M. *The Appomattox Campaign, March 29–April 9, 1865.* Con-shohocken, Pa.: Combined Books, 1997.

———. *The Battles of Appomattox Station and Appomattox Court House, April 8–9, 1865.* Lynchburg, Va.: H. E. Howard, 1987.

———. *The Final Bivouac: The Surrender Parade at Appomattox and the Dis-banding of the Armies, April 1 to May 20, 1865.* Lynchburg, Va.: H. E. Howard, 1988.

———. *Thirty-six Hours before Appomattox: April 6 and 7, 1865.* Farmville, Va.: Farmville Herald Publishing Co., 1980.

The Campaign Life of Lt.-Col. Henry Harrison Young . . . Providence, R.I.: Sid-ney S. Rider, 1882.

Campbell, John A. *Recollections of the Evacuation of Richmond, April 2d, 1865.* Baltimore: John Murphy & Co., 1880.

Carpenter, J. Edward, comp. *A List of Battles, Engagements, Actions and Important Skirmishes in Which the Eighth Pennsylvania Cavalry Partici-pated* . . . Philadelphia: Allen, Lane & Scott, 1886.

Carter, Samuel, III. *The Last Cavaliers: Confederate and Union Cavalry in the Civil War.* New York: St. Martin's Press, 1979.

Carter, William Harding. *From Yorktown to Santiago with the Sixth U.S. Cav-alry.* Baltimore: Lord Baltimore Press, 1900.

Casualties in the Union Forces in the Appomattox Campaign, March 28– April 9, 1865 . . . Washington, D.C.: War Records Office, n.d.

Catton, Bruce. *A Stillness at Appomattox.* Garden City, N.Y.: Doubleday & Co., 1953.

Cauble, Frank P. *Biography of Wilmer McLean.* Lynchburg, Va.: H. E. Howard, 1987.

Chamberlain, Joshua L. *The Passing of the Armies: An Account of the Final Campaign of the Army of the Potomac* . . . New York: G. P. Putnam's Sons, 1915.

Cheney, Newel. *History of the Ninth Regiment, New York Volunteer Cavalry, War of 1861 to 1865* . . . Jamestown, N.Y.: Martin Merz & Son, 1901.

Chewning, Charles A. *The Journal of Charles A. Chewning, Company E, 9th Virginia Cavalry, C.S.A.* Edited by Richard B. Armstrong. n.p.: privately issued, n.d.

Clark, Walter, ed. *Histories of the Several Regiments and Battalions from North Carolina in the Great War, 1861–'65* . . . 5 vols. Goldsboro, N.C.: Nash Brothers; Raleigh, N.C.: E. M. Uzzell, 1901.

Cleaves, Freeman. *Meade of Gettysburg.* Norman: University of Oklahoma Press, 1960.

Coltrane, Daniel B. *The Memoirs of Daniel Branson Coltrane, Co. I, 63rd Reg., N.C. Cavalry, C.S.A.* Raleigh, N.C.: Edwards & Broughton Co., 1956.

Cooke, John Esten. *Wearing of the Gray: Being Personal Portraits, Scenes and Adventures of the War.* Baton Rouge: Louisiana State University Press, 1997.

Cormany, Samuel E., and Rachel B. Cormany. *The Cormany Diaries: A Northern Family in the Civil War.* Edited by James C. Mohr and Richard E. Winslow, III. Pittsburgh: University of Pittsburgh Press, 1982.

Corson, William Clark. *My Dear Jennie: A Collection of Love Letters from a Confederate Soldier to His Fiancée during the Period 1861–1865.* Edited by Blake W. Corson. Richmond: Dietz Press, 1982.

Cowles, Calvin D., comp. *Atlas to Accompany the Official Records of the Union and Confederate Armies.* Washington, D.C.: Government Printing Office, 1891–95.

Cresap, Bernarr. *Appomattox Commander: The Story of General E. O. C. Ord.* San Diego: A. S. Barnes & Co., 1981.

Crook, George. *General George Crook: His Autobiography.* Edited by Martin F. Schmitt. Norman: University of Oklahoma Press, 1960.

Crosland, Charles. *Reminiscences of the Sixties.* Columbia, S.C.: State Co., ca. 1910.

Crowninshield, Benjamin W., and D. H. L. Gleason. *A History of the First Regiment of Massachusetts Cavalry Volunteers.* Boston: Houghton Mifflin & Co., 1891.

Cruikshank, George L. *Back in the Sixties: Reminiscences of the Service of Co. A, 11th Pennsylvania [Cavalry] Regiment.* Fort Dodge, Iowa: Times Printing House, 1893.

Crumb, DeWitt. *22d Regiment N.Y. Vol. Cav.: Historical Address . . .* South Otselic, N.Y.: W. M. Reynolds, 1887.

Cummings, Charles M. *Yankee Quaker, Confederate General: The Curious Career of Bushrod Rust Johnson.* Rutherford, N.J.: Fairleigh Dickinson University Press, 1971.

Custer, George Armstrong, and Elizabeth Bacon Custer. *The Custer Story: The Life and Intimate Letters of General George A. Custer and His Wife Elizabeth.* Edited by Marguerite Merington. New York: Devin-Adair Co., 1950.

Daly, Louise Porter. *Alexander Cheves Haskell: The Portrait of a Man.* Norwood, Mass.: Plimpton Press, 1934.

Davies, Henry E. *General Sheridan.* New York: D. Appleton & Co., 1899.

Davis, Burke. *To Appomattox: Nine April Days, 1865.* New York: Rinehart & Co., 1959.

Davis, Julia. *Mount Up: A True Story Based on the Reminiscences of Major E. A. H. McDonald of the Confederate Cavalry.* New York: Harcourt, Brace & World, 1967.

Davis, William C. *Breckinridge: Statesman, Soldier, Symbol.* Baton Rouge: Louisiana State University Press, 1974.

Dawson, Francis W. *Reminiscences of Confederate Service, 1861–1865.* Charleston, S.C.: News and Courier Book Presses, 1882.

Dawson, Henry Barton. *The Colors of the United States First Raised over the Capitol of the Confederate States, April 3, 1865.* Morrisania, N.Y.: privately issued, 1866.

Dawson, John Harper. *Wildcat Cavalry: A Synoptic History of the Seventeenth Virginia Cavalry . . .* Dayton: Morningside House, 1982.

dePeyster, John Watts. *La Royale, Parts I, II, III, IV, V, & VI: The Grand Hunt of the Army of the Potomac, on the 3d-7th April [1865], Petersburg to High Bridge . . .* New York: Julius R. Huth, 1872.

———. *La Royale, Part VII: Cumberland Church . . . 7th April, 1865 . . .* New York: Julius R. Huth, 1874.

dePeyster, Jonathan L. *Colors of U.S. First Raised over Richmond.* Morrisania, N.Y.: privately issued, 1866.

Dickinson, Jack L. *16th Virginia Cavalry.* Lynchburg, Va.: H. E. Howard, 1989.

———. *Records of the 16th Virginia Cavalry.* Barboursville, W. Va.: privately issued, 1984.

Divine, John E. *35th Battalion Virginia Cavalry.* Lynchburg, Va.: H. E. Howard, 1985.

Dixon, David. *Hero of Beecher Island: The Life and Military Career of George A. Forsyth.* Lincoln: University of Nebraska Press, 1994.

Doster, William E. *Lincoln and Episodes of the Civil War.* New York: G. P. Putnam's Sons, 1915.

Driver, Robert J., Jr. *5th Virginia Cavalry.* Lynchburg, Va.: H. E. Howard, 1997.

———. *First & Second Maryland Cavalry, C.S.A.* Charlottesville, Va.: Rockbridge Publishing Co., 1999.

———. *1st Virginia Cavalry.* Lynchburg, Va.: H. E. Howard, 1991.

———. *10th Virginia Cavalry.* Lynchburg, Va.: H. E. Howard, 1992.

Driver, Robert J., Jr., and H. E. Howard. *2nd Virginia Cavalry.* Lynchburg, Va.: H. E. Howard, 1995.

Dulany, Richard H., et al. *The Dulanys of Welbourne: A Family in Mosby's Confederacy.* Edited by Margaret Ann Vogtsberger. Berryville, Va.: Rockbidge Publishing Co., 1995.

Dwight, Charles S. *A South Carolina Rebel's Recollections . . . of the Evacuation of Richmond and the Battle of Sailor's Creek, April 1865.* Columbia, S.C.: State Co., 1917.

Dyer, Frederick H. *A Compendium of the War of the Rebellion . . .* 3 vols. New York: Thomas Yoseloff, 1959.

Edmonds, Howard O. *Owen-Edmonds Incidents of the American Civil War, 1861–1865, Prepared from Family Records.* Chicago: Lakeside Press, 1928.

Eggleston, George Cary. *A Rebel's Recollections.* New York: G. P. Putnam's Sons, 1878.

Faust, Patricia L., ed. *Historical Times Illustrated Encyclopedia of the Civil War.* New York: Harper & Row, 1986.

Featherston, Nathaniel R. *The History of Appomattox, Virginia.* Marceline, Mo.: Walsworth Brothers, 1948.

First Maine Cavalry Association: Record of Proceedings of the First Annual Re-Union . . . Augusta, Maine: privately issued, 1872.

Flint, Joseph. *Regimental History of the First New York Dragoons . . .* Washington, D.C.: Gibson Brothers, 1865.

Fortier, John. *15th Virginia Cavalry.* Lynchburg, Va.: H. E. Howard, 1993.

Foster, Alonzo. *Reminiscences and Record of the 6th New York V. V. [Veteran Volunteer] Cavalry.* Brooklyn, N.Y.: privately issued, 1892.

Freeman, Douglas Southall. *Lee's Lieutenants: A Study in Command.* 3 vols. New York: Charles Scribner's Sons, 1942–44.

———. *R. E. Lee: A Biography.* 4 vols. New York: Charles Scribner's Sons, 1934–35.

Frye, Dennis E. *12th Virginia Cavalry.* Lynchburg, Va.: H. E. Howard, 1988.

Fuller, J. F. C. *The Generalship of Ulysses S. Grant.* Bloomington: Indiana University Press, 1958.

Gallaher, DeWitt C. *A Diary Depicting the Experiences of DeWitt Clinton Gallaher in the War Between the States While Serving in the Confederate Army.* Charleston, W. Va.: privately issued, 1945.

Gardiner, William. *Operations of the Cavalry Corps . . . from February 27 to March 8, 1865 . . .* Providence, R. I.: privately issued, 1896.

Garraty, John A., and Mark C. Carnes, eds. *American National Biography.* 24 vols. New York: Oxford University Press, 1999.

Gaston, John T. *Confederate War Diary of John Thomas Gaston.* Compiled by Alifaire Gaston Walden. Columbia, S.C.: Vogue Press, 1960.

Gause, Isaac. *Four Years with Five Armies . . .* New York: Neale Publishing Co., 1908.

Gibbon, John. *Personal Recollections of the Civil War.* New York: G. P. Putnam's Sons, 1928.

Gills, Mary Louise. *It Happened at Appomattox: The Story of an Historic Virginia Village.* Richmond: Dietz Press, 1948.

Goldsborough, W. W. *The Maryland Line in the Confederate States Army.* Baltimore: Kelly, Piet & Co., 1869.

Gordon, John Brown. *The Last Days of the Confederacy: A Lecture . . .* Philadelphia: John D. Morris & Co., 1900.

————. *Reminiscences of the Civil War.* New York: Charles Scribner's Sons, 1905.

Gorman, John C. *Lee's Last Campaign . . .* Raleigh, N.C.: Wm. B. Smith & Co., 1866.

Gracey, S. L. *Annals of the Sixth Pennsylvania Cavalry.* Philadelphia: E. H. Butler & Co., 1868.

Grant, Ulysses S. *Personal Memoirs of U. S. Grant.* 2 vols. New York: Charles L. Webster & Co., 1885–86.

————. *Report of Lieutenant-General U. S. Grant, of the Armies of the United States, 1864–'65.* Washington, D.C.: privately issued, 1865.

The Grayjackets and How They Lived, Fought and Died, for Dixie. Richmond: Jones Brothers & Co., 1867.

Greene, A. Wilson. *Breaking the Backbone of the Rebellion: The Final Battles of the Petersburg Campaign.* Mason City, Iowa: Savas Publishing Co., 2000.

Hackley, Woodford B. *The Little Fork Rangers: A Sketch of Company "D," Fourth Virginia Cavalry.*: Dietz Printing Co., 1927.

Haden, B. J. *Reminiscences of J. E. B. Stuart's Cavalry.* Charlottesville, Va.: Progress Publishing Co., ca. 1890.

Hall, Hillman A., W. B. Besley, and Gilbert G. Wood, comps. *History of the Sixth New York Cavalry . . .* Worcester, Mass.: Blanchard Press, 1908.

Harris, Nathaniel E. *Autobiography: The Story of an Old Man's Life, with Reminiscences of Seventy-Five Years.* Macon, Ga.: J. W. Burke Co., 1925.

Harris, Nelson. *17th Virginia Cavalry.* Lynchburg, Va.: H. E. Howard, 1994.

Harris, Samuel. *Major General George A. Custer: Stories Told around the Camp Fire of the Michigan Brigade of Cavalry.* Chicago: privately issued, 1898.

————. *Personal Reminiscences of Samuel Harris.* Chicago: Rogerson Press, 1897.

Harrison, Walter. *Pickett's Men: A Fragment of War History.* New York: D. Van Nostrand, 1870.

Harvey, Marshall S. *Recollections of 1864–5 after Forty Years . . .* Columbus, Ohio: privately issued, 1904.

Haskin, William L., comp. *The History of the First Regiment of Artillery from Its Organization in 1821, to January 1st, 1876.* Portland, Me.: B. Thurston & Co., 1879.

Hatcher, Edmund N. *The Last Four Weeks of the War.* Columbus, Ohio: Co-operative Publishing Co., 1892.

Heitman, Francis B., comp. *Historical Register and Dictionary of the United States Army . . .* 2 vols. Washington, D.C.: Government Printing Office, 1903.

Hendrickson, Robert. *The Road to Appomattox.* New York: John Wiley & Sons, 1998.

Hergesheimer, Joseph. *Sheridan: A Military Narrative.* Boston: Houghton Mifflin Co., 1931.

Hewett, Janet, et al., eds. *Supplement to the Official Records of the Union and Confederate Armies.* 99 vols. Wilmington, N.C.: Broadfoot Publishing Co., 1994–2001.

Hinds, Thomas. *Tales of War Times: Being the Adventures of Thomas Hinds during the American Civil War.* Watertown, N.Y.: Herald Printing Co., 1904.

History of the Eleventh Pennsylvania Volunteer Cavalry. Philadelphia: Franklin Printing Co., 1902.

History of the Third Pennsylvania Cavalry . . . in the American Civil War, 1861–1865. Philadelphia: Franklin Printing Co., 1905.

Hoehling, A. A., and Mary Hoehling. *The Day Richmond Died.* San Diego: A. S. Barnes & Co., 1981.

Hoge, John M. *A Journal by John Milton Hoge, 1862–5 . . .* Cincinnati: M. H. Bruce, 1961.

Holland, Darryl. *24th Virginia Cavalry.* Lynchburg, Va.: H. E. Howard, 1997.

Hopkins, Luther W. *From Bull Run to Appomattox: A Boy's View.* Baltimore: Fleet-McGinley Co., 1908.

Howard, McHenry. *Recollections of a Maryland Confederate Soldier and Staff Officer under Johnston, Jackson and Lee.* Baltimore: Williams & Wilkins Co., 1914.

Hudgins, Robert S., II. *Recollections of an Old Dominion Dragoon: The Civil War Experiences of Sgt. Robert S. Hudgins II, Company B, 3rd Virginia Cavalry.* Edited by Garland C. Hudgins and Richard B. Kleese. Orange, Va.: Publisher's Press, 1993.

Humphreys, Andrew A. *The Virginia Campaign of '64 and '65: The Army of the Potomac and the Army of the James.* New York: Charles Scribner's Sons, 1883.

Humphreys, Charles A. *Field, Camp, Hospital and Prison in the Civil War, 1863–1865.* Boston: George H. Ellis Co., 1918.

Huntington, Albert. *8th New York Cavalry: Historical Paper.* Palmyra, N.Y.: privately issued, 1902.

Hyde, Thomas W. *Following the Greek Cross; or, Memories of the Sixth Army Corps.* Boston: Houghton, Mifflin & Co., 1894.

Hyndman, William. *History of a Cavalry Company: A Complete Record of Company "A," 4th Penn'a Cavalry.* Philadelphia: James B. Rodgers Co., 1870.

Isham, Asa B. *An Historical Sketch of the Seventh Regiment Michigan Volunteer Cavalry, from its Organization, in 1862, to its Muster Out, in 1865.* New York: Town Topics Publishing Co., 1893.

Jacobs, Lee, comp. *The Gray Riders: Stories from the Confederate Cavalry.* Shippensburg, Pa.: Burd Street Press, 1999.

Johnson, Curt. *Cavalry Battles of the American Civil War.* Washington, D.C.: Brassey's, 1999.

Johnston, Angus James, II. *Virginia Railroads in the Civil War.* Chapel Hill: University of North Carolina Press, 1961.

Johnston, David E. *The Story of a Confederate Boy in the Civil War.* Portland, Ore.: Glass & Prudhomme Co., 1914.

Jones, Katharine M. *Ladies of Richmond, Confederate Capital.* Indianapolis: Bobbs-Merrill Co., 1962.

Jordan, David M. *"Happiness Is Not My Companion": The Life of General G. K. Warren.* Bloomington: Indiana University Press, 2001.

Keifer, Joseph W. *Slavery and Four Years of War . . . A Narrative of the Campaigns and Battles of the Civil War in Which the Author Took Part, 1861–1865.* 2 vols. New York: G. P. Putnam's Sons, 1900.

Keyes, C. M., ed. *The Military History of the 123rd Regiment Ohio Volunteer Infantry.* Sandusky, Ohio: Register Steam Press, 1874.

Keys, Thomas B. *Tarheel Cossack: W. P. Roberts, Youngest Confederate General.* Orlando, Fla.: privately issued, 1983.

King, Katherine Gray, comp. *The Seven Gray Brothers of the Confederate Cavalry, 1861–1865.* Rochester, N.Y.: St. Vincent Press, 1983.

King, Matthew W. *To Horse: With the Cavalry of the Army of the Potomac, 1861–1865.* Cheboygan, Mich.: privately issued, 1926.

Kinsley, Ardyce, comp. *The Fitzhugh Lee Sampler.* Lively, Va.: Brandylane Publishers, 1992.

Knapp, David, Jr. *The Confederate Horsemen.* New York: Vantage Press, 1966.

Krick, Robert K. *Lee's Colonels: A Biographical Register of the Field Officers of the Army of Northern Virginia.* Dayton: Morningside Bookshop, 1979.

———. *9th Virginia Cavalry.* Lynchburg, Va.: H. E. Howard, 1982.

———. *30th Virginia Infantry.* Lynchburg, Va.: H. E. Howard, 1983.

LeConte, Emma. *When the World Ended: The Diary of Emma LeConte.* Edited by Earl Schenck Miers. New York: Oxford University Press, 1957.

Lee, Fitzhugh. *General Lee.* New York: D. Appleton & Co., 1894.

Lee, Robert E. *Lee's Dispatches: Unpublished Letters of General Robert E. Lee, C.S.A., to Jefferson Davis and the War Department of the Confederate States of America, 1862–65.* Edited by Douglas Southall Freeman and Grady McWhiney. New York: G. P. Putnam's Sons, 1957.

———. *The Wartime Papers of R. E. Lee.* Edited by Clifford Dowdey and Louis H. Manarin. Boston: Little, Brown & Co., 1961.

Lee, William O., comp. *Personal and Historical Sketches and Facial History of . . . the Seventh Regiment Michigan Volunteer Cavalry, 1862–65.* Detroit: Ralston-Stroup Co., 1903.

Lewis, Charles E. *War Sketches . . . With the First [New York] Dragoons in Virginia . . .* London: Simmons & Botten, 1897.

Lincoln, Abraham. *The Collected Works of Abraham Lincoln.* Edited by Roy P. Basler, et al. 8 vols. New Brunswick, N.J.: Rutgers University Press, 1953.

Lincoln, William S. *Life with the Thirty-fourth Mass. Infantry in the War of the Rebellion.* Worcester, Mass.: Noyes, Snow & Co., 1879.

Long, E. B., and Barbara Long. *The Civil War Day by Day: An Almanac, 1861–1865.* Garden City, N.Y.: Doubleday & Co., 1971.

Longacre, Edward G. *Army of Amateurs: General Benjamin F. Butler and the Army of the James, 1861–1865.* Mechanicsburg, Pa.: Stackpole Books, 1997.

———. *Custer and His Wolverines: The Michigan Cavalry Brigade, 1861–1865.* Conshohocken, Pa.: Combined Publishing, 1997.

———. *Jersey Cavaliers: A History of the First New Jersey Volunteer Cavalry, 1861–1865.* Hightstown, N.J.: Longstreet House, 1992.

———. *Lee's Cavalrymen: A History of the Mounted Forces of the Army of Northern Virginia, 1861–1865.* Mechanicsburg, Pa.: Stackpole Books, 2002.

———. *Lincoln's Cavalrymen: A History of the Mounted Forces of the Army of the Potomac, 1861–1865.* Mechanicsburg, Pa.: Stackpole Books, 2000.

———. *Pickett, Leader of the Charge: A Biography of General George E. Pickett, C.S.A.* Shippensburg, Pa.: White Mane Publishing Co., 1995.

Longstreet, James. *From Manassas to Appomattox: Memoirs of the Civil War in America.* Philadelphia: J. B. Lippincott Co., 1896.

Lyman, Theodore. *Meade's Headquarters, 1861–1865: Letters of Colonel Theodore Lyman from the Wilderness to Appomattox.* Edited by George R. Agassiz. Boston: Atlantic Monthly Press, 1922.

Mansfield, James R. *Robert Henry Jerrell (1843–1907) (Pvt. Co. E, 9th Virginia Cal [Cav.] C.S.A.)* . . . n.p.: privately issued, 1966.

Marshall, Charles. *An Aide-de-Camp of Lee: Being the Papers of Colonel Charles Marshall* . . . Edited by Sir Frederick Maurice. Boston: Little, Brown & Co., 1927.

Marvel, William. *A Place Called Appomattox.* Chapel Hill: University of North Carolina Press, 2000.

McCabe, W. Gordon. *A Brief Sketch of Andrew Reid Venable, Jr., Formerly A. A. and Inspector General, Cavalry Corps, A.N.V.* Richmond: Wm. Ellis Jones, 1909.

———. *Theodore Stanford Garnett, Jr., 1844–1915.* Richmond: Virginia Historical Society, 1916.

McClellan, Carswell. *Notes on the Personal Memoirs of P. H. Sheridan.* St. Paul: William E. Banning, Jr., 1889.

———. *The Personal Memoirs and Military History of U. S. Grant versus the Record of the Army of the Potomac.* Boston: Houghton, Mifflin Co., 1887.

McClellan, Henry B. *The Life and Campaigns of Maj. Gen. J. E. B. Stuart, Commander of the Cavalry of the Army of Northern Virginia.* Boston: Houghton, Mifflin & Co., 1885.

McDonald, William N. *A History of the Laurel Brigade, Originally The Ashby Cavalry of the Army of Northern Virginia, and Chew's Battery.* Edited by Bushrod C. Washington. Baltimore: Sun Job Printing, 1907.

McGuire, Judith W. *Diary of a Southern Refugee during the War, by a Lady of Virginia.* New York: E. J. Hale & Son, 1867.

McKim, Randolph H. *A Soldier's Recollections: Leaves from the Diary of a Young Confederate* . . . New York: Longmans, Green, and Co., 1910.

McKinney, Edward P. *Life in Tent and Field, 1861–1865.* Boston: Richard G. Badger, 1922.

Meade, George G. *The Life and Letters of George Gordon Meade, Major-General, United States Army.* 2 vols. New York: Charles Scribner's Sons, 1913.

Merrill, Samuel H. *The Campaigns of the First Maine and First District of Columbia Cavalry.* Portland, Me.: Bailey & Noyes, 1866.

Miers, Earl Schenck. *The Last Campaign: Grant Saves the Union.* Philadelphia: J. B. Lippincott Co., 1972.

Miller, Millard J. *My Grandpap Rode with Jeb Stuart: Experiences of James Knox Polk Ritchie, Company H, Twelfth Virginia Cavalry, Laurel Brigade, Army of Northern Virginia, Civil War, 1861–1865.* Westerville, Ohio: privately issued, 1974.

Monaghan, Jay. *Custer: The Life of General George Armstrong Custer.* Boston: Little, Brown & Co., 1959.

Moncure, Eustace C. *Reminiscences of the Civil War.* n.p.: privately issued, ca. 1914.

Moore, Frank, ed. *The Rebellion Record: A Diary of American Events.* 12 vols. New York: various publishers, 1861–68.

Moore, Robert H., II. *The 1st and 2nd Stuart Horse Artillery.* Lynchburg, Va.: H. E. Howard, 1985.

Morgan, James Morris. *Recollections of a Rebel Reefer.* Boston: Houghton Mifflin Co., 1917.

Morris, Roy O. *Sheridan: The Life and Wars of General Phil Sheridan.* New York: Crown Publishers, 1992.

Moyer, H. P., comp. *History of the Seventeenth Regiment Pennsylvania Volunteer Cavalry.* Lebanon, Pa.: Sowers Printing Co., 1911.

Musick, Michael P. *6th Virginia Cavalry.* Lynchburg, Va.: H. E. Howard, 1990.

Myers, Frank M. *The Comanches: A History of White's Battalion, Virginia Cavalry, Laurel Brig., Hampton ['s] Div., A.N.V., C.S.A.* Baltimore: Kelly, Piet & Co., 1871.

Naisawald, L. Van Loan. *Grape and Canister: The Story of the Field Artillery of the Army of the Potomac, 1861–1865.* New York: Oxford University Press, 1960.

Nanzig, Thomas P. *3rd Virginia Cavalry.* Lynchburg, Va.: H. E. Howard, 1989.

Neese, George M. *Three Years in the Confederate Horse Artillery.* New York: Neale Publishing Co., 1911.

Nelson, Horatio. *"If I Am Killed on This Trip, I Want My Horse Kept for My Brother": The Diary of the Last Weeks in the Life of a Young Confederate Cavalryman.* Edited by Harold Howard. Manassas, Va.: Manassas Chapter, United Daughters of the Confederacy, 1980.

Newhall, Frederic C. *With General Sheridan in Lee's Last Campaign, by a Staff Officer.* Philadelphia: J. B. Lippincott & Co., 1866.

Nichols, James L. *General Fitzhugh Lee: A Biography.* Lynchburg, Va.: H. E. Howard, 1989.

Norton, Chauncey S. *"The Red Neck Ties," or, History of the Fifteenth New York Volunteer Cavalry . . .* Ithaca, N.Y.: Journal Book and Job Printing House, 1891.

Norton, Henry, comp. *Deeds of Daring; or History of the Eighth N.Y. Volunteer Cavalry . . .* Norwich, N.Y.: Chenango Telegraph Printing House, 1889.

O'Connor, Richard. *Sheridan, the Inevitable*. Indianapolis: Bobbs-Merrill Co., 1953.

O'Ferrall, Charles T. *Forty Years of Active Service . . . from Private to Lieutenant-Colonel and Acting Colonel in the Cavalry of the Army of Northern Virginia . . .* New York: Neale Publishing Co., 1904.

Olson, John E. *21st Virginia Cavalry*. Lynchburg, Va.: H. E. Howard, 1989.

Opie, John N. *A Rebel Cavalryman with Lee, Stuart, and Jackson*. Chicago: W. B. Conkey Co., 1899.

Owen, William Miller. *In Camp and Battle with the Washington Artillery of New Orleans . . .* Boston: Ticknor & Co., 1885.

Paris, Comte de. *History of the Civil War in America*. 4 vols. Philadelphia: Porter & Coates, 1876–88.

Parker, William L. *General James Dearing, C.S.A.* Lynchburg, Va.: H. E. Howard, 1990.

Parmelee, Uriah N. *The Civil War Diary of Captain Uriah Nelson Parmelee*. Edited by Charles Lewis Biggs. Guilford, N.H.: privately issued, 1940.

Patrick, Rembert W. *The Fall of Richmond*. Baton Rouge: Louisiana State University Press, 1960.

Peck, Rufus H. *Reminiscences of a Confederate Soldier of Co. C, 2nd Va. Cavalry*. Fincastle, Va.: privately issued, 1913.

Pennypacker, Isaac. *General Meade*. New York: D. Appleton & Co., 1901.

Pfanz, Donald C. *Richard S. Ewell: A Soldier's Life*. Chapel Hill: University of North Carolina Press, 1998.

Pickerill, William N. *History of the Third Indiana Cavalry*. Indianapolis: Aetna Printing Co., 1906.

Pickett, George E. *The Heart of a Soldier, as Revealed in the Intimate Letters of Genl. George E. Pickett, C.S.A.* New York: Seth Moyle, 1913.

Pickett, La Salle Corbell. *Pickett and His Men*. Atlanta: Foote & Davies Co., 1900.

Pollard, Henry R. *Memoirs and Sketches of the Life of Henry Robinson Pollard: An Autobiography*. Richmond: Lewis Printing Co., 1923.

Porter, Burton B. *One of the People: His Own Story*. Colton, Calif.: privately issued, 1907.

Porter, Horace. *Campaigning with Grant*. Edited by Wayne C. Temple. Bloomington: Indiana University Press, 1961.

Power, J. Tracy. *Lee's Miserables: Life in the Army of Northern Virginia from the Wilderness to Appomattox*. Chapel Hill: University of North Carolina Press, 1998.

Preston, N. D. *History of the Tenth Regiment of Cavalry, New York State Volunteers, August, 1861, to August, 1865*. New York: D. Appleton & Co., 1892.

Price, George F., comp. *Across the Continent with the Fifth [United States] Cavalry.* New York: D. Van Nostrand, 1883.

Pyne, Henry R. *The History of the First New Jersey Cavalry.* Trenton: J. A. Beecher, 1871.

Randol, Alanson M. *Last Days of the Rebellion: The Second New York Cavalry (Harris Light) at Appomattox Station and Appomattox Court House, April 8 and 9, 1865.* San Francisco: Presidio of San Francisco, 1883.

Report of the . . . Annual Reunion of the Sixth Ohio Veteran Volunteer Cavalry Association . . . 52 vols. n.p.: various publishers, 1865–1917.

Rhodes, Charles D. *History of the Cavalry of the Army of the Potomac . . .* Kansas City, Mo.: Hudson-Kimberly Publishing Co., 1900.

Ripley, Edward H. *Vermont General: The Unusual War Experiences of Edward Hastings Ripley, 1862–1865.* Edited by Otto Eisenschiml. New York: Devin-Adair Co., 1960.

Ripley, Warren. *Artillery and Ammunition of the Civil War.* New York: Van Nostrand-Reinhold Co., 1970.

Robbins, Walter R. *War Record and Personal Experiences of Walter Raleigh Robbins from April 22, 1861, to August 4, 1865.* Edited by Lilian Rea. Chicago: privately issued, 1923.

Roberts, John N. *Reminiscences of the Civil War.* n.p.: privately issued, 1925.

Robertson, James I., Jr. *18th Virginia Infantry.* Lynchburg, Va.: H. E. Howard, 1984.

Robertson, John, comp. *Michigan in the War.* Lansing, Mich.: W. S. George & Co., 1882.

Robinson, Charles F. *My Enlistment and Service in the Civil War.* Takoma Park, Md.: Takoma Journal, 1929.

Rockwell, Alphonso. *Rambling Recollections: An Autobiography.* New York: Paul B. Hober, 1920.

Rodenbough, Theophilus F., comp. *From Everglade to Cañon with the Second Dragoons . . .* New York: D. Van Nostrand, 1875.

Rodick, Burleigh Cushing. *Appomattox: The Last Campaign.* New York: Philosophical Library, 1965.

Rosser, Thomas L. *Addresses of Gen'l T. L. Rosser, at the Seventh Annual Reunion of the Association of the Maryland Line . . .* New York: L. A. Williams Printing Co., 1889.

———. *Riding with Rosser.* Edited by S. Roger Keller. Shippensburg, Pa.: White Mane Publishing Co., 1997.

Royall, William L. *Some Reminiscences.* New York: Neale Publishing Co., 1909.

Ryan, David D. *Four Days in 1865: The Fall of Richmond.* Richmond: Cadmus Communications Corp., 1993.

Sanford, George B. *Fighting Rebels and Redskins: Experiences in Army Life of Colonel George B. Sanford, 1861–1892.* Edited by E. R. Hagemann. Norman: University of Oklahoma Press, 1969.

Schaff, Morris. *The Sunset of the Confederacy.* Boston: John W. Luce & Co., 1912.

Scott, Henry Bruce. *The Surrender of General Lee and the Army of Northern Virginia at Appomattox, Virginia, April 9, 1865.* Boston: privately issued, ca. 1916.

Scruggs, Philip L. *The History of Lynchburg, Virginia.* Lynchburg, Va.: J. P. Bell Co., n.d.

Sheridan, Philip H. *Appendix to Reports of Operations in the Appomattox Campaign . . .* n.p.: privately issued, n.d.

———. *Personal Memoirs of P. H. Sheridan.* 2 vols. New York: Charles L. Webster & Co., 1888.

———. *Report of Operations of the 1st and 3d Divisions [of] Cavalry, Army of the Shenandoah . . . from Feb. 27th to March 28th, 1865.* New Orleans: privately issued, 1865.

———. *Report of Operations of the United States Forces under Command of Major General P. H. Sheridan, from March 29, 1865, to April 9, 1865 . . .* n.p.: privately issued, 1865.

Simmons, Sampson S. *Memories of Sampson Sanders Simmons, a Confederate Veteran.* Edited by Naomi Sanders Klipstein. Pasadena, Calif.: Publications Press, 1954.

Smith, Joshua. *From Gettysburg to Appomattox: Map and Description of the Main Battlefields, Routes, Camps and Headquarters in the Gettysburg, Wilderness, and Appomattox Campaigns . . .* Chicago: privately issued, 1900.

Snyder, Edwin. *Adventures and Misadventures, Civil and Military, of a Union Veteran of the Civil War.* Topeka, Kans.: Cavanaugh Printing Co., 1909.

Stanley, James C. *The Union Cavalry in West Virginia for the Civil War: Thrilling and Dangerous Service of the Second Virginia Cavalry . . .* August, Ill.: privately issued, n.d.

Stanley, Vara Smith. *Appomattox County, Organized 1845: Past—Present—Future . . .* Appomattox, Va.: privately issued, 1965.

Starr, Stephen Z. *The Union Cavalry in the Civil War.* 3 vols. Baton Rouge: Louisiana State University Press, 1979–85.

Stern, Philip Van Doren. *An End to Valor: The Last Days of the Civil War.* Boston: Houghton Mifflin Co., 1958.

Stevens, George T. *Three Years in the Sixth Corps . . .* New York: D. Van Nostrand, 1870.

Stevenson, James H. *"Boots and Saddles": A History of . . . the First New York (Lincoln) Cavalry . . .* Harrisburg, Pa.: Patriot Publishing Co., 1879.

Stiles, Kenneth L. *4th Virginia Cavalry.* Lynchburg, Va.: H. E. Howard, 1985.

Stiles, Robert. *Four Years under Marse Robert.* New York: Neale Publishing Co., 1903.

Stine, J. H. *History of the Army of the Potomac.* Philadelphia: J. B. Rodgers Printing Co., 1892.

Stribling, Robert M. *Gettysburg Campaign and the Campaigns of 1864 and 1865 in Virginia.* Petersburg, Va.: Franklin Press Co., 1905.

Sutton, J. J. *History of the Second Regiment, West Virginia Cavalry Volunteers during the War of the Rebellion.* Portsmouth, Ohio: privately issued, 1892.

Swank, Walbrook D., ed. *Confederate Letters and Diaries, 1861–1865.* Shippensburg, Pa.: White Mane Publishing Co., 2000.

Swett, Joel B. *Deeds of the Eighth New York Cavalry . . .* Rochester, N.Y.: Robert Dransfield, 1865.

Swinton, William. *Campaigns of the Army of the Potomac.* New York: Charles B. Richardson, 1866.

Sypher, J. R. *History of the Pennsylvania Reserve Corps . . .* Lancaster, Pa.: Elias Barr & Co., 1865.

Taylor, Nelson. *Saddle and Saber: Civil War Letters of Corporal Nelson Taylor, Ninth New York State Volunteer Cavalry . . .* Edited by Gray Nelson Taylor. Bowie, Md.: Heritage Books, 1993.

Taylor, Walter H. *Four Years with General Lee . . .* New York: D. Appleton & Co., 1877.

————. *General Lee: His Campaigns in Virginia, 1861–1865 . . .* Norfolk, Va.: Nusbaum Book & News Co., 1906.

————. *Lee's Adjutant: The Wartime Letters of Colonel Walter Herron Taylor.* Edited by R. Lockwood Tower. Columbia: University of South Carolina Press, 1995.

Tenney, Luman H. *War Diary of Luman Harris Tenney, 1861–1865.* Edited by Frances Andrews Tenney. Cleveland: Evangelical Publishing House, 1914.

Thaxter, Sidney W. *Sidney Warren Thaxter.* Portland, Me.: Marks Printing House, 1909.

Thomas, Emory M. *The Confederate State of Richmond: A Biography of the Capital.* Austin: University of Texas Press, 1971.

Thomas, Hampton S. *Some Personal Reminiscences of Service in the Cavalry of the Army of the Potomac.* Philadelphia: L. R. Hammersly & Co., 1889.

Tobie, Edward P. *History of the First Maine Cavalry, 1861–1865.* Boston: Emery & Hughes, 1887.

Tremain, Henry E. *The Closing Days about Richmond . . .* New York: privately issued, 1884.

———. *Last Hours of Sheridan's Cavalry: A Reprint of War Memoranda.* New York: Bonnell, Silver & Bowers, 1904.

———. *Sailors' Creek to Appomattox Court House, 7th, 8th, 9th April, 1865 . . .* Edited by J. Watts de Peyster. New York: Charles H. Ludwig, 1885.

Trout, Robert J. *In the Saddle with Stuart.* Gettysburg, Pa.: Thomas Publications, 1998.

Trudeau, Noah Andre. *Out of the Storm: The End of the Civil War, April-June 1865.* Boston: Little, Brown & Co., 1994.

Trueheart, Charles W., and Henry M. Trueheart. *Rebel Brothers: The Civil War Letters of the Truehearts.* Edited by Edward B. Williams. College Station: Texas A&M University Press, 1995.

Turner, George E. *Victory Rode the Rails: The Strategic Place of the Railroads in the Civil War.* Indianapolis: Bobbs-Merrill Co., 1953.

Vaill, Theodore F. *History of the Second Connecticut Volunteer Heavy Artillery . . .* Winsted, Conn.: Winsted Printing Co., 1868.

Vinter, Thomas H. *Memoirs of Thomas H. Vinter.* Philadelphia: Walter H. Jenkins, 1926.

Wagner, Arthur L., comp. *Cavalry Studies from Two Great Wars.* Kansas City, Mo.: Hudson-Kimberly Publishing Co., 1896.

Wainwright, Charles S. *A Diary of Battle: The Personal Journals of Colonel Charles S. Wainwright, 1861–1865.* Edited by Allan Nevins. New York: Harcourt, Brace & World, 1962.

Walker, Francis A. *History of the Second Army Corps in the Army of the Potomac.* New York: Charles Scribner's Sons, 1886.

Wallace, Lee A., Jr. *3rd Virginia Infantry.* Lynchburg, Va.: H. E. Howard, 1986.

Wallace, Robert C. *A Few Memories of a Long Life.* Helena, Mont.: privately issued, 1916.

Warner, Ezra J. *Generals in Blue: Lives of the Union Commanders.* Baton Rouge: Louisiana State University Press, 1964.

———. *Generals in Gray: Lives of the Confederate Commanders.* Baton Rouge: Louisiana State University Press, 1959.

The War of the Rebellion: A Compilation of the Official Records of the Union and Confederate Armies. 4 series, 70 vols. in 128. Washington, D.C.: Government Printing Office, 1880–1901.

Warren, Gouverneur K. *An Account of the Operations of the Fifth Army Corps, Commanded by Maj.-Gen. G. K. Warren, at the Battle of Five Forks, April 1, 1865 . . .* New York: William M. Franklin, 1866.

Watson, George W. *The Last Survivor: The Memoirs of George William Watson, a Horse Soldier in the 12th Virginia Cavalry (Confederate States Army).* Edited by Brian Stuart Kesterton. Washington, W. Va.: Night Hawk Press, 1993.

Watts, Charles. *A War Friendship: "Bill and Me".* Library, Pa.: Springbrook Printery, 1906.

Weaver, Augustus C. *Third Indiana Cavalry: A Brief Account of the Actions in Which They Took Part . . .* Greenwood, Ind.: privately issued, 1919.

Weaver, Jeffrey C. *22nd Virginia Cavalry.* Lynchburg, Va.: H. E. Howard, 1991.

Wellman, Manly Wade. *Rebel Boast: First at Bethel—Last at Appomattox.* New York: Henry Holt & Co., 1956.

Wensyel, James W. *Appomattox: The Passing of the Armies.* Shippensburg, Pa.: White Mane Books, 2000.

Wert, Jeffry. *Custer: The Controversial Life of George Armstrong Custer.* New York: Simon & Schuster, 1996.

———. *General James Longstreet, the Confederacy's Most Controversial Soldier: A Biography.* New York: Simon & Schuster, 1993.

Wheeler, Richard. *Witness to Appomattox.* New York: Harper & Row, 1989.

Whittaker, Frederick. *A Complete Life of Gen. George A. Custer . . .* New York: Sheldon & Co., 1876.

———. *Volunteer Cavalry—The Lessons of a Decade, by a Volunteer Cavalryman.* New York: privately issued, 1871.

Williams, Kenneth P. *Lincoln Finds a General: A Military Study of the Civil War.* 5 vols. New York: Macmillan Co., 1949–59.

Wilson, William L. *A Borderland Confederate.* Edited by Festus P. Summers. Pittsburgh: University of Pittsburgh Press, 1962.

Winik, Jay. *April 1865: The Month That Saved America.* New York: Harper Collins, 2001.

Wise, Jennings Cropper. *The Long Arm of Lee; or, The History of the Artillery of the Army of Northern Virginia . . .* 2 vols. Lynchburg, Va.: J. P. Bell, 1915.

Wise, John S. *The End of an Era.* Boston: Houghton, Mifflin & Co., 1899.

INDEX